Women and Incarceration

Recent Titles in Women and Society around the World

Women and Violence
Kathleen Nadeau and Sangita Rayamajhi, Editors

Women and Health
AnnJanette Alejano-Steele, Editor

Women and the Military
Ruth Margolies Beitler and Sarah M. Gerstein

Women and Religion
Susan M. Shaw, Editor

Women and Sexuality
Kelly Campbell and M. L. Parker, Editors

Women and Politics
Malliga Och, Editor

Women and Education
Erin Kenny

Women and Incarceration

Global Lives in Focus

Francesca Spina

BLOOMSBURY ACADEMIC
NEW YORK • LONDON • OXFORD • NEW DELHI • SYDNEY

BLOOMSBURY ACADEMIC
Bloomsbury Publishing Inc, 1359 Broadway, New York, NY 10018, USA
Bloomsbury Publishing Plc, 50 Bedford Square, London, WC1B 3DP, UK
Bloomsbury Publishing Ireland, 29 Earlsfort Terrace, Dublin 2, D02 AY28, Ireland

First published in the United States of America 2026

A catalog record for this book is available from the Library of Congress.

ISBN: HB: 979-8-7651-2487-1
ePDF: 979-8-7651-2488-8
eBook: 979-8-7651-2489-5

Series: Women and Society around the World

Typeset by Integra Software Services Pvt. Ltd.
Printed and bound in the United States of America

For product safety-related questions, contact productsafety@bloomsbury.com.

To find out more about our authors and books visit www.bloomsbury.com and sign up for our newsletters.

Contents

Series Foreword vi
Preface viii
Chronology x

Introduction 1

1 North America 15
2 Latin America and the Caribbean 47
3 Europe 81
4 North Africa and the Middle East 115
5 Sub-Saharan Africa 149
6 Central and East Asia 185
7 South and Southeast Asia 221
8 Oceania 257

Glossary 293
Bibliography 297
Index Term List 302

Series Foreword

Women make up half the population of the world, impacting all spheres of society in innumerable ways. Despite sharing some similarities in the issues they face, women's agency and their engagement in their cultural communities, political life, and economies vary greatly across the world. In some places, women are denied the right to an education and to political participation; while in others, women are pioneers in their professional fields and encouraged into leadership roles in all areas of society. Gender inequality looms in all aspects of life, from employment to education to opportunities in sports and the military. What are the challenges, issues, and achievements women face?

The Women and Society around the World series investigates key topics in women's experiences and offers a cross-regional and cross-cultural comparison of how women are living and of the unique structures that hinder their freedoms. The volumes cover topics such as

- Health;
- Violence;
- Religion;
- Sexuality;
- The military;
- Sports;
- Education; and
- Technology, among others.

Each volume begins with an introductory background essay on the volume's topic and is followed by a general chronology of significant world events pertaining to the topic. Eight chapters follow, focusing on the world's regions: the United States and Canada, Latin America and the Caribbean, Europe, North Africa and the Middle East, Sub-Saharan Africa, Central and East Asia, South and Southeast Asia, and Oceania. All chapters include a list of further reading resources, and a selected bibliography at the end of each volume provides students with additional print and electronic resources for further research needs.

The chapters examine women in each region with broad brushstrokes, highlighting specific examples of key customs and policies in specific countries that help to illuminate cultural nuances among countries within each region. They can be read alone or be reviewed cumulatively to make cross-cultural comparisons. The volumes are ideal for high school students doing projects, undergraduate students writing research papers, and even general readers interested in learning about women's lives.

The goal of the Women and Society around the World series is to depict the roles of women worldwide by exploring the major issues they face and the accomplishments they have made, especially in terms of bridging the gap in gender inequality and fighting for basic human rights. While readers will learn about the challenges that half of the world's population face, they will also discover the empowering ways women succeed and overcome social and cultural barriers in their daily lives.

Preface

Examining women who are incarcerated around the world is a considerable undertaking. There are over 700,000 women and girls incarcerated throughout the world. Yet, while women make up a little over half of the world's population, they only comprise about 7 percent of the world's incarcerated. Thus, the focus of incarceration has historically been on men's experiences. In some countries, there has been little research conducted about women's experiences behind bars. This book intends to provide a framework for seeing how women across the world experience incarceration. In order to explore a topic of this scale within the confines of one book, each chapter begins with a general discussion of the region, followed by three examples of countries examined in more depth. Sparing Antarctica, the book covers all continents, concentrating on crucial countries within each region. It serves as a starting point for additional research on the experiences of incarcerated women worldwide.

Women constitute a growing segment of the incarcerated population, with their pathways into the criminal justice system shaped by poverty, trauma, discrimination, and systemic inequality. Economic marginalization, substance abuse, histories of trauma and abuse, and structural inequities push many women into conflict with the law. Once inside prison, they encounter environments shaped by systems designed with men in mind, often ill-equipped to address their needs, including reproductive health, childcare responsibilities, or trauma recovery. Across different regions, there are also variations in legal frameworks, societal attitudes, and institutional practices that further shape the experiences of incarcerated women. Each country presents its own challenges and responses to the experiences of these women.

This book examines the gendered dimensions of imprisonment, inviting readers to consider questions of justice, equity, and human rights in the context of women's imprisonment. It explores how women from different regions of the world experience the challenges of incarceration and how systems are working to create more just responses for incarcerated women. This book is intended for students, scholars, and practitioners in criminal justice and anyone concerned with human rights, gender equality, and social justice. It can contribute to awareness of these issues and inspire new ideas for addressing the needs of incarcerated women across the globe.

Chronology

***c.* AD 304**	Agnes of Rome, a Christian martyr, is one of the first recorded cases of a woman being incarcerated.
1430	Joan of Arc, a peasant girl from France, is accused of heresy and imprisoned by the English during the Hundred Years' War.
1500s–1700s	During the Colonial era, incarcerated women across the globe are housed in the same facilities as men and are subject to harsh punishments.
1823	The Parliament of the UK establishes the Gaols Act of 1823. This act mandates sex-segregated prisons, as well as female wardens, for incarcerated women in the British Empire.
1827	Elizabeth Fry, an English prison reformer, publishes her seminal book, *Observations on the Visiting, Superintendence, and Government of Female Prisoners*, which discusses the need for penal reform in women's prisons.
1839	The first facility for women, the Mount Pleasant Female Prison, is opened in New York. It is part of Sing Sing, the facility that houses men.
1870s	Women in the United States begin being housed in separate correctional facilities from men. Countries across the globe also begin to open separate correctional facilities for women during this period.
1878	The first meeting of the International Conference of Women convenes in Paris from July 25 to August 9. Groups of women participating in the suffrage movement worldwide come together to discuss issues affecting women.
1909	National Women's Day, still recognized yearly, is started to promote gender equality and equal rights. On February 28, the event is initiated in New York City by Theresa Malkiel, a labor activist, to protest against poor working conditions for women working in the garment industry.

1917 In the United States, over forty suffragettes are arrested for protesting outside of the White House. Alice Paul and Lucy Burns, prominent figures in the National Woman's Party, lead the protests. The group seeks a federal suffrage amendment so that women can vote.

1920 Women in the United States are granted the right to vote, influencing prison reform. The suffrage movement gains momentum in many countries throughout the world, including Czechoslovakia, Austria, Germany, Poland, Canada, the Netherlands, and the UK.

1927 The first federal reformatory for women, Federal Prison Camp Alderson, opens in the United States.

1945 The United Nations is officially formed on October 24 to establish international peace and security, following the devastation after the Second World War. At first, there are fifty-one member countries, including the United States, the UK, and the Soviet Union.

1948 The United Nations adopts the Universal Declaration of Human Rights, recognizing these inherent rights for people worldwide.

1950 The European Convention on Human Rights is signed on November 4 in Rome, Italy by twelve member countries, including Italy, France, and the UK. It emphasizes fundamental rights for everyone, including the treatment of people who are incarcerated.

1955 The United Nations adopts the Standard Minimum Rules for the Treatment of Prisoners (now also known as the Nelson Mandela Rules) on August 30 in Geneva, Switzerland. These Rules influence both men and women who are incarcerated across the globe.

1969 The Canadian Association of the Elizabeth Fry Societies is established, which advocates for women's rights in the criminal justice system. Other countries adopt similar models to advocate for women, including the UK, New Zealand, Australia, and Ireland.

The American Convention on Human Rights is adopted on November 22 in San Jose, Costa Rica by the member states of the Organization of American States. It emphasizes human rights protections in Latin America and influences advocacy efforts to improve conditions for incarcerated women.

1970s Feminist movements around the world highlight issues for incarcerated women. In the United States, activists support the Attica Prison Uprising, highlighting the systemic abuse and challenges faced by incarcerated women, such as sexual violence. In the UK, movements focus on harsh conditions at Holloway Prison, advocating for reforms and alternatives to incarceration for women.

1971 The War on Drugs begins in the United States as a result of President Richard Nixon's policies. Consequently, the female prison population increases, which lasts for decades. Furthermore, the War on Drugs has an impact on drug policy throughout much of the world.

1974 The United Nations adopts the Declaration on the Protection of Women and Children in Emergency and Armed Conflict on December 14. This declaration highlights the importance of addressing the needs of vulnerable populations in times of war, including incarcerated women.

1975 The United Nations designates this year as International Women's Year. This initiative involves all UN member states, leading to the first World Conference on Women, held in Mexico City from June 19 to July 2. The conference addresses gender equality, reproductive rights, and the economic empowerment of women.

1985 The Nairobi Forward-Looking Strategies for the Advancement of Women advocates for gender equality worldwide and brings awareness to incarcerated women's issues. The initiative advocates for better prison conditions, gender-responsive legal reforms, and better rehabilitation programs for incarcerated women, bringing global attention to these issues.

1993 The Vienna Declaration and Programme of Action is adopted on June 25 to strengthen human rights work around the world. This plan also advocates for the humane treatment of people within criminal justice systems. It was signed by representatives from 171 UN member states.

1994 The United States passes the Violence Against Women Act (VAWA). VAWA impacts legal protections and services for incarcerated women and influences global policies.

1995 The Beijing Declaration and Platform for Action helps advance women's rights worldwide and was endorsed by 189 UN member states. This effort promotes gender equality and advocates for women's rights and dignity, including those imprisoned.

1996 In Britain, incarcerated women no longer have to be restrained when giving birth. Other countries begin to reconsider this practice.

1999 The United Nations adopts the Optional Protocol to the Convention on the Elimination of All Forms of Discrimination against Women (CEDAW) on October 6. This protocol provides guidance for incarcerated women to seek redress for human rights violations.

2000s Countries across the world begin to focus more on gender-responsive programming, trying to address the unique needs of women who are incarcerated.

2003 The Prison Rape Elimination Act (PREA) passes in the United States to deter sexual assaults within prisons. PREA serves as a model for other countries, as ideas about sexual abuse within correctional settings are increasingly being recognized as human rights violations.

2007 The United States passes the Second Chance Act, which focuses on rehabilitation and reentry programs for people leaving prison, including women. This act serves as a model for countries around the world.

2008 The United Nations Office on Drugs and Crime (UNODC) publishes the Handbook for Prison Managers and Policymakers on Women and Imprisonment. This handbook provides guidance about best practices for managing women's prisons.

2010 The United Nations adopts the Bangkok Rules, or more formally, "United Nations Rules for the Treatment of Women Prisoners and Non-custodial Measures for Women Offenders." These rules provide international guidance about treating incarcerated women.

2015 The United Nations Sustainable Development Goals are established. One of the goals is to achieve gender equality, including for those who are incarcerated.

2019 The United Nations publishes the Global Study on Children Deprived of Liberty, discussing how children of incarcerated parents, especially mothers, are impacted by their imprisonment.

2020 The COVID-19 pandemic impacts incarcerated women across the globe. Incarcerated people are many of the first people to contract the virus, as it is easily transmissible within correctional facilities.

2020s There is ongoing advocacy for criminal justice reform and improving the conditions for incarcerated women across the globe. Countries continue to work on gender-responsive programming and addressing the unique needs of women. Those leading the efforts are Canada, New Zealand, Australia, Norway, and the UK.

Introduction

Women and Incarceration: Global Lives in Focus investigates women's incarceration experiences around the world, offering a cross-regional and cross-cultural comparison of how women experience incarceration. It compares how women experience incarceration in North America, Latin America and the Caribbean, Europe, North Africa and the Middle East, Sub-Saharan Africa, Central and East Asia, South and Southeast Asia, and Oceania.

Women make up over half the world's population but only about 7 percent of the incarcerated population across the globe (Fair and Walmsley 2022). The issue of women and incarceration is a complex one, encompassing various social, economic, and systemic factors. Moreover, countries should abide by the Bangkok Rules, which are the United Nations Rules for the Treatment of Women Prisoners and Non-custodial Measures for Women Offenders (Thailand Institute of Justice 2018). These rules were created in 2010, and they established guidelines for the humane treatment of incarcerated women. However, as you will learn throughout the book, women still face human rights violations in many prisons across the globe.

Each chapter examines three countries within each region, following a similar structure and examining similar topics. Every chapter discusses the historical context for women within the given countries, including the roles of women, how women are treated in society, and how the criminal justice system views women. It then examines female incarceration rates and trends for the country, laws contributing to these incarceration rates, crimes for which women are incarcerated, and demographics of those who are incarcerated. It then discusses women's prisons, including the facilities where women are housed. The chapters then examine related policy reforms countries are taking to improve conditions for incarcerated women. Lastly, each chapter concludes with a synthesis of the examples that were taken for the region.

Compared to their male counterparts, women worldwide face unique challenges behind bars. They face histories of abuse, mental illness, and substance abuse. They also face different health challenges compared to men, including a higher likelihood of being sexually abused in prison and being pregnant while incarcerated. Moreover, they are often the caretakers for children and face a more significant burden of being separated from their children during incarceration. Furthermore, they also have different needs for programming while incarcerated and when they leave prison. Each chapter examines these issues, along with problems that are unique to a particular country. Below is an outline of the countries you will learn about in this book.

Chapter 1 examines women experiencing incarceration in North America, specifically the United States, Canada, and Mexico. The United States has the highest rates of incarceration in the world for both men and women. At the end of 2021, 660 of every 100,000 people in the United States were incarcerated in prisons or jails. For women, that figure is 120 out of every 100,000 people (Carson and Kluckow 2023). The United States has a complex criminal justice system with varying laws and policies across the federal government and the fifty states. Starting with the War on Drugs in the 1970s and the "get tough" on crime policies of the 1980s and 1990s, US prisons experienced significant increases in their populations. Women, especially women of color, faced higher rates of incarceration for drug crimes during this period. While incarceration rates in the United States have been declining in the recent decade, incarcerated women still face issues related to overcrowding, inadequate healthcare, and a lack of programming.

Canada also has a considerable rate of incarcerated individuals, but not as high as the United States. Currently, 112 out of every 100,000 adults are incarcerated in either the federal or provincial/territorial system. Of the individuals admitted to the country's provincial/territorial system, 14 percent are women, and over 40 percent are Indigenous (Government of Canada 2024). This chapter examines the overrepresentation of Indigenous women in the Canadian prison system and issues related to decolonization and systemic discrimination that impact these women (Department of Justice 2023). There are the challenges faced by incarcerated mothers, as well as a lack of adequate healthcare and access to services in many facilities in Canada.

In Mexico, 174 out of every 100,000 people are incarcerated, and almost 6 percent of that population is women (World Prison Brief 2024a). There is a recent trend of increasing involvement of women in organized crime in Mexico. Many of these women are single mothers from low-income backgrounds who are recruited into these groups through personal relationships or drug dependency (Loaiza 2023). Thus, many women who are incarcerated in Mexico have been convicted of drug trafficking, drug dealing, and violent offenses. Women in Mexican prisons face harsh conditions that are worsened by overcrowding and inadequate facilities. Moreover, many of these women are in pre-trial detention centers and lack the resources and social support to navigate legal challenges. As most of these women are single mothers, their imprisonment impacts their children, who often suffer from socioeconomic instability and increased vulnerability to criminal groups (Valle 2024).

Chapter 2 examines Latin America and the Caribbean. This chapter explores women incarcerated in Brazil, Colombia, and Jamaica. The Latin American country of Brazil has a considerable incarceration rate, with 390 of every 100,000 people behind bars, and women constitute about 5 percent of this population (World Prison Brief 2022). Punitive drug laws have disproportionately affected women in Brazil, with over 60 percent of these women imprisoned for crimes related to drug trafficking. Moreover, 35 percent of them are in pre-trial detention (Dolabela and Roncetti 2022), which means they have been deprived of their liberties without being convicted. Women incarcerated in Brazil face issues of overcrowding, lack of gender-specific programming, and inadequate healthcare, especially for Black women.

Colombia, another Latin American country, has experienced decades of internal conflict related to drug trafficking, violence against civilians, and violations of human rights (Human Rights Watch 2023a). This conflict has impacted its criminal justice system and the experiences of people who are incarcerated. Colombia has an incarceration rate of 197 per 100,000 people, and 6 percent are women (Institute for Crime and Justice Policy Research 2024). Moreover, because Colombia is a "source country" for drugs entering the United States, almost half of the women incarcerated in Colombia are there because of policies related to the United States' War on Drugs (The National Council 2022). Like many countries, women in Colombian prisons face issues such as overcrowding, physical abuse, and inadequate healthcare and sanitation.

Furthermore, Jamaica offers a notable context for examining the experiences of incarcerated women in the Caribbean. With 125 out of every 100,000 people, Jamaica has one of the highest incarceration rates in the Caribbean, and 4 percent of those incarcerated are women ("Jamaica | World Prison Brief" 2022). There is a lack of medium security facilities for women in Jamaica, and their rehabilitative and programmatic needs are rarely met. Facilities are outdated, leading to safety concerns and inhumane conditions in custody (Leslie 2020).

Jamaica faces many social and economic challenges related to extreme poverty, inequality, and corruption, contributing to women's involvement in crime. Many women imprisoned in Jamaica have been convicted of drug-related crimes that violate the Dangerous Drugs Act.

Chapter 3 looks at Europe, specifically Russia, Norway, and Italy. The Russian Federation imprisons 300 out of every 100,000 people, and 9 percent of this population is women ("Russian Federation | World Prison Brief" 2023). Furthermore, 26 percent of people in Russia are in pre-trial detention and have not been convicted. Recently, Russian prisons came to the attention of the media when Brittney Griner, a professional women's basketball player in the United States, was arrested and detained for drug smuggling in 2022. She has since been released, but her detainment highlighted how women imprisoned in Russia face challenges such as overcrowding, inadequate healthcare, and human rights violations.

Norway offers a contrasting perspective compared to Russia. It has a low prison rate, with only 55 out of every 100,000 incarcerated, and 5 percent of this population is women (World Prison Brief 2024b). Norway is known for its progressive approach to criminal justice, emphasizing human rights and reintegration. Since the 1990s, Norwegian prisons have made reforms to prioritize education, vocational training, and interventions to help people reintegrate into society upon release from prison (Kirby 2019). Moreover, Norwegian facilities focus on the professionalism of staff members and the effects the physical buildings have on people housed in them. As a result of these reforms, there have been reductions in recidivism rates after individuals return to their communities.

Italy, a Southern European country, has an incarceration rate of 105 people out of every 100,000, and a little over 4 percent of that population is women ("Italy | World Prison Brief" 2024). Italy has a long history related to legal philosophy and reform, yet much of it has been designed with male needs and norms in mind. Thus, like many countries, incarcerated women in Italy face challenges that go neglected because the system has been intended for men. Nearly two-thirds of these women regularly use psychotropic drugs, and incarcerated women are twice as likely as their male counterparts to engage in self-harm (Riggi 2024). Italy lacks a dedicated office for women's detention, and it is deficient in access to healthcare, vocational training, and gender-based violence support services for incarcerated women.

Chapter 4 examines North Africa and the Middle East. It delves into the lives of incarcerated women in Egypt, Tunisia, and Iran. Egypt, a North African country, incarcerates 116 out of every 100,000 people, 4 percent of whom are women ("Egypt | World Prison Brief" 2022). The experiences of incarcerated women in Egypt provide awareness into the connection of gender, politics, and the criminal justice system. Many of these women are political prisoners, including journalists, human rights activists, or those who have criticized Egyptian authorities (The Tahrir Institute for Middle East Policy 2023). Egypt's prison conditions have been criticized for overcrowding, lack of access to healthcare, and allegations of abuse and mistreatment. Women in these prisons face challenges related to societal norms regarding gender and are also impacted by ongoing political unrest and government crackdowns on civil liberties, as experienced by political prisoners.

Tunisia, another North African country, offers a perspective from a more progressive country which transitioned to a democracy in 2011 after the Arab Spring (Grewal 2021). Since then, Tunisia has instituted considerable legal and policy reforms, including improving prison conditions. Tunisia's national prison service, the General Directorate of Prisons and Rehabilitation, took measures to upgrade the infrastructure of facilities to prevent overcrowding and create more humane conditions for people housed within them (MENA Prison Forum 2023). However, the imprisonment rate remains relatively high at 196 out of every 100,000 people incarcerated, and 3 percent of this population is women ("Tunisia | World Prison Brief" 2021).

Examining the experiences of incarcerated women in Iran offers insight into the connection between gender, law, and culture in the Middle East. Iran's legal system is influenced by Islamic law, along with its societal norms, and shapes the experiences of women imprisoned in this country. The incarceration rate in Iran is 228 out of every 100,000 people, and approximately 3 percent of that population is women ("Iran | World Prison Brief" 2020). Many of these women are political prisoners, including activists, lawyers, or anyone else criticizing the regime (United States Institute of Peace 2023). Women in Iran are often sentenced to long prison terms, charged with vague crimes against the state, and denied access to counsel. They are frequently sent into exile, denied their basic needs, and face human rights violations (National Council of Resistance of Iran 2021).

Chapter 5 examines Sub-Saharan Africa, specifically South Africa, Nigeria, and Kenya. With a history of apartheid and socioeconomic disparities, South Africa's criminal justice system faces intersecting issues related to race, class, and gender. South Africa has a prison rate of 258 out of every 100,000 people, and approximately 3 percent of this population is women

("South Africa | World Prison Brief" 2023). Typically, women in South Africa are incarcerated for drug crimes or economic offenses, often driven by poverty and exploitation (United Nations Office on Drugs and Crime 2021). Women in South African prisons face issues related to overcrowding, inadequate healthcare services, and unhygienic sleeping conditions (SAHRC 2023). There is a great need to improve gender-responsive programming in South African prisons.

Overall, Nigeria faces considerable challenges, including violence, repression of rights, and corruption (Human Rights Watch 2021a), which impact the criminal justice system. The prison rate in Nigeria is relatively low at thirty-five people incarcerated per 100,000, with 2 to 3 percent of that population being women ("Nigeria | World Prison Brief" 2024). Nearly 70 percent of people in Nigerian prisons are in pre-trial detention, housed in detention centers as they await trial. These centers do not adequately address the health needs of individuals, and women have limited access to basic healthcare or hygiene products. However, the Nigerian Correctional Service recently partnered with the United Nations Office on Drugs and Crime (UNODC) and United Nations Population Fund (UNFPA) to provide dignity kits to women awaiting trial in Nigeria (United Nations Office on Drugs and Crime 2022).

Kenya, a country in East Africa, has an incarceration rate of 103 people per 100,000, and 5 percent of that population is women ("Kenya | World Prison Brief" 2022). Women's incarceration in Kenya has been linked to a patriarchal society, which leads women to have few economic or educational opportunities. In contrast to their male counterparts, who are incarcerated for property and violent crimes, over 30 percent of women in Kenya are behind bars for violating the Liquor Act, which means they brewed and sold alcohol without a license (IEA Kenya 2016). While Kenya has many non-governmental organizations that advocate for the rights of the incarcerated, people behind bars still face overcrowding, food and water shortages, and inadequate sanitary conditions ("Kenya" 2023).

Next, Chapter 6 examines the experiences of incarcerated women in Central and East Asia, specifically Uzbekistan, China, and Japan. Uzbekistan, a country in Central Asia, has a history of authoritarian rule and government crackdowns on dissent, so many people have been incarcerated for political crimes. Uzbekistan has an incarceration rate of 85 per 100,000 people ("Uzbekistan | World Prison Brief" 2022), although the percentage of women is not available. Women incarcerated in Uzbekistan face many issues, including lack of water and food, lack of heating in the winter months, and insufficient conditions for pregnant people (Review of Uzbekistan 2023 Human Rights Report 2023). However, since electing a new President in 2016, Uzbekistan has taken steps to release political prisoners and promote gender equality throughout its society.

In East Asia, China's context is unique, given its one-party rule by the Chinese Communist Party (CCP), which imposes considerable restrictions on civil liberties. China has an incarceration rate of 119 per 100,000, who are sentenced in Ministry of Justice prisons, and nearly 9 percent of this population is women. It is also estimated that there are over 200,000 people in pre-trial detention, but the figures are unreliable (World Prison Brief 2018). Aside from the United States, China incarcerates the second-largest number of women, and these numbers have been rising. Most women have been imprisoned for non-violent crimes, engaging in sex work, or crimes related to drugs. These women face overcrowding, limited access to programming, and long working hours. Additional facilities have been built in suburban areas to accommodate the growing number of incarcerated women.

Another East Asian country, Japan, offers another perspective on the experiences of incarcerated women in East Asia. Japan has a relatively low rate of incarceration, with thirty-three out of every 100,000 people behind bars, and approximately 9 percent of this population is women ("Japan | World Prison Brief" 2023). Many women in Japanese prisons have been convicted of simple drug possession because alternatives to incarceration are rarely used (Human Rights Watch 2023b). These women face challenges such as limited access to substance abuse and mental health services, along with the mistreatment of transgender people. Furthermore, women in Japanese prisons also face stigma and discrimination related to cultural norms and expectations regarding women's roles and behaviors.

Chapter 7 examines South and Southeast Asia, particularly India, the Philippines, and Cambodia. With its considerable population and diversity, India, in South Asia, provides a context for studying factors such as caste, class, and regional differences that influence women's pathways to incarceration. India has a relatively low incarceration rate, with forty-one people out of every 100,000 behind bars. Approximately 4 percent of this population is women, and three-quarters of these people are pre-trial detainees ("India | World Prison Brief" 2022). Most women in Indian prisons are from marginalized communities, and their social and economic situations prevent them from obtaining proper legal defense (Citizens for Justice and Peace 2019). Incarcerated women face challenges such as overcrowding, lack of sanitation and hygiene, and limited access to mental health services. However, children up to six years old can live with their mothers in prisons.

The Southeast Asian country of the Philippines faces social and political challenges, including poverty, inequality, and corruption. The country's drug war, started by President Rodrigo Duterte in 2016, has been characterized by aggressive policing, led to thousands of deaths and raised issues related to human rights violations (Human Rights Watch 2021b). It has led to increases in the prison population and has adversely affected women. The Philippines has an incarceration rate of 162 people per 100,000, and almost 10 percent of that population is women ("Philippines | World Prison Brief" 2022). Women in Philippine prisons face issues such as overcrowding and a lack of gender-responsive programming. However, the Philippines has recently taken steps to address human rights concerns and to improve the effectiveness of services for incarcerated women (United Nations Office on Drugs and Crime 2023).

Cambodia, another Southeast Asian country, has been shaped by a history of conflict, genocide, and a one-party government. The country is characterized by significant human rights issues, including unlawful killings, cruel and inhumane imprisonment, holding political prisoners, and problems with the judiciary. Moreover, the government can legally monitor all telephone conversations and online correspondence and imprison anyone they find to threaten national security. It also prohibits peaceful assembly, as well as political discussions in schools (United States Department of State 2022). All these issues have impacted incarcerated women in Cambodia. The incarceration rate is 320 out of every 100,000 people, and a little over 6 percent of that population is women (Institute for Crime and Justice Policy Research 2025). Women in Cambodian prisons face issues of considerable overcrowding, a lack of food and water, and inadequate healthcare.

Lastly, Chapter 8 examines Oceania and the experiences of incarcerated women in Australia, Papua New Guinea (PNG), and New Zealand. Australia provides insight into a Western-style prison system as a developed country with a well-established legal system. The incarceration rate in Australia is 157 per 100,000 people, and nearly 8 percent of that population is women (World Prison Brief 2023). Incarceration rates for women have been rising for the past fifteen years in Australia, and it has disproportionately affected marginalized and First Nations women with mental health and substance abuse issues (Meyer 2021). While incarcerated women in Australian prisons do not face the conditions that many of the other countries covered do, they still face problems of overcrowding, loss of rights, and a lack of gender-responsive programming.

PNG is a resource-rich country, but 40 percent of its people live in poverty (Human Rights Watch 2023c). Women in PNG face a range of gender-specific issues, including high rates of gender-based violence, limited access to education and healthcare, and gender inequalities, especially in rural areas. For instance, women in PNG can be incarcerated for having an abortion. PNG has a relatively low incarceration rate, with 57 out of every 100,000 people incarcerated, and women comprise a little over 4 percent of that population ("Papua New Guinea | World Prison Brief" 2023). Conditions in prisons in PNG are harsh and can be life-threatening. Incarcerated women face overcrowding, poor sanitation, and a lack of medical treatment.

In New Zealand, the incarceration rate is 179 out of 100,000 people, and approximately 7 percent of that population is women ("New Zealand | World Prison Brief" 2024). The incarceration experience of women in New Zealand is approached with a focus on rehabilitation and addressing their gender-specific needs through their Women's Strategy, which aims to improve services and support for women, particularly the Indigenous wāhine Māori, who are disproportionately represented in prison (New Zealand Department of Corrections 2021). This strategy also addresses systemic challenges such as bail conditions impacted by domestic violence. Furthermore, women's prisons in New Zealand have mothers with babies units and feeding and bonding facilities to help mothers bond with their young children (New Zealand Department of Corrections 2022).

Once you have finished this book, you will better understand the similarities and differences incarcerated women face in these regions. By studying their experiences, researchers can contribute to a nuanced understanding of the intersection of gender, politics, and the criminal justice systems in different regions while also identifying opportunities for legal and policy reform and the protection of women's rights.

References

Carson, E. Ann, and Rich Kluckow. 2023. "Correctional Populations in the United States, 2021—Statistical Tables." Bureau of Justice Statistics. Washington, DC: Bureau of Justice Statistics. https://bjs.ojp.gov/document/cpus21st.pdf.

Citizens for Justice and Peace. 2019. "Plight of Women in Indian Prisons." March 9, 2019. https://cjp.org.in/plight-of-women-in-indian-prisons/.

Department of Justice. 2023. "Understanding the Overrepresentation of Indigenous People—State of the Criminal Justice System Dashboard." Justice.gc.ca. Government of Canada. April 13, 2023. https://www.justice.gc.ca/socjs-esjp/en/ind-aut/uo-cs.

Dolabela, Sofia, and Angela Roncetti. 2022. "Review of the Massive Incarceration of Women in Brazil: A Cycle of Violence and Exclusion." Global Human Rights Defence. The Hague: Global Human Rights Defence. https://www.ghrd.org/wp-content/uploads/2024/03/The-Massive-Incarceration-Of-Women-In-Brazil-A-Cycle-Of-Violence-And-Exclusion-25-May-2022.pdf.

"Egypt | World Prison Brief." 2022. https://www.prisonstudies.org/country/egypt.

Fair, Helen, and Roy Walmsley. 2022. "World Female Imprisonment List Fifth Edition Women and Girls in Penal Institutions, Including Pre-Trial Detainees/Remand Prisoners." https://www.prisonstudies.org/sites/default/files/resources/downloads/world_female_imprisonment_list_5th_edition.pdf.

Government of Canada, Statistics Canada. 2024. "Correctional Services Statistics: Interactive Dashboard." https://www150.statcan.gc.ca/n1/pub/71-607-x/71-607-x2019018-eng.htm.

Grewal, Sharan. 2021. "Ten Years in, Tunisian Democracy Remains a Work in Progress." Brookings. January 22, 2021. https://www.brookings.edu/articles/ten-years-in-tunisian-democracy-remains-a-work-in-progress/.

Human Rights Watch. 2023a. "Colombia: Events of 2022." January 12, 2023. https://www.hrw.org/world-report/2023/country-chapters/colombia.

Human Rights Watch. 2023b. "Japan: Women Seriously Abused in Prisons." November 14, 2023. https://www.hrw.org/news/2023/11/14/japan-women-seriously-abused-prisons.

Human Rights Watch. 2023c. "Papua New Guinea: Events of 2022." January 12, 2023. https://www.hrw.org/world-report/2023/country-chapters/papua-new-guinea.

Human Rights Watch. 2021a. "Nigeria: Events of 2021." December 16, 2021. https://www.hrw.org/world-report/2022/country-chapters/nigeria.

Human Rights Watch. 2021b. "Philippines: Events of 2021." 2021. https://www.hrw.org/world-report/2022/country-chapters/philippines.

IEA Kenya. 2016. "Liquor Laws Effect on Women's Conviction." Accessed July 16, 2024. https://ieakenya.or.ke/blog/liquor-laws-effect-on-womens-conviction/.

"India | World Prison Brief." 2022. https://www.prisonstudies.org/country/india.

Institute for Crime & Justice Policy Research. 2025. "Cambodia." *World Prison Brief.* https://www.prisonstudies.org/country/cambodia.

Institute for Crime & Justice Policy Research. 2024. *Colombia | World Prison Brief.* https://www.prisonstudies.org/country/colombia.

"Iran | World Prison Brief." 2020. https://www.prisonstudies.org/country/iran.

"Italy | World Prison Brief." 2024. https://www.prisonstudies.org/country/italy.

"Jamaica | World Prison Brief." 2022. https://www.prisonstudies.org/country/jamaica.

"Japan | World Prison Brief." 2023. https://www.prisonstudies.org/country/japan.

"Kenya." 2023. United States Department of State. Accessed July 16, 2024. https://www.state.gov/reports/2023-country-reports-on-human-rights-practices/kenya/.

"Kenya | World Prison Brief." 2022. https://www.prisonstudies.org/country/kenya.

Kirby, Emma Jane. 2019. "How Norway Turns Criminals into Good Neighbours." *BBC News*, July 7, 2019. https://www.bbc.com/news/stories-48885846.

Leslie, Dacia Latoya. 2020. "Reassessing Conditions of 'Prison' in Jamaica." *International Criminal Justice Review*, May, 105756772092228.

Loaiza, Lara. 2023. "Women Increasingly Participating in Organized Crime in Mexico: Report." InSight Crime. December 14, 2023. https://insightcrime.org/news/women-increasingly-participating-organized-crime-mexico-report/.

MENA Prison Forum. 2023. "'Prison Reform' in the Middle East and North Africa | Part II." Accessed May 16, 2024. https://www.menaprisonforum.org/observer_detail/13/.

Meyer, Silke. 2021. "Why More Women Are Doing Time in Australia." Monash Lens. July 30, 2021. https://lens.monash.edu/@politics-society/2021/07/30/1383557/rethinking-female-incarceration-road-to-prison-paved-with-domestic-abuse.

National Council of Resistance of Iran. 2021. "The Conditions of Women in Iranian Prisons." December 9, 2021. https://women.ncr-iran.org/2021/12/09/the-conditions-of-women-iran-prisons/#:~:text=The%20conditions%20of%20women%20in%20Iranian%20prisons%20are%20deplorable.

"New Zealand | World Prison Brief." 2024. https://www.prisonstudies.org/country/new-zealand.

New Zealand Department of Corrections. 2022. "Women in Prison." November 2, 2022. https://www.corrections.govt.nz/our_work/in_prison/being_in_prison/women_in_prison.

New Zealand Department of Corrections. 2021. *Wāhine: E Rere Ana Ki Te Pae Hou Women's Strategy 2021–2025*. October 28, 2021. https://www.corrections.govt.nz/resources/strategic_reports/wahine_e_rere_ana_ki_te_pae_hou_womens_strategy.

"Nigeria | World Prison Brief." 2024. https://www.prisonstudies.org/country/nigeria.

"Papua New Guinea | World Prison Brief." 2023. https://www.prisonstudies.org/country/papua-new-guinea.

"Philippines | World Prison Brief." 2022. https://www.prisonstudies.org/country/philippines.

Review of Uzbekistan 2023 Human Rights Report. 2023. Washington, DC: United States Department of State. https://www.state.gov/wp-content/uploads/2024/01/528267_UZBEKISTAN-2023-HUMAN-RIGHTS-REPORT.pdf.

Riggi, Erika. 2024. "Discriminated, Even in Prison: The First Report on Women in Prison in Italy and Antigone's 10 Proposals." Il Secondo Mestiere. March 2, 2024. https://www.ilsecondomestiere.org/en/discriminated-even-in-prison-the-first-report-on-women-in-prison-in-italy-and-antigones-10-proposals/.

"Russian Federation | World Prison Brief." 2023. https://www.prisonstudies.org/country/russian-federation.

SAHRC. 2023. "Women in Prison Deserve Better Treatment." Accessed May 20, 2024. https://www.sahrc.org.za/index.php/sahrc-media/news-2/item/3447-women-in-prison-deserve-better-treatment.

"South Africa | World Prison Brief." 2023. https://www.prisonstudies.org/country/south-africa.

Thailand Institute of Justice. 2018. *About Bangkok Rules | TIJ Bangkok Rules.* Accessed May 28, 2024. https://www.tijbangkokrules.org/en/about-bangkok-rules#:~:text=The%20Bangkok%20Rules&text=adopted%20by%20the%20United%20Nations.

The National Council. 2022. "Reducing Women's Incarceration in Colombia." Accessed May 15, 2024. https://www.nationalcouncil.us/blog/reducing-womens-incarceration-in-colombia.

The Tahrir Institute for Middle East Policy. 2023. "Women in Egypt's Prisons: Tales of Oppression, Abuse and Human Rights Violations." April 19, 2023. https://timep.org/2023/04/19/women-in-egypts-prisons-tales-of-oppression-abuse-and-human-rights-violations.

"Tunisia | World Prison Brief." 2021. https://www.prisonstudies.org/country/tunisia.

United Nations Office on Drugs and Crime. 2023. "The Philippines Addresses Jails and Prisons Overcrowding." https://www.unodc.org/roseap/en/philippines/2023/12/jails-prisons-overcrowding/story.html.

United Nations Office on Drugs and Crime. 2022. "Nigerian Correctional Service Partners with UNODC, UNFPA to Provide Dignity Kits to Women in Custodial Centres in Nigeria." Accessed May 20, 2024. https://www.unodc.org/conig/en/documents/nigerian-correctional-service-partners-with-unodc–unfpa-to-provide-dignitary-kits-to-women-in-custodial-centres-in-nigeria.html.

United Nations Office on Drugs and Crime. 2021. *An Assessment of Relevant National Laws, Policies and Practices Used to Apply Non-Custodial Measures, with a Focus on Women in Conflict with the Law.* Accessed May 20, 2024. https://www.unodc.org/documents/southernafrica/Publications/CriminalJusticeIntegrity/GBV/focus_on_women_detained_web_version.pdf.

United States Department of State. 2022. "Cambodia." https://www.state.gov/reports/2022-country-reports-on-human-rights-practices/cambodia/#:~:text=Significant%20human%20rights%20issues%20included.

United States Institute of Peace. 2023. "Notable Women Detained in Iran." *The Iran Primer*, November 17, 2023. https://iranprimer.usip.org/blog/2023/nov/17/notable-women-detained-iran.

"Uzbekistan | World Prison Brief." 2022. Accessed May 20, 2024. https://www.prisonstudies.org/country/uzbekistan.

Valle, Daniela. 2024. "Why Are There More Women in Mexican Prisons for Organized Crime?" InSight Crime. May 13, 2024. https://insightcrime.org/news/why-more-women-mexican-prisons-organized-crime/.

World Prison Brief. 2024a. "Mexico | World Prison Brief." 2024. https://www.prisonstudies.org/country/mexico.
World Prison Brief. 2024b. "Norway | World Prison Brief." 2024. https://www.prisonstudies.org/country/norway.
World Prison Brief. 2023. "Australia | World Prison Brief." 2023. https://www.prisonstudies.org/country/australia.
World Prison Brief. 2022. "Brazil | World Prison Brief." 2022. https://www.prisonstudies.org/country/brazil.
World Prison Brief. 2018. "China | World Prison Brief." 2018. https://www.prisonstudies.org/country/china.

1

North America

This chapter explores the experiences of incarcerated women in the United States, Canada, and Mexico. It offers a comparative analysis of the historical context, incarceration trends, demographics, and crimes leading to their incarceration. It also examines laws and policies contributing to their imprisonment, prison conditions in each country, and the impact on their families. This chapter stresses how marginalized women, especially those of color and Indigenous women, experience harsher penalties and face additional challenges than their white counterparts. Overall, it emphasizes the need to address the root causes of why women offend, such as poverty and **systemic inequalities**, by promoting **gender-responsive, trauma-informed strategies** to support these women.

The United States

Historical Context

The US penal system was not designed for women, who historically made up a smaller portion of the prison population. It, therefore, has not always adequately addressed the needs of women housed in jails and prisons. The first all-female facility was the Mount Pleasant Female Prison in New York, which opened in 1839, but it was still connected to the men's facility at Sing Sing (Mount Pleasant 2022). Before that, women were housed in the same facilities as men. Unfortunately, the conditions were deplorable (Pishko 2015), and women often experienced physical and sexual abuse, as well as neglect in these early facilities.

Society realized that these issues were problematic, and more women's prisons began opening in the United States in the late 1800s. For example, the Indiana Women's Prison, the first separate institution for women, opened in 1873 (IDOA 2022). These early institutions revolved around a reformatory model intended to help rehabilitate women, and they tried to teach them moral and domestic training. Women were thought to engage in crime because they lacked proper morals. Since their role was to be homemakers, early facilities focused on these skills (Pishko 2015). This outdated model did not address women's underlying causes of criminality, like histories of abuse or structural inequalities; rather, it supported the patriarchal views of the time. Furthermore, the reformatories were designed for white women, while women of color faced harsher punishments.

However, by the 1960s, there were societal changes in the United States with the Civil Rights movement and the feminist movement. There was a rise in awareness related to incarcerated women, especially those of color (Knight 2024). Then, beginning in the 1980s, the female incarceration rate skyrocketed as a result of the War on Drugs and policies aimed to "get tough on crime." From 1980 to 2010, the number of women in prison rose by nearly 650 percent (Pishko 2015), which will be discussed more in the next section.

Female Incarceration Rates and Trends

With over 168,000 adult women behind bars in jails and prisons, the United States has the highest female incarceration rate (120 out of every 100,000 people) (Carson and Kluckow 2023) globally. To put it in perspective, the United States holds about 5 percent of the world's female population but houses almost one-third of the world's female incarcerated population (Bandele 2017). These women are housed in 446 state prisons, 27 federal prisons, and 3,116 local jails nationwide (Kajstura and Sawyer 2024). The majority of this increase occurred after 1980, when there were only 12,300 women behind bars (ACLU 2007).

The War on Drugs, which targeted many low-level drug crimes, was one of the primary factors leading to the increases in the female prison population over the past few decades. Once convicted of drug offenses, women were sentenced to longer prison terms as a result of mandatory minimum sentencing. Moreover, women's incarceration has increased at twice the rate of men's in the past few decades (Kajstura and Sawyer 2024), much of which has been within local jails. Jails house people convicted of lesser crimes, as well as those who have not been convicted. In fact, 60 percent of people in local jails are still awaiting trial (Kajstura and Sawyer 2024). These individuals often have difficulty affording bail, leaving them waiting in detention until their trial.

Furthermore, similar to incarcerated men, women of color are disproportionately affected by incarceration. For instance, the imprisonment rate for African-American women is 1.6 times that of white women; for Latina women, it is 1.2 times that of white women (Budd 2023). These disparities are a result of a history of systemic inequalities, such as biases in policing and sentencing, in addition to greater economic and social problems that women of color face.

Beginning in 2008, there have been decreases in the women's prison population in the United States. This pattern is similar to a decline in the number of incarcerated men, as well. Yet, these declines are small in comparison to the increases of previous decades. For instance, female state imprisonment rates decreased by about 10 percent in the decade after the 2007 peak but increased by almost 30 percent in the prior decade (Heimer, Malone, and De Coster 2023). These decreases have been caused by policy reforms, as well as budgetary concerns.

Demographics of Incarcerated Women

As noted, women of color are incarcerated at higher rates than white women in the United States. Additionally, many women behind bars are from economically disadvantaged backgrounds. For instance, in state prisons, 53 percent of women did not have a job before their arrest and 26 percent reported being homeless prior to their arrest (Kajstura and Sawyer 2024). Furthermore, many women await trial in jail, and the economically disadvantaged face longer criminalization. As they wait in jail, they are likely to lose their jobs or their housing, contributing to their marginalization (Bandele 2017).

There is variation in female incarceration rates among the different states. For instance, Idaho has the highest female incarceration rate, with 132 out of every 100,000 women behind bars. In comparison, Massachusetts has the lowest rate, with seven out of every 100,000 women incarcerated (Budd 2023).

It makes sense that the majority of women behind bars are mothers, as three-quarters of incarcerated women are between the ages of eighteen and forty-four (Johns Hopkins Medicine 2019). Nearly 60 percent of women in prison (Bertram and Sawyer 2021) and over 80 percent of women in jail (Bandele 2017) are mothers of minor children.

Furthermore, over two-thirds of incarcerated women in the United States have a history of mental health problems (Villa 2017), nearly twice as many as incarcerated men. Additionally, up to 90 percent of incarcerated women have experienced sexual or physical abuse. This history of abuse contributes to their mental health problems, as well as substance abuse issues. In fact, nearly 70 percent of women in state facilities meet the criteria for drug or alcohol dependence or abuse (Women's Health Care in Correctional Settings 2020).

Crimes Leading to Incarceration

Most women in the United States are incarcerated for non-violent crimes, such as drug offenses, property crimes, or public order crimes. However, there are different breakdowns of crime types depending on the type of facility in which women are housed. Recall that about 60 percent of women in jails are still awaiting trial. Of the 40 percent of women in jails who have been convicted, approximately 33 percent are there for property crimes, 27 percent for drug crimes, 24 percent for public order crimes, and 15 percent for violent crimes (Kajstura and Sawyer 2024).

In state prisons, approximately 45 percent of women are imprisoned for violent crimes, 25 percent for drug crimes, 19 percent for property crimes, and 10 percent for public order crimes. Furthermore, in federal prisons, approximately 65 percent of women have been convicted of drug offenses, 22 percent for public order crimes, 9 percent for property crimes, and less than 5 percent for violent crimes (Kajstura and Sawyer 2024).

Property crimes, such as theft, fraud, and larceny, are usually committed as a result of poverty or addiction. Women typically commit these crimes out of necessity and are trying to provide for their families. Unlike men, women are much less likely to be imprisoned for committing violent offenses. Yet, when they are convicted of violent crimes, it is often related to domestic violence and trying to protect themselves from an abuser (Schwartz 2024).

Contributing Laws and Policies

There have been different policies and laws contributing to the large number of women imprisoned in the United States. The most detrimental are related to the War on Drugs and its associated laws during the 1980s and 1990s. Mandatory minimum sentencing laws mandated that people convicted of certain crimes, many low-level drug offenses, including possession, spend a minimum amount of time in prison. These laws disproportionately affected women, especially women of color (Pecorara n.d.). In particular, the Anti-Drug Abuse Act of 1986 imposed mandatory minimum sentences for drug offenses, leading to longer prison sentences for non-violent female offenders (Congress.Gov 2019).

Furthermore, the "get tough on crime" era criminalized behaviors related to addiction and poverty, which are problems that disproportionately impact women. The Violent Crime Control and Law Enforcement Act of 1994 expanded these measures by limiting opportunities for parole and creating longer prison sentences for women with histories of non-violent crimes (United States Congress 2019).

Additionally, there were welfare policies created in the 1990s that impacted women. For example, the Personal Responsibility and Work Opportunity Reconciliation Act of 1996 established stipulations denying housing assistance and welfare benefits to people with felony drug convictions (Kasich 1996). This act negatively impacted people who were already in poverty, making it more likely they would engage in more criminal activity.

It is important to note that the Fair Sentencing Act of 2010 reduced the sentencing disparity for crack cocaine and powder cocaine, which had adversely affected African-American communities as a result of the War on Drugs. Before this act was passed, people convicted of possession of crack faced the same sentences as people convicted of possession of 100 times the amount of powder cocaine. This act reduced the disparity from 100:1 to 18:1, and it also eliminated mandatory minimums for possessing crack (U.S. Congress, 2010). While this piece of legislation helped reduce sentencing disparities, they still exist.

Conditions in Women's Prisons

The conditions in women's prisons have been criticized for not addressing the needs of women. Many facilities are overcrowded and have limited access to healthcare and programming, contributing to the traumas these women experienced before their imprisonment. This is especially true in jails, which often have limited programming and services because they were designed for shorter stays and are less apt to prevent recidivism upon release (Kajstura and Sawyer 2024).

One of the most challenging issues in women's prisons in the United States is inadequate reproductive healthcare. Approximately 4 percent of women in prison are pregnant (Johns Hopkins Medicine 2019), but access to prenatal and postpartum care varies by state. Furthermore, while most states restrict shackling during childbirth, there are still some states that allow it (Hernandez 2022). In addition, many prisons still lack adequate menstrual hygiene products, and some women must pay for them (Straughan 2021).

Additionally, mental health services and programming in US prisons are not adequate for women, especially given their histories of mental illness, trauma, and substance abuse. A study on incarcerated women found they had frustrations related to program restrictions, limited vocational training, and a lack of gender-responsive approaches (Pederson et al. 2024). All of these limitations prevent incarcerated women from successful rehabilitation and stress the need for more targeted interventions to help them be successful in prison and upon release.

Furthermore, physical and sexual abuse by staff or other inmates is another concern in women's prisons. There are supposed to be protections in place related to the **Prison Rape Elimination Act**, but there are still issues. For example, a recent investigation found evidence of sexual abuse in at least two-thirds of federal facilities housing women (Johnson 2022). There is also the issue of transgender women who are housed in male prisons in the United States because they face even higher rates of sexual violence (Jenness 2021). These women experience systemic violence in prison, and there is a need for better housing practices to ensure their safety.

Health and Mental Health Issues

Incarcerated women's health and mental health issues are exacerbated by inadequate prison conditions and the lack of proper care (Anderson et al. 2020). About two-thirds of incarcerated women have mental health issues, including depression, anxiety, and post-traumatic stress disorder related to previous traumas. Unfortunately, the conditions of prison can make these issues worse. For instance, Fedock et al. (2024) found that prison-based mental health treatment can cause harm rather than providing care for incarcerated women. In this study, the women experienced insufficient care and coercion, especially when they were forced to take psychotropic medicine. This medicine was often administered to the women without explaining its side effects. Some of the women said it made them feel like "zombies," and they lost their sense of self. As a result, some of them refused treatment because it felt dehumanizing. While some facilities have mental health services, they are often inadequate and not trauma-informed.

Furthermore, many prisons do not have healthcare providers trained in obstetrics and gynecology, leading to lower rates of screenings and incorrect interpretation of test results. Women are also not always screened early enough for preventable diseases such as breast cancer (Ziazadeh 2019). Untreated physical and mental health issues negatively impact health outcomes, and without proper care, incarcerated women face ongoing struggles with their physical and emotional well-being.

Impact on Families and Children

Incarceration does not just impact these women; it also affects their families. Since the War on Drugs began, the rate of children with incarcerated mothers has increased by 100 percent (Martin 2017). Furthermore, African American children are nearly eight times as likely as white children to have an incarcerated parent (Martin 2017). These women are often the primary caregivers for their children, and the children are left with emotional, psychological, and financial difficulties upon their mother's imprisonment.

Because incarcerated women are often the primary caregivers, their children are likely to end up in foster care if they are not able to live with another relative, which presents problems of instability. Being separated from their mothers weakens their bonds, negatively impacting their development (Dargis and Mitchell-Somoza 2021). Furthermore, the stigma of having a parent who is incarcerated can also be problematic for children, leading to bullying and struggles in school.

Many incarcerated women are from economically disadvantaged backgrounds, and imprisonment makes it harder for their families (Martin 2017). Their incarceration leads to loss of income and the potential for housing instability. These financial burdens also make it hard to maintain contact with incarcerated women because phone calls and visits can be expensive, especially if the facility is not geographically close to their home.

Because so many incarcerated women are mothers, it is important to have programs that help them become better parents. For example, at the Bedford Hills Correctional Facility in New York, there is a parenting program that supports incarcerated mothers. It provides services that help mothers strengthen their bonds with their children and includes workshops to improve their parenting skills. It also has a prison nursery, which allows mothers to live with their children for up to eighteen months. This program has been shown to improve outcomes, such as reducing recidivism, promoting healthy childhood development, and fostering nurturing relationships, for incarcerated mothers and their children (Prison-Based Family Services Programs n.d.).

Policy Reforms and Recommendations

Policy reforms must address the needs of incarcerated women and the challenges they face. There remains a need for gender-responsive policies that consider women's histories of trauma, poverty, and substance abuse. Similarly, there is a need for trauma-informed care during incarceration to address these challenges. Without using rehabilitation to help incarcerated women with these issues, they will not be able to successfully reintegrate into society upon release from prison (Anderson et al. 2020).

Additionally, it is necessary to improve access to healthcare and mental health services for incarcerated women. Ensuring better access to preventative screening measures, prenatal care, and menstrual hygiene products are necessary steps for the well-being of incarcerated women (Straughan 2021) throughout the United States. Furthermore, it is necessary to expand the number of trained mental healthcare professionals within correctional facilities who can help address the unique needs of women with trauma-informed approaches. In addition to improving mental health services within the prison setting, it is also important for these women to have connections to mental health services upon release so they are successful in the community.

It is also important to have programs that help connect incarcerated mothers and their children. Several prisons nationwide, including the program at Bedford Hills and the Washington Corrections Center for Women, have prison nurseries where newborns can stay with their mothers for the first year or two of their lives (Corley 2019). Prison nurseries help strengthen the bond between mothers and children, reducing the impact that incarceration has on women and their families. However, prison nurseries must operate under strict guidelines and be reserved for non-violent offenders.

Sentencing reform is also needed to reduce the number of incarcerated women in the United States, especially for drug crimes. There is a need to re-examine mandatory minimums, which disproportionately impact women of color. While the **EQUAL Act** has not been approved yet, it has been proposed to reduce mandatory minimums (Siegler 2021) and their associated racial disparities. It would eliminate the sentencing disparity between crack and powder cocaine that started during the War on Drugs and permit retroactive reductions in sentencing. However, progress on sentencing reform can often be slow due to political opposition and fear that reducing harsh sentences will increase crime rates.

Furthermore, Cox and Malkin (2023) discuss the lack of diverse representation in convict criminology, which considers the lived experiences of people who have been incarcerated. They suggest integrating feminist epistemology into convict criminology to account for the intersectional experiences of incarcerated women, including women of color and LGBTQ+ populations. This will ensure that the voices of these women, who are over-represented in the system, are heard.

Canada

Historical Context

Similar to what we saw in the United States, the criminal justice system in Canada was designed for men because women made up such a small percentage of those in prison. Before becoming a country in 1867, the system was one of punishment, whereby people who broke the law, including women and children, suffered harsh consequences. They were often whipped, branded, or put in pillories or stocks for the public to see (Canada Correctional Service 2007).

In the mid-1800s, the federal penitentiary system was established in Canada. However, women were housed in separate sections in the same facilities as men during this period. The first women incarcerated in a Canadian penitentiary were at the Provincial Penitentiary of Upper Canada in Kingston in 1835 (Canada Correctional Service 2024). They faced harsh punishment, including isolation, and received no educational training. Also, their living conditions were deplorable, with common bug infestations, and they used buckets for toilets.

The first separate facility for women in Canada, the Kingston Prison for Women, opened in 1934. It was a maximum-security federal facility that housed all women in Canada, regardless of their security level (Correctional Service Canada 2020). With nearly 4 million square miles, Canada is the second-largest country behind Russia (World Data Editors n.d.), making it challenging for incarcerated women throughout Canada to be housed in only one facility.

As a result of the geographic challenges and issues with housing women of all security levels together, there were changes to the system in the late twentieth century. In 1990, a task force commissioned by the federal government reviewed the situation of incarcerated women and brought it in a new direction (Correctional Service Canada 2020). As a result of this task force, the

Correctional Service of Canada (CSC) began to focus more on rehabilitating women and establishing additional facilities for them. The Kingston Prison for Women closed in 2000, and there are now six federal facilities throughout Canada for women (Correctional Service Canada 2020).

Female Incarceration Rates and Trends

Let's now take a look at what the population of women looks like in these facilities. While there are far fewer women incarcerated in Canada than in the United States, there has been an increase in recent decades, and this increase has grown faster than for men. In 1980, there were 200 women housed in Canada's federal system (Canada 2024), and it reached its peak in 2019 with 693 incarcerated women (Canada Correctional Service 2019). That number has been decreasing in recent years, as there were 558 incarcerated women in the federal system in 2022 (Correctional Service Canada 2024).

Aside from the federal system, many people are housed in Canada's Provincial/Territorial System, which is managed by the thirteen Canadian provinces. This system is similar to local jails in the United States, where people convicted of crimes with lesser sentences and those detained before trial are housed. There has also been an increase in the number of women housed in this system. In 2000, there were nearly 20,000 women, and it peaked in 2017 with approximately 35,500 women. Since then, the number has been decreasing, and there are now almost 23,000 women housed here (Government of Canada 2024). About two-thirds of people in this system are detained as they await trial, many of whom are Indigenous, so they are imprisoned even though they are not convicted (Robinson et al. 2023).

In general, there is an overrepresentation of Indigenous women behind bars in Canada, which has also been increasing at a much higher rate than non-Indigenous women in recent years. Indigenous women make up almost half of the women's prison population (Major 2021), but they comprise only 5 percent of the general population (Government of Canada 2023).

Similar to the United States, harsh sentencing laws, such as **Mandatory Minimum Penalties** (MMPs) for non-violent offenses, like drug-related crimes or property offenses, have driven the rise in female incarceration in Canada. These laws have disproportionately affected women, especially those from marginalized communities, including Indigenous women (Department of Justice Canada 2021).

Demographics of Incarcerated Women

The overrepresentation of Indigenous women is due to the lasting impacts of colonialism and systemic racism (Bird 2024). Indigenous women often come from disadvantaged backgrounds, and they face poverty and a lack of education, especially those living in remote areas (Government of Canada 2022). Colonial policies date back to the **Indian Act of 1896**, which marginalized Indigenous people, disrupting their governance, and making them more vulnerable to structural disadvantages (The Indian Act and Why You Need to Know about It 2023). Other colonial policies, like residential schools and the **Sixties Scoop**, aimed to take Indigenous children away from their homes and infiltrate them with Euro-Canadian values, contributing to a breakdown of Indigenous families (Department of Justice 2023).

The impact of these colonial practices has left a legacy of forced assimilation that has led to poverty, higher rates of substance abuse, and mental health issues among Indigenous populations, making them more apt to be involved in the criminal justice system. Furthermore, when in prison, Indigenous women are more likely to be subjected to harsher conditions like solitary confinement and higher security classifications (Bird 2024), making them less likely to receive programming and rehabilitation.

In regard to age, most incarcerated women in Canada are under forty-five years old (Correctional Service Canada 2019). There is a lack of research on the number of women who are mothers, but it is estimated that approximately 80 percent of incarcerated women in Canada have been pregnant

The Sixties Scoop

Between the 1960s and 1980s, thousands of Indigenous children in Canada were taken from their families and placed in non-Indigenous foster or adoptive homes. This policy, now called the "Sixties Scoop," was part of a pattern of colonial control that destabilized Indigenous families. The Canadian government has since acknowledged the harms of the Sixties Scoop, issuing formal apologies and compensation agreements to survivors, though many argue that these efforts have not fully addressed the lasting effects of displacement and inequality. Its legacy contributes to higher rates of poverty, trauma, and substance abuse, which are factors linked to the overrepresentation of Indigenous women in Canadian prisons today.

(Paynter et al. 2022). Historically, there has been a lack of data on this topic. There is also a lack of attention on children with incarcerated parents, indicating that they are "invisible" in the criminal justice system. As a result of this invisibility, some argue that it is a way the criminal justice system avoids addressing the challenges that these children face (Paynter et al., 2022).

Mental health and substance abuse are also prevalent among incarcerated women in Canada. Almost 80 percent of Indigenous women and nearly 60 percent of white women in Canadian prisons have had a moderate to severe problem with substances. In addition, about two-thirds of Indigenous women and almost half of all white women reported frequent poly-substance use in the year leading up to their arrest (Correctional Service Canada 2023). Furthermore, nearly 80 percent of incarcerated women in Canada have at least one DSM-IV-TR diagnosis (Cameron et al. 2020). Many of them have depression, anxiety, and post-traumatic stress disorder, often because they have a history of abuse or trauma.

Crimes Leading to Incarceration

Over three-quarters of the time, adult women in Canada are incarcerated for non-violent offenses (Canada 2015), such as property crimes, public order offenses, or drug crimes. Property crimes, such as theft and fraud, are the most common type of crime women are convicted of, comprising about 35 percent of all crimes (Canada 2015). Substance use is often a factor that influences women's involvement with crime, as many women commit property crimes to financially support their addiction. Moreover, economic conditions, such as single parenting, living in poverty, and lack of employment opportunities, affect women more than men (Understanding Women's Experiences with the Criminal Justice System as Accused and Offenders 2024). Consequently, women often commit crimes as a result of poverty so that they can meet the needs to support their families.

About 10 percent of female crime in Canada is drug-related (Canada 2015). Many of these women are involved in low-level drug trafficking or possession, often caused by addiction or the need to survive. Furthermore, women in the drug trade usually played minor roles but faced long sentences as a result of MMPs (Malinowska and Rychkova 2015).

Violent crimes are not common for women, but when they engage in violence, it is usually related to intimate partner violence when trying to defend themselves or their children. Thus, the most common victims when women engage in violence are spouses or intimate partners (Understanding Women's Experiences with the Criminal Justice System as Accused and Offenders 2024).

Contributing Laws and Policies

Laws and policies have contributed to the incarceration of women in Canada, especially women from marginalized communities. Stricter sentencing laws, like MMPs, for non-violent and drug crimes have disproportionately impacted women. MMPs have been used for drug crimes under Canada's Controlled Drugs and Substances Act (CDSA) beginning in 2006 (Government of Canada 2016). They eliminate judicial discretion, so judges cannot consider the defendant's circumstances when sentencing. These practices have particularly impacted Indigenous women, who often engage in crimes of survival rather than crimes of violence.

Note that the Supreme Court of Canada tried to address these disparities for Indigenous people in *R. v. Gladue* (1999) by requiring judges to consider an Indigenous individual's background during sentencing (R. V. Gladue, 1999 CanLII 679 (SCC) 1999). However, there remains an overrepresentation of Indigenous women in the system, which has continued to increase, showing that this ruling has not been adequately implemented.

Moreover, Bill C-5 was passed in 2022, removing MMPs for many drug-related crimes under the CDSA. This allows judges more discretion for individualized sentencing, especially for non-violent or drug crimes involving marginalized women. However, MMPs remain for crimes like murder and other serious violent offenses (Department of Justice Canada 2021).

Furthermore, the over-policing of marginalized communities, including Indigenous women, has contributed to female incarceration in Canada. Indigenous women experience more surveillance by the police, such as racial profiling and disproportionate use of force. Yet, they are under-policed when they are the victims of crimes (McKay 2021). Indigenous Services Canada has funded programs like the Pathways to Safe Indigenous Communities Initiative to reduce over-policing and to use culturally appropriate approaches to support these communities—however, over-policing remains (Canada 2021).

Conditions in Women's Prisons

The conditions for incarcerated women in Canada vary, but since the early 1990s, there has been a greater focus on rehabilitation in the CSC (Correctional Service

Canada 2020). However, there are instances when the needs of incarcerated women in Canada are not met, especially concerning programming and rehabilitation.

For instance, women with mental illness are sometimes placed in solitary confinement, which can make their conditions worse. In one study, Prevost and Kilty (2020) looked at the use of solitary confinement in federal prisons, noting that it is disproportionately used on Indigenous women. They critiqued how the CSC often considers mental illness as something that is managed through segregation rather than rehabilitation.

Additionally, access to healthcare is a concern in some facilities, especially related to reproductive needs. For example, Jones and colleagues (2024) found that incarcerated women in Ontario faced inconsistent healthcare and a lack of contraceptive options. These women wanted access to contraception and to be better educated about it, necessitating a need for the prison system to look into these concerns.

Lastly, in 2017, the CSC updated its policy for housing transgender individuals, letting them be housed in a facility that aligns with their gender identity. This policy stresses the protection and equal treatment of transgender inmates. It also ensures confidentiality about gender identity and allows for preferred pronouns (CBC n.d.). While transgender individuals are still subject to discrimination in the prison system, the new policy is safer, especially for transgender women who were previously housed in men's facilities and at greater risk of sexual violence (Boyer et al. 2019).

Health and Mental Health Issues

Many Canadian women enter the prison system with mental health needs, and they often have physical health problems, as well. Despite the need for mental health services, there has historically been inadequate access to care within the prison system. However, the CSC has been trying to improve mental health services in prison. Amendments to the Corrections and Conditional Release Act mandate mental health assessments when people are admitted, and there must also be regular monitoring of people with mental illness in the system. Yet, issues remain with limited mental health staffing and varied levels of care across the provinces (Cameron et al. 2020).

Similar to many countries, pregnant women in Canada do not always receive adequate care. A recent study found that prenatal care for women in Ontario jails was below international standards. Pregnant women in these jails received about half of the number of prenatal visits than the general population, and only over one-third of them received care in the first trimester, which is when many problems occur (Craggs 2020). There were also reports of pregnant women being shackled during examinations.

Furthermore, there are problems with sexually transmitted diseases among incarcerated women in Canada. Erickson and colleagues (2020) found that recently imprisoned women living with HIV in Vancouver were significantly less likely to reach viral suppression. This was a result of challenges they faced before incarceration, such as homelessness, drug use, and limited access to healthcare. Thus, there should be interventions to improve HIV care during incarceration.

Impact on Families and Children

More than 375,000 children have a parent who is incarcerated in Canada ("Kids with Incarcerated Parents Canada" 2020), and as a result, they face family instability, economic insecurity, and social isolation. However, there is a Mother-Child Program in Kitchener, Ontario, that lets eligible mothers raise their infants and toddlers in a unit of the prison. The program was created in 2001, allowing mothers to bond with their children in dormitory-style housing. To date, this program has helped over 150 women and their children have more positive relationships. Eligibility criteria for the program are strict, so it has been criticized for being difficult to participate in, especially for Indigenous women. (Howorun 2023). Regrettably, being separated from their children in prison perpetuates the family separation that occurred with Indigenous families during the time of **residential schools**.

There are organizations in Canada that are working to meet the needs of children of incarcerated parents. Kids with Incarcerated Parents (KIP) is an organization that aims to help children with parents who are in prison (Our Mission | KIP 2020). KIP provides programming and services for these children to foster self-esteem and to give them a sense of security while they deal with the incarceration of a parent. This organization tries to break the cycle of crime and give kids the tools they need to create a better future for themselves. Furthermore, the Canadian Coalition for Children with Incarcerated Parents (CCCIP) is a network that advocates for the rights of children with incarcerated parents. CCCIP also tries to minimize the overrepresentation of Indigenous people in prison and the impacts parental incarceration has on Indigenous children (Our Work | CCCIP 2023). By educating decision-makers, government officials, and the public, CCCIP has raised awareness about the impact of parental incarceration.

Policy Reforms and Recommendations

Policy reforms are needed for incarcerated women in Canada to address the issues that this population faces. There must be more alternatives to incarceration, especially for women convicted of non-violent crimes. Community programs and **restorative justice** initiatives help keep women out of prison, focusing on rehabilitation and offering support to treat the root of their problems rather than just punishing them. One suggestion is the use of Stride Circles, which are community-based groups that help women foster a sense of inclusion and belonging. They focus on restorative justice, emphasizing community collaboration and support instead of punishment (Fortune et al. 2020).

There is also a need for better healthcare and mental health services for incarcerated women in Canada. For instance, because many women have sexually transmitted diseases and do not have adequate access to contraception, there is a need to address these issues and educate women about these diseases (Taylor et al. 2021). Also, it is necessary to increase access to counseling and therapy in prison, with a focus on addressing trauma, addiction, and mental health conditions common among incarcerated women. Similar to the United States, it is important to not only increase access to these services during incarceration but also provide support upon their release so that they can thrive in the community.

Lastly, culturally appropriate services are needed for Indigenous women. For example, more Indigenous women should be able to participate in the Okimaw Ohci Healing Lodge in Saskatchewan, Canada (Canada 2013). This federal facility operates based on Indigenous cultural and spiritual values, providing a trauma-informed approach to rehabilitation, and it has been linked to lower recidivism rates. It integrates Indigenous healing practices, teachings, and ceremonies into the women's recovery and rehabilitation, including cultural programming that addresses the root of their problems (Department of Justice 2023).

Mexico

Historical Context

Imprisonment practices began evolving in Mexico in 1849, following the country's loss of territory to the United States. Early prisons were designed to moralize political rebels and social deviants, and this approach was codified in the first Mexican Federal Penal Code during President Benito Juárez's government (Bucerius and Sandberg 2022). These practices shaped Mexico's penitentiary system, including the treatment of incarcerated women, who were often viewed as moral failures for violating strict gender roles (Sandberg, Agoff, and Fondevila 2021).

Throughout the Penitentiary Reform Movement of the 1930s, women's prisons focused on restoring relationships with family, and some of these practices continue today (Bucerius and Sandberg 2022). The first prison for women in Mexico was the Centro Femenil de Readaptación y Rehabilitación Social Femenil Tepepan (Women's Social Rehabilitation Center of Tepepan), which opened in the late 1970s. This facility encouraged the women housed there to strengthen the bonds with their families. For instance, young children could live with their mothers, older children could occasionally spend the night, and there were spaces where families could gather together and engage in activities, like cooking together (Pearson 1993).

Over the past twenty years, economic instability, rising violence, and organized crime have contributed to an increase in female incarceration, with many women coerced into low-level roles in criminal networks. Some of this coincided with Mexico's participation in the War on Drugs in the United States (Puyana et al. 2017), which targeted low-level drug offenses, disproportionately affecting women.

Women incarcerated in Querétaro, Mexico, making tortillas, *c.* 1905–1910. (California Historical Society Collection via Wikimedia Commons)

Currently, there are 280 prisons in Mexico (14 federal and 266 state), and approximately 13 are designated explicitly as women's correctional centers. There are also 338 municipal jails throughout Mexico which house people convicted of minor offenses or those awaiting trial (Instituto Nacional de Estadística y Geografía 2024). Moreover, only about 30 percent of all incarcerated women in Mexico are housed in female facilities. The other 70 percent are housed in units of men's prisons, even though Article 18 of Mexico's Constitution mandates gender segregation in prisons ("Mexico 1917 (Rev. 2015) Constitution—Constitute" n.d.). Thus, despite the Mexican prison system's emphasis on family connections, it was designed for men, leaving the unique needs of women unaddressed (Sandberg, Agoff, and Fondevila 2021).

Female Incarceration Rates and Trends

In recent decades, female incarceration in Mexico has increased largely due to drug and organized crime. In 2000, there were nearly 7,000 incarcerated women, but that number has almost doubled to approximately 13,500 as a result of drug crimes and the marginalization of women coerced into low-level roles within criminal organizations (World Prison Brief 2024).

Over half of the women incarcerated at the federal level have been convicted of drug crimes. Aside from the War on Drugs in the United States, Mexico also declared a similar "war" in 2006 by former president Felipe Calderon (Moshan et al. 2024). During Calderon's six-year term as president, approximately 3,000 women were incarcerated for drug crimes, and the federal prison population grew nearly twice as much for women than men.

Since 2017, there has also been an increase in the number of women imprisoned for involvement in organized crime (Valle 2024), but most of these women are low in the ranks of these organizations. They are often involved in transporting or selling drugs as a result of social and economic difficulties that forced them into illegal activities to survive.

Furthermore, nearly 40 percent of the Mexican prison population is awaiting trial and has not been convicted (World Prison Brief 2024). Women in pre-detention centers or municipal jails often lack legal support and are detained for extended periods (Valle 2024). For example, Ana Georgina Dominguez has been in jail for over thirteen years on charges of money laundering, which prosecutors have still not proven she has committed (Woodford 2022). She is one of thousands of women in Mexico who have not seen their children for years as they await their trial in jail.

Lastly, another trend is the increasing imprisonment of Indigenous people. Over 6,500 Indigenous people are incarcerated in Mexico, many of whom face significant language barriers, lack access to interpreters, and suffer from inadequate legal representation. For instance, in 2015, Carlota, a 66-year-old Indigenous speaker from Oaxaca, was arrested and received legal documents that she was unable to read. After being flown nearly 300 miles to Mexico City, she was asked to give her statements in Spanish, which she minimally spoke. It was not until days later that she was read her charges of human trafficking in her native language. Similar to many Indigenous people facing incarceration, Carlota faced language barriers and discrimination in the system. Although Mexico's 2020 Amnesty Law intended to address these issues, its implementation has been hindered due to bureaucratic delays. Unfortunately, these problems have not been resolved despite over 1,000 amnesty requests, including Carlota's (Lopez Sarabia 2021).

Demographics of Incarcerated Women

There are social and economic disparities in Mexico, which are reflected in the population of incarcerated women, as most of them come from poverty, are uneducated, and unemployed (Ballesteros 2018). The vast majority of these women are single mothers whose involvement in crime is associated with economic survival or coercion by men involved in organized crime (Garsd 2018).

Many of these women became mothers very young, between thirteen and sixteen years old. This pattern is the result of abortion being illegal in most Mexican states and because Mexican society opposes abortion (Bucerius and Sandberg 2022). Because these women were so young when they had their children, they were often economically dependent on their children's fathers, making it difficult to leave even if they were being abused. Many of these women experienced severe sexual and physical abuse before incarceration, often as children, and were also involved in abusive relationships as adults (Bucerius and Sandberg 2022).

About 40 percent of women in Mexican prisons are in their twenties and thirties (Mexico: Prison Population by Age and Gender 2022 2024), reflecting a younger population drawn into crime. As many of these women are serving time for drug-related offenses, there is an emphasis on the socioeconomic factors and gender dynamics that influence their pathways to crime.

Crimes Leading to Incarceration

Similar to women in the United States and Canada, women in Mexico are usually incarcerated for non-violent crimes, such as drug and property crimes. About 43 percent of incarcerated women in Mexico are serving time for crimes related to drug trafficking and narcotics. Moreover, approximately 21 percent are imprisoned for property crimes like theft, burglary, and fraud, while violent crimes, like homicide or assault, comprise only about 12 percent of their crimes (International Crisis Group 2023).

Poverty and a lack of opportunities are the main reasons women engage in crime in Mexico. They are typically involved in crimes of survival, like transporting drugs or engaging in property crimes, so that they can provide for their families. Although not as common as non-violent crimes, violent offenses do occur, especially as more women are becoming involved in organized crime (Valle 2024). Often recruited by men, once they are involved in organized crime, they may participate in violent crimes to prove their loyalty to the group. Organized crime groups may also coerce some of them to engage in violence. Furthermore, some women engage in violence as a means of self-defense if they have been the victims of domestic violence (International Crisis Group 2023).

Contributing Laws and Policies

Harsh laws and mandatory sentencing policies for drug and organized crimes in Mexico have contributed to women's incarceration. Mexico's efforts to curtail drug trafficking and organized crime officially began in 2006 under former President Calderón. At this time, thousands of troops were used to fight drug cartels that had taken over parts of Mexico. The hope was to demolish drug-trafficking organizations that produced and transported drugs in the United States. Unfortunately, Mexico's War on Drugs has led to more violence as cartels fought back against the government. It has also contributed to more government corruption. Yet, it has not addressed the root causes of drug production and consumption (Mexico's Long War 2022).

The Código Penal Federal (Federal Penal Code) provides mandatory minimum penalties for drug crimes in Mexico, which have intensified since the country's War on Drugs. For instance, crimes like drug trafficking, manufacturing, and distribution impose sentences of up to thirty years, and violent crimes related to drug trafficking can result in life imprisonment. Conversely, lesser drug possession offenses can result in fines or imprisonment of up to five years (Mexico

2024). Additionally, the Ley Federal Contra la Delincuencia Organizada (Federal Law Against Organized Crime) imposes penalties for organized crime. These sentences range from ten to forty years in prison, depending on the individual's role within the network. Fines are often imposed along with imprisonment, ranging from 250 to 25,000 days' worth of minimum wage (Mexico 2021).

Women in Mexico have been disproportionately impacted by these mandatory penalties. However, there tends to be more judicial discretion under the Federal Penal Code than the Federal Law Against Organized Crime. Articles 51 and 52 of the Federal Penal Code stress how judges can consider aggravating or mitigating circumstances, as well as an individual's background during sentencing (Mexico 2024). Although these penalties have tried to reduce organized crime and drug trafficking, they have adversely impacted women engaged in low-level crimes, making it necessary to explore reforms that address the root causes of their criminality.

Conditions in Women's Prisons

Women in Mexican prisons often face harsh conditions, such as overcrowding and a lack of access to necessities and services. For instance, 37 percent of Mexican prisons are overcrowded, 30 percent of people do not have drinking water in their cells, and only 8 percent receive personal hygiene items (Q&A 2020).

Moshan and colleagues (2024) examined the stories of formerly incarcerated women to show the injustices faced by women in Mexican prisons, finding a lack of necessities like food, feminine hygiene products, and healthcare services, including prenatal care. They also found that Indigenous women are especially vulnerable, as they have language barriers and face cultural isolation because most prisons do not have culturally appropriate services.

Furthermore, an Amnesty International investigation (Latimer 2016) found that almost three-quarters of incarcerated women in Mexico had experienced sexual violence during their arrest or while they were being interrogated. In addition, 97 percent experienced physical abuse, such as beatings. There is also a lack of mental health services for these incarcerated women to deal with these traumas at the hands of the state. Moreover, even though there have been investigations into these allegations, there is a lack of accountability, as rarely does anyone face consequences for engaging in these types of abuses.

Programs to help reintegrate into society are also limited, especially in pre-trial detention centers. Vocational training and educational opportunities, which could help imprisoned women with the skills they need to be successful upon release, are lacking (Latimer 2016). There have been limited attempts at improving conditions in Mexican prisons, making it hard to address the needs of incarcerated women (Moshan et al. 2024).

Health and Mental Health Issues

There are health and mental health concerns for incarcerated women in Mexico. Many women have health conditions that are worsened by past trauma and coercion into crime. They are at risk of developing diseases like hypertension and obesity, which are further exacerbated by a poor diet, overcrowded conditions, and a lack of physical activity. Also, much of their food is from prison stores or brought in by visitors and is unhealthy and processed, contributing to further health complications (Silverman-Retana et al. 2018).

Another issue is substance abuse. Upward of 60 percent of incarcerated women have reported drug use (Silverman-Retana et al. 2018), and many women have substance abuse issues. However, rehabilitation programs are usually lacking in Mexican facilities. Furthermore, the presence of alcohol and cocaine in Mexican prisons makes it hard to overcome addictions since these substances are widely available.

Furthermore, the mental health of women in Mexico is impacted by the violence that is a regular part of life. Many women are in constant fear of sexual assault and femicide (i.e., killing women for their gender), given the rampant gendered violence throughout many parts of the country. In 2021, one in five women was exposed to sexual violence, and between 2007 and 2021, the number of femicides tripled (Ospina-Escobar 2023). This fear is worsened for incarcerated women, who face gender-based violence from the state, as noted above (Latimer 2016), as well as the trauma they experienced before incarceration. Thus, there is a need for more mental health services, as well as protection for women inside and outside of prison.

Impact on Families and Children

The incarceration of women in Mexico impacts their families, especially their children, as many of these women are single mothers. However, the situation for mothers and children differs between the United States and Canada. In Mexico, children can stay in prison with their mothers until they are three years old, and there are upward of 600 children in Mexico's federal and state prisons

Children Growing Up in Prison

In Mexico, children can remain with their mothers in prison until age three. Currently, more than 600 children live in federal and state prisons. Proponents argue this allows mother–child bonding, especially since many incarcerated women are single mothers with no alternatives for childcare. However, critics suggest that prison is not a place for children, warning that it perpetuates trauma and cycles of incarceration. This debate illustrates the conflict between protecting family ties and ensuring children's healthy development.

(White 2023). For example, Nancy Polanco Najera is housed in a prison in Mexico City, but she can be with her son, who was born in prison. Najera met her son's father in prison and stresses that her son helps her get through the challenges of incarceration. Yet, she knows that her son will soon be separated from her as he is reaching the age limit when a child can remain with his imprisoned mother under the law (Garsd 2018).

However, there is debate about whether children should be raised in prison. While children need to bond with their mothers, some question the ethics of raising young children in prison. They argue that caregivers like grandparents or aunts would provide a better environment for the children of incarcerated mothers, as living in prison may perpetuate the familial cycle of incarceration. Unfortunately, many women have no viable alternatives for their children (Garsd 2018).

Policy Reforms and Recommendations

There are several necessary policy reforms to address the issues facing incarcerated women in Mexico. Most importantly, incarcerating women for non-violent crimes has not been effective because it disproportionately impacts marginalized communities, disrupts families, and does not address the root cause of their offending (EQUIS 2021). Thus, it is essential to increase alternatives to incarceration for non-violent offenders, such as **restorative justice** programs, like what was discussed in Canada, or drug courts. For example, in 2009, Mexico introduced drug courts, known as Tribunales para Tratamiento de Adicciones, as an alternative to incarceration to reduce drug use and recidivism. As long as people complete the drug court program, they do not have to go to prison. While the use of drug courts shows a focus on rehabilitation and treatment, their use remains limited throughout the country due to insufficient resources and bureaucratic delays (Transnational Institute 2020).

Reforms must also focus on drug policy, such as decriminalizing minor drug crimes and reducing mandatory minimum sentences. There has been some movement in this direction. In 2018, Mexico's Supreme Court ruled that prohibiting recreational cannabis was unconstitutional, and there are proposals for new cannabis laws. However, the implementation of these laws remains unresolved (Transnational Institute 2020).

Furthermore, women incarcerated in Mexico need better access to gender-specific services and programming. For example, a program called La Cana provides employment and therapeutic activities to help women be productive (Ancira 2017). This type of programming prepares women to reintegrate into society, giving them tools to make them less apt to reoffend. Without this type of programming, the prison system continues to perpetuate the cycle of poverty and crime.

Conclusion

The experiences of incarcerated women in the United States, Canada, and Mexico have shared challenges and unique circumstances, stressing the importance of addressing women's needs within each country. In all of these countries, women are often incarcerated for non-violent crimes, such as property or drug crimes. However, their reasons for incarceration and the conditions of their imprisonment are different. In the United States, the impact of the War on Drugs and mandatory minimums has led to the highest incarceration rates in the world and has disproportionately affected women of color. In Canada, there has been an increase in the number of Indigenous women who are over-represented in the justice system as a result of colonialism. Mexico has also seen a rise in female incarceration rates, primarily from drug crimes, and Indigenous women and women coerced into organized crime face additional challenges.

These countries all lack adequate healthcare, mental health services, and programming for rehabilitation. In the United States, facilities often lack gender-responsive programming, including sufficient access to mental health and reproductive care. While Canada has a greater focus on rehabilitation, it still has inadequate mental health services, along with limited culturally appropriate services for Indigenous women. Mexico has harsher prison conditions, and women face overcrowding, violence, and limited access to basic necessities. Moreover, Indigenous women in Mexico also face cultural isolation and language barriers.

It is necessary to address the unique needs of these women to encourage rehabilitation and minimize recidivism. Gender-responsive, trauma-informed approaches are required to help them be successful during their incarceration and upon release. These strategies must provide them with access to healthcare, mental health services, vocational training, and parenting programs. In addition, policy reforms must explore alternatives to incarceration for non-violent crimes, which are necessary to break the cycle of poverty and crime. The struggles incarcerated women face in these countries stress how important it is for reforms to prioritize their specific needs. Justice systems throughout North America must focus more on rehabilitation and models that recognize how gender, race, and class impact women's imprisonment.

References

ACLU. 2007. "Facts About the Over-Incarceration of Women in the United States." American Civil Liberties Union. December 12, 2007. https://www.aclu.org/documents/facts-about-over-incarceration-women-united-states.

Ancira, Daniela. 2017. *La Cana, Mexico: Providing Female Prisoners with Employment and Reintegration Opportunities.* Penal Reform International. https://www.penalreform.org/blog/la-cana-mexico-how-prison-labour-programmes-with/.

Anderson, Joi D., Ronald O. Pitner, and Nikki R. Wooten. 2020. "A Gender-Specific Model of Trauma and Victimization in Incarcerated Women." *Journal of Human Behavior in the Social Environment* 30 (2): 191–212.

Ballesteros, Cecilia. 2018. "Mexico's Women Prisoners: Doubly Punished for Not Living up to Female Roles." EL PAÍS. February 12, 2018. https://english.elpais.com/elpais/2018/02/12/inenglish/1518440239_829884.html.

Bandele, Monifa. 2017. "Here's How Prison and Jail Systems Brutalize Women, Especially Mothers | News & Commentary." American Civil Liberties Union. October 23, 2017. https://www.aclu.org/news/womens-rights/heres-how-prison-and-jail-systems-brutalize-women.

Bertram, Wanda, and Wendy Sawyer. 2021. "Prisons and Jails Will Separate Millions of Mothers from Their Children in 2021." Prison Policy Initiative. May 5, 2021. https://www.prisonpolicy.org/blog/2021/05/05/mothers-day-2021/.

Bird, Danielle. 2024. "Indigenous Incarceration and Settler Colonial Genocides." *Journal of Prisoners on Prisons* 33 (2): 92–111.

Boyer, Yvonne, Ayoola S. Odeyemi, Erin Fletcher, and Jade Fletcher. 2019. "Vulnerable Targets: Trans Prisoner Safety, the Law, and Sexual Violence in the Prison System." *Canadian Journal of Women and the Law/Revue Femmes et Droit* 31 (2): 387–409.

Bucerius, Sandra, and Sveinung Sandberg. 2022. "Women in Prisons." *Crime and Justice* 51: 137–86.

Budd, Kristen. 2023. "Incarcerated Women and Girls." The Sentencing Project. April 3, 2023. https://www.sentencingproject.org/fact-sheet/incarcerated-women-and-girls/.

Cameron, Colin, Najat Khalifa, Andrew Bickle, Hira Safdar, and Tariq Hassan. 2020. "Psychiatry in the Federal Correctional System in Canada." *BJPsych International* 18 (2): 42–46.

Canada. 2024. "Information Archivée Dans Le Web | Information Archived on the Web." Publications.gc.ca. https://publications.gc.ca/collections/collection_2010/scc-csc/PS83-3-99-eng.pdf.

Canada. 2021. "Pathways to Safe Indigenous Communities Initiative." Sac-Isc.gc.ca. https://sac-isc.gc.ca/eng/1646747630193/1646747651080.

Canada. 2015. "Table 8 Rates of Criminal Code and Other Federal Statute Violations by Sex and Age of Accused, 2015." Statcan.gc.ca. https://www150.statcan.gc.ca/n1/pub/89-503-x/2015001/article/14785/tbl/tbl08-eng.htm.

Canada. 2013. "Okimaw Ohci Healing Lodge." February 11, 2013. https://www.canada.ca/en/correctional-service/corporate/facilities-security/institutional-profiles/prairie/okimaw-ohci-healing-lodge.html.

Canada Correctional Service. 2024. "Crime, Punishment, and Prison for Women." https://www.canada.ca/en/correctional-service/lets-talk/read/2024/03-04-prison-for-women.html.

Canada Correctional Service. 2019. "Statistics and Research on Women Offenders." https://www.canada.ca/en/correctional-service/programs/offenders/women/statistics-research-women-offenders.html.

Canada Correctional Service. 2007. "Pre-1920: From Punishment to Penance." November 15, 2007. https://www.canada.ca/en/correctional-service/corporate/history-csc/timeline/pre-1920.html.

Carson, E. Ann, and Rich Kluckow. 2023. "Correctional Populations in the United States, 2021—Statistical Tables." Bureau of Justice Statistics. Washington, DC: Bureau of Justice Statistics. https://bjs.ojp.gov/document/cpus21st.pdf.

CBC. n.d. "Canada's Prison System Overhauls Transgender Inmate Policy | CBC News." https://www.cbc.ca/news/politics/transgender-inmates-csc-policy-1.4512510.

Congress.Gov. 2019. "H.R.5484—99th Congress (1985–1986): Anti-Drug Abuse Act of 1986." Congress.gov. https://www.congress.gov/bill/99th-congress/house-bill/5484.

Corley, Cheryl. 2019. "NPR Choice Page." Npr.org. https://www.npr.org/2018/12/06/663516573/programs-help-incarcerated-moms-bond-with-their-babies-in-prison.

Correctional Service Canada. 2024. "Regional Profiles of Canadian In-Custody Women Federal Offenders—Canada.ca." Canada.ca. https://www.canada.ca/en/correctional-service/corporate/library/research/glance/467.html.

Correctional Service Canada. 2023. "Substance Use Patterns of Women Offenders Across Ethnocultural Groups—Canada.ca." Canada.ca. https://www.canada.ca/en/correctional-service/corporate/library/research/research-brief/23-18.html.

Correctional Service Canada. 2020. "History of Women's Corrections—Canada.ca." Canada.ca. https://www.canada.ca/en/correctional-service/programs/offenders/women/history-womens-corrections.html.

Correctional Service Canada. 2019. "Pandemic Era Changes in Federal Corrections Age Structures—Canada.ca." Canada.ca. https://www.canada.ca/en/correctional-service/corporate/library/research/research-brief/22-28.html.

Cox, Alison, and Michelle L. Malkin. 2023. "Feminist Convict Criminology for the Future." *Critical Criminology* 31: 685–705.

Craggs, Samantha. 2020. "Pregnant Inmates Are Getting Prenatal Care Far Below Health Standards, Study Shows." CBC. https://www.cbc.ca/news/canada/hamilton/costescu-1.5692144.

Dargis, Monika, and Arielle Mitchell-Somoza. 2021. "Challenges Associated with Parenting While Incarcerated: A Review." *International Journal of Environmental Research and Public Health* 18 (18): 9927.

Department of Justice. 2023. "Understanding the Overrepresentation of Indigenous People—State of the Criminal Justice System Dashboard." Justice.gc.ca. Government of Canada. https://www.justice.gc.ca/socjs-esjp/en/ind-aut/uo-cs.

Department of Justice Canada. 2021. "Bill C-5: Mandatory Minimum Penalties to Be Repealed." https://www.canada.ca/en/department-justice/news/2021/12/mandatory-minimum-penalties-to-be-repealed.html.

EQUIS. 2021. "Criminalización de Mujeres y Políticas Punitivas." *EQUIS Justicia para las Mujeres*. https://equis.org.mx/criminalizacion/.

Erickson, Margaret, Neora Pick, Flo Ranville, Melissa Braschel, Mary Kestler, Karen Kinvig, Andrea Krüsi, and Kate Shannon. 2020. "Recent Incarceration as a Primary Barrier to Virologic Suppression Among Women Living with HIV: Results from a Longitudinal Community-Based Cohort in a Canadian Setting." *AIDS and Behavior* 24 (4): 1243–51.

Fedock, Gina L., Sheila Shankar, Celina Doria, and Marion Malcome. 2024. "'You Have to Take Care of Your Own Mental Status': Incarcerated Women Seeking Care Within and Beyond Mental Health Treatment." *Affilia: Feminist Inquiry in Social Work* 39 (2): 302–19.

Fortune, Darla, Susan M. Arai, and Kimberly J. Lyons. 2020. "Relational Possibilities for Women Leaving Prison: Renewed Hope for Inclusion and Belonging." *Contemporary Justice Review* 23 (1): 3–21.

Garsd, Jasmine. 2018. "As More Women Are Incarcerated in Mexico, so Are Their Babies." *The World from PRX*. https://theworld.org/stories/2018/03/31/smallest-inmates-children-who-live-mexicos-prison-system.

Government of Canada, Department of Justice. 2016. "1.0 Introduction: An Overview of Canadian Mandatory Minimum Penalties—Mandatory Minimum Penalties in Canada: Analysis and Annotated Bibliography." https://www.justice.gc.ca/eng/rp-pr/jr/mmp-pmo/p1.html.

Government of Canada, Statistics Canada. 2024. "Correctional Services Statistics: Interactive Dashboard." https://www150.statcan.gc.ca/n1/pub/71-607-x/71-607-x2019018-eng.htm.

Government of Canada, Statistics Canada. 2023. "Canada's Indigenous Population." https://www.statcan.gc.ca/o1/en/plus/3920-canadas-indigenous-population.

Government of Canada, Statistics Canada. 2022. "Indigenous Women and Girls: Socioeconomic Conditions in Remote Communities Compared with More Accessible Areas." https://www150.statcan.gc.ca/n1/pub/75-006-x/2022001/article/00005-eng.htm.

Heimer, Karen, Sarah E. Malone, and Stacy De Coster. 2023. "Trends in Women's Incarceration Rates in US Prisons and Jails: A Tale of Inequalities." *Annual Review of Criminology* 6: 85–106.

Hernandez, Joe. 2022. "More States Are Restricting the Shackling of Pregnant Inmates, but It Still Occurs." NPR. https://www.npr.org/2022/04/22/1093836514/shackle-pregnant-inmates-tennessee.

Howorun, Cristina. 2023. "Program Allows Incarcerated Women to Raise Their Children Inside Canadian Prisons." *CityNews Toronto*. https://toronto.citynews.ca/2023/05/24/program-incarcerated-women-raise-their-children-prisons-canada/.

IDOA. 2022. "Randolph Street Campus." https://www.in.gov/idoa/state-property-and-facilities/public-works/capital-projects/randolph-street-campus/.

Instituto Nacional de Estadística y Geografía (INEGI). 2024. "Censo Nacional de Sistema Penitenciario Federal y Estatales 2024." Resultados. https://www.inegi.org.mx/temas/penitenciarias/.

International Crisis Group." 2023. "Partners in Crime: The Rise of Women in Mexico's Illegal Groups. Latin America Report No. 103. International Crisis Group. https://www.crisisgroup.org.

Jenness, Valerie. 2021. "The Social Ecology of Sexual Victimization Against Transgender Women Who Are Incarcerated: A Call for (More) Research on Modalities of Housing and Prison Violence." *Criminology & Public Policy* 20 (1): 3–18.

Johns Hopkins Medicine. 2019. "First of Its Kind Statistics on Pregnant Women in U.S. Prisons." *Johns Hopkins Medicine News Release*. March 21, 2019. https://www.hopkinsmedicine.org/news/newsroom/news-releases/2019/03/first-of-its-kind-statistics-on-pregnant-women-in-us-prisons.

Johnson, Carrie. 2022. "Male Prison Employees Assault Women in at Least Two-Thirds of U.S. Prisons." NPR. https://www.npr.org/2022/12/13/1142594198/male-prison-employees-assault-women-in-at-least-two-thirds-of-u-s-prisons.

Jones, Reilly, Sasha Lemberg-Pelly, Brigid Dineley, Jessica Jurgutis, Fiona G. Kouyoumdjian, and Jessica Liauw. 2024. "We Wish We Had the Option: A Qualitative Study of Women's Perspectives and Experiences with Contraception in a Provincial Prison in Ontario, Canada." *Health & Justice* 12 (15): 1–8.

Kajstura, Aleks, and Wendy Sawyer. 2024. "Women's Mass Incarceration: The Whole Pie 2024." https://www.prisonpolicy.org/reports/pie2024women.html.

Kasich, John R. 1996. "H.R.3734—104th Congress (1995–1996): Personal Responsibility and Work Opportunity Reconciliation Act of 1996." https://www.congress.gov/bill/104th-congress/house-bill/3734.

Kids with Incarcerated Parents Canada. 2020. *Kids with Incarcerated Parents Canada.* KIP. https://www.kipcanada.org/.

Knight, Kiana. 2024. "Black Women's Activism and the Long 1960s: A CBFS Interview—AAIHS." https://www.aaihs.org/black-womens-activism-and-the-long-1960s-a-cbfs-interview/.

Latimer, Brian. 2016. "Sexual Abuse, Torture Used Against Women in Mexico Prisons, Arrests: Report." NBC News. https://www.nbcnews.com/news/latino/sexual-abuse-torture-used-against-women-mexico-prisons-arrests-report-n600576.

Lopez Sarabia, Tomas. 2021. "Indigenous People Can't Wait." *Voices* (blog), Open Society Foundations. August 9, 2021. https://www.opensocietyfoundations.org/voices/a-travesty-of-justice-for-indigenous-people-in-mexicos-prisons.

Major, Darren. 2021. "Indigenous Women Make up Almost Half the Female Prison Population, Ombudsman Says." CBC. https://www.cbc.ca/news/politics/indigenous-women-half-inmate-population-canada-1.6289674.

Malinowska, Kasia, and Olga Rychkova. 2015. "Getting Drug Policy Right for Women and Girls." *Voices* (blog), Open Society Foundations. June 11, 2015. https://www.opensocietyfoundations.org/voices/getting-drug-policy-right-women-and-girls.

Martin, Eric. 2017. "Hidden Consequences: The Impact of Incarceration on Dependent Children." National Institute of Justice. https://nij.ojp.gov/topics/articles/hidden-consequences-impact-incarceration-dependent-children.

McKay, John. 2021. "Systemic Racism in Policing in Canada Report of the Standing Committee on Public Safety and National Security." https://www.ourcommons.ca/Content/Committee/432/SECU/Reports/RP11434998/securp06/securp06-e.pdf.

Mexico. 2024. "Cámara de Diputados del H. Congreso de la Unión. Código Penal Federal." Últimas Reformas DOF 07–06–2024. https://www.gob.mx/sfp/documentos/codigo-penal-federal.

Mexico. 2021. "Cámara de Diputados del H. Congreso de la Unión. Ley Federal contra la Delincuencia Organizada." Última Reforma DOF 20–05–2021. https://www.diputados.gob.mx/LeyesBiblio/pdf/101_200521.pdf.

Mexico 1917 (Rev. 2015) Constitution—Constitute. n.d. https://www.constituteproject.org/constitution/Mexico_2015.

Mexico: Prison Population by Age and Gender 2022. 2024. Statista. https://www.statista.com/statistics/1281077/prison-population-age-gender-mexico/.

Mexico's Long War: Drugs, Crime, and the Cartels. 2022. Council on Foreign Relations. September 7, 2022. https://www.cfr.org/backgrounder/mexicos-long-war-drugs-crime-and-cartels.

Moshan, M. S., A. V. N. Ordaz, D. Mondragón, L. Bell, and Joseph Whitfield. 2024. "Sorority Inside and Outside as a Means of Survival and Resistance: Experiences of Women Imprisoned in Mexico." *Prison Service Journal* 272: 41–9.

Mount Pleasant—the Female Prison at Sing. 2022. Sing Prison Museum. https://www.singsingprisonmuseum.org/blog/mount-pleasant-female-prison-at-sing-sing.

Ospina-Escobar, Angélica. 2023. "'I Don't Want to Disappear': How Mexico's Criminal Violence Reshapes Women's Lives." https://www.crisisgroup.org/latin-america-caribbean/mexico/i-dont-want-disappear-how-mexicos-criminal-violence-reshapes-womens-lives.

Our Mission | KIP. 2020. https://www.kipcanada.org/our-mission.

Our Work | CCCIP. 2023. https://www.childrenofincarceratedparents.ca/our-work.

Paynter, Carla, Shonna Heggie, Margaret Matheson, Jessica Rillie, Raissa Beals, and Jonathan Bray. 2022. *Exploring the Experiences of Incarcerated Women in a Provincial Prison in Nova Scotia*. Halifax: Dalhousie University.

Pearson, Jennifer M. 1993. "Centro Femenil: A Women's Prison in Mexico." *Social Justice* 20 (3/4) (Fall–Winter): 85–128.

Pecorara, Michael. n.d. "Time's up for Mandatory Minimums." *Harvard Undergraduate Law Review*. https://hulr.org/spring-2022/times-up-mandatory-minimums.

Pederson, Kaitlyn M., Wesley T. Smith, Kiarra Fortney, Janet L. Mullings, and Ashley G. Blackburn. 2024. "A Qualitative Examination of Correctional Programming Perceptions and Experiences Among Incarcerated Women." *Crime & Delinquency* 70 (3): 947–74.

Pishko, Jessica. 2015. "A History of Women's Prisons | JSTOR Daily." https://daily.jstor.org/history-of-womens-prisons/.

Prevost, Haleigh, and Jennifer M. Kilty. 2020. "You Start to Feel Like You're Losing Your Mind: An Intersectionality-Based Policy Analysis of Federal Correctional Segregation Policy and Practice." *Canadian Journal of Women and the Law/Revue Femmes et Droit* 32 (1): 163–80.

Prison-Based Family Services Programs. n.d. Hour Children. https://hourchildren.org/how-we-help/prison-based-family-services-programs/.

Puyana, Juan Carlos Jacob, Andres Mariano Rubiano, Jorge Hernan Montenegro, Glyn O. Estebanez, Alvaro Ignacio Sanchez, and Felipe Vega-Rivera. 2017. "Drugs, Violence, and Trauma in Mexico and the USA." *Medical Principles and Practice* 26 (4): 309–15.

Q&A: The COVID-19 Crisis in Mexico's Prisons. 2020. Opensocietyfoundations.org. https://www.opensocietyfoundations.org/voices/q-and-a-the-covid-19-crisis-in-mexicos-prisons.

Robinson, Paul, Taylor Small, Anna Chen, and Mark Irving. 2023. "Over-Representation of Indigenous Persons in Adult Provincial Custody, 2019/2020 and 2020/2021." https://www150.statcan.gc.ca/n1/pub/85-002-x/2023001/article/00004-eng.htm.

R. V. Gladue, 1999 CanLII 679 (SCC). 1999. CanLII. https://www.canlii.org/en/ca/scc/doc/1999/1999canlii679/1999canlii679.html.

Sandberg, Sveinung, Carolina Agoff, and Gustavo Fondevila. 2021. "Doing Marginalized Motherhood: Identities and Practices Among Incarcerated Women in Mexico." *International Journal for Crime, Justice and Social Democracy* 10 (1): 15–29.

Schwartz, Alexandra. 2024. "When Women Commit Violence: 'The Furies' and 'If Love Could Kill.'" The New Yorker. https://www.newyorker.com/magazine/2024/02/12/the-furies-by-elizabeth-flock-review-if-love-could-kill-by-anna-motz.

Siegler, Alison. 2021. "End Mandatory Minimums | Brennan Center for Justice." Brennan Center for Justice at NYU Law. https://www.brennancenter.org/our-work/analysis-opinion/end-mandatory-minimums.

Silverman-Retana, Omar, Edson Servan-Mori, Stefano Michele Bertozzi, Emanuel Orozco-Nuñez, Sergio Bautista-Arredondo, and Ruy Lopez-Ridaura. 2018. "Prison Environment and Non-Communicable Chronic Disease Modifiable Risk Factors: Length of Incarceration Trend Analysis in Mexico City." *Journal of Epidemiology and Community Health* 72 (4): 342–8.

Straughan, David. 2021. "U.S. Prisons Still Don't Have Adequate Menstrual Supplies in 2021." Interrogating Justice. https://interrogatingjustice.org/prisons/prisons-menstrual-supplies-2021/.

Taylor, Susie, Margaret Haworth-Brockman, and Yoav Keynan. 2021. "Slipping Through: Mobility's Influence on Infectious Disease Risks for Justice-Involved Women in Canada." *Health & Justice* 9 (35): 1–9.

The Indian Act and Why You Need to Know About It. 2023. Live & Learn: A Project of English Online Inc. https://livelearn.ca/article/about-canada/the-indian-act-and-why-you-need-to-know-about-it/.

Transnational Institute. 2020. "About Drug Law Reform in Mexico." https://www.tni.org/en/publication/about-drug-law-reform-in-mexico.

Understanding Women's Experiences with the Criminal Justice System as Accused and Offenders. 2024. https://www.justice.gc.ca/socjs-esjp/en/women-femmes/ao-ad.

United States Congress. 2019. "H.R.3355—103rd Congress (1993–1994): Violent Crime Control and Law Enforcement Act of 1994." Congress.gov. https://www.congress.gov/bill/103rd-congress/house-bill/3355.

U.S. Congress. 2010. *Fair Sentencing Act of 2010*, Pub. L. No. 111–220, 124 Stat. 2372 (August 3, 2010). https://www.congress.gov/111/plaws/publ220/PLAW-111publ220.pdf.

Valle, Daniela. 2024. "Why Are There More Women in Mexican Prisons for Organized Crime?" InSight Crime. https://insightcrime.org/news/why-more-women-mexican-prisons-organized-crime/.

Villa, Manuel. 2017. "The Mental Health Crisis Facing Women in Prison." The Marshall Project. https://www.themarshallproject.org/2017/06/22/the-mental-health-crisis-facing-women-in-prison.

White, Heather. 2023. "Born Inside: Montessori Gives Hope to Children Living Their First Years of Life in Mexico's Prisons." *Montessori Life Blog*, American Montessori Society. August 18, 2023. https://amshq.org/Blog/2023-08-18-Montessori-in-Prisons-in-Mexico.

Women's Health Care in Correctional Settings. 2020. National Commission on Correctional Health Care. https://www.ncchc.org/position-statements/womens-health-care-in-correctional-settings-2020/.

Woodford, Isabel. 2022. "'I Have to Keep Fighting': Mexicans Wait for Years Behind Bars for a Trial." Reuters. https://www.reuters.com/world/americas/i-have-keep-fighting-mexicans-wait-years-behind-bars-trial-2022-09-28/.

World Data Editors. n.d. "List of the Total Areas of the World's Countries, Dependencies, and Territories." Encyclopedia Britannica. https://www.britannica.com/topic/list-of-the-total-areas-of-the-worlds-countries-dependencies-and-territories-2130540.

World Prison Brief. 2024. "Mexico | World Prison Brief." Prisonstudies.org. https://www.prisonstudies.org/country/mexico.

Ziazadeh, Danya. 2019. "Inadequate Health Care: A Significant Problem Affecting Incarcerated Women." Sph.umich.edu. https://sph.umich.edu/pursuit/2019posts/inadequate-healthcare-a-significant-problem-affecting-incarcerated-women.html.

2

Latin America and the Caribbean

The incarceration of women in Latin America and the Caribbean reveals socioeconomic inequality and systemic discrimination. This chapter examines the challenges women imprisoned in Brazil, Colombia, and Jamaica face. It explores the role of colonialism, drug policies, and gendered violence that influence their experiences. By examining incarceration trends, demographics, and the conditions in women's prisons, the chapter explores the structural inequities that contribute to female imprisonment in these countries. It also considers the impact on families and communities, suggesting reforms to address these issues. By focusing on these regional circumstances, the chapter provides an understanding of the factors contributing to female incarceration and the need for gender-responsive policies in these countries.

Brazil

Historical Context

The historical context of women's imprisonment in Brazil is shaped by colonization, slavery, and structural inequalities. From the sixteenth century, the Portuguese imported enslaved Africans to Brazil, with the number of enslaved people surpassing that of North America (Brown University 2019). This legacy of exploitation fostered systemic racialized violence against marginalized groups, especially women. The trauma endured by enslaved women continues in modern prisons, where incarcerated women face violence, neglect, and limited rights.

Brazil's legal system, influenced by patriarchal and elitist ideas, has historically reinforced gender and economic inequalities. During the military dictatorship (1964–85), women who opposed the regime were targeted and

Outdoor Mass celebrating abolition of slavery, Brazil, 1888 (Wikimedia Commons)

incarcerated, reflecting institutional gender biases (Napolitano 2018). Economic disparities, racial inequalities, and limited access to education have further marginalized women, especially those from impoverished communities, while wealth remains concentrated among the elite (Pimental 2022). This inequality continues to worsen challenges for women with experiences in the criminal justice system.

The post-dictatorship period brought democracy in 1985, but it also saw rising incarceration rates, particularly among women convicted of low-level drug crimes. Strict drug policies in the 1990s, combined with economic hardship, drove many women to participate in the drug trade to survive (De Azevedo and Cifali 2017). Inequality, police violence, and racial disparities persisted during this period, reflecting failures in public security and justice (Interviews and Perspectives 2020). The Lula and Dilma Administrations' efforts to address poverty (2003–16) unintentionally worsened prison overcrowding and penalties for marginalized women due to a lack of rehabilitative alternatives.

In 2018, Jair Bolsonaro's presidency strengthened the punitive nature of Brazil's criminal justice system. His policies encouraged excessive police violence and reinforced racial discrimination, disproportionately incarcerating Black women for drug-related offenses (Interviews and Perspectives 2020). The militarization of police forces and lack of attention to prison reform worsened conditions. While Lula's reelection in 2023 has reignited promises to reduce poverty and discrimination, Brazil's justice system continues to reflect social inequalities, leaving the specific needs of incarcerated women unaddressed (Watson and Davies 2023).

Female Incarceration Rates and Trends

There were 27,608 incarcerated women in Brazil in 2023, and this percentage fluctuates between 3 and 7 percent of the country's prison population (SISDEPEN 2023). Furthermore, over 30 percent of incarcerated women are pretrial detainees who have not yet received a trial (SISDEPEN 2023). **Pretrial detention** contributes to overcrowding and disproportionately affects women from low-income backgrounds. Many of these women are detained for non-violent crimes and face lengthy time in custody without having been convicted due to delays in the system and lack of access to adequate legal representation.

In Brazil, the prison system is divided into the federal system, managed by the Ministry of Justice and Public Security, and the state and Federal District systems, overseen by their respective executive branches (Miranda, Goldberg, and Díaz Bermúdez 2024). There are approximately fifteen facilities for women nationwide (De Araújo et al. 2020), but the exact number is unclear because women are often incarcerated in facilities for men due to overcrowding. Additionally, many women are housed in annexes attached to male prisons, complicating statistics. The São Paulo Women's Penitentiary is the largest women's prison in the country. It has a total capacity of 256, although it has held up to 400 women (HRW 2024). In addition, the Women's House of Detention in Tatuapé, in São Paulo, also holds over 200 people. However, most women's prisons in Brazil hold fewer than 100 people.

Brazil has the fourth largest female incarceration rate in the world (Medeiros 2021). Similar to worldwide trends, female incarceration rates in Brazil have also increased over the past few decades. Between 2005 and 2009, the female incarceration rate increased by 184 percent, while the rate for men only rose by 31 percent. During this time, women's participation in drug trafficking crimes increased by 200 percent (Baltieri 2014). Furthermore, at its peak in 2016, the female prison population totaled 42,000, indicating a 656 percent increase over the population in 2000 (De Araújo et al. 2020).

Demographics of Incarcerated Women

The demographics of incarcerated women in Brazil show that there are social inequalities in terms of race, class, and education. Fifty percent of these women

The Toll on Black Women

Racial inequality defines women's imprisonment in Brazil. Although Black women make up just over 10 percent of the national population, they comprise more than 60 percent of the female prison population. They are also twice as likely as white women to be the victims of homicide. These disparities signal long-standing structural inequalities, economic exclusion, and discriminatory policing. Additionally, the justice system's harsh drug sentencing worsens these racial gaps.

are young, between the ages of eighteen and twenty-nine. Furthermore, over 60 percent of incarcerated women in Brazil are Black (Prison Insider 2020), compared to just 10 percent of the general population, indicating racial disparities within the nation's justice system (Belandi and Gomes 2023).

Additionally, most incarcerated women come from low-income communities with limited access to education. Two-thirds have not completed high school (Faquim et al. 2020), and many were unemployed at the time of their arrest. This economic marginalization often pushes women into involvement with crime, particularly drug-related offenses, as a means of survival. Also, approximately 70 percent of incarcerated women are mothers (Female Incarceration in Brazil and the United States 2021), many of whom are the primary caregivers for their children. Their incarceration has negative consequences for their families, often leading to children being placed in foster care or with relatives.

Moreover, the lack of official data complicates efforts to determine the number of LGBTQ+ individuals in Brazilian prisons, but societal marginalization and criminalization likely contribute to their higher incarceration rates (Daken et al. 2023). A 2020 penitentiary survey revealed that out of 1,499 facilities, only 106—all male prisons—had designated spaces for cisgender homosexual men, bisexuals, transgender women, and transgender men, serving a total LGBTQ+ population of 12,356 individuals (Brasil 2020). Despite a 2019 Supreme Federal Court mandate requiring the transfer of transgender women to female prisons or designated areas in male prisons, many facilities have not complied, reflecting challenges in ensuring their dignity and human rights (Miranda, Goldberg, and Díaz Bermúdez 2024).

Lastly, many incarcerated women also have histories of domestic violence, sexual abuse, and exploitation. One woman is killed every four hours in Brazil, and female homicides are double the global average. Moreover, the homicide rate for Black women in states like Alagoas is seven times higher than for non-Black women (Wilson 2021). These intersecting vulnerabilities contribute to the pathways leading women into the criminal justice system.

Crimes Leading to Incarceration

Crimes leading to incarceration for women in Brazil are often related to the country's strict drug laws and social inequalities. Over 60 percent of women are imprisoned for drug-related offenses (Medeiros 2021). These women are usually involved in low-level trafficking, acting as **drug mules**, often under coercion or because of poverty.

For instance, Helena, a 26-year-old from São Tomé and Príncipe in Guinea, was offered a job as a cook in Brazil in 2018. However, when she arrived, she was forced to swallow cocaine to smuggle to Africa. She was arrested at Guarulhos International Airport outside of São Paulo and sentenced to five years in jail (Adams 2020). This is one of many stories highlighting how women from marginalized backgrounds are more apt to be drawn into drug-related crimes to survive.

Other crimes leading to their incarceration involve small-scale offenses, such as petty theft (26 percent), as women try to meet the needs of their families (Faquim et al. 2020). Violent crimes, such as homicide, are less common among incarcerated women in Brazil, though when they do occur, they are often linked to self-defense in situations of domestic violence (Penal Reform International 2016). Overall, the criminalization of poverty and harsh sentencing laws for drug-related offenses have driven the disproportionate incarceration of women.

Contributing Laws and Policies

The Drug Law of 2006 (Law 11.343) has contributed to high rates of incarceration for women in Brazil, increasing the mandatory minimum for trafficking from three to five years. This law was intended to distinguish between drug users and traffickers, but it has resulted in the mass incarceration of women involved in low-level trafficking. Article 28 of this law states that drug users can be given warnings, community service, or education as an alternative to incarceration (TNI 2024). However, the law has been criticized for its unclear criteria to distinguish between use and trafficking, leaving the decision up to the police or judges. Unfortunately, it has disproportionately impacted poor women, who are often classified as traffickers, even for small amounts of drugs.

Furthermore, drug crimes are classified under Brazil's **Heinous Crimes Law** of 1990, which equates them with violent crimes like murder. People convicted of drug crimes receive longer prison sentences, as well as restrictions on their parole. Opponents of these punitive measures stress that they adversely affect women, who often engage in drug offenses out of necessity (TNI 2024). These harsh sentencing laws do not consider mitigating factors like economic hardship or coercion.

While the harsh drug laws are still in place, there have been some recent reforms. In 2024, Brazil's Supreme Federal Court (STF) established that people found with up to 40 grams of marijuana or cultivating up to six cannabis plants would be considered personal users rather than traffickers. This ruling provides some guidelines to distinguish between personal use and trafficking (Brazil's STF Sets 40 Grams of Marijuana Cap between Users and Traffickers 2024). Cannabis is still illegal in Brazil, but this ruling ensures that people with amounts of marijuana within specified guidelines will not be prosecuted, indicating a shift toward a less punitive approach.

Conditions in Women's Prisons

The conditions in women's prisons in Brazil are inadequate, often due to overcrowding, as many facilities hold far more people than they were designed to accommodate. Overcrowding leads to a lack of resources such as food, clean water, and hygiene supplies, negatively impacting the health and well-being of incarcerated women (HRW 2024).

In a country with one of the highest levels of inequality globally, the system responsible for mass incarceration creates a prime environment for the violation of human rights (Miranda, Goldberg, and Díaz Bermúdez 2024). To illustrate, the facility with the worst conditions that Human Rights Watch saw was São Paulo's third police precinct. This facility is a precinct lockup located in an area called "Crackolandia" because of the drugs sold and used there. It does not have a women's annex, so women are confined to a holding cell located at the entrance of the men's section. Human Rights Watch reported that ten women were confined in a small, cramped cell measuring about sixteen feet long and three feet wide, with part of the space taken up by a hole-in-the-floor toilet. The only light came through a barred metal gate since the overhead bulb was broken. Among the inmates was a woman five months pregnant who was experiencing illness and discomfort, but her complaints were disregarded by the guards (HRW 2024).

Women often face challenges in accessing healthcare, particularly mental health, reproductive, and maternal care. Pregnant women and new mothers are especially vulnerable, as medical facilities are inadequate, and there is often a lack of specialized care. For example, a nurse at Bom Pastor Women's Prison told "Wiviane," a 28-year-old mother of two serving seven years for trafficking crack cocaine, that she had symptoms of the Zika virus, but she was never tested. Zika is especially dangerous for pregnant women and can cause neurological damage in fetuses. While Wiviane was not pregnant, testing her could have shown if virus-carrying mosquitoes were present at the facility, which had at least six pregnant women at that time (Canineu 2017).

In addition, incarcerated women often face sexual abuse and verbal harassment by male correctional officers despite national laws that prohibit male guards in women's prisons. Furthermore, in a 2015 riot in Minas Gerais, male inmates broke into a women's wing and raped several of them (Canineu 2017). This highlights the disregard for legal protections and worsens the situation for women in already inhumane conditions.

Health and Mental Health Issues

Similar to other countries, health and mental health issues are challenges for incarcerated women in Brazil. Many women experience physical health problems as a result of overcrowding, unsanitary conditions, and a lack of access to medical care. Additionally, cardiovascular diseases are over four times more prevalent in incarcerated women under thirty in Brazil. Women in prison also experience cancer and stroke at over twice the rate of the general population (Leal et al. 2023).

Furthermore, research shows that over half of incarcerated women in Brazil have not received preventive cervical cancer screenings, and more than 85 percent have never had a mammogram in prison. Additionally, over half have experienced sexually transmitted diseases (De Araújo et al. 2020), highlighting a lack of access to basic preventive and gynecological care. With only thirty-seven gynecologists for the entire prison system—about one per 800 women (Canineu 2017)—this shortage worsens these issues. Additionally, pregnant women often face inadequate nutrition and medical care, increasing risks during pregnancy and childbirth, while postpartum care is lacking, and mothers are separated from their newborns six months after birth (De Araújo et al. 2020).

Mental healthcare is also deficient despite the high prevalence of trauma, domestic violence, and mental health disorders among incarcerated women. Upward of 80 percent of incarcerated women globally, including in Brazil, experience mental health issues, including depression, anxiety, and post-traumatic stress disorder (De Araújo et al. 2020). Yet, there are few mental health professionals or treatment programs available. Some facilities have less than one psychologist available per 1,000 people (De Araújo et al. 2020).

Substance abuse is another issue, as many incarcerated women in Brazil struggle with addiction. Over half of incarcerated women have a drug or alcohol misuse history, and they are more likely than men to test positive for cocaine at the time of arrest (Baltieri 2014). Unfortunately, there is limited access to rehabilitation or drug treatment programs. Furthermore, despite efforts to enhance rehabilitation initiatives within the prison system, issues like overcrowding, insufficient resources, and violence frequently undermine their success (Miranda, Goldberg, and Díaz Bermúdez 2024).

Impact on Families and Children

The incarceration of women in Brazil has a considerable impact on their families and children, mainly because many incarcerated women are the primary caregivers. Approximately 40 percent of these children are under ten years old (De Araújo et al. 2020). In many cases, they are placed with relatives, often their grandmothers. In other situations, they are placed in the care of the state, which increases their risk of neglect or abuse.

While there are some prison nurseries in Brazil, they are available in less than 20 percent of women's facilities (Stella, Sequeira, and Rosa 2016). In these facilities, children can stay with their mothers for six months after birth, but they spend most of their time in overcrowded cells with their mothers. The nurseries also have minimal resources (e.g., toys, stimulation), poor food quality, and inadequate healthcare. Although there are challenges in this environment, babies can bond with their mothers for six months. In facilities without nurseries, they are immediately separated from their mothers.

Brazilian law does allow pregnant women and mothers of children under twelve to apply for house arrest so that they can remain in the community with their children. However, the eligibility criteria are strict (e.g., no repeat offenders, must have a permanent address, etc.), excluding many women from this option. Unfortunately, these barriers result in children being raised without their mothers, leading to further marginalization (De Araújo et al. 2020).

Policy Reforms and Recommendations

Policy reforms for incarcerated women in Brazil are needed to address many issues. First, drug laws need to be revised because they heavily contribute to female incarceration. The 2006 Drug Law, for instance, has adversely impacted marginalized women incarcerated for low-level drug crimes. Revising these laws to lessen sentences, focus more on rehabilitation, and enhance alternatives to incarceration would reduce the prison population and more effectively get to the root of why women commit crimes (TNI 2024).

Similarly, alternatives to incarceration for women with young children must be expanded. While Brazilian law allows pregnant women and mothers of young children to apply for house arrest, the eligibility criteria are so strict that many women are excluded from this opportunity (De Araújo et al. 2020). Reforming the criteria to make house arrest more accessible would help mothers and children bond, reduce the negative impacts of incarceration on these families, and allow mothers to remain in the community.

Improving healthcare in prisons is another area that needs reform. The lack of medical and mental health professionals in women's prisons, including only thirty-seven gynecologists for the entire prison system, indicates that the country needs to invest in more practitioners (HRW 2024). Improving healthcare access, especially for prenatal, postpartum, and mental healthcare, is necessary, given the prevalence of trauma and health issues among women in Brazilian prisons.

Lastly, it is necessary to address overcrowding and conditions in women's prisons. The nation needs to invest in better infrastructure, ensuring that facilities can provide clean water, hygiene supplies, and adequate food for people housed in prisons (Medeiros 2021). Furthermore, as noted above, steps must be taken to enhance alternatives to incarceration for non-violent offenders to not only help these women in the community but also to alleviate overcrowded conditions in Brazilian prisons.

Colombia

Historical Context

The context of women's incarceration in Colombia is related to the country's history of armed conflict, inequality, and oppression. A history of violence, including the actions of guerrilla groups like the **Fuerzas Armadas Revolucionarias de Colombia (FARC)**, has adversely affected women in Colombia. Many women were coerced into these groups, with more than 18,000 children, including many girls, recruited by the FARC (Colombia's FARC Rebels Recruited More than 18,000 Children: Court 2021). Other women joined voluntarily, as they were driven by poverty, lack of opportunities, or needed protection. Over 11,000 women were part of guerrilla efforts, making up approximately 40 percent of FARC members (From War to Economic Reintegration 2023).

Furthermore, since the 1980s, Colombia's drug wars have influenced the country's criminal justice system. The rise of cartels like Medellín and Cali has caused violence, leading the government to respond with aggressive anti-drug strategies (Britto 2020). Supported by allies like the United States, Colombia authorized policies to eradicate coca, dismantle cartels, and criminalize drug-related activities (Lee 2020).

Overall, the involvement of women in armed groups and the drug trade has led to increases in their incarceration, regardless of whether their participation was voluntary or coerced. Moreover, female human rights defenders, especially Afro-Colombians, have faced wrongful imprisonment because of their activism in war zones (Kirby 2019). The country's transition to peace agreements, such as with the FARC in 2016, has not improved this situation for women. Many who were formerly involved in the violence have been further stigmatized and have had trouble reintegrating into society.

Social inequality plays a large role in the incarceration of women in Colombia. Women from poor communities are disproportionately represented in prison. These groups face systemic disadvantages, including limited access to education and economic opportunities, which often drive them into non-violent crimes like drug trafficking (Women, Drug Policies, and Incarceration n.d.).

Female Incarceration Rates and Trends

Colombia's prison system has 125 facilities, which are operating at 127 percent occupancy (Colombia | World Prison Brief 2024). The National Penitentiary and Prison Institute (INPEC) manages these facilities, and most house both men and women in separate sections (Colombia 2023 Human Rights Report 2024). Because most of these prisons were designed for men, they do not adequately meet the needs of women. Currently, Colombia's prison system houses more than 17,000 women, approximately 7,800 of whom have been convicted but the rest are awaiting trial (Agencia EFE 2023).

Female incarceration rates in Colombia have increased over the past few decades, similar to global trends. Between 2000 and 2017, the number of women in Colombian prisons increased by 53 percent (Rendón González 2022), and drug-related crimes were most common (46 percent) (García-Sayan 2024). Many of these women are imprisoned for low-level drug trafficking offenses, often acting as mules out of necessity or under coercion by organized crime groups (Women, Drug Policy, and Imprisonment 2016).

In response to rising female incarceration rates, Colombia has implemented some reforms to address the issues contributing to women's imprisonment. One is the introduction of alternatives to incarceration for non-violent offenders. In 2022, the nation enacted a law allowing women who are single heads of households meeting certain conditions to be sentenced to community service rather than prison. This reform is meant to reduce the negative effects of incarceration on women and children (Youngers 2022).

Additionally, efforts have been made to improve prison experiences and provide educational and vocational training to incarcerated women. Programs like the Centro Universitario Devoto (CUD) in Buenos Aires offer incarcerated women the opportunity to pursue higher education and participate in workshops that enhance their opportunities upon release (Salomón 2024). However, these reforms have been limited in scope and implementation across Colombia.

Demographics of Incarcerated Women

The demographics of incarcerated women in Colombia show the intersection of poverty, gender, and social inequality. Approximately 80 percent of women in Colombian prisons belong to the lowest socioeconomic level, often coming from areas with limited infrastructure and access to basic services (Del Pozo Serrano and Jiménez Ramírez 2017). These women typically lack education and stable employment, making them particularly vulnerable to criminalization. Almost 70 percent did not attend secondary school, indicating the relationship between a lack of education and incarceration (Rendón González 2022).

Additionally, about 59 percent of incarcerated women identify as mixed race, 32 percent as Caucasian, and 9 percent as Afro-Colombian (Del Pozo Serrano and Jiménez Ramírez 2017). Data on the age ranges of incarcerated women in Colombia is limited, but available statistics indicate that 54 percent of women incarcerated for drug offenses are between thirty and fifty-four years old, and the remaining 46 percent are under thirty (Colombia: Share of Females Incarcerated for Drug Offenses by Age Group 2016). Eighty-five percent of women in Colombia's prisons are mothers, and 75 percent are single heads of household, leading to disruptions for their families once they are incarcerated (Youngers 2022).

Additionally, two-thirds of these women have histories of gendered violence, including domestic violence, sexual abuse, and abuse as a result of armed conflict. Moreover, two-thirds reported regular consumption of substances, including cocaine, marijuana, and alcohol (Del Pozo Serrano and Jiménez Ramírez 2017). These experiences are often linked to their involvement in criminal activity, as many women turn to illegal means to escape abusive environments or provide for their families.

Crimes Leading to Incarceration

In Colombia, the majority of women are incarcerated for non-violent crimes. Almost 60 percent of these women engage in drug-related crimes to provide for their families due to a lack of legitimate income sources (UNODC 2019). Many were influenced by close relationships, such as spouses or friends, and they assumed roles like couriers.

For instance, in 2017, Cassandra Sainsbury, a 22-year-old Australian woman, was arrested at El Dorado International Airport in Bogotá after authorities discovered 5.8 kilograms of cocaine in headphone boxes in her luggage (ABC News 2017a). She had been struggling financially and was working at a brothel in Australia where she was introduced to drug traffickers and became a mule (Yahoo 2017). Sainsbury accepted a plea deal, resulting in a six-year sentence, which she served three years at El Buen Pastor women's prison in Bogotá after being released early (ABC News 2017b). Her case highlights the socioeconomic factors, in Colombia and globally, that push people into trafficking.

Aside from drug-related offenses, women are also imprisoned for other crimes. For example, theft constitutes approximately 31 percent of crimes committed by women (Rendón González 2022), making it one of the most common non-drug-related offenses. Women involved in theft are often just trying to meet their families' needs.

A smaller percentage of women in Colombia are incarcerated for violent crimes, often linked to domestic abuse or self-defense. Many of these women have histories of trauma and domestic violence, acting in response to ongoing abuse. For example, in 2024, Colombia's Constitutional Court cancelled a 28-year sentence against Virgelina Aguiar, who killed her rapist, pointing out that the ruling failed to account for prolonged sexual violence. This case highlights how violence committed by women is frequently related to their experiences of abuse (Reynoso 2024).

Contributing Laws and Policies

There have been several laws and policies that have contributed to the rise of incarceration rates for women in Colombia. One of the largest contributors is Law 30 of 1986, the National Narcotics Statute, which calls for strict, mandatory sentences that target all levels of the drug trade, even low-level, high-risk jobs performed by impoverished women. This law has contributed to a 5.5-fold increase in the incarceration of women since 1991 (UNODC 2016). Moreover, it gives authority to the Ministry of Health and Social Protection and the National Drug Council to regulate controlled substances, but critics argue it does not address the causes of drug-related offenses (Details 2024).

Other laws have reinforced these punitive measures. For instance, Law 599 of 2000, the Colombian Penal Code, classifies drug-related offenses and penalties based on the type and quantity of the substance (Criminal Code of Colombia: Law 599 of 2000 2020). Additionally, Law 1453 of 2011, the Citizen Security Law, strengthened penalties for organized crime and drug trafficking, also leading to higher rates of incarceration for women. Within one year of its enactment, the prison population increased by 15 percent, with much of this increase being women convicted of low-level drug offenses. This also worsened overcrowding and conditions in women's prisons (UNODC 2016).

Law 1760 of 2015 was intended to help reduce prison overcrowding by establishing maximum lengths for pretrial detention and encouraging alternatives to incarceration for people convicted of non-violent crimes. However, it has not been implemented consistently nationwide because of limited awareness among lawyers, insufficient training on alternative sentencing, and preferences for punitive measures. As a result, many people who could participate, particularly impoverished women, still experience lengthy stays in pre-trial detention (La Comisión de Seguimiento de la Sentencia 2016).

Furthermore, in 2023, Colombia introduced another reform offering alternatives to incarceration for women with caregiving responsibilities. This law allows people sentenced to up to eight years for non-violent crimes to replace their prison term with unpaid community service. It is applicable retroactively and could lead to the release of 5,000 women, which would help address some of the issues caused by previous laws and policies (Colombia—Penal Reform International 2023).

Conditions in Women's Prisons

The conditions in women's prisons in Colombia exhibit overcrowding, poor sanitation, and insufficient healthcare. As a result, women do not have adequate sleeping space, hygiene, or nutrition. For instance, the Reclusión de Mujeres de Bogotá El Buen Pastor, Colombia's largest women's prison, houses 1,888 people, far surpassing its capacity. Carolay Bayona, who was formerly housed there, said that the prison violated basic rights, offered no rehabilitation, and subjected women to "double punishment" because of their gender. She reported not receiving menstrual supplies or being able to have visitors, highlighting the neglect impacting incarcerated women (Hiller 2023).

Furthermore, sanitation in Colombian women's prisons is not adequate. Many facilities have limited access to clean water, toilets, and bathing facilities. Inadequate hygiene and insufficient medical supplies make it easy to spread diseases and infections, especially when they go untreated because of inadequate medical services (Colombia 2023 Human Rights Report 2024).

Similarly, it is difficult for incarcerated women in Colombia to receive reproductive healthcare. Pregnant women face insufficient prenatal and postnatal care, poor nutrition, and unsatisfactory medical treatment during childbirth. Many prisons lack the facilities to address maternal health needs, putting mothers and infants at risk. This stresses the need for reforms to ensure the well-being of incarcerated women, especially mothers (Cardona 2024).

In addition to poor conditions, incarcerated women in Colombia face sexual and physical violence, often at the hands of correctional officers. For

Life Inside El Buen Pastor

El Buen Pastor in Bogotá is Colombia's largest women's prison, housing nearly 1,900 people in a facility built for far fewer. Women describe sleeping in shifts, lacking basic supplies like menstrual products, and facing restrictions on visits. Consequently, some women formed a peer-support group called *El Mal Rebaño* ("The Bad Flock") to cope with trauma and long waits for mental healthcare. The group offers a space for women to talk about their families, children, and emotions, becoming a source of psychological support in the absence of adequate institutional care. Conditions demonstrate the "double punishment" of incarceration: being penalized for crimes and for being women in a system designed for men.

instance, between January and August 2023, disciplinary investigations were initiated against twenty-six guards for physical abuse, with one case involving sexual abuse. This abuse, combined with a lack of mental health resources to address trauma from gender-based violence and armed conflict, leaves many incarcerated women without the support needed to rehabilitate (Colombia 2023 Human Rights Report 2024).

Health and Mental Health Issues

Incarcerated women in Colombia face many physical health challenges, including malnutrition, respiratory illnesses, and infectious diseases. Overcrowded prisons often fail to provide sufficient food, leading to malnutrition. For instance, at the El Pesebre prison in Puerto Triunfo, fifteen people (mostly men) died from malnutrition over an eighteen-month period (Lugo 2024). Poor food quality and quantity, compounded by substance abuse where food is traded for drugs, worsen these issues. Additionally, limited access to clean drinking water causes illnesses among the incarcerated population.

In addition, poor ventilation in living spaces increases the risk of respiratory illnesses. Many incarcerated people live in tight spaces with inadequate airflow, creating environments conducive to respiratory infections and chronic conditions. The lack of preventive healthcare and insufficient medical attention leaves many incarcerated women without treatment, making their conditions even worse (Colombia: Rights Do Not End behind Bars 2024).

Mental health challenges are widespread among incarcerated women in Colombia. In Bogotá's El Buen Pastor prison, the scarcity of permanent psychologists and prolonged wait times (up to ten months) led women to form a peer-support group, El Mal Rebaño. Suicides in Colombian prisons are also a serious concern. In 2023 alone, there were eighteen confirmed cases across the prison system (including both men and women, though women were disproportionately affected), a rate nearly three times higher than that of the general population (Parada Lugo 2025). Substance use disorders are another widespread problem. Yet, despite the prevalence of addiction among incarcerated women in Colombia, the prison system offers limited rehabilitation programs or access to treatment. Instead, treatment for substance use disorders is usually self-funded and provided by psychologists, psychiatrists, and social workers. Non-governmental organizations (NGOs) often deliver these services, indicating a lack of state-provided rehabilitation programs within the prison system (Colombia Country Profile 2024).

Impact on Families and Children

In Colombia, pregnant and lactating women can substitute house arrest for incarceration, starting two months before their due date until six months after giving birth. Additionally, after returning to prison, mothers can choose to have their child live with them until the child's third birthday or be placed with relatives or in foster care under the care of the Colombian Family Welfare Institute (ICBF) (Paurus 2017). This policy is intended to support the bonding process at birth and during lactation.

However, critics argue that this policy encourages some women to become pregnant while incarcerated. Children conceived during conjugal visits may later be separated from their mothers, which can ultimately make the situation worse. While living with their mothers in prison may help with the bonding process, the prison environment has little access to educational opportunities, which is not in the best interest of the child. Also, when separated from their mothers at age three, children often experience emotional and attachment difficulties, which disrupt family bonds and cause psychological distress to mothers and children (Paurus 2017).

Furthermore, under Colombian constitutional law, women who are mothers of minor children or children with disabilities may be eligible for house arrest as an alternative to incarceration. In 2012, this stipulation was also given to fathers who are the primary caregivers when the mother is absent. However, this option is not available to people convicted of serious crimes (Paurus 2017).

Programs that provide alternatives to incarceration can lessen the adverse effects of a mother's incarceration on the family. Allowing mothers to remain with their children in the community supports families and reduces the stigma children face when they have an incarcerated parent. Studies suggest that children who remain in a home environment with their mothers are less likely to experience behavioral issues or problems at school. Thus, expanding and consistently implementing these alternatives, particularly for non-violent offenders, could improve outcomes for more families affected by incarceration (Colombia—Penal Reform International 2023).

Policy Reforms and Recommendations

Policy reforms for incarcerated women in Colombia are needed to address the issues that affect them. For one, it is necessary to have more alternatives to incarceration. While there are house arrest options for mothers of minor children and children with disabilities, these alternatives should be offered to more non-violent offenders so that they can remain in the community (Paurus 2017). These programs should be implemented nationwide, ensuring that legal professionals are familiar with such alternatives.

It is also necessary to improve the conditions for women in Colombian prisons by addressing overcrowding, unsanitary environments, and inadequate healthcare. There should be more funding for prisons so women have adequate sleeping arrangements, clean water, hygiene supplies, and better nutrition. Moreover, there should be more spaces and educational programs for mothers with children so children have an environment more conducive to their development (Hiller 2023).

Furthermore, with a high prevalence of trauma, mental health issues, and substance use disorders, mental health and addiction services need to be prioritized. For instance, the state should establish mental health programs and work with NGOs to provide services to incarcerated women throughout Colombia (Colombia: Rights Do Not End behind Bars 2024).

Lastly, helping women to better reintegrate into society is needed to break the cycle of poverty and crime. Better access to vocational training, education, and employment should exist during incarceration and after release. Initiatives should focus on helping women get out of armed conflict or the drug trade, offering more support so they can positively contribute to society (Salomón 2024).

Jamaica

Historical Context

Colonialism, economic challenges, and gender-based discrimination influence women's imprisonment in Jamaica. In colonial times, Jamaica's criminal justice system was based on British laws, and it imposed harsh penalties on disadvantaged groups, including impoverished women (Lemonius 2017). Even after independence in 1962, these colonial ideas continued, contributing to the incarceration of women, mainly for minor, non-violent offenses. This legacy reflects systemic inequality and a lack of reforms to address the circumstances that drive women into the criminal justice system.

Research indicates that 86 percent of incarcerated women in Jamaica are imprisoned for drug offenses (PIOJ 2005). Many of these women have histories of domestic violence, sexual abuse, and trauma, which often lead to criminal behaviors as coping mechanisms. According to the World Bank, four in ten Jamaican women experience intimate partner violence, which can push them to crime either through coercion or as a means for survival (Brief Country Profile 2023). Jamaica's location in the Caribbean further worsens this issue, as its role in the regional drug trade has disproportionately impacted women. Many are recruited as drug couriers, often single mothers facing financial hardship who are enticed by promises of large payments for smuggling drugs into countries like the UK and North America (BBC News 2002).

Historically, Jamaica's prison system has lacked gender-specific policies, resulting in inadequate healthcare, poor living conditions, and little support for incarcerated women. The closing of the Fort Augusta Adult Correctional Centre in 2017 stressed this, as the facility was overcrowded, had poor infrastructure, and lacked proper sanitation (Leslie 2022). People housed there were relocated to the South Camp Adult Correctional Centre, which was renovated to provide modern facilities and improved rehabilitation programs (South Camp Rehabilitation Centre a Better Rehabilitation Centre than Fort Augusta 2017). In 2024, the first prison nursery for incarcerated mothers was opened at South Camp, representing a step toward addressing the needs of incarcerated women and their children (First-Ever Infant Nursery for Incarcerated Expectant Mothers Opened 2024). However, despite these improvements, the system continues to struggle with addressing the root causes of female incarceration like poverty, violence, and inequality.

Female Incarceration Rates and Trends

Female incarceration rates in Jamaica are mostly influenced by socioeconomic factors and the country's role in the drug trade. Women represent about 4 percent of the overall prison population, but their numbers have fluctuated over the years. In 2004, female incarceration peaked at 270, but by 2005, the number had dropped to 175, representing a 35 percent decrease (PIOJ 2005). In 2012, there were 195 incarcerated women, but by 2014, the number had declined to 140. By 2022, the number had further decreased to 106 (Countryeconomy 2022). These women are currently held at the South Camp Adult Correctional Centre.

Jamaica has been criticized for its limited use of alternatives to incarceration, especially for non-violent offenders and women. Despite evidence that these alternatives (e.g., community service, probation, or house arrest) can lessen the impact on families and reduce recidivism, they are underutilized. Thus, many women are incarcerated for minor offenses, leading to family separations and disruptions (Roach-Spencer 2013).

However, the Department of Correctional Services (DCS) has recognized the need for alternatives to incarceration, suggesting ideas like Probation Orders for rehabilitation and Community Service Orders to replace custodial sentences (Jamaica Information Service 2010). Yet, the implementation of these alternatives has been limited. Similarly, Drug Treatment Courts, which were created to rehabilitate non-violent drug offenders, offer another alternative approach but are only used in a few of the country's parishes (The Gleaner 2017). Expanding access to these alternatives to incarceration would be effective for many people, especially women and mothers convicted of non-violent crimes.

Demographics of Incarcerated Women

The demographics of incarcerated women in Jamaica indicate social inequalities, particularly concerning poverty and gender. Most of these women come from economically disadvantaged communities, with many engaging in petty crimes or drug-related crimes resulting from financial insecurity. For instance, research has found that 86 percent of incarcerated women had committed offenses linked to economic hardship (PIOJ 2005). Additionally, most (80 percent) of these women are mothers (Robinson 2019).

The story of Georgette, a Jamaican single mother arrested at Heathrow Airport in 2002 for smuggling cocaine, illustrates how poverty can force women into drug trafficking. Promised £1,500 (approximately 3,850 current USD) to transport drugs, she faced an eight-year sentence in the UK. While her arrest occurred abroad, her circumstances reflect the problems of many Jamaican women incarcerated domestically for similar reasons. Economic struggles and limited opportunities often push women into low-level drug roles to support their families. Jamaica's criminal justice system worsens the issue with its limited use of alternatives to incarceration, leaving many women trapped in a cycle of poverty and incarceration (Ash 2006).

Additionally, Afro-Jamaican women are disproportionately represented in the prison population, mirroring societal inequalities. Although specific incarceration rates by race are not readily available, it is notable that approximately 92 percent of Jamaica's population identifies as Black (Jamaica 2023). Also, many incarcerated women have histories of domestic violence and trauma, which often contribute to their involvement in criminal activities. Studies indicate that nearly one in three women in Jamaica has experienced gender-based violence (UNSDG 2024). Overall, these intersecting factors (i.e., poverty, gender inequality, racial disparities, and histories of trauma) stress the need for reforms that address the root causes of female incarceration in Jamaica.

Crimes Leading to Incarceration

Aside from drug crimes, detailed statistical breakdowns of the specific offenses committed by incarcerated women in Jamaica are limited. Yet, available information indicates that, in addition to drug-related crimes, women are involved in offenses such as simple larceny, fraudulent activities, and domestic-related murders (Roach-Spencer 2013).

Poverty is an issue in Jamaica, with a poverty rate of 20 percent (Owens 2021). It disproportionately affects women, especially those in rural areas, leading some to engage in minor crimes to survive. The Jamaica National Crime Victimisation Survey (JNCVS) provides data on theft-related crimes. While it does not disaggregate data by gender, it reports that 5.5 percent of people experienced larceny in the previous year (Statistical Institute of Jamaica 2019). Given the economic challenges faced by many women, it is likely that impoverished women committed a large portion of these incidents.

However, a couple of recent cases represent high-profile cases of financial fraud involving women in Jamaica. Andrea Gordon, a former National Commercial Bank (NCB) manager with thirty years of service, was sentenced to seven and a half years in prison for embezzling over J$34 million (about 221,000 USD) between 2017 and 2020. She transferred funds to finance extravagant items and renovate her home, ultimately ruining her career and generating conversations about ethics and accountability (Mundle 2021). Similarly, Khadene Thomas, an NCB wealth advisor, was sentenced to two years for embezzling J$74.5 million (484,250 USD) from clients' accounts between 2019 and 2022. Using forged signatures, she transferred funds to support her personal needs despite later repaying some of the stolen money (Davis 2024).

In Jamaica, while violent crimes are less common among women, some women are imprisoned for offenses linked to domestic violence, often involving self-defense against abusive partners. According to the 2016 Women's Health Survey, 28 percent of Jamaican women have experienced intimate partner violence in their lifetime (UN Women 2018). Despite this prevalence, a 2022 report revealed that 80 percent of women confide in informal networks rather than seeking help from formal institutions (The Gleaner 2022). Prolonged abuse can lead some women to defend themselves, sometimes resulting in injury or death of their abusers, which may lead to criminal charges due to limited consideration of the context. Although Jamaica's Domestic Violence Act offers protection orders, enforcement and accessibility remain challenging (Generis Legal Intelligence 2024).

Contributing Laws and Policies

The Dangerous Drugs Act applies penalties for drug-related crimes in Jamaica. It was established in 1948, imposing severe penalties for drug offenses like possession and trafficking (Jamaica Information Service n.d.). Despite amendments from 2015 that aimed to decriminalize small quantities of marijuana, the act still has strict penalties for other drug-related offenses. Between 2015 and 2020, over 5,000 people were arrested for violating this act, with approximately 9 percent being women (The Gleaner 2020).

For example, under the Dangerous Drugs Act, Andrea Getters, a 22-year-old from Westmoreland Parish, was sentenced to two years in prison in Jamaica after pleading guilty to importing cocaine. She was arrested after arriving from Trinidad and Tobago, having swallowed two pounds of cocaine-filled pellets (Radio Jamaica News Online 2009). This case stresses how the Dangerous Drug Act can impact drug couriers, many of whom are impoverished women.

Furthermore, mandatory minimum sentencing laws, mainly for violent crimes and those involving illegal firearms, have negative effects on incarcerated women. These laws eliminate judicial discretion, leading to penalties that do not consider individual circumstances. For example, the Firearms (Prohibition, Restriction, and Regulation) Act requires a mandatory minimum sentence of fifteen years for illegal firearm possession (Hyatt 2023). This sentence is applied in all cases, affecting women who may possess firearms under coercion or for self-defense in cases of domestic violence. The lack of discretion in such cases can result in sentences that do not consider the context of the crime.

Conditions in Women's Prisons

As mentioned, the Fort Augusta Adult Correctional Centre was previously the primary facility for female inmates. This facility was reported to have nearly 300 inmates at one point with no indoor water supply, requiring people to obtain water from a central source using their own containers (U.S. Department of State 2013) and use buckets for toilets (Robottom 2011).

While the facility at Fort Augusta has since closed and women have been moved to South Camp Adult Correctional Centre (SCACC), there are still challenges. In early 2021 during the COVID-19 pandemic, SCACC reported thirty-six new positive COVID-19 cases within twenty-four hours. The outbreak called attention to the facility's challenges when managing a health crisis (The Gleaner 2021a). During this time, people expressed dissatisfaction with living conditions, including limited access to healthcare and inadequate sanitation, leading to protests and hunger strikes (The Gleaner 2021b).

Although the pandemic highlighted ongoing concerns about living conditions at SCACC, this facility has been an improvement over Fort Augusta. This facility has recently opened the aforementioned prison nursery. In addition, the Human Employment and Resource Training/National Service Training Agency Trust (HEART/NSTA Trust) of Jamaica provides training and job certification in cosmetology, sewing, data operations, customer service delivery, and other courses to women at SCACC. Recently, fifty women graduated from this program, which aims to help them reintegrate into society and be productive upon release (Angus 2023).

Health and Mental Health Issues

Health and mental health issues can be a problem for incarcerated women in Jamaica, which are worsened by prison conditions and limited access to services (Urgent Need to Address Prison Conditions 2024). Physical health problems are common due to overcrowding, unsanitary conditions, and a lack of necessities like proper nutrition and hygiene. Typical health issues include respiratory infections worsened by poorly ventilated cells and skin diseases resulting from inadequate sanitation. Gastrointestinal problems are also common because of poor nutrition. Additionally, chronic illnesses, like hypertension and diabetes, can worsen because of insufficient medical care (Prison Conditions and Inhumane Treatment of Prisoners 2023).

Moreover, incarcerated women experience higher rates of mental health issues compared to their male counterparts. These problems include depression, anxiety, and post-traumatic stress disorder (PTSD), which are often the result of past trauma, abuse, and the stress of imprisonment, especially for mothers. Nevertheless, the Ministry of Health has recently partnered with the Ministry of National Security to strengthen mental health services for people incarcerated in Jamaica (Prison Conditions and Inhumane Treatment of Prisoners 2023).

Furthermore, more women in Jamaica are using substances (Survey Finds Increased Substance Use in Jamaica in Last 7 Yrs 2024), so many women struggled with addiction before their imprisonment. Research indicates there are high-risk patterns of alcohol, cannabis, and tobacco use across Jamaica. These substances can adversely impact the health of incarcerated women who already have compromised health due to poor prison conditions (High-Risk Patterns of Substance Use Detected among Jamaicans 2024). Unfortunately, there are limited rehabilitation or treatment programs available within Jamaican prisons to address this problem (Sowande 2023).

Lastly, incarcerated women often face inadequate prenatal and postnatal care. In Jamaica, women incarcerated while pregnant are separated from their newborns up to six months after giving birth (Hendricks 2020). This separation leads to anxiety and depression, worsening health risks for mothers and children. The impact of mother's incarceration on families is discussed in more detail below.

Impact on Families and Children

The incarceration of women in Jamaica has an overwhelming impact on them and their families. One woman, who had been imprisoned at twenty-four and was pregnant with her first child, spoke of her struggles:

> Imagine being eight months pregnant and have to be sleeping on a bunk bed. Every time I move I fear rolling off the bed because it wasn't very wide and I wasn't exactly small bodied ... Then, on top of that, I was stressed thinking about my trial, and as you know, stress isn't good for anyone, much less pregnant women who already have high blood pressure. (Hendricks 2020)

She also recounted the added stress when her baby was taken away: "When they took him I cried for weeks and months. My pressure went through the roof. I thought I was going to die. I lost so much weight in such a short space of time it was ridiculous. I couldn't eat. I couldn't sleep, I couldn't breathe or think properly" (Hendricks 2020).

This emotional and psychological toll is increased by the separation from their children who are often left in the care of extended family members, such as grandparents or aunts, or placed in state care. Both situations can lead to trauma for the children. Moreover, after separation, incarcerated women face limitations on contact with their children, being allowed to see them only twice per year and make one five-minute phone call each week (Hendricks 2020).

However, introducing the recent prison nursery program offers hope for these women. This program allows incarcerated mothers to bond with their young children, promoting a sense of connection and lessening the trauma of separation. While still in its early stages, the nursery represents a step toward addressing the needs of incarcerated mothers and their children (First-Ever Infant Nursery for Incarcerated Expectant Mothers Opened 2024).

Policy Reforms and Recommendations

Policy reforms for incarcerated women in Jamaica are needed to address the issues that impact them. First, it is essential to encourage alternatives to incarceration. Many women are imprisoned for non-violent, drug-related offenses, often driven by poverty or coercion. Alternatives like probation or participating in drug treatment courts can be helpful to keep families intact. Thus, it is recommended that the availability of Drug Treatment Courts, which are available in less than 40 percent of parishes, be expanded throughout the country (The Gleaner 2017). Additionally, utilizing the option of house arrest with electronic monitoring would allow more mothers to care for their children while serving their sentences in the community.

Next, it is necessary to improve family support programs. The separation of mothers from their children causes emotional trauma. Therefore, allowing mothers to care for their young children in the nursery program beyond their first six months is suggested. Furthermore, there should be more opportunities for contact between incarcerated mothers and their children, such as more frequent visits and additional phone calls (Hendricks 2020).

Finally, it is crucial to keep developing economic and educational opportunities because poverty and lack of opportunity are the primary reasons for female incarceration. Programs like those offered by the HEART/NSTA Trust have proven effective in preparing women for reintegration (Angus 2023). Consequently, there should be expanded vocational and educational programs focusing on skills that provide employment opportunities post-release. The SCACC could partner with more local organizations to support women in securing jobs and housing after incarceration. These reforms would help address the inequalities driving female incarceration in Jamaica while reducing its impacts on families and communities.

Conclusion

This chapter has examined the challenges related to the incarceration of women in Brazil, Colombia, and Jamaica, which are primarily associated with socioeconomic factors, gendered violence, and systemic inequalities. A commonality is the disproportionate incarceration of women for non-violent, drug-related crimes related to poverty or coercion. In Brazil, strict drug laws and overcrowded prisons indicate failures to address the needs of incarcerated women. Additionally, Colombia's history of armed conflict and the drug trade contributes to women's incarceration. In Jamaica, women's imprisonment is rooted in colonialism and worsened by insufficient alternatives to incarceration, leaving many mothers separated from their children.

There are similarities and differences in how these countries approach the incarceration of women. Brazil's prison system illustrates overcrowding and inadequate healthcare, with only thirty-seven gynecologists available for the entire incarcerated population. Colombia, while similarly affected by overcrowding and poor sanitation, has begun to implement reforms, such as alternatives to incarceration for non-violent offenders who are primary caregivers. Jamaica has similar struggles, especially in its lack of community-based and rehabilitative options. Each country demonstrates a need for reforms to help address the challenges faced by incarcerated women.

Addressing these needs will help reduce recidivism, support reintegration, and lessen the effects of imprisonment on families and communities. Gender-responsive policies that focus on alternatives to incarceration, improve prison conditions, and expand access to healthcare and training programs are needed. Furthermore, working with local organizations can strengthen these reforms. By recognizing the social, economic, and historical factors that contribute to female incarceration, these countries can take steps to improve the experiences of imprisoned women.

References

ABC News. 2017a. "Cassandra Sainsbury: Accused Cocaine Smuggler 'Would Have Known Drugs Were in Her Bag.'" ABC News. May 2, 2017. https://www.abc.net.au/news/2017-05-03/cassandra-sainsbury-knew-drugs-were-in-her-bad-colombian-police/8491966.

ABC News. 2017b. "Cassandra Sainsbury Could Serve Six Years' Jail in Colombia After Plea Deal Reportedly Struck." ABC News. October 20, 2017. https://www.abc.net.au/news/2017-10-21/cassie-sainsbury-faces-six-years-after-reported-plea-deal/9072884.

Adams, David. 2020. "Criminal or Victim?: Female Drug Mules Trapped as 'Legal Zombies' in Brazil—Sight Magazine." Sight Magazine. January 11, 2020. https://sightmagazine.com.au/features/criminal-or-victim-female-drug-mules-trapped-as-legal-zombies-in-brazil/.

Agencia EFE. 2023. "Colombia Opens a Window to Freedom for Imprisoned Women—EFE." EFE Noticias. September 17, 2023. https://efe.com/en/latest-news/2023-09-17/colombia-opens-a-window-to-freedom-for-imprisoned-women/.

Angus L., Garfield. 2023. "Women Graduate at South Camp Adult Correctional Centre—Jamaica Information Service." Jis.gov.jm. December 1, 2023. https://jis.gov.jm/women-graduate-at-south-camp-adult-correctional-centre/.t.

Ash, Lucy. 2006. "Hard Return for Jamaica Drugs Mule." *BBC News*. http://news.bbc.co.uk/2/hi/americas/4629282.stm.

Baltieri, Danilo Antonio. 2014. "Predictors of Drug Use in Prison Among Women Convicted of Violent Crimes." *Criminal Behaviour and Mental Health* 24 (2): 113–28.

BBC News UK. 2002. "Jamaica Battles UK Drugs 'Mules.'" Bbc.co.uk. January 4, 2002. http://news.bbc.co.uk/2/hi/uk_news/1741283.stm.

Belandi, Caio, and Irene Gomes. 2023. "2022 Census: Self-Reported Brown Population Is the Majority in Brazil for the First Time | News Agency." Agência de Notícias—IBGE. December 22, 2023. https://agenciadenoticias.ibge.gov.br/en/agencia-news/2184-news-agency/news/38726-2022-census-self-reported-brown-population-is-the-majority-in-brazil-for-the-first-time.

Brasil. 2020. *LGBT nas prisões do Brasil: Diagnóstico dos procedimentos institucionais e experiências de encarceramento*. Ministério da Mulher, Família e Direitos Humanos.

"Brazil's STF Sets 40 Grams of Marijuana Cap Between Users and Traffickers." 2024. MercoPress. 2024. https://en.mercopress.com/2024/06/27/brazil-s-stf-sets-40-grams-of-marijuana-cap-between-users-and-traffickers?

"Brief Country Profile: Gender-Based Violence in Jamaica." 2023. World Bank. https://www.worldbank.org/en/news/infographic/2023/07/26/brief-country-profile-gender-based-violence-in-jamaica.

Britto, Lina. 2020. "The Drug Wars in Colombia." *Oxford Research Encyclopedia of Latin American History*. https://doi.org/10.1093/acrefore/9780199366439.013.504.

Brown University. 2019. "The African Slave Trade and Slave Life | Brazil: Five Centuries of Change." Brown.edu. 2019. https://library.brown.edu/create/fivecenturiesofchange/chapters/chapter-2/african-slavery/.

Canineu, Maria Laura. 2017. "Brazil's Illegal Treatment of Women in Prison." *Human Rights Watch*. March 6, 2017. https://www.hrw.org/news/2017/03/06/brazils-illegal-treatment-women-prison.

Cardona, Claudia Alejandra. 2024. "Opening Doors for Women in Prison." *Open Society Foundations.* May 22, 2024. https://www.opensocietyfoundations.org/voices/the-fight-for-women-s-rights-behind-bars-in-colombia.

Colombia—Penal Reform International. 2023, May 19. Penal Reform International. https://www.penalreform.org/issues/women/bangkok-rules/bangkok-rules-map/colombia/.

"Colombia | World Prison Brief." 2024. https://www.prisonstudies.org/country/colombia.

"Colombia: Rights Do Not End Behind Bars." 2024. International Committee of the Red Cross. March 3, 2024. https://www.icrc.org/en/document/colombia-rights-do-not-end-behind-bars.

"Colombia: Share of Females Incarcerated for Drug Offenses by Age Group 2016 | Statista." 2024. Statista. December 2, 2016. https://www.statista.com/statistics/914869/colombia-females-incarcerated-drug-offenses-age-group/.

"Colombia 2023 Human Rights Report." 2024. State.gov. https://www.state.gov/wp-content/uploads/2024/02/528267_COLOMBIA-2023-HUMAN-RIGHTS-REPORT.pdf.

"Colombia Country Profile | International Society of Substance Use Professionals." 2024. https://www.issup.net/national-chapters/issup-colombia/country-profile.

"Colombia's FARC Rebels Recruited More than 18,000 Children: Court." 2021. https://www.aljazeera.com/news/2021/8/10/colombia-farc-rebels-recruited-more-than-18000-children-court.

Countryeconomy. 2022. "Jamaica—Total Prison Population 2022." Countryeconomy.com. https://countryeconomy.com/demography/prison-population/jamaica.

"Criminal Code of Colombia: Law 599 of 2000." 2020. Cejamericas.org. http://desa1.cejamericas.org:8080/handle/2015/4225.

Daken, Kirstie, Tarra Excell, Kirsty A. Clark, Jaclyn M. W. Hughto, Tait Sanders, Joseph Debattista, Carol du Plessis, Amy B. Mullens, Tania M. Phillips, Jessica Gildersleeve, and Annette Brömdal. 2023. "Correctional Staff Knowledge, Attitudes and Behaviors Toward Incarcerated Trans People: A Scoping Review of an Emerging Literature." *International Journal of Transgender Health* 10 (2): 149–66.

Davis, Akera. 2024. "Convict and Lawyer Unhappy with Custodial Sentence." Jamaicaobserver.com. June 28, 2024. https://www.jamaicaobserver.com/2024/06/28/convict-lawyer-unhappy-custodial-sentenceformer-ncb-wealth-advisor-gets-24-months-stealing-74-5-million/.

De Araújo, Priscila França, Ligia Regina Franco Sansigolo Kerr, Carl Kendall, George W. Rutherford, David W. Seal, Roberto da Justa Pires Neto, Patrícia Neyva da Costa Pinheiro, Marli Teresinha Gimeniz Galvão, Larissa Fortunato Araújo, Francisco Marto Leal Pinheiro, and Ana Zaira da Silva. 2020. "Behind Bars: The Burden of Being a Woman in Brazilian Prisons." *BMC International Health and Human Rights* 20: 28.

De Azevedo, Rodrigo Ghiringhelli, and Ana Claudia Cifali. 2017. "Public Security, Criminal Policy and Sentencing in Brazil During the Lula and Dilma Governments, 2003–2014: Changes and Continuities." *International Journal for Crime, Justice, and Social Democracy* 6 (1): 146–63.

Del Pozo Serrano, Francisco José, and Magdalena Jiménez Ramírez. 2017. "Women Prisoners in the Colombian Caribbean and Social-Educative Action: Multicultural Faces in the Feminization of Poverty, Conflict and Social Exclusion." *Procedia—Social and Behavioral Sciences* 237: 216–22.

"Details." 2024. Unodc.org. https://www.unodc.org/LSS/Country/DetailsLegalSystem?code=DLIL&country=CO&utm_.

Faquim, Juliana, Juliana Macedo, Juliana Oliveira, Silvia Machado, Gabriela Ivancko, Karina Costa, Mariana Alves, and Thais Oliveira. 2020. "Profile of Incarcerated Women in the Interior of Brazil and the Challenge of Education in Prison." *European Journal of Public Health* 30 (suppl. 5): ckab164.001.

"Female Incarceration in Brazil and the United States." 2021. Instituto Terra, Trabalho E Cidadania—ITTC. January 14, 2021. https://ittc.org.br/female-incarceration-brazil-and-us/.

"First-Ever Infant Nursery for Incarcerated Expectant Mothers Opened." 2024. Jamaica-Gleaner.com. September 27, 2024. https://jamaica-gleaner.com/article/news/20240927/first-ever-infant-nursery-incarcerated-expectant-mothers-opened.

"From War to Economic Reintegration: The Challenges for Women Ex-Combatants in Colombia." 2023. International Growth Centre. March 20, 2023. https://www.theigc.org/blogs/gender-equality/war-economic-reintegration-challenges-women-ex-combatants-colombia.

García-Sayan, Diego. 2024. "El Fracaso de La 'Guerra Contra Las Drogas': La Despenalización." El País América. December 7, 2024. https://elpais.com/america/2024-12-07/el-fracaso-de-la-guerra-contra-las-drogas-la-despenalizacion.html.

Generis Legal Intelligence. 2024. "Understanding Domestic Violence Protection Measures in Jamaica." Generis Global Legal Services. November 19, 2024. https://generisonline.com/understanding-domestic-violence-protection-measures-in-jamaica/.

Hendricks, Sharlene. 2020. "The Agony of Serving Time in Prison While Pregnant." Jamaicaobserver.com. March 8, 2020. https://www.jamaicaobserver.com/2020/03/08/the-agony-of-serving-time-in-prison-while-pregnant/.

"High-Risk Patterns of Substance Use Detected among Jamaicans—Ministry of Health & Wellness, Jamaica." 2024. Moh.gov.jm. https://www.moh.gov.jm/high-risk-patterns-of-substance-use-detected-among-jamaicans/.

Hiller, Joseph. 2023. "Women Organize Against the 'Double Punishment' of Colombian Prisons." NACLA. December 8, 2023. https://nacla.org/women-organize-against-double-punishment-colombian-prisons.

"HRW: Behind Bars in Brazil (Women Prisoners)." 2024. Hrw.org. https://www.hrw.org/legacy/reports98/brazil/Brazil-12.htm.

Hyatt, Matthew. 2023. "Why Mandatory Minimum Sentences Won't Work." *The Gleaner.* October 27, 2023. https://jamaica-gleaner.com/article/

commentary/20231027/matthew-hyatt-why-mandatory-minimum-sentences-wont-work.

Interviews and Perspectives. 2020. "Public Security, Identity, and Democracy in Brazil: Interview with Ilona Szabó." Harvard International Review. September 11, 2020. https://hir.harvard.edu/illona-szabo-security-democracy-brazil/.

"Jamaica." 2023. United States Department of State. https://www.state.gov/reports/2023-country-reports-on-human-rights-practices/jamaica/.

Jamaica Information Service. 2010. "Department of Correctional Services Looking at Alternatives to Incarceration." January 14, 2010. https://jis.gov.jm/department-of-correctional-services-looking-at-alternatives-to-incarceration/.

Jamaica Information Service. n.d. "Dangerous Drugs Act: The Facts." Accessed December 26, 2024. https://jis.gov.jm/features/dangerous-drugs-act-facts/.

Kirby, Jenni Monet. 2019. "Facing Wrongful Detention and Threats, Afro-Colombian Women Call for Justice." Truthout. March 17, 2019. https://truthout.org/articles/facing-wrongful-detention-and-threats-afro-colombian-women-call-for-justice/.

La Comisión de Seguimiento de la Sentencia T-388 de 2013. Comunicado sobre la Ley 1760 de 2015 y su Impacto en la Población Penitenciaria en Colombia. Bogotá: La Comisión de Seguimiento de la Sentencia T-388 de 2013, 2016. https://www.dejusticia.org/wp-content/uploads/2017/04/fi_name_recurso_837.pdf.

Leal, Marto, Ligia Kerr, Rosa Maria Salani Mota, Roberto da Justa Pires Neto, David Seal, and Carl Kendall. 2023. "Differences in Non-Communicable Diseases Between Women in Prison and the General Population in Brazil." *Scientific Reports* 13.

Lee, Brendon. 2020. "Not-So-Grand Strategy: America's Failed War on Drugs in Colombia." *Harvard International Review*. January 10, 2020. https://hir.harvard.edu/americas-failed-war-on-drugs-in-colombia/.

Lemonius, Michele. 2017. "Deviously Ingenious: British Colonialism in Jamaica." *Peace Research: The Canadian Journal of Peace and Conflict Studies* 49 (2): 79–103.

Leslie, Dacia. 2022. "Reassessing Conditions of 'Prison' in Jamaica." *International Criminal Justice Review* 32 (1): 48–67.

Lugo, Valentina Parada. 2024. "Los Presos Que Mueren de Hambre En La Prisión Que Fue Parte de La Opulenta Hacienda de Pablo Escobar." El País América Colombia. September 2024. https://elpais.com/america-colombia/2024-09-01/los-presos-que-mueren-de-hambre-en-la-prision-que-fue-parte-de-la-opulenta-hacienda-de-pablo-escobar.html.

Medeiros, Leonardo. 2021. "Brazil Has the World's 3rd Largest Prison Population." Conectas. April 8, 2021. https://www.conectas.org/en/noticias/brazil-worlds-3rd-largest-prison-population/.

Miranda, Raquel B., Alejandro Goldberg, and Ximena Pamela Díaz Bermúdez. 2024. "Social Reintegration of Cisgender and Transgender Women Post-Incarceration in Brazil: Policies and Challenges." *Health & Justice* 12 (29): 1–14.

Mundle, Tanesha. 2021. "Bowed with Shame, Ex-Banker Gets 71/2 Yrs for Fraud." Jamaica-Gleaner.com. June 1, 2021. https://jamaica-gleaner.com/article/lead-stories/20210601/bowed-shame-ex-banker-gets-712-yrs-fraud.

Napolitano, Marcos. 2018. "The Brazilian Military Regime, 1964–1985." Oxford Research Encyclopedia of Latin American History. April 26, 2018. Accessed December 19, 2024. https://oxfordre.com/latinamericanhistory/view/10.1093/acrefore/9780199366439.001.0001/acrefore-9780199366439-e-413.

Owens, Nia. 2021. "The Push for Improved Women's Rights in Jamaica." The Borgen Project. April 25, 2021. https://borgenproject.org/womens-rights-in-jamaica/.

Parada Lugo, Valentina. 2025. "Mal rebaño", el colectivo de presas que promueve la salud mental en la cárcel El Buen Pastor. *El País (América Colombia)*. February 8, 2025. https://elpais.com/america-colombia/2025-02-08/mal-rebano-el-colectivo-de-presas-que-promueve-la-salud-mental-en-la-carcel-el-buen-pastor.html

Paurus, Melanie. 2017. "International Report on the Conditions of Children of Incarcerated Parents a Survey of Prison Nurseries." https://cicmn.org/wp-content/uploads/2017/03/Melanie-Report-Edited.pdf.

Penal Reform International, and Linklaters LLP. 2016. *Women Who Kill in Response to Domestic Violence: How Do Criminal Justice Systems Respond?* London: Penal Reform International and Linklaters LLP. www.penalreform.org/resource/women-who-kill-in-response-to-domestic-violence/.

Pimental, Renan. 2022. "'Equal Before the Law,' but Not in Practice: Brazil's Social Inequality Crisis." *Harvard Political Review*. February 9, 2022. https://harvardpolitics.com/brazil-social-inequality/.

"PIOJ Launches First Study on Impact of Imprisonment of Women—Jamaica Information Service." 2005. Jis.gov.jm. December 20, 2005. https://jis.gov.jm/pioj-launches-first-study-on-impact-of-imprisonment-of-women/.

"Prison Conditions and Inhumane Treatment of Prisoners." 2023. Jamaica-Gleaner.com. February 6, 2023. https://jamaica-gleaner.com/article/news/20230206/prison-conditions-and-inhumane-treatment-prisoners.

Prison Insider. 2020. "Brazil: Drugs, Walls and Being a Woman." September 7, 2020. https://www.prison-insider.com/en/articles/bresil-pour-les-femmes-la-drogue-et-les-murs.

Radio Jamaica News Online. 2009. "Two Given Long Sentences for Importing Cocaine." April 7, 2009. https://radiojamaicanewsonline.com/local/two-given-long-sentences-for-importing-cocaine.

Rendón González, Nataly. 2022. "Colombia: Example of Increased Criminality by Women." *AULA Blog*. January 28, 2022. https://aulablog.net/2022/01/28/colombia-example-of-increased-criminality-by-women/.

Reynoso, Lucas. 2024. "La Corte Constitucional de Colombia Anula Por Sesgos Machistas La Alta Condena Contra Una Mujer Que Mató a Su Violador." El País América Colombia. November 20, 2024. https://elpais.com/america-colombia/2024-11-20/la-corte-constitucional-de-colombia-anula-por-sesgos-machistas-la-alta-condena-contra-una-mujer-que-mato-a-su-violador.html.

Roach-Spencer, Joycelyn. 2013. "Treatment of Female Offenders in Jamaica." Resource Material Series No. 90. United Nations Asia and Far East Institute for the Prevention of Crime and the Treatment of Offenders (UNAFEI). https://unafei.or.jp/publications/pdf/RS_No90/No90_16PA_Roach-Spencer.pdf.

Robinson, Corey. 2019. "Mother's Day Behind Bars—Domestic Abuse, 'Survival Crimes' Major Factors Why Moms Imprisoned." *Jamaica Gleaner*. May 12, 2019. http://past.jamaica-gleaner.com/article/lead-stories/20190512/mothers-day-behind-bars-domestic-abuse-survival-crimes-major-factors

Robottom, James. 2011. " Prison Conditions in Jamaica: A Report Based on James Robottom's Visit in August 2009." London: The Death Penalty Project. https://www.deathpenaltyproject.org.

Salomón, Josefina. 2024. "La Universidad Se Mete a La Cárcel En América Latina." El País América. October 14, 2024. https://elpais.com/america-futura/2024-10-14/la-universidad-se-mete-a-la-carcel-en-america-latina.html.

SISDEPEN. 2023. Secretaria Nacional de Políticas Penais. https://www.gov.br/senappen/pt-br/servicos/sisdepen.

"South Camp Rehabilitation Centre a Better Rehabilitation Centre than Fort Augusta — Charles." 2017. Jamaicaobserver.com. March 5, 2017. https://www.jamaicaobserver.com/2017/03/04/south-camp-rehabilitation-centre-a-better-rehabilitation-centre-than-fort-agusta-charles/.

Sowande, Olufemi. 2023. "Rehabilitation for Incarcerated Should Be Top Priority." Jamaica-Gleaner.com. January 30, 2023. https://jamaica-gleaner.com/article/news/20230130/rehabilitation-incarcerated-should-be-top-priority.

Statistical Institute of Jamaica. 2019. *Jamaica National Crime Victimisation Survey (JNCVS) 2019 Report*. Kingston: Statistical Institute of Jamaica, 2020. ISBN 978-976-8252-56-2.

Stella, Claudia, Vania C. Sequeira, and Thais La Rosa. 2016. "Mothers and Babies in a Brazilian Prison: A Study Exploring the Impact of Prison Conditions." *Forensic Research & Criminology International Journal* 2 (3): 104–10.

"Survey Finds Increased Substance Use in Jamaica in Last 7 Yrs." 2024. Jamaica-Gleaner.com. November 12, 2024. https://jamaica-gleaner.com/article/lead-stories/20241112/survey-finds-increased-substance-use-jamaica-last-7-yrs.

The Gleaner. 2022. "Near 100 Per Cent Rise in Domestic Violence Reports in Five Years." The Gleaner. July 20, 2022. https://jamaica-gleaner.com/article/news/20220720/near-100-cent-rise-domestic-violence-reports-five-years.

The Gleaner. 2021a. "36 New COVID Cases at South Camp Adult Correctional Centre." February 15, 2021. https://jamaica-gleaner.com/article/news/20210215/36-new-covid-cases-south-camp-adult-correctional-centre.

The Gleaner. 2021b. "'We Are Living Like Dogs': Inmates Enraged as Female Prison Leads COVID-19 Caseload." February 28, 2021. https://jamaica-gleaner.com/article/

news/20210228/we-are-living-dogs-inmates-enraged-female-prison-leads-covid-19-caseload.

The Gleaner. 2020. "Big Fish Among Us: Foreign Drug Cartels Handling Business on Jamaican Soil." The Gleaner. December 20, 2020. https://jamaica-gleaner.com/article/lead-stories/20201220/big-fish-among-us-foreign-drug-cartels-handling-business-jamaican-soil.

The Gleaner. 2017. "Chuck: Drug Treatment Court an Alternative to Incarceration." Last modified September 8, 2017. https://jamaica-gleaner.com/article/lead-stories/20170908/chuck-drug-treatment-court-alternative-incarceration.

TNI. 2024. "Brazil." https://www.druglawreform.info/en/country-information/latin-america/brazil/item/201-brazil.

UN Women. 2018. "Jamaican National Gender-Based Violence Survey." UN Women. June 26, 2018. https://www.unwomen.org/en/news/stories/2018/6/announcement-jamaican-national-gender-based-violence-survey.

United Nations Office on Drugs and Crime (UNODC). 2019. *Estudio: Las Mujeres Privadas de la Libertad por Delitos de Drogas*. Bogotá: UNODC. https://www.unodc.org/documents/colombia/2019/Octubre/Estudio_Las_mujeres_Privadas_de_la_Libertad_por_Delitos_de_Drogas.pdf.

United Nations Office on Drugs and Crime (UNODC). 2016. *Informe sobre la Ley 30 de 1986 y su Impacto en las Mujeres Privadas de la Libertad en Colombia*. Bogotá: UNODC.

"UNSDG | The Changing Face of Domestic Violence Intervention in Jamaica." 2024. Un.org. November 19, 2024. https://unsdg.un.org/latest/stories/changing-face-domestic-violence-intervention-jamaica.

"Urgent Need to Address Prison Conditions." 2024. Jamaicaobserver.com. December 2, 2024. https://www.jamaicaobserver.com/2024/12/02/urgent-need-address-prison-conditions/.

U.S. Department of State. 2013. "Country Reports on Human Rights Practices for 2013: Jamaica." Washington, DC: U.S. Department of State. https://2009-2017.state.gov/documents/organization/220666.pdf.

Watson, Katy, and Alys Davies. 2023. "Lula Sworn in as Brazil President as Predecessor Bolsonaro Flies to US." BBC News. January 1, 2023. sec. Latin America & Caribbean. https://www.bbc.com/news/world-latin-america-64138739.

Wilson, Rebecca. 2021. "Understanding Violence Against Women and Girls in Brazil." Latin America Bureau. September 24, 2021. https://lab.org.uk/understanding-violence-against-women-and-girls-in-brazil/.

"Women, Drug Policies, and Incarceration." n.d. https://www.oas.org/en/cim/docs/womendrugsincarceration-en.pdf.

"Women, Drug Policy, and Imprisonment: A Guide for Reforming Policy in Colombia." 2016. IDPC. November 22, 2016. https://idpc.net/publications/2016/11/women-drug-policy-and-imprisonment-a-guide-for-reforming-policy-in-colombia.

Yahoo. 2017. "Debt and a Failed Dream: Past Life of Accused Adelaide Drug Mule Revealed." Yahoo News. May 3, 2017. https://au.news.yahoo.com/debt-and-failed-dream-past-life-of-accused-adelaide-drug-mule-cassie-sainsbury-revealed-35273411.html.

Youngers, Coletta. 2022. "Colombia to Implement Law on Alternatives to Incarceration for Women Heads of Household." WOLA. August 11, 2022. https://www.wola.org/analysis/colombia-law-alternatives-incarceration-women-heads-household/.

3

Europe

This chapter explores the experiences of incarcerated women in Europe, focusing on the challenges they face and the issues that shape their incarceration. Highlighting Russia, Norway, and Italy, it discusses the historical, legal, and social factors influencing the treatment of women in these prison systems. From the harsh conditions in Soviet-era Gulags to the progressive, rehabilitative approaches in Scandinavian countries and the patriarchal ideas impacting Italy's prison system, the chapter examines the complex experiences of incarceration for women. Emphasizing economic challenges, gender-based violence, and the need for reform, it investigates how incarceration affects women, their families, and their outlooks for reintegrating into society.

Russia

Historical Context

The history of incarcerated women in Russia is influenced by the country's political and social upheavals. Women convicted of crimes in the Tsarist period were often sentenced to Siberian labor camps, which were characterized by extreme weather and physical demands, similar to men's camps (Gheith and Jolluck 2011). Women were also exiled to these camps for political reasons, including members of groups like Narodnaya Volya, who opposed the monarchy, and they faced significant difficulties, such as being separated from their families. These practices laid the foundation for the Soviet-era penal system, where people suffered from similar conditions (Applebaum 2003).

Under Soviet rule, especially during Stalin's Great Purges in the 1930s and 1940s, the incarceration of women increased, with many imprisoned as part of the **Gulag** system (e.g., forced labor camps). Women arrested under **Article 58**

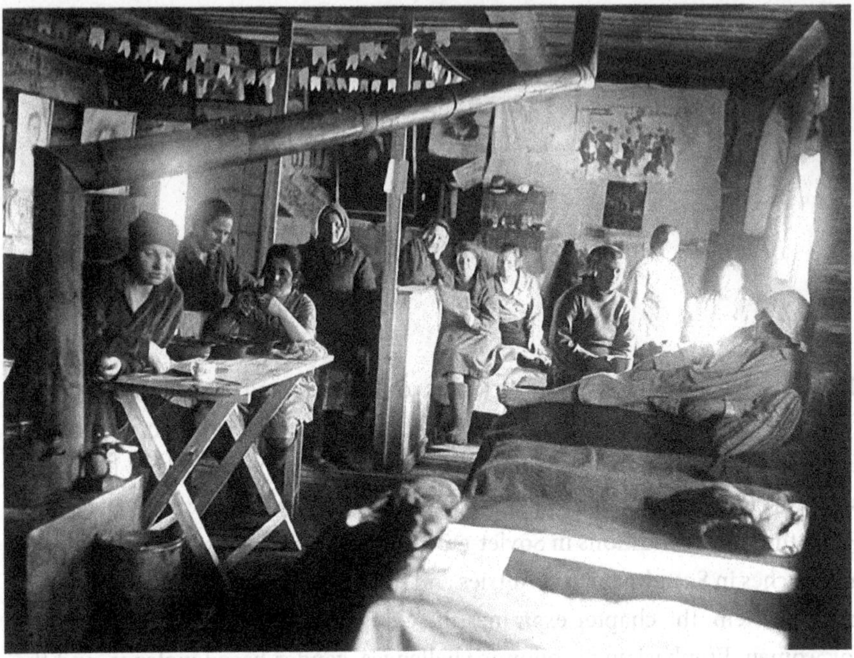

Female prisoners in a Soviet Gulag, 1930s (Laski Diffusion/Getty Images)

of the Soviet Penal Code faced charges of counter-revolutionary activities or espionage (Viola 2007). At this time, women made up about 7 percent of the Gulag population, which meant there were tens of thousands of incarcerated women.

In the Gulags, women endured severe conditions, performing physical labor like logging and mining with inadequate clothing and insufficient food (Applebaum 2003). Sexual violence was also common, as incarcerated women were often abused by male correctional officers and incarcerated men, leading to pregnancies and trauma. Women were also assigned to less physically demanding tasks, like sewing, which often had quotas and penalties if they did not reach them (Viola 2007).

Unfortunately, the collapse of the Soviet Union in 1991 did not improve the lives of incarcerated women, as the economic instability of the time contributed to rising crime rates and an increase in female incarceration (Pallot and Piacentini 2012). Many women were imprisoned for non-violent offenses, like theft, fraud, or drug-related crimes, showing the socioeconomic problems of that time (Sudoplatov and Wistrich 1994). By the mid-1990s, women made up approximately 9 percent of Russia's prison population (Pallot and Piacentini 2012).

Women in the Gulag

During Stalin's Great Purges (1936–8), thousands of women were imprisoned in the Gulag system. Many were accused of "counter-revolutionary" activities under Article 58, including espionage or aiding enemies of the state. Incarcerated women endured forced labor, inadequate food, and abuse. Some were assigned to sewing factories with punishing quotas. Others worked in logging or mining under extreme conditions. Additionally, sexual violence was widespread, leaving many with lifelong trauma. Their experiences show the gendered factors of Soviet repression.

Post-Soviet policies have maintained a punitive approach, and incarcerated women have faced overcrowding, unsanitary living conditions, and insufficient healthcare (Pallot and Piacentini 2012). Women often reside in shared cells designed for fewer people, do not have access to hygiene products, and have inadequate prenatal care (Roth 2006). Moreover, there are few rehabilitation programs to help women gain educational or vocational training. The treatment of incarcerated women in Russia shows patterns of neglect and marginalization.

Female Incarceration Rates and Trends

Over time, female incarceration rates in Russia have made up between 8 and 10 percent of the total prison population (Pallot and Piacentini 2012). Despite recent decreases in the number of incarcerated individuals, Russia's incarceration rate is still one of the highest in Europe. The current rate is 328 per 100,000 people, with about 45,000 women incarcerated (World Prison Brief 2023). In 2024, Russia's prison system had 872 facilities, including penal colonies, prisons, and detention centers (Prison Insider 2024). The current number of facilities entirely for women is not indicated. However, in 2003, Russia had twenty-six prisons for women, with most of them serving their sentences far from home (Pravda 2004).

Poverty, unemployment, and stringent drug policies have disproportionately affected women, who are typically imprisoned for non-violent crimes like theft, fraud, or drug crimes. Similar to other countries, impoverished women in Russia may resort to theft or become involved in low-level drug crimes to survive. Moreover, tough-on-crime policies from the early 2000s under Vladimir Putin's administration led to increases in female incarceration, with especially strict sentences for minor crimes like drug possession (Pallot and Piacentini 2012).

Russia has since implemented ways to reduce the prison population using alternatives to incarceration (e.g., fines, community service, and house arrest). Between 2010 and 2020, reforms reduced the female prison population by almost 25 percent, from 59,000 to 45,000 (World Prison Brief 2023). However, these alternatives have not been consistent, with women from marginalized communities being less apt to utilize them (Pallot and Piacentini 2012), often because they exclude people without stable housing. While these reforms are a step in the right direction, the overuse of incarceration shows that these alternatives could be more widely used.

Furthermore, recidivism rates among women in Russia are high, mainly due to the limited availability of rehabilitation programs and the struggles of reintegrating into society. About 40 percent of women released from Russian prisons reoffend within three years, which is worsened by stigma and a lack of economic opportunities (Pallot and Piacentini 2012). Many women face discrimination in the job market because of their criminal records, and inadequate rehabilitative programs make this situation worse, especially for impoverished women with substance abuse issues.

Demographics of Incarcerated Women

Many women in Russia commit crimes as a result of economic insecurity. Research indicates that 68 percent of women did not have permanent sources of income at the time they committed their crimes. Regarding education, 34 percent of women graduated from only nine classes of general education school, 34 percent completed secondary vocational education, 18 percent received a certificate of full general education, and only 14 percent obtained higher education. Research also shows that 56 percent of women commit crimes between the ages of 30–49 years, 27 percent between the ages of 18–29, and 15 percent over the age of 50 (Ukrainchik et al. 2022). Statistics indicate that about 80 percent of these women are mothers, most of whom committed crimes to support their families (Penal Reform International 2021).

About 40 percent of women are imprisoned for drug-related crimes, often tied to coping with poverty and trauma (Margo 2020). Russia's strict drug laws worsen the issue by imposing severe penalties based on the weight of the drug mixture rather than the pure substance. For example, possession of a "significant" quantity can result in up to three years of imprisonment, with penalties of up to fifteen years for larger amounts (Drug Policy Facts n.d.). These harsh penalties contribute to the incarceration of women for minor drug offenses, often without addressing their problems with addiction or economic disadvantage.

Furthermore, domestic violence is widespread in Russia, affecting women and contributing to the incarceration of many who have histories of abuse. At least 20 percent of women in Russia experience physical violence from a partner, including physical and psychological abuse (Human Rights Watch 2018). Incarcerated women frequently have histories of trauma as a result of this domestic violence, with some criminalized for acts of self-defense.

Crimes Leading to Incarceration

The most common crimes committed by women in Russia include property-related offenses such as theft, fraud, and embezzlement. Other crimes include running brothels, promoting prostitution, and distributing pornographic materials (Ukrainchik et al. 2022). However, it was not possible to determine an exact breakdown of the percentage incarcerated for these different crimes.

As noted, 40 percent of women are incarcerated for drug-related crimes, including the sale, storage, and transportation of drugs. Addiction plays a role in these offenses, with over 30 percent of women committing crimes under the influence of alcohol or drugs (Ukrainchik et al. 2022). High rates of recidivism increase this problem, with over 40 percent of women returning to criminal behavior after serving their sentences, often due to unaddressed addiction issues.

Violent crimes committed by women are less common but still notable. In many cases, these involve acts of self-defense or retaliation against domestic abusers. Approximately 12 percent of women incarcerated in Russia have committed murder, usually related to these circumstances (Ukrainchik et al. 2022). Furthermore, human trafficking remains an issue, with women being both victims and perpetrators, although the percentage of women incarcerated for human trafficking is not known. The country's law criminalizes human trafficking under Articles 127.1 and 127.2 of the Russian Criminal Code, which address trafficking in persons and the use of slave labor, respectively (U.S. Department of State 2024).

Contributing Laws and Policies

Laws and policies in Russia contribute to women's incarceration, mainly through harsh sentencing and limited legal protections. Strict drug laws are problematic for women, as minor possession and low-level trafficking can result in severe penalties. For example, the possession of over six grams of cannabis is considered a crime that carries strict penalties, including imprisonment. Moreover, the unauthorized manufacturing, distribution, or sale of cannabis, which is punishable under Article 228.1 of the Russian Criminal Code, can result in imprisonment of up to twenty years (Morris 2024).

In 2022, United States WNBA player Brittney Griner was arrested at Moscow's Sheremetyevo International Airport when authorities found cannabis oil in her luggage. Griner was charged with drug possession and smuggling. She pleaded guilty, claiming she had unintentionally put the cartridges in her bag and did not mean to break the law. Despite her plea, she was sentenced to nine years and fined 1 million rubles (about 13,000 USD). Her case got international attention, as many people thought it was politically motivated by tensions between the United States and Russia. In the end, Griner was released as part of a prisoner exchange between the countries (AlBaroudi et al. 2023).

Domestic violence laws are also a problem in Russia. Laws that decriminalize acts of domestic violence were amended in 2017, reclassifying first-time crimes resulting in minor injuries as violations punishable by fines or short-term imprisonment. This change lessened protections for victims and survivors (Amnesty International 2017) and has been criticized for supporting abusers and reducing reporting, as many women now fear protection from the system.

Furthermore, Russia uses incarceration as the main form of punishment, with few opportunities for alternatives to incarceration, particularly for women. Although there have been reforms to reduce the prison population, including other options for non-violent offenders, they have not been consistently applied. This often leaves women with few options for rehabilitation or chances to serve their sentence in the community (Penal Reform International 2013).

Conditions in Women's Prisons

Conditions in Russian women's prisons are known to be harsh, exhibiting overcrowding, poor sanitation, and inadequate access to necessities. Many facilities are located in remote areas, making it hard for people to maintain contact with their families. Additionally, overcrowded conditions limit people's privacy and space. For instance, women's prisons can have up to sixty people in a dormitory-style room, with bunk beds arranged in rows, and each woman is given a bed, chair, and small bedside table. Access to hygiene is limited, with only one shower per week (Penal Reform International 2013).

Forced labor is standard in Russian prisons, and despite working long hours, women are barely compensated (e.g., 196 rubles, about 5.50 USD per day). Nadezhda Tolokonnikova, a member of the group Pussy Riot, reported being forced to work seventeen hours per day in a Mordovian prison, only getting one day off every two months. She said the work conditions were torturous, and people were starving and sleep-deprived (Abarinov 2014).

Moreover, the work environments are unsafe and unhealthy, typically lacking ventilation or safety precautions. Worse, the work rarely provides skill development, leaving many women unprepared for reintegration into society upon release. Hard labor, rather than educational or vocational training, contributes to high recidivism rates and prevents these women from being successful when they return to the community (Riddle Russia 2021).

Furthermore, women in Russian prisons are often the victims of abuse by staff. A 2021 investigation exposed torture and sexual violence in prisons across Russia, with authorities often looking the other way or participating in the abuse. For example, videos from a prison hospital in Saratov showed incarcerated people being sexually assaulted, which led to the discharge of several prison officials (France 24 2021). However, most people who engage in this type of abuse never face consequences.

Health and Mental Health Issues

Incarcerated women in Russia face many health and mental health challenges, worsened by underfunded and poorly equipped prison healthcare systems. Chronic illnesses, such as tuberculosis and HIV, are rampant, and the prison environment, with its overcrowding and poor sanitation, only worsens the spread of infectious diseases. Research indicates a high occurrence of drug-resistant tuberculosis in Russian prisons, with rates up to sixteen times higher than average (Droznin et al. 2017). The treatment is intensive, and access to these medications is limited. Therefore, many incarcerated women do not receive proper treatment, contributing to higher mortality rates.

Additionally, about 20 percent of women in Russian prisons have an HIV diagnosis (Women in Prison Initiative n.d.), and they do not receive adequate care. For instance, Elena Paltseva was an HIV-positive woman in a Russian prison who was failed by the system. Between 2011 and 2016, she was denied diagnostic tests, including CD4 and viral load analyses, and she experienced interruptions in her antiretroviral therapy. Her treatment lacked proper medical justification, monitoring, and compliance with national healthcare standards, leaving her without adequate care for nearly five years. In 2018, the European Court of Human Rights (ECHR) ruled in her favor, awarding her €15,000 (about 16,500 USD). This case reflects larger issues in Russian prisons, where shortages of infectious disease specialists, inadequate diagnostics, and reliance on low-cost medications with severe side effects are common (Women in Prison Initiative n.d.).

Incarcerated women in Russia also face mental health challenges, often entering the system with histories of trauma, including domestic violence and addiction. Research has found that almost three-quarters of these women suffer from mental health issues, with depression, anxiety, and post-traumatic stress disorder (PTSD) being prevalent (Bardenshteyn and Shaklein 2017). Despite the high incidence of mental health disorders, services within Russian women's prisons are nearly non-existent. The lack of adequate mental healthcare means that these conditions often go undiagnosed and untreated, worsening their psychological distress (Penal Reform International 2013).

Impact on Families and Children

The incarceration of women in Russia affects their families, especially their children. Currently, 564 babies and toddlers live in thirteen children's homes within women's penal colonies, staying with their mothers until the age of three. In rare cases, extensions are granted if the mother has less than one year left on her sentence. However, mothers are often separated from their children immediately after birth. While some experimental programs, such as those in Nizhny Novgorod, allow mothers to live with their children, these are exceptions. Even within the designated children's homes, mother–child interactions are highly regulated, with mothers required to wear prison uniforms and adhere to strict visitation schedules (Riddle Russia 2021).

While children under three years old can live in designated correctional units, these facilities are often underfunded and not equipped to meet children's developmental needs. Additionally, programs allowing children to stay with their mothers are limited, increasing the difficulties these families face. Moreover, after the children have reached the age limit, they are placed with relatives or in state care institutions, leading to emotional and psychological challenges (Penal Reform International 2013).

Furthermore, for women with children under fourteen years old, Russian law allows for the deferral of prison sentences until the child reaches this age. The idea behind this law is to preserve the family unit during the child's formative years. However, this provision is applied inconsistently. For instance, Anna Shavenkova, who was sentenced to 2.5 years for vehicular manslaughter, had her sentence deferred until 2024, when her child would turn fourteen. This case shows how the law is unequally enforced because Shavenkova's mother was a high-ranking regional official, and most women are not granted the privilege of a deferred sentence (The Moscow Times 2011).

Policy Reforms and Recommendations

Several reforms would help address the issues women face within Russia's prison system. First, there is a need for more alternatives to incarceration. These alternatives must be applied uniformly, assuring they are accessible to marginalized women, including those without housing. This approach would not only reduce incarceration rates, but also allow more women who have committed non-violent offenses to be sentenced in the community (Pallot and Pallot and Piacentini 2012).

Next, it is necessary to focus on the shortage of healthcare resources by increasing the number of infectious disease specialists and providing diagnostic tools and treatments, especially for tuberculosis and HIV. Cases like Elena Paltseva's, where healthcare failures led to someone's unnecessary suffering, indicate the need for reforms that comply with healthcare standards. There is also a need for improved mental health services for incarcerated women, many of whom suffer from trauma and addiction (Droznin et al. 2017).

Moreover, it is also essential to improve programs for incarcerated mothers and their children. One suggestion is to have more experimental programs, such as those in Nizhny Novgorod, to allow mothers to live with their children, allowing for maternal bonding. Additionally, it is necessary to address the inconsistencies in deferred sentencing for mothers by creating guidelines that assure the law benefits all eligible women, not just those with political connections (The Moscow Times 2011).

Lastly, Russian prisons must better promote education, vocational training, and addiction programs for women to confront the causes of their criminal behavior. Replacing forced labor with programs that focus on developing marketable skills will better prepare incarcerated women for reintegration into society and improve their employment opportunities after release (Riddle Russia 2021).

Norway

Historical Context

The history of incarcerated women in Norway signifies its shift from punitive practices to a rehabilitative and humane justice system. In the early 1800s, Norway reflected Europe's harsh penal practices. Women often faced severe penalties like men, including lengthy prison terms and forced labor. However, by the late nineteenth and early twentieth centuries, social reform movements, including suffrage efforts, advocated for improved prison conditions and enhancements to women's rights (Pratt and Eriksson 2013).

In the 1990s, Norway adopted a rehabilitative social welfare model, displaying Scandinavian progressive values (Pratt and Eriksson 2013). Because women often enter the criminal justice system due to non-violent crimes related to economic hardship, addiction, or domestic violence, policymakers concentrated on ways to address these causes. Programs addressed trauma, addiction, and vocational training for reintegration (Bucerius and Sandberg 2022). Norway also introduced alternatives like community service and electronic monitoring to reduce imprisonment (Pratt and Eriksson 2013). These reforms addressed the factors contributing to women's criminal behavior and also supported the goal of reducing recidivism and promoting reintegration.

Norway's contemporary penal philosophy emphasizes dignity and respect. Women's prisons are designed to be less punitive and more rehabilitative, providing environments similar to communities rather than prisons. For instance, Halden Prison has private rooms with bathrooms, shared kitchens, and outdoor areas, promoting independence and a sense of normalcy for the people living there (Pratt and Eriksson 2013). Programs focus on giving women the tools they need for reintegration, including vocational training and education. They also recognize the high rates of victimization among incarcerated women, so they concentrate on substance abuse and mental health challenges (Bucerius and Sandberg 2022).

Furthermore, the current system still frequently uses alternatives to incarceration for people who have committed non-violent crimes (Øster and Rokkan 2008). Norway's recidivism rate is around 20 percent, one of the lowest in the world (First Step Alliance 2022), highlighting the effectiveness of its practices. By prioritizing rehabilitation, Norway's ideas are a model for balancing justice with reintegration, showing how a system built on respect can be effective for incarcerated individuals and, ultimately, societies.

Halden Prison's "Normality" Principle

Halden Prison is often called the world's most humane prison, reflecting Norway's philosophy of "normality." Incarcerated people live in private rooms with bathrooms, shared kitchens, and landscaped outdoor areas. The design is similar to life outside prison, with the goal of reducing the "shock" of release and encouraging reintegration. Staff are trained to interact as mentors instead of enforcers, emphasizing respect and responsibility. This approach highlights Norway's belief that taking away freedom (not dignity) is the punishment.

Female Incarceration Rates and Trends

Female incarceration rates in Norway are among the lowest in the world, indicating the country's commitment to rehabilitation and alternative sentencing. Women comprise about 5 percent of Norway's 3,000-person prison population, or about 160 people (World Prison Brief 2024). This low rate is credited to the country's emphasis on tackling the causes of criminal behavior rather than focusing only on punishment. Women are housed in fourteen facilities across the country, five of which are exclusively for women (APT 2024).

Most women incarcerated in Norway are serving time for non-violent crimes, including drug-related offenses, fraud, and theft (Øster and Rokkan 2008). Norway's lenient drug policy offers treatment over punishment, keeping female incarceration rates low (Bucerius and Sandberg 2022). Additionally, alternative sentencing also contributes to low incarceration rates. People convicted of non-violent crimes often receive community service, like working with local organizations or participating in cleanup initiatives. This option allows them to be held accountable for their actions without imprisonment. Additionally, probation and restorative justice, including victim-offender mediation, also reduce the need for incarceration by promoting rehabilitation and repairing harm (Øster and Rokkan 2008).

Norway's correctional system also stresses the importance of maintaining family ties and minimizing the trauma of separation for incarcerated mothers. The Norwegian Correctional Service has established ways to help women during incarceration, including considerations for those with dependent children (UNODC 2022). For instance, Norway's use of electronic monitoring as an alternative to incarceration allows certain people to serve their sentences at home. This approach enables them to maintain employment and family ties, supporting the rehabilitative philosophy (Øster and Rokkan 2008).

Demographics of Incarcerated Women

The demographics of incarcerated women in Norway indicate that many of them come from disadvantaged backgrounds, often struggling with poverty, mental health issues, and substance abuse. Research shows that 58 percent of these women come from low-income households (Svendsen et al. 2023). Moreover, 75 percent of them have psychiatric disorders, with substance use disorders affecting 56 percent of them and dual diagnoses (i.e., co-occurring substance use and other psychiatric disorders) present in 38 percent of this population (Svendsen et al. 2023). These findings highlight the combined vulnerabilities that often lead women into the criminal justice system.

The majority of incarcerated women are Norwegian citizens; however, 26 percent of the overall prison population is foreign-born (World Prison Brief 2024). Many of these foreign-born women are involved in trafficking or immigration-related offenses, reflecting global patterns of marginalization and exploitation. Human trafficking, a significant issue in Norway, disproportionately affects foreign-born women, who are often abused in labor and sex industries (U.S. Department of State 2023). Trafficking victims are often coerced into criminal activities like drug couriering. Despite their victimization, these women frequently find themselves incarcerated for crimes they engaged in due to coercion or desperation.

In terms of age, incarcerated women in Norway are predominantly middle-aged, with only 16 percent under thirty, 61 percent between thirty and forty-nine, and 23 percent over fifty (Statistics Norway 2023a). Family dynamics are also a crucial part of the demographics, as approximately 44 percent of incarcerated women are mothers to underage children (Svendsen et al. 2023). This stresses the importance of family-oriented policies within Norway's prison system, such as maintaining family ties through extended visits and family-friendly accommodations (Barrow Cadbury Trust 2014).

Crimes Leading to Incarceration

Crimes leading to the imprisonment of women in Norway are primarily non-violent (52 percent) (Statistics Norway 2023b). Common offenses for which women are incarcerated include drug-related crimes (26 percent), as well as property crimes and offenses for profit (16 percent) (Statistics Norway 2023b). Concerning drug-related crimes, many of these women struggle with addiction, and their criminal behavior is often linked to substance abuse. Norway's approach to drug offenses, which focuses more on rehabilitation, has contributed to lower incarceration rates, but women involved in drug trafficking, especially foreign nationals, still face imprisonment. Furthermore, economic crimes such as theft, fraud, and embezzlement are often due to financial hardship, with many women committing these crimes to support their families.

However, 48 percent of women are incarcerated for violent crimes, typically assault or domestic violence (Statistics Norway 2023b). The relatively high percentage of women incarcerated for violent crimes in Norway shows an interaction between violence and domestic abuse. Many of these women are involved in domestic violence cases, with acts often committed in response to prolonged abuse. While the justice system allows for self-defense claims, including in cases involving battered woman syndrome, the success of these defenses depends on the specific circumstances, including the proportionality between the violence used in self-defense and the risk of being abused. In many cases, women who have acted in self-defense against extended abuse may not meet the legal criteria for justified self-defense, resulting in their incarceration despite the context of their actions (Baker McKenzie 2024c).

Furthermore, Norway's broad legal definition of violent crimes also contributes to the higher proportion of women classified as violent offenders. This category includes a wide range of acts, from minor altercations to severe assaults, which may escalate to incarceration due to repeat offenses or violations of restraining orders (Baker McKenzie 2021). However, Norway's rehabilitative prison system tries to address underlying factors through interventions. Facilities like Bredtveit Prison, which houses most women incarcerated for violent offenses, offer trauma-informed care, mental health support, and counseling programs focusing on anger management and the impacts of abuse (Norwegian Parliamentary Ombudsman 2016).

Contributing Laws and Policies

Norway's laws and policies regarding incarceration reflect a progressive approach that minimizes imprisonment, particularly for women. Several laws and initiatives emphasize rehabilitation, alternative sentencing, and addressing the causes of criminal behavior. For instance, Norway's approach to drug-related offenses prioritizes treatment, especially for non-violent crimes like drug possession or small-scale trafficking. Initiatives like the Drug Court Program, known as **Narkotikaprogram med domstolskontroll** (**ND**), allow people to participate in treatment in the community instead of imprisonment. ND was established first in Oslo and Bergen in 2006 and was implemented nationwide in 2016. It provides participants with supervision, drug testing, and addiction treatment services, aiming to treat the causes of crime so that people do not reoffend (Justice Speakers International 2016).

Norway also uses alternative sentencing options for non-violent offenders, which benefits women involved in minor crimes such as theft or fraud. Community service, probation, and restorative justice initiatives are often used in place of prison. These community sentences are used to help people keep their jobs and connections to their families, which helps reduce rates of recidivism (Statistics Norway 2013). The National Mediation Service runs restorative justice programs, which repair harm and reintegrate people into their communities. Approximately 8,000 to 9,000 cases are referred to mediation annually, often replacing traditional sentences (Council of Europe Probation 2018).

Lastly, while Norway's judicial system considers the context of domestic abuse in cases where women act in self-defense against abusive partners, women may still face legal consequences. Domestic violence is criminalized under Sections 282 and 283 of the Norwegian Penal Code, and penalties include restraining orders or imprisonment for up to six years (Baker McKenzie 2024b). While self-defense is a recognized defense, its success depends on the proportionality of the response to the threat of abuse, and it often fails as a defense. However, to help with cases of domestic violence, policies like the Shelter Act of 2010 mandate municipalities to provide crisis centers to ensure that victims of domestic violence receive necessary support and protection (Bergman et al. 2022).

Conditions in Women's Prisons

Prisons in Norway are often small, and there is a goal of creating a normalized environment similar to the outside world. They typically have about seventy cells, and the smallest facilities house as few as thirteen people, allowing for a stronger sense of community. Each person usually has a private room and bathroom, rather than traditional prison cells. This design aims to respect people's dignity and promote responsibility (Johnsen et al. 2018).

Furthermore, Norway has been known to offer adequate medical services to incarcerated women. Norwegian prisons provide mental healthcare services equivalent to those available to the general population, and incarcerated people receive individualized assessments to ensure that services fit their needs. Yet, challenges persist in adequately supporting people with mental health problems, who are a particularly vulnerable group (Sivilombudet 2017).

Additionally, incarcerated women have access to different educational programs, including literacy courses and other learning opportunities similar to what is available to the general population. Vocational training in fields like carpentry, welding, and culinary arts is also provided, equipping people with skills to increase their chances of employment upon release (Esplaguera 2024). These initiatives address gaps in their prior learning experiences. Many incarcerated people have had inadequate schooling compared to the general population, stressing the importance of education and training within the prison system. By offering these opportunities, Norway aims to empower people to secure meaningful employment post-incarceration, facilitating successful reintegration (Langelid et al. 2003).

However, while Norway takes a progressive approach, there is still progress to be made. For instance, compared to their male counterparts, incarcerated women have less access to outdoor spaces, physical activities, and employment training opportunities. Additionally, many women's prisons are located in older buildings, which can impact the quality of life for these women (Sivilombudet 2017).

Health and Mental Health Issues

Norway's correctional system provides comprehensive healthcare to incarcerated women, ensuring services equivalent to those available to the general population. This includes regular medical check-ups, screenings, vaccinations, specialist services, and treatment for acute and chronic conditions. The "import model" used in Norwegian prisons assures that healthcare services are managed by municipal authorities, maintaining independence from the Correctional Service and supporting the medical personnel's autonomy (Sivilombudet 2024).

Pregnant women incarcerated in Norway receive adequate prenatal and postnatal care. Furthermore, the Norwegian Health and Care Services Act allows for the involuntary admission of pregnant women who have substance abuse issues into special facilities. For example, Borgestadklinikken is a facility specialized in treating pregnant women with drug and alcohol problems, ensuring the health of mothers and children. These efforts focus on the health of incarcerated mothers and support the well-being of their babies. However, critics argue that this approach is coercive and raises ethical concerns about the autonomy of women (Crewe 2020).

Mental healthcare, including counseling and therapy, is a vital component of Norway's rehabilitative philosophy, helping women address the emotional and psychological challenges of imprisonment. Despite these services, a recent study has highlighted gaps in mental healthcare access, indicating barriers that prevent incarcerated people from seeking and receiving mental health support (Psychreg 2024). They often face delays in receiving mental healthcare due to administrative inefficiencies and a shortage of specialists, along with inconsistencies in service delivery when integrating municipal health services into the prison system. Moreover, specialized care, like treatment for dual diagnoses, is limited in smaller or older facilities (Psychreg 2024).

Lastly, addiction treatment programs are essential to Norway's approach, as substance dependency impacts many women who commit crimes. The Norwegian Correctional Services have implemented cognitive behavioral drug treatment programs and drug treatment units in prisons to support people's rehabilitation efforts (Bukten et al. 2015). These programs support opiate agonist treatments (e.g., methadone, buprenorphine), facilitate routine screening for substance issues, and aim to sustain treatment continuity post-release. These are part of a strategy to ensure that people are drug-free or can control their substance use when reintegrating into society (Bukten et al. 2020).

Impact on Families and Children

The incarceration of women in Norway impacts them and their families. Unlike many other countries, Norway does not allow infants or young children to live with their mothers in prison. Instead, it focuses on community-based solutions or foster care to prioritize the child's welfare outside prison (Crewe 2020). Children of incarcerated mothers are usually cared for by fathers, relatives, or foster families. Research shows that while some children adjust, many experience stress, with 29 percent having severe distress (JURK 2007). Additionally, prison visits, although intended to maintain bonds, often leave children feeling upset, and logistical and emotional barriers exacerbate the strain. Dissatisfaction with visiting arrangements, particularly at facilities like Bredtveit Prison, worsens the challenges families face.

Incarcerated women have little opportunities for direct contact with their children, which is worsened by challenges related to mental health (JURK 2007). The emotional toll of separation is serious, and the lack of support services to maintain family bonds during incarceration often leaves mothers and children struggling to reconnect. These difficulties suggest that interventions should support the child's welfare and also assist the mother's role in their lives during and after imprisonment.

Maternal incarceration also imposes financial strain on families. Many incarcerated women in Norway come from disadvantaged backgrounds, and their imprisonment worsens economic problems like affording childcare or household expenses. Travel costs for prison visits add to these difficulties, especially for families living far from facilities. A JURK (2007) survey found that only 12 percent of incarcerated women received visits from their children, with financial issues cited as a major reason for not visiting. While Norwegian sentencing laws encourage alternatives to incarceration for mothers with young children, these measures are inconsistently applied, stressing a need for better consistency.

Policy Reforms and Recommendations

Norway emphasizes rehabilitation and family welfare, but there are still challenges in addressing the needs of incarcerated women. Several reforms could help with the negative impacts of their incarceration while aligning with Norway's commitment to humane treatment. First, it is necessary to expand and consistently apply the use of alternatives to incarceration, especially for mothers with young children (Øster and Rokkan 2008). Increased access to these alternatives would reduce unnecessary family separations, allowing mothers to remain caregivers while serving their sentences in the community.

Improving support for maintaining family bonds is another area for reform. Separation from their mothers causes severe distress for 29 percent of children of incarcerated women, and inadequate visiting amenities make this situation worse (JURK 2007). Facilities like Bredtveit Prison often lack family-friendly arrangements, limiting opportunities for meaningful interactions. Expanding child-friendly spaces and providing better accommodations for families would promote deeper relationships.

Maternal incarceration also imposes financial strain on families, especially those already struggling with economic problems. The loss of maternal income and the high costs of travel for prison visits are barriers to maintaining family connections (JURK 2007). Financial support for travel, prison facilities closer to family homes, and childcare assistance could lessen these burdens and help families maintain stability during incarceration.

Finally, it is necessary to increase access to mental health services. Three-quarters of incarcerated women in Norway have psychiatric disorders (Svendsen et al. 2023), so it is crucial to strengthen these services. Increasing access to psychologists and prioritizing care for dual diagnoses would help address the reasons for criminal behavior, supporting rehabilitation. These reforms would improve the experiences of incarcerated women and their families, which aligns with Norway's approach to justice.

Italy

Historical Context

The history of women's incarceration in Italy has been influenced by the social and political forces that have shaped the country's justice system. In the early 1900s, the prison system was punitive, similar to other European nations. It was overcrowded and treated men and women alike. Women faced harsh, patriarchal conditions, with pregnant inmates often giving birth under inhumane circumstances with minimal medical care (Gibson 2009).

During the fascist era (1920s–40s), Italy's prisons became tools of political repression, targeting those who opposed Benito Mussolini's regime. Women associated with anti-fascism, like Ada Gobetti, a prominent educator, writer, and activist, faced torture, imprisonment, or exile for their political dissent (Thomson 2014). Political prisons, including the Santo Stefano penitentiary, housed women with men in deplorable conditions (Stano Stefano 2024). Mussolini's policies aimed to increase birth rates and reinforce gender roles, offering financial motivations to women with large families and discouraging them from working. Women who fought these expectations with activism were often imprisoned, a measure enforced by the Special Tribunal for the Defense of the State to maintain the regime's authoritarian and patriarchal ideology (Barocci 2022).

After the Second World War, Italy's approach to incarceration changed and was influenced by the feminist movements of the 1960s and 1970s. These movements brought awareness to problems like inadequate healthcare, limited accommodations for mothers, and a lack of vocational programs for women. They led to reforms encouraging alternatives to incarceration for non-violent offenders and addressing the needs of incarcerated mothers (Barocci 2022). By the 1980s, Italy introduced community-based sanctions for some incarcerated women, allowing them to serve sentences outside of prisons (Women's Prison Association 2009). Although there have been reforms, modern prisons still face issues like overcrowding, with some facilities being 180 percent above capacity

(Statista 2024). While Italy has moved from a punitive to a more rehabilitative model, reforms are still required to address the needs of incarcerated women.

Female Incarceration Rates and Trends

According to the Italian Ministry of Justice, the total prison population in Italy in 2023 was 60,637, with 2,615 being women (DM 2024), or about 4.3 percent of the total, reflecting historical trends in female incarceration. Italy has forty-nine prisons that house women, only six of which are entirely for women (Italian Penitentiary Administration 2024). The largest women's prison is Rebibbia, located in Rome. This facility houses 334 women and is known for overcrowding, with a capacity of 275 (Antigone Onlus Association 2023).

Over the past two decades, Italy has introduced reforms to reduce imprisonment rates by promoting alternatives to incarceration for people convicted of non-violent crimes. For instance, Law 67 of 2014 established alternatives to incarceration, allowing for probation for crimes with sentences of up to four years and reclassifying certain offenses as administrative violations rather than crimes. These reforms aimed to reduce overcrowding, promote rehabilitative justice, and better match penalties with the severity of offenses (Italy: Overhaul of Criminal Penalties 2015).

However, foreign nationals in Italy face challenges in receiving alternative sentencing options. Criteria like stable housing, employment, and community ties often exclude them. Moreover, language barriers and limited access to legal representation further prevent them from these options (The Issue n.d.). Among women in Italian prisons, foreign-born individuals, particularly from Eastern Europe and Africa, represent a growing demographic. As of 2024, foreign nationals accounted for about 28 percent of incarcerated women (Italian Penitentiary Administration 2024). These trends suggest that, despite Italy's low female incarceration rate, social disparities influence who is incarcerated.

Demographics of Incarcerated Women

The demographics of incarcerated women in Italy indicate social inequalities, with many coming from economically marginalized backgrounds. Most of these women are imprisoned for non-violent crimes, with drug-related offenses accounting for about one-third of their convictions (Montanari 2020). Approximately 30 percent of these women are between the ages of thirty-four and forty-four, and their crimes, like theft, extortion, and drug trafficking, signify their economic problems (Maglie et al. 2021).

As noted, many incarcerated women in Italy are foreign-born, facing unique challenges within the country's justice system. Many of these women are coerced or economically forced into crime, such as drug trafficking. Human trafficking victims, often from Africa or Eastern Europe, are coerced into illegal activities such as sex work or forced labor, frequently leading to their incarceration (Criminality in Italy 2023). The connection between victimization and criminalization is clear, as these women often find themselves in cycles of abuse and punishment with no support. Moreover, many incarcerated women in Italy have histories of trauma, including domestic violence and sexual abuse, which play a role in their paths to crime (Antigone 2023).

To illustrate this cycle, a case from 2022 highlighted the exploitation of foreign-born women in Italy. Two Chinese nationals, Yang Yun Xia (known as Sofía) and Li Yan Rong (known as Lia), were among three women found murdered in apartments linked to illegal activities. They were the victims of human trafficking and coerced into sex work by Chinese criminal organizations in Italy. The murders exposed the unsafe conditions trafficked women experience in Italy and around the world. While these women were not imprisoned, this case emphasizes the need for measures to combat trafficking and protect victims who often end up in the system (Sanchez 2022).

Worsening these challenges, many incarcerated women in Italy are mothers, which adds further stress to their imprisonment. Nearly two-thirds are mothers (Antigone Onlus Association 2023), and as of 2024, twenty-three women were living in Italian prisons with their children (Italian Penitentiary Administration 2024). Despite this, data on incarcerated women in Italy remains limited, making it difficult to understand the scope of their challenges and needs. Moreover, the lack of gender-responsive services exacerbates their difficulties, as addressing trauma is necessary for successful reintegration (Giacomi 2017).

Crimes Leading to Incarceration

In Italy, a large portion of incarcerated women are imprisoned for non-violent offenses, with drug-related crimes accounting for 33 percent and property crimes accounting for 29 percent (Antigone Onlus Association 2023). These offenses are often driven by economic hardship, particularly among single mothers. Make Mothers Matter (2022) stresses the economic insecurity faced by single mothers across Europe, including Italy, which can drive them to commit non-violent crimes to survive.

Furthermore, the COVID-19 pandemic worsened these economic problems for single mothers in Italy. Guetto and colleagues (2021) found that single parents experienced increased stress and financial instability during and after the pandemic, making them more susceptible to committing crimes out of economic desperation.

Women's involvement in violent crimes in Italy is rare, but sometimes incidents happen due to prolonged domestic violence. Those who commit violent acts against their abusers face challenges in the system, which does not consistently account for domestic abuse. Italian self-defense laws require an immediate threat and proportional response, which can disadvantage women acting in response to cumulative abuse (Baker McKenzie n.d.). This often fails to address the realities of abuse, leading to convictions that do not consider their history of victimization.

An example is the case of Milena Quaglini, who suffered violence in her childhood at the hands of her father, as well as abuses in her relationships as an adult. In 1988, after enduring years of abuse in her marriage, she killed her husband in self-defense but was sentenced to fourteen years in prison. Later, she killed two other men, a loan shark who attempted to coerce her into sex and a man who raped her while she was under house arrest. Her crimes were related to her history of victimization and a lack of support. Unfortunately, she ended her life in prison in 2001. This story highlights the importance of addressing the impacts of abuse and trauma to prevent outcomes like Quaglini's (Balsamo 2023).

Contributing Laws and Policies

Similar to many countries, drug laws have impacted the incarceration of women in Italy. The Jervolino-Vassalli Act of 1990 introduced strict drug control policies, with severe penalties for possession and trafficking, including prison sentences of seven to twenty years. Then, in 1993, a referendum decriminalized personal drug use. However, the 2006 Fini-Giovanardi law reclassified cannabis as a "hard drug," increasing penalties until it was overturned in 2014, leading to reduced sentences and reclassification of cannabis as a Schedule II drug. Despite these reforms, Italy still needs to balance punitive and rehabilitative approaches because foreign nationals and coerced women continue to be disproportionately impacted by these laws (Long and Perduca 2019).

In addition to drug laws, while Italy has alternatives to incarceration, their application varies across regions and cases due to judicial discretion and resource availability. Women often face barriers to accessing these alternatives because eligibility depends on having established housing, employment, and social support. For instance, house arrest could help more mothers maintain family ties with their children, but it is underused because of strict requirements and a lack of oversight to support greater access (Marietti 2015).

Furthermore, domestic violence is a widespread issue in Italy, affecting approximately one in three women (Generis Legal Intelligence 2024). Although Italian law permits self-defense, its application requires proof of an immediate threat and a proportionate response. Women who act in self-defense against abusive partners often face criminalization, and cultural attitudes and inconsistent judicial practices do not adequately address these concerns (Baker McKenzie n.d.). Legal developments, like the introduction of the **Code Red Law** in 2019, have strengthened penalties for gender-based violence and domestic abuse by allowing victims to call emergency services and activate immediate protective responses, including restraining orders and police intervention (Baker McKenzie 2024a). However, there remains a need for reforms, including consistent enforcement of laws, judicial training on the subtleties of domestic abuse, and efforts to change norms preserving victim-blaming.

The Code Red Law

Italy's *Codice Rosso* ("Code Red") law was enacted in 2019. It strengthens protections against domestic violence and gender-based abuse by allowing victims to report abuse and receive immediate responses from police and prosecutors, including protective orders. While it is a step forward, critics note inconsistent enforcement or barriers that still discourage women from reporting. This law represents Italy's continued struggle to address gender violence. For example, the 2023 murder of university student Giulia Cecchettin, who had previously sought help against her ex-boyfriend, sparked national outrage and renewed calls for stronger implementation of this law.

Conditions in Women's Prisons

Conditions in women's prisons in Italy are a problem, with overcrowding and a lack of programming being some of the main concerns. Italy's prison system operates at over 120 percent of its capacity, which aggravates the stresses of incarceration. This problem is even worse in mixed-gender facilities, where women are often confined to separate units that are smaller and less equipped with amenities than men's units (Antigone 2023).

Incarcerated women in Italy also have limited access to hygiene products and other necessities. They are often expected to clean their own cells, but there is a lack of cleaning tools, leading to poor sanitation. Additionally, personal hygiene items, like toilet paper or menstrual supplies, are often lacking. Even though laws mandate showers in every cell, many facilities have not been updated to comply with this legislation, so people often only get two showers per week (What are Prisons like in Italy 2022). The European Union Agency for Fundamental Rights notes that common showers are often situated in degraded buildings, and there is a need to furnish all sleeping quarters with showers to ensure hygienic conditions (Italy—Sanitary Conditions 2024).

Furthermore, rehabilitation and education programs for incarcerated women in Italy remain lacking, preventing their successful reintegration into society. Vocational training is often limited to sewing or cooking instead of offering modern employment opportunities, leaving many women unprepared to work upon release (ViP n.d.). While prison law mandates equal access to cultural and professional training, the reality is different, especially in mixed-gender facilities, where women's smaller numbers limit their access. For example, only 7 percent of women participated in literacy courses, and just 2.5 percent attended secondary school programs (Italian Penitentiary Administration 2024). These challenges indicate inequalities in educational and vocational opportunities, maintaining a need for better access to programming for these women.

Health and Mental Health Issues

Incarcerated women in Italy face health and mental health challenges, often entering prison with chronic diseases and untreated mental illnesses. Psychiatric disorders are the most common health issues in the prison population, affecting

41 percent of people (Voller et al. 2016). These conditions, which include depression, anxiety, and psychotic disorders, are frequently linked to histories of trauma and abuse and are worsened by incarceration. Women experience higher rates of psychiatric diagnoses than men and are more likely to use psychotropic medications, with 64 percent using them (Antigone Onlus Association 2023). Unfortunately, the lack of mental health resources makes it difficult for these women to manage their conditions.

Physical health issues are also widespread among incarcerated women in Italy. They commonly suffer from physical health issues, including digestive system diseases (15 percent), infectious diseases (12 percent), and cardiovascular diseases (11 percent) (Voller et al. 2016). Incarcerated women are also more likely than men to suffer from asthma. Other factors contributing to poor health include high smoking rates (71 percent), sedentary lifestyles, and stress. Despite these problems, the healthcare system in Italian prisons focuses on emergency care, leaving preventive care unaddressed, and failing to meet the needs of incarcerated women (Zoia 2005).

Gynecological and obstetric care in Italian prisons is also deficient. Gynecological services are unavailable in one-third of prisons, and obstetrics services are provided in less than one-third of facilities (Antigone Onlus Association 2023). This lack of access leaves many reproductive health issues untreated. Moreover, transferring prison healthcare management to the National Health Service is intended to improve care, but there are still problems (Vanzan 2023). Underfunding for health services continues to prevent care, stressing the need for reforms that address the physical and mental health needs of women imprisoned in Italy.

Impact on Families and Children

The incarceration of women in Italy impacts their families, especially their children. Italian law permits mothers to live with their children under three, but facilities are under-resourced (Ferrara et al. 2007). For instance, in Lecce Prison, a mother and her two-year-old daughter were housed in a separate area, but the lack of a proper nursery section meant only a makeshift space was available for the child (Antigone Onlus Association 2023).

Additionally, separation from their mothers often leads to emotional and psychological trauma for children. The absence of a primary caregiver disrupts family stability, leaving children in the care of extended family or state institutions. This separation results in symptoms such as anxiety, depression, and behavioral problems, with children vulnerable to feelings of abandonment. These challenges affect their emotional and social development (Robertson 2007). Even for children allowed to remain with their mothers in facilities like Rebibbia Women's Prison in Rome, which provides nurseries to foster bonds during early years, the confined environment often contributes to issues like sleep disorders and apathy for them (Lai et al. 2022).

Visitation conditions also present barriers to maintaining parent–child relationships. Initiatives like Bambinisenzasbarre's (translated "Children Without Borders") "Yellow Spaces" provide child-friendly areas to reduce the emotional impact of the prison environment, offering support and play areas to help children feel more comfortable during visits (Children of Prisoners Europe n.d.). However, these programs are not available in all prisons, many of which lack the resources to support this type of contact (Pompei 2019).

Policy Reforms and Recommendations

There are several policy reforms and recommendations to improve the experiences of women incarcerated in Italy. First, according to the Antigone Onlus Association (2023), a specialized office focused on women's detention, led by experts in gender policies, should be created to address the needs of incarcerated women. This office could oversee reforms, such as ensuring access to better healthcare and improving mother–child programs. Establishing this centralized office would ensure that policies are adapted to the challenges faced by women and implemented consistently across facilities.

Italian prisons must also prioritize healthcare reforms to address women's health needs. This includes offering cancer prevention and screening services, such as Pap tests and breast exams, at the same standard as those available to women in the community. Additionally, screening for experiences of sexual violence or abuse should be conducted at the time of admission, with follow-up care and psychological support provided during and after incarceration. Properly trained staff specialized in gender-based violence should be employed so that women receive trauma-informed care (Vanzan 2023).

Additionally, expanding the use of alternatives to incarceration would help reduce overcrowding and minimize the disruption to families. These alternatives are especially important for non-violent offenders and mothers with young children, allowing them to maintain caregiving roles and access to community resources. Programs like Italy's "custodia attenuata" (low-security custody) model could be enhanced to create more rehabilitative and supportive environments that align with community life (Italy: Overhaul of Criminal Penalties 2015).

Lastly, there needs to be better access to education, vocational training, and employment opportunities for incarcerated women in Italy. These programs should focus on modern skills that will help women become employable after they leave prison rather than offering courses in sewing or cooking. These suggestions will help support rehabilitation, reduce recidivism, and improve women's lives after incarceration (Italian Penitentiary Administration 2024).

Conclusion

This chapter has examined the experiences of incarcerated women in Russia, Norway, and Italy, including the challenges they face and the factors influencing their imprisonment. In Russia, women experience overcrowding, inadequate healthcare, and forced labor. There are high incarceration rates, which are driven by strict drug laws and economic instability. Norway provides a contrast, emphasizing rehabilitation and humane treatment. This country has low incarceration rates and focuses on alternatives to incarceration. Italy offers a middle ground between Russia and Norway. Its system has shown some progress with alternatives to incarceration but still exhibits overcrowding, gender disparities, and limited access to services and programming for women.

Overall, Russia's punitive model worsens challenges for incarcerated women, perpetuating cycles of poverty, recidivism, and trauma. Norway demonstrates the value of a rehabilitative and community-oriented justice system, showing how dignity and support can reduce recidivism and promote reintegration. Italy illustrates the conflict between punitive practices and modern reforms, with initiatives to reduce incarceration rates for non-violent crimes hindered by inconsistent application and resource limitations. Across all three countries, socioeconomic vulnerability, victimization, and a lack of gender-responsive policies contribute to women's incarceration.

Incarcerated women face challenges related to economic instability, gender-based violence, and limited access to healthcare and programming. Reforms, like enhanced alternatives to incarceration, better access to healthcare and mental health services, and gender-responsive rehabilitation programs, will improve the experiences of these women. Understanding the different experiences of women imprisoned in these countries can help policymakers improve systems to create safer, more equitable communities.

References

Abarinov, Vladimir. 2014. "Russia's Prison Labor: A Struggle to Survive." *Radio Free Europe/Radio Liberty*. August 13, 2014. https://www.rferl.org/a/russia-prison-labor/26525003.html.

AlBaroudi, Wajih, Isabel Gonzalez, and Shanna McCarriston. 2023. "Brittney Griner Situation Explained: WNBA All-Star Released from Russian Custody After Prisoner Swap." CBS Sports. https://www.cbssports.com/wnba/news/brittney-griner-situation-explained-wnba-all-star-released-from-russian-custody-after-prisoner-swap/.

Amnesty International. "Russia: Domestic Violence Law Puts Women at Greater Risk." February 7, 2017. https://www.amnesty.org/en/latest/news/2017/02/russia-domestic-violence-law-puts-women-at-greater-risk-2/.

Antigone. 2023. *Rapporto di Antigone sulle condizioni di detenzione*. https://www.antigone.it.

Antigone Onlus Association. 2023. *By the Side of Antigone: First Report on Detained Women in Italy, Press Kit*. Rome. https://www.antigone.it.

Applebaum, Anne. 2003. *Gulag: A History*. New York: Anchor Books.

Association for the Prevention of Torture (APT). 2024. Norway Country Report. https://www.apt.ch/sites/default/files/2024-12/norway_country_report.pdf.

Balsamo, Massimo. 2023. "Milena Quaglini, La Storia Della Vedova Nera Del Pavese." IlGiornale.it. June 2023. https://www.ilgiornale.it/news/cronaca-nera/milena-quaglini-storia-vedova-nera-pavese-2159083.html.

Bardenshteyn, Leonid, and Konstantin N. Shaklein. 2017. "The Prevalence of Mental Disorders Among Women Serving a Sentence in Penal Colony." *Russian Medicine* 23 (1): 23–6.

Barocci, Antonio. 2022. "Political Arrests of Women Under Fascism: Gender and the Special Tribunal in Italy 1926–1928." *GeoJournal* 87: 749–64.

Barrow Cadbury Trust. 2014. "Norway Embraces Family Visits for Prisoners." https://barrowcadbury.org.uk/news-and-opinion/news/norway-embraces-family-visits-for-prisoners/.

Bergman, Solveig, Margunn Bjørnholt, and Hannah Helseth. 2022. "Norwegian Shelters for Victims of Domestic Violence in the COVID-19 Pandemic—Navigating the New Normal." *Journal of Family Violence* 37 (6): 927–37.

Bucerius, Sandra, and Sveinung Sandberg. 2022. *Women in Prisons*. Chicago: University of Chicago Press.

Bukten, Anne, Ingunn Olea Lund, Stuart A. Kinner, Eline Borger Rognli, Ingeborg A. Havnes, Anne Elise Muller, and Marianne Riksheim Stavseth. 2020. "Factors Associated with Drug Use in Prison: Results from the Norwegian Offender Mental Health and Addiction (NorMA) Study." *Health & Justice* 8 (1): 10.

Bukten, Anne, Ingunn Olea Lund, Eline Borger Rognli, Marianne Riksheim Stavseth, Philipp Lobmaier, Svetlana Skurtveit, Thomas Clausen, and Nikolaj Kunøe. 2015. "The Norwegian Offender Mental Health and Addiction Study—Design and

Implementation of a National Survey and Prospective Cohort Study." *Substance Abuse: Research and Treatment* 9 (S2): 59–66.

Children of Prisoners Europe. n.d. "Spazio Giallo (Yellow Spaces)." https://childrenofprisoners.eu/database/spazio-giall/.

Council of Europe Probation. 2018. *Mediation and Restorative Justice Sanctions in Norway*. https://www.cep-probation.org/wp-content/uploads/2018/10/DG13CEP-DG-Oslo-2013-Mediation-and-restorative-justice-sanctions-in-Norway.pdf.

Crewe, Helen. 2020. "No Babies in Prison: Norway's Exception Explained." Cambridge Core. https://www.cambridge.org/engage/api-gateway/coe/assets/orp/resource/item/5f94c2a58f3ba900111bdc84/original/no-babies-in-prison-norway-s-exception-explained.pdf.

"Criminality in Italy—the Organized Crime Index." 2023. Ocindex.net. https://ocindex.net/country/italy?

DM. 2024. "Ministero Della Giustizia | Statistiche." Giustizia.it. https://www.giustizia.it/giustizia/it/mg_1_14_1.page?contentId=SST459008&utm.

Droznin, Maxwell, Allen Johnson, and Asal Mohamadi Johnson. 2017. "Multidrug Resistant Tuberculosis in Prisons Located in Former Soviet Countries: A Systematic Review." *PLoS ONE* 12 (3): 1–13.

Drug Policy Facts. n.d. "Russian Drug Laws and Penalties." https://www.drugpolicyfacts.org/node/4370.

Esplaguera, Shang. 2024. "Norwegian Prison System: A Model for Rehabilitation." https://marites.net/norwegian-prison-system-a-model-for-rehabilitation/.

Ferrara, Pietro, Valentina Emmanuele, Alessandra Nicoletti, Alessandro Mastrangelo, Giuseppe Marrone, and Giuseppe Pedote. 2007. "Mothers with Their Babies in Prison: The First Italian Experience." *Archives of Disease in Childhood* 92 (2): 183.

First Step Alliance. 2022. "Lessons from Norway's Prison System." https://www.firststepalliance.org/post/norway-prison-system-lessons.

France 24. 2021. "Russia Fires Prison Officials, Investigates Reports of Systemic Abuse." October 7, 2021. https://www.france24.com/en/europe/20211007-russia-fires-prison-officials-investigates-reports-of-systemic-abuse.

Generis Legal Intelligence. 2024. "Understanding Domestic Violence Protection Measures in Italy." Generis Global Legal Services. November 19, 2024. https://generisonline.com/understanding-domestic-violence-protection-measures-in-italy/.

Gheith, Jehanne, and Katherine R. Jolluck, eds. 2011. *Gulag Voices: Women's Stories*. New York: Palgrave Macmillan.

Giacomi, Ilaria. 2017. "Women: The Invisible Inmates in Italy's Prisons." Liberties.eu. June 19, 2017. https://www.liberties.eu/en/stories/invisible-women-in-italian-prisons/12221?.

Gibson, Mary. 2009. "Women's Prisons in Italy: A Problem of Citizenship." *Crime, Histoire & Sociétés* 13 (2): 27–40.

Guetto, Raffaele, Elena Pirani, and Patrizio Lodetti. 2021. "The Wellbeing of Single Parents in Italy Before and After the COVID-19 Pandemic." *Rivista Italiana di Economia Demografia e Statistica* 75 (4): 122–32. https://www.rivista-statistica.unifi.it/.

Human Rights Watch. 2018. *"I Could Kill You and No One Would Stop Me": Weak State Response to Domestic Violence in Russia.* October 25, 2018. https://www.hrw.org/report/2018/10/25/i-could-kill-you-and-no-one-would-stop-me/weak-state-response-domestic-violence.

Italian Penitentiary Administration. 2024. *Women in Prison: Analysis from the National Preventive Mechanism.* August 2024. https://www.garantenazionaleprivatiliberta.it/gnpl/pages/it/homepage/pub_rel_par/.

"Italy: Overhaul of Criminal Penalties." 2015. The Library of Congress. https://www.loc.gov/item/global-legal-monitor/2014-05-28/italy-overhaul-of-criminal-penalties/.

"Italy—Sanitary Conditions." 2024. Italy—Sanitary Conditions | Criminal Detention in the EU. December 6, 2024. https://fra.europa.eu/en/databases/criminal-detention/node/7995.

Johnsen, Berit, Marianne Vollan, and Bjørn C. Myhrer. 2018. *Normality Behind the Walls: Examples from the Norwegian Prison Service.* Oslo: Correctional Service of Norway Staff Academy. https://krus.brage.unit.no/krus-xmlui/bitstream/handle/11250/2577862/Normality%20behind%20the%20walls.pdf.

Juridisk Rådgivning for Kvinner (JURK). 2007. Country Report: Norway. February 2007. https://www.jurk.no/rapporter/kvinners_soningsforhold.pdf.

Justice Speakers International. 2016. "Norway Sentences Drug Addicts to Treatment Rather than Prison." https://www.justicespeakersinternational.com/norway-sentence-drug-addicts-treatment-rather-prison/.

Lai, Carlo, Linda Elisabetta Rossi, Federica Scicchitano, Chiara Ciacchella, Mariarita Valentini, Giovanna Longo, and Emanuele Caroppo. 2022. "Motherhood in Alternative Detention Conditions: A Preliminary Case-Control Study." *International Journal of Environmental Research and Public Health* 19 (10): 6000.

Langelid, Torfinn, Svenolov Svensson, and Kaj Raundrup. 2003. *Nordic Prison Education: A Lifelong Perspective.* Oslo: County Governor of Hordaland, Department of Education. https://www.oppikrim.no.

Long, Guido, and Marco Perduca. 2019. "From Jervolino-Vassalli to CBD Light: An Overview of Cannabis in Italy." *Talking Drugs.* https://www.talkingdrugs.org/from-jervolino-vassalli-to-cbd-light-an-overview-of-cannabis-in-italy/.

Maglie, Rosita Belinda, Pierpaolo Basile, Marco Polignano, Claudia Marin, and Ignazio Grattagliano. 2021. "Women and Prison in Italy: Wor(l)ds and (E)motions." *Membro del Collaboration Group.*

Make Mothers Matter. 2022. *Single Mothers Policy Paper: Recommendations to Support Single Mothers in Europe.* Brussels: Make Mothers Matter. December 2022. https://

makemothersmatter.org/wp-content/uploads/2022/12/SINGLE-MOTHERS-POLICY-PAPER.pdf.

Margo, Giavana. 2020. "Policing and Sentencing Practices in Russia and Their Impacts on Women Who Use Drugs." In *The Impact of Global Drug Policy on Women: Shifting the Needle*, edited by Julia Buxton, Giavana Margo, and Lona Burger, 113–21. Bingley: Emerald Publishing Limited.

Marietti, Susanna. 2015. *Alternatives to Prison in Europe: Italy*. European Prison Observatory. Rome: Antigone Edizioni.

McKenzie, Baker. 2024a. "Legal Provisions on Domestic Violence in Italy." Resource Hub. https://resourcehub.bakermckenzie.com/en/resources/fighting-domestic-violence/europe/italy/topics/1legal-provisions.

McKenzie, Baker. 2024b. "Legal Provisions on Domestic Violence: Norway." https://resourcehub.bakermckenzie.com/en/resources/fighting-domestic-violence/europe/norway/topics/1legal-provisions.

McKenzie, Baker. 2024c. "Special Issues in Domestic Violence: Norway." https://resourcehub.bakermckenzie.com/en/resources/fighting-domestic-violence/europe/norway/topics/6-special-issues.

McKenzie, Baker. 2021. Fighting Domestic Violence: Norway. 2021_FDV_Norway.pdf.

McKenzie, Baker. n.d. "Prosecutorial Considerations: Italy." Fighting Domestic Violence—Resource Hub. https://resourcehub.bakermckenzie.com/en/resources/fighting-domestic-violence/europe/italy/topics/5-prosecutorial-considerations.

Montanari, Linda. 2020. "Women Offenders in Europe: Drug Problems and Drug Offences and/or Gender-Based Violence." *European Journal of Public Health* 30, Supplement 5: ckaa165.1366.

Morris, Meagan. 2024. "Is Marijuana Legal in Russia?" *Leafwell*. https://leafwell.com/blog/is-marijuana-legal-in-russia.

Norwegian Parliamentary Ombudsman. 2016. "Visit Report: Bredtveit Prison 2016." https://www.sivilombudet.no/wp-content/uploads/2017/05/2016-Bredtveit-prison-Visit-report-EN.pdf.

Øster, Marianne Kylstad, and Tore Rokkan. 2008. "Curfew as a Means, Not as an End: Electronic Monitoring in Norway." *EuroVista* 2 (2): 90–6.

Pallot, Judith, and Laura Piacentini. 2012. *Gender, Geography, and Punishment: The Experience of Women in Carceral Russia*. Oxford: Oxford University Press.

Penal Reform International. 2021. "Double Punishment: The Situation, Challenges and Adversities Faced by Mothers in Prison Around the World." https://www.penalreform.org/blog/double-punishment-the-situation-challenges-and-adversities-faced-by-mothers-in-prison-around-the-world/.

Penal Reform International. 2013. "Women in Prison in Russia." May 2013. https://cdn.penalreform.org/wp-content/uploads/2013/05/Women-in-Prison-in-Russia_0.pdf.

Pompei, Francesca. 2019. "The Women of Rebibbia: Walls of Stories." https://phmuseum.com/projects/the-women-of-rebibbia-walls-of-stories-1.

Pratt, John, and Anna Eriksson. 2013. *Contrasts in Punishment: An Explanation of Anglophone Excess and Nordic Exceptionalism*. Abingdon: Routledge.

Pravda. 2004. "Russian Women's Prisons." https://english.pravda.ru/society/5147-prison/.

Prison Insider. 2024. "Russia." https://www.prison-insider.com/en/countryprofile/russie-2024.

Psychreg. 2024. "Mental Health Barriers Persist in Norway Prisons Despite Reforms." https://www.psychreg.org/mental-health-barriers-persist-norway-prisons-despite-reforms/.

Riddle Russia. 2021. "The Brutal Treatment of Women in Russian Prisons." February 25, 2021. https://ridl.io/the-brutal-treatment-of-women-in-russian-prisons/.

Robertson, Oliver. 2007. *The Impact of Parental Imprisonment on Children*. Quaker United Nations Office. April 2007. https://www.quno.org/sites/default/files/resources/QUNO-Impact-of-Parental-Imprisonment-on-Children.pdf.

Roth, Mitchel P. 2006. *Prisons and Prison Systems: A Global Encyclopedia*. Westport, CT: Greenwood Publishing Group.

Sanchez, Gonzalo. 2022. "The Women Caught in the Web of Chinese Organized Crime in Rome." December 6, 2022. https://efe.com/en/latest-news/2022-12-06/the-women-caught-in-the-web-of-chinese-organized-crime-in-rome/.

"Santo Stefano: The Panopticon Island—Abandoned Daily." 2024. Abandoned Daily. June 13, 2024. https://abandoneddaily.com/santo-stefano-the-panopticon-island/.

Sivilombudet. 2024. *Women in Prison: Analysis from the National Preventive Mechanism*. Norway: Sivilombudet. March 2024. https://www.sivilombudet.no/en/.

Sivilombudet. 2017. *Women in Prison: A Thematic Report About the Conditions for Female Prisoners in Norway*. Oslo: Parliamentary Ombudsman. https://www.sivilombudet.no/wp-content/uploads/2017/05/2016-Bredtveit-prison-Visit-report-EN.pdf.

Statista. 2024. "Prisons in Italy." 2024. https://www.statista.com/topics/7628/prisons-in-italy/.

Statistics Norway. 2023a. "Imprisoned Persons, by Age and Sex." https://www.ssb.no/en/statbank/table/10530/tableViewLayout1/.

Statistics Norway. 2023b. "Prisoners by Main Offense and Sex." https://www.ssb.no/en/statbank/table/10532/tableViewLayout1/.

Statistics Norway. 2013. "Execution of Community Sentences in Norway." https://www.ssb.no/en/sosiale-forhold-og-kriminalitet/artikler-og-publikasjoner/straffegjennomforing-med-samfunnsstraff-i-norge.

Sudoplatov, Pavel, and Robert Wistrich. 1994. *Special Tasks: The Memoirs of an Unwanted Witness*. Boston: Little, Brown and Company.

Svendsen, Vegard G., Marianne Riksheim Stavseth, Torbjørn Skardhamar, and Anne Bukten. 2023. "Psychiatric Morbidity Among Women in Norwegian Prisons, 2010–2019: A Register-Based Study." *BMC Psychiatry* 23: 390.

"The Issue." n.d. Penal Reform International. https://www.penalreform.org/issues/foreign-nationals/the-issue/.

The Moscow Times. 2011. "Top Court Approves 14-Year Jailing Delay." November 22, 2011. https://www.themoscowtimes.com/2011/11/22/top-court-approves-14-year-jailing-delay-a10943.

Thomson, Ian. 2014. "The Woman Who Invented the Italian Resistance." *The Spectator*. https://www.spectator.co.uk/article/the-woman-who-invented-the-italian-resistance/.

Ukrainchik, Alevtina V., Natalia M. Selezneva, Valentina V. Gorbunova, Kira D. Bondarenko, and Svetlana I. Bondarenko. 2022. "Female Crime in Modern Russia: Features, Main Trends, and Problems of Prevention." In *Business 4.0 as a Subject of the Digital Economy*, edited by Elena G. Popkova, 1195–202. Advances in Science, Technology & Innovation. Cham: Springer.

United Nations Office on Drugs and Crime (UNODC). 2022. *Reducing Reoffending Through Rehabilitation and Reintegration: Norway*. https://www.unodc.org/documents/justice-and-prison-reform/ReducingReoffending/MS/Norway_-_31st_CCPCJ_Reducing_reoffending_through_rehabilitation_and_reintegration.pdf.

U.S. Department of State. 2024. *2024 Trafficking in Persons Report: Russia*. U.S. Department of State.https://www.state.gov/reports/2024-trafficking-in-persons-report/russia/.

U.S. Department of State. 2023. *2023 Trafficking in Persons Report: Norway*. https://www.state.gov/reports/2023-trafficking-in-persons-report/norway/.

Vanzan, Sofia. 2023. "The Right to Mental Healthcare in Italian Prisons: Obligations of Italy Under the AAAQ Framework." University of Groningen. February 21, 2023. https://www.rug.nl/rechten/onderzoek/expertisecentra/gchl/student-blog/the-right-to-mental-healthcare-in-italian-prison-obligations-of-italy-under-the-aaaq-framework?lang=en.

Viola, Lynne. 2007. *The Unknown Gulag: The Lost World of Stalin's Special Settlements*. Oxford: Oxford University Press.

"ViP | Vocational Training in Prison !" n.d. Conseil-Recherche-Innovation.net. https://vip.conseil-recherche-innovation.net/.

Voller, Fabio, Caterina Silvestri, Gianrocco Martino, Eleonora Fanti, Giorgio Bazzerla, Fabio Ferrari, Marco Grignani, Sandro Libianchi, Antonio Maria Pagano, Franco Scarpa, Cristina Stasi, and Teresa Di Fiandra. 2016. "Health Conditions of Inmates in Italy." *BMC Public Health* 16 (1162): 1–10.

"What Are Prisons like in Italy?" 2022. MyVeniceLife. https://myvenicelife.com/blogs/news/what-are-prisons-like-in-italy-with-photos.

Women in Prison Initiative. n.d. "HIV in Russian Prisons." https://women-in-prison.ru/hivzonerussia.

Women's Prison Association. 2009. *Mothers, Infants, and Imprisonment: A National Look at Prison Nursery Programs and Community-Based Alternatives*. New York: Women's Prison Association. www.wpaonline.org.

World Prison Brief. 2024. "Norway | World Prison Brief." Prisonstudies.org. https://www.prisonstudies.org/country/norway.

World Prison Brief. 2023. "World Prison Population List." Institute for Crime & Justice Policy Research.

Zoia, Donatella. 2005. "Women and Healthcare in Prison: An Overview of the Experiences of Imprisoned Women in Italy." *International Journal of Prisoner Health* 1 (2/3/4): 117–26.

4

North Africa and the Middle East

This chapter examines the experiences of women incarcerated in North Africa and the Middle East, focusing on Egypt, Tunisia, and Iran. It explores the historical, social, and political circumstances influencing how these countries' justice systems treat women. For these nations, inequalities, patriarchal ideas, and political repression heavily impact women's imprisonment. Many of these women are economically marginalized and culturally stigmatized before being incarcerated, and then they experience harsh conditions in prison, including overcrowding, poor healthcare, and violence. Furthermore, the chapter investigates the health and mental health challenges incarcerated women face, as well as the impact of incarceration on their families. Overall, there is an urgent need for reforms addressing these issues and protecting the rights and dignity of women in these regions.

Egypt

Historical Context

During British colonial rule in the early 1900s, Egypt's criminal justice system emphasized control and punitive measures (Joseph 2016). Women were disproportionately targeted for **moral offenses** like adultery and prostitution, reinforcing patriarchal ideas. This continued after Egypt gained independence in 1952, as legal reforms did little to address the gender biases in the justice system. Women accused of moral crimes were judged harshly and stigmatized because they were thought to have dishonored their families (Biancani 2018).

Under Gamal Abdel Nasser's regime (1950s and 1960s), political imprisonment was widespread, and the government targeted women who opposed the regime's ideas. Members of groups like the Muslim Brotherhood were exposed to harsh penalties, such as isolation, abuse, and a lack of legal representation. For example, Zaynab al-Ghazali, a known member of the Muslim Brotherhood and critic of the regime, was arrested and imprisoned for her political activism. During her incarceration, she recounted enduring psychological pressure and physical mistreatment intended to break her will and silence dissent. Her testimony brought attention to the forms of abuse female **political prisoners** faced, including threats to their dignity and safety (Booth 1987).

In recent decades, Egypt's prison system continues to be criticized for its treatment of women, particularly those from economically disadvantaged backgrounds. Many women are incarcerated for non-violent crimes such as theft, drug-related offenses, or prostitution, usually as a result of economic marginalization. For instance, women in debt or coerced into illegal activities because of financial problems are criminalized rather than helped (Douah 2023). Women in Egyptian prisons encounter overcrowding, limited access to healthcare, and abuse. Pregnant women lack prenatal care, and overcrowded facilities worsen the spread of disease and mental health issues (Amnesty International 2021a).

Furthermore, women incarcerated for moral offenses continue to face stigma and bias. Such crimes subject women to moral rehabilitation programs intended to "reform" their behavior. After release, many of these women are further ostracized and subjected to isolation in the community (Nazra for Feminist Studies 2017). Political repression continues, and activists like Hoda Abdel-Moneim, an Egyptian human rights lawyer, are often detained without trials, showing how the government still uses imprisonment to prevent dissent

Zaynab al-Ghazali

Zaynab al-Ghazali, an Islamist activist and writer, was arrested in 1965 for opposing President Nasser's regime. She experienced beatings, solitary confinement, and death threats while incarcerated. Her writing described the mistreatment of women prisoners and how Egypt used incarceration to silence dissenting voices. After her release in the early 1970s, she continued to advocate for women's roles in Islamic society and published her influential memoir, *Return of the Pharaoh*, recounting her imprisonment. Al-Ghazali lived until 2005, remaining a prominent and controversial figure in Egypt's religious and political landscape. She represents a symbol of female resistance against political repression.

(Amnesty International 2021b). Overall, Egypt's prison system reveals gender biases, inequalities, and marginalization of incarcerated women.

Female Incarceration Rates and Trends

In 2006, Egypt's female prison population was approximately 2,386 (Fair and Walmsley 2022), although the country has not released statistics in recent years. Human Rights Watch (2023) has called for transparency in prison data, advocating for the Egyptian government to release detailed, updated data. While women make up a small percentage (between 3 and 5 percent) of Egypt's total prison population, the number has been rising due to various factors, primarily due to poverty-related crimes and political repression (Human Rights Watch 2020).

Incarcerated women in Egypt are housed across several facilities, with each serving different regions of the country (Euro-Mediterranean Human Rights Monitor 2019). The largest facility, Al-Qanater Women's Prison, serves the Greater Cairo area. There is also the Damanhour Prison in the Delta region, Tanta Prison in the central Delta, Minya Prison in Upper Egypt, and Port Said Prison, which houses women from the northeastern part of the country.

Economic problems contribute to the incarceration of women in Egypt, with many imprisoned for non-violent offenses related to poverty. For example, over 30,000 people in Egypt (referred to as **gharemat**) are incarcerated for not repaying loans, often incurred for necessities like medical treatment or school (Douah 2023). This indicates the criminalization of poverty and lack of support for economically disadvantaged people. Additionally, the Egyptian government's crackdown on political activism since the Arab Spring of 2011, a series of pro-democracy uprisings, has contributed to women's incarceration. Hundreds of women were arrested when President Mohamed Morsi was overthrown in 2013, and those involved in protests, activism, or opposition still face an increased risk of imprisonment (Tahrir Institute for Middle East Policy 2023a).

Demographics of Incarcerated Women

Many incarcerated women in Egypt come from marginalized backgrounds. They often lack access to education and employment, which can lead to crimes like theft, fraud, and drug-related offenses. Poverty disproportionately affects women, especially those in rural areas, with nearly 30 percent of the population living in poverty (CAPMAS 2020). A lack of resources and limited access to legal representation worsen their susceptibility to being incarcerated for these types of crimes (Nazra for Feminist Studies 2017). Additionally, many incarcerated women are also single mothers or primary caregivers. There are over 12 million single mothers in Egypt, many of whom are economically disadvantaged and turn to crime for survival (Fahmy 2019).

In addition to the challenges of poverty and caregiving, many incarcerated women in Egypt have experienced gender-based violence. Reports estimate that nearly 8 million women in Egypt suffer from various forms of violence each year, whether from intimate partners, family members, or strangers (UNFPA n.d.). Some women are incarcerated for retaliating against abusive partners or for actions taken in self-defense. This gender-based violence intersects with issues of criminalization, where women often face harsh penalties for crimes tied to their efforts to protect themselves or escape abusive situations.

Foreign-born women also make up a portion of Egypt's female prison population. These women are often incarcerated for drug trafficking or immigration-related crimes since Egypt is a hub for drug smuggling and sex trafficking. Comprehensive statistics on the number of foreign-born incarcerated women are limited, but reports indicate that many women are trafficked from regions like Sub-Saharan Africa and Asia (U.S. Department of State 2023b).

Furthermore, substance abuse among incarcerated women is an issue. Many women struggle with addiction and have limited access to treatment programs. In 2022, heroin was the drug most commonly abused by women, affecting 55 percent of cases (Van Hout et al. 2022). These challenges indicate a need for reforms and gender-responsive interventions in Egypt's prison system.

Crimes Leading to Incarceration

While there are no official statistics on the current number of incarcerated women in Egypt, they are typically behind bars because of poverty or political repression. Economic hardship, especially in rural areas with limited job opportunities, often pushes women toward crime. Many of these women are imprisoned due to debt, typically for borrowing money to support their families or purchase marriage supplies for their children. They often face imprisonment when they cannot repay loans, particularly when they act as guarantors for relatives who default on their payments (Egypt Today 2020b).

As a result, the Egyptian government has created ways to reduce female incarceration due to debt. The government started the "Prisons Without

Debtors" initiative in 2018, providing 30 million Egyptian pounds (nearly 1 million USD) to support the release of incarcerated women and provide social, economic, and educational support to facilitate their success in the community. The state has also worked to encourage women to develop small businesses and has established the National Committee for the Welfare of Debtors to raise awareness and prevent debt-related incarcerations (Egypt Today 2020b).

As noted, political activism has also become a major reason for female incarceration in Egypt. As of 2023, over 200 female political prisoners, including human rights activists, journalists, and political opponents, were held in Egyptian prisons, where they experience abuse such as strip searches, beatings, and deprivation of personal belongings (Magdy 2023). Moreover, seventeen activists were recently arrested during a protest outside the United Nations Women's Headquarters in Cairo in support of women in Gaza and Sudan, showing that the government is still suppressing peaceful demonstrations (Center for Justice and Accountability 2024).

Contributing Laws and Policies

Laws and policies in Egypt contribute to the incarceration of women, particularly through criminal statutes, inadequate legal protections for gender-based violence victims, and the government's stance on political dissent. For example, Egypt's drug laws disproportionately affect women, especially those from impoverished communities. Even minor offenses, such as possession or small-scale trafficking, can lead to severe penalties. These systemic issues are compounded by the lack of gender-responsive approaches in drug policy and criminal justice. A 2022 study by the United Nations Office on Drugs and Crime (UNODC) found that women in Egypt who use or inject drugs experience barriers to receiving addiction treatment and harm-reduction services, which remain limited throughout the country (Van Hout et al. 2022).

Additionally, Egypt's legal system does not adequately protect victims of gender-based violence, especially women incarcerated for harming their abusive spouses. Although the Penal Code (No. 58 of 1937, amended in 2018) addresses violence against women, enforcement is inconsistent, and many women lack access to legal representation (Tahrir Institute for Middle East Policy 2023a). As a result, women who commit violent acts, such as assault or homicide, in self-defense against an abusive partner often face harsh legal consequences without the courts properly considering the context of their abuse.

The Egyptian government's crackdown on political dissent has also contributed to the growing number of female political prisoners detained for non-violent activities such as protests and speaking out against the government. These women face harsh treatment, including physical abuse and denial of legal representation. Magdy (2023) highlighted such abuses, emphasizing how political repression has contributed to women's incarceration in Egypt.

Lastly, despite how many women in Egypt are incarcerated for non-violent crimes like theft, there is a lack of alternatives to incarceration. Although there is a need for these alternatives, Egypt's justice system rarely offers community-based options. The United Nations Office on Drugs and Crime (2007) promotes non-custodial measures such as community service, probation, and restorative justice programs, which can address the causes of criminal behavior more effectively than prison sentences, especially for women who commit non-violent crimes.

Conditions in Women's Prisons

Conditions in women's prisons in Egypt are known to be harsh, with overcrowding, inadequate sanitation, and limited access to healthcare. Many of them house far more people than they were intended to, resulting in limited privacy and the ability to maintain basic hygiene. Overcrowding can also lead to life-threatening conditions due to insufficient access to medical care, sanitation, ventilation, food, or potable water (U.S. Department of State 2023a). Also, because of overcrowding, there are no formal rehabilitation or training programs for women imprisoned in Egypt, but some incarcerated women volunteer to teach activities. However, these opportunities are limited, and they are not offered to political prisoners (Nazra for Feminist Studies 2017).

Additionally, the health and well-being of incarcerated women are often disregarded. The families of the incarcerated are typically responsible for providing them with medication, food, and other necessities (Amnesty International 2021a). Furthermore, women are often denied medical treatment or hospital visits, which could result in preventable deaths or avoiding serious health problems. The Egyptian Initiative for Personal Rights (EIPR 2014) has found that many incarcerated women, particularly pregnant ones, lack access to medical care, worsening their complications during pregnancy and childbirth.

Furthermore, women in Egypt experience harassment and abuse by prison staff, including strip searches, beatings, and the removal of their belongings. In many cases, women are placed in solitary confinement as punishment for minor violations. Many women also report experiencing sexual violence, either from other inmates or prison staff, without adequate procedures to seek justice (Nazra for Feminist Studies 2017). This mistreatment is a violation of human rights. It harms both their physical and mental health, particularly pregnant or nursing women, whose vulnerable health conditions are worsened by the stresses of this abuse (Tahrir Institute for Middle East Policy 2023b).

Health and Mental Health Issues

There are numerous health and mental health issues for incarcerated women in Egypt. Many of these women come into prison with pre-existing conditions, and overcrowding and unsanitary conditions only worsen these problems. The US Department of State's 2023 Human Rights Report indicates that insufficient medical care and poor sanitation lead to the spread of diseases like tuberculosis, hepatitis, and scabies in detention centers.

Mental health is another concern, as many incarcerated women suffer from trauma and abuse, but they receive no psychological care in prison. The mental health needs of these women are ignored or inadequately addressed (Amnesty International 2021a). Furthermore, the harsh prison environment, including experiences of abuse and a lack of privacy, worsens conditions like depression, anxiety, and suicidal ideation. Conditions in Egyptian detention centers have led to repeated suicide attempts, with human rights organizations documenting multiple cases in a single month, including detainees driven to self-harm by overcrowding, torture, and denial of medical care (Committee for Justice 2023). A lack of psychiatric care exacerbates these issues, leaving many women untreated and their conditions worsening over time (Tahrir Institute for Middle East Policy 2023b).

To illustrate the dire state of healthcare in Egypt's prisons is the case of Alia Awad. Awad, a journalist from Cairo, was arrested in 2014 and again in 2017. During her time in detention, she was exposed to torture, including beatings and forced confessions. She was also diagnosed with a uterine tumor, but despite repeated requests, she was denied surgery (Alkarama 2020). This delay led to severe bleeding, anemia, and weight loss, eventually requiring blood transfusions. The prison administration only responded after her health deteriorated drastically. Her case highlights the neglect of medical care and the psychological toll of prolonged torture and deprivation in the Egyptian prison system. Awad was eventually able to undergo surgery, but she still suffers from psychological stress from her incarceration.

Additionally, pregnant women face health challenges because of inadequate medical facilities and staff, which can lead to health risks for mothers and children. Many prisons do not provide them with essential medical care, including regular prenatal visits, which violates legal standards. There have been incidents of pregnant women giving birth without medical assistance or losing their babies because of negligence, illustrating the severity of these healthcare shortcomings (Euro-Mediterranean Human Rights Monitor 2019).

Furthermore, women imprisoned in Egypt lack basic health needs, such as menstrual hygiene products, which contributes to poor sanitation and an increased risk of disease. Malnutrition is also a concern, especially for pregnant or breastfeeding women who rely on family visits to meet their nutritional needs. These many health-related issues indicate the need for improved healthcare services addressing the needs of women incarcerated in Egypt, especially for pregnant women (Nazra for Feminist Studies 2017).

Impact on Families and Children

The incarceration of women in Egypt has an overwhelming impact on their families and children. The Egyptian Child Law (Article 31) allows for a nursery in women's prisons to house children until age four. It also ensures mothers can be with their babies during their first year. However, despite this law, conditions in Egyptian women's prisons are inadequate to house children. Overcrowding, a lack of healthcare, and physical abuse affect mothers and their children, raising questions about the efficacy of the law that is intended to help them stay together (Egypt Today 2020a).

Moreover, many incarcerated women report not being allowed to have contact with their families. For example, Sharifa, a woman who was formerly incarcerated, discussed how she was unable to communicate with her children, husband, or family during her five-year detention. She described how she was denied all visits and correspondence (Tahrir Institute for Middle East Policy 2023b). Similar to Sharifa's story, the Egyptian Initiative for Personal Rights (2014) reports that women in prison typically encounter arbitrary visitation restrictions, with visits being infrequent or denied altogether. This lack of contact worsens the stress on both mothers and children. Additionally, the social stigmatization of maternal incarceration and financial burdens make it even more challenging for families to visit. This isolation also makes reintegration more difficult for mothers and their children because a lengthy separation makes it difficult to repair broken bonds (Nazra for Feminist Studies 2017).

Furthermore, the lack of data on the number of incarcerated women and their children in Egypt makes it difficult to understand the scope of this problem. However, the information that is known demonstrates a need for policies that better support children affected by their mothers' incarceration, including regular visits and correspondence.

Policy Reforms and Recommendations

There are several recommendations to address the issues that women face in Egypt's prisons to ensure their fundamental human rights are protected. First, it is suggested to revise the Penal Code to provide more alternatives to incarceration, especially for women convicted of non-violent crimes. Applying the International Covenant on Civil and Political Rights (ICCPR), which states that no one should be imprisoned because they cannot fulfill a contractual obligation, such as defaulting on a loan, would help reduce incarceration rates for non-violent crimes (Nazra for Feminist Studies 2017).

Additionally, healthcare must be improved. All prisons should have appropriate medical staff and facilities to care for incarcerated women, particularly pregnant women and those with chronic conditions. Implementing routine medical checkups, improving access to medications, and providing mental health services in Egyptian prisons are urgently needed. For instance, many women suffer from untreated health conditions like tuberculosis, hepatitis, and malnutrition (U.S. Department of State 2023a), and these measures would help improve these conditions. Furthermore, introducing regular access to mental health professionals would address the psychological toll of abuse and stresses of incarceration.

Furthermore, the lack of regular contact between incarcerated women and their families is a considerable issue in Egyptian prisons. Limits on visitation rights and the lack of communication worsen the stress for everyone involved. Recommendations include allowing more frequent family visits to ensure children maintain relationships with their incarcerated mothers (Egypt Today 2020a). The financial burden on families, which often prevents visits, should also be addressed through government subsidies for those with economic hardships.

Lastly, training for prison staff is needed to implement gender-sensitive practices. This includes hiring female staff in women's prisons and offering training to avoid mistreatment. Additionally, reforms should address overcrowded conditions and make sure that all women have access to proper hygiene, adequate food, and educational or rehabilitative activities (Nazra for

Feminist Studies 2017). These steps will improve the experiences of incarcerated women in Egypt, promoting rehabilitation, reducing recidivism, and supporting their reintegration.

Tunisia

Historical Context

The history of incarcerated women in Tunisia is influenced by colonialism and gender norms. When the country was under French colonial rule (1881–1956), the prison system was punitive, but women's incarceration rates were low because of their restricted roles in society. Those who were imprisoned were often punished for poverty-related crimes, such as theft, or moral offenses like prostitution, reflecting colonial and patriarchal repression (Davis 2007). Gender norms were conservative, with laws restricting women's rights, aiming to keep them at home to raise children.

After Tunisia's independence in 1956, President Habib Bourguiba introduced legal reforms to modernize the country. For example, the *Code of Personal Status* granted women rights related to marriage and divorce. It gave them the right to ask for a divorce, as well as more protections against forced marriages. These reforms made Tunisia a leader in women's rights in the Arab world, with a more progressive position on gender roles (Charrad 2001).

The 2011 Tunisian Revolution was another important moment in the country's history, bringing greater political freedoms but also worsening economic instability. Women played a role in this revolution, participating in protests and advocating for democratic reforms. However, many were detained for dissenting against the Ben Ali regime (Tunisia's president from 1987 to 2011), risking their freedom for expressing their views (Beardsley 2011). After the revolution, there were economic problems throughout the country, which disproportionately affected women. For instance, in 2020, unemployment rates for women were 25 percent versus 14 percent for men (UN Women 2021).

Although Tunisia has made some progressive legal reforms over the years, inequalities remain, especially among impoverished women. Poverty often drives these women to commit non-violent crimes for their families to survive. Additionally, moral codes still criminalize women for offenses like prostitution, which continue to be influenced by patriarchal views (Ben Salah

2020). Women incarcerated for moral offenses face societal stigmatization, which limits their opportunities for rehabilitation and reintegration, indicating a gap between Tunisia's progress and the realities of these marginalized women (Mkaouar 2022).

Female Incarceration Rates and Trends

Female incarceration rates in Tunisia are low, with women making up approximately 3 percent of the total prison population (Boukhayatia 2022), or approximately 1,000 women (National Authority for the Prevention of Torture 2024). One-third of these women have been sentenced, while the other two-thirds are in pre-trial detention as they await their trials. With such a high percentage in pre-trial detention, this trend brings up concerns about access to legal representation and the effectiveness of the legal process. Furthermore, women are housed in eight prisons throughout Tunisia, but only one (the Manouba Prison) is strictly a women's prison (National Authority for the Prevention of Torture 2024).

Female rates of incarceration in Tunisia have been steady over time. However, while the percentage is consistently low, the number of incarcerated women indicates socioeconomic challenges, including poverty and limited access to education and employment (Boukhayatia 2022). As a result, women often turn to non-violent crimes to support themselves.

Another ongoing trend is that Tunisian prisons lack gender-specific rehabilitation programs. Incarcerated women often encounter violence and socioeconomic challenges, which contribute to their incarceration (Boukhayatia 2022). Recognizing these challenges, initiatives have been started to address their needs. For example, the Tunisian Ministry of Justice and the UNODC recently introduced a project to improve gender-responsive correctional services for incarcerated women to better support their reintegration (UNODC 2024). Despite these efforts, many women still face stigma upon release, preventing their success in society.

Demographics of Incarcerated Women

The demographics of incarcerated women in Tunisia indicate social and economic marginalization. Education levels among them are low, with one-third reporting only primary school education. Economic problems are widespread, as two-thirds describe being poor or very poor, and nearly half (49 percent) have children. The median age of these women is 33.3 years, and 42 percent are single, which often limits their support in the community (Boukhayatia 2022).

Many incarcerated women in Tunisia have experienced trauma and mental health challenges. For instance, 70 percent have been victims of domestic violence, and 45 percent report having been sexually abused on numerous occasions. Mental health concerns are also common, with 71 percent suffering from depression, 40 percent confirming self-harm or suicide attempts, and one-third receiving treatment for psychological problems while incarcerated. Furthermore, 28 percent of these women have been drug or alcohol dependent (Boukhayatia 2022).

Moreover, foreign-born women in Tunisian prisons represent a part of the incarcerated population who face challenges due to their non-citizen status. As of 2021, there were fifty-six foreign women incarcerated in Tunisia, which is about 6 percent of the total female prison population (National Authority for the Prevention of Torture 2024). Many of these women are detained on charges related to drug trafficking or are victims of human trafficking. Traffickers often exploit these women, who may have entered the country on valid visas but found themselves in coercive situations (U.S. Department of State 2024).

Crimes Leading to Incarceration

The incarceration of women in Tunisia is linked to non-violent crimes related to economic and social marginalization. Many women are imprisoned for crimes like theft, fraud, and issuing checks without sufficient funds. They are often criminalized because of their financial instability, and many face imprisonment due to debt-related offenses (Human Rights Watch 2024b). A survey conducted by Penal Reform International (2014) found that only 17 percent of incarcerated women were charged with violent crimes.

Prostitution and other "moral" offenses, such as adultery, also contribute to female incarceration in Tunisia. Prostitution is legally confined to regulated zones like Sidi Abdallah Guech in Tunis, and parts of Sfax, and women operating outside these areas are subject to penalties, including imprisonment. When many red-light districts closed after the 2011 Revolution, sex workers were forced into unregulated environments, increasing their risks of arrest and exploitation (Ben Salah 2020). Additionally, adultery is still criminalized under Tunisia's Penal Code, demonstrating how conservative social norms still influence the country's

Chaima Issa, Political Prisoner

Chaima Issa, a Tunisian journalist and activist, was the first female political prisoner under President Kais Saied's rule. Arrested in 2023 for criticizing the regime's authoritarian policies, she symbolizes the repression of dissent in post-revolution Tunisia. Her detention drew attention from human rights groups worldwide since Tunisia was once seen as a leader in women's rights in the Arab world. Issa was released in 2024 after more than a year in detention, but she remains banned from travel and public appearances, continuing to face charges that limit her political activity. Despite these restrictions, she has vowed to keep advocating for democracy and human rights in Tunisia.

legal system even though there have been steps toward advancing women's rights (The Advocates for Human Rights and Mobilising for Rights Associates 2022).

Drug-related offenses are another cause of female incarceration, with reports indicating that about 15 percent of women in Tunisia are behind bars for these crimes (Human Rights Watch 2016b). These cases often involve women playing small roles in drug trafficking or acting as couriers, typically under coercion. Tunisia's drug laws, particularly before reforms in 2017, imposed severe penalties for minor drug-related crimes, disproportionately affecting marginalized women (Human Rights Watch 2016b).

Furthermore, political dissent continues to be a factor in female incarceration. Activist Chaima Issa became the first female political prisoner under President Kais Saied's regime in 2023, detained for criticizing the government's authoritarian policies (El Atti 2023). Moreover, in 2024, during National Women's Day, protests highlighted the detention of over thirty female judges and activists critical of Saied (El Atti 2024). Lastly, although Tunisia has passed laws to combat violence against women, inadequate enforcement and societal stigmas often lead to the criminalization of women who act in self-defense against their abusers (Human Rights Watch 2022).

Contributing Laws and Policies

Legal frameworks and policies in Tunisia contribute to the incarceration of women through harsh drug laws, regulations on moral offenses, and insufficient protections against gender-based violence. Tunisia's drug laws, mainly Law

No. 92-52 (of 1992), inflicted strict penalties for minor drug-related crimes, including mandatory minimum sentences for possession. Courts were required to sentence people to at least one year in prison for their first offense and five years for subsequent offenses, with no room for judicial discretion (Human Rights Watch 2016a).

Before reforms in 2017, the enforcement of these drug laws also had other consequences, including prison overcrowding. In 2016, people convicted of drug offenses made up nearly one-third of Tunisia's prison population (Vinchon 2017), with women being disproportionately affected. Recognizing these issues, Tunisia amended Law 52 in 2017 to introduce proportional sentencing and alternatives to incarceration for minor drug offenses. While these reforms represent progress, their effective implementation remains critical (Badri 2017).

Additionally, the criminalization of unregulated sex work subjects women to violence, exploitation, and health risks. Those who work outside of regulated zones are more likely to face abuse and lack access to healthcare services in the absence of legal protections (Ben Salah 2020). Furthermore, Organic Law 2016-61, the country's anti-trafficking law, was intended to impose severe penalties (up to ten years in prison) on people engaged in human trafficking (U.S. Department of State 2024). However, it has not been implemented effectively, with unclear lines between human trafficking and consensual sex work. This has led to the further closing of regulated brothels, leaving many women in unsafe working conditions (International Federation for Human Rights 2016).

Tunisia has also struggled to protect women from gender-based violence. The enactment of Law No. 58 (of 2017) was a step toward eliminating violence against women, but stigma and insufficient implementation have made it ineffective. Unfortunately, many women who defend themselves against abusive partners are criminalized. Limited financial resources and varying attitudes among police and judges worsen these inconsistencies. Legal reforms are needed so that victims of gender-based violence are protected rather than punished (Human Rights Watch 2022).

Conditions in Women's Prisons

There are several issues plaguing the conditions of incarceration for women in Tunisia. For one, overcrowding is an issue, especially in Manouba Prison, which exceeds its capacity by 24 percent (National Authority for the Prevention of Torture 2024). Overcrowding is problematic because it often prevents women from getting the care they need. For instance, many essential hygiene products, including those for genital infections, are rarely provided in Tunisian prisons. This shows neglect, as untreated infections can lead to further complications.

Additionally, security measures like strip searches violate people's dignity. These searches are invasive and leave women feeling humiliated. Also, while solitary confinement is rarely used for discipline, it is used to isolate women with contagious diseases because there is a lack of proper healthcare (National Authority for the Prevention of Torture 2024). Disturbing accounts, such as that of Asma, a university-educated woman who was incarcerated, stress the severity of these conditions. She described overcrowded cells, limited access to water, and degrading practices such as invasive body searches and sleeping on insect-infested mattresses (Boukhayatia 2022).

Furthermore, suicide attempts, made out of desperation or used as a form of protest, are frequent. Opportunities for rehabilitation and reintegration are minimal, leaving most women sitting in their cells, increasing their sense of despair and isolation. After release, women face stigmatization and rejection by their families and communities, and they often lose custody of their children (Boukhayatia 2022).

Health and Mental Health Issues

Health and mental health issues are challenges for incarcerated women in Tunisia. Many women enter prison with untreated health conditions like malnutrition, infectious diseases, or chronic illnesses. Inadequate access to healthcare worsens these problems, as there are insufficient medical facilities and a lack of trained healthcare personnel. This often results in delayed treatment, which puts these women at risk of complications. For example, there were six women with HIV and thirteen with hepatitis C in 2024, indicating the presence of infectious diseases that could spread if not properly treated and managed (National Authority for the Prevention of Torture 2024).

Pregnant women and mothers face challenges as laws mandating prenatal and postnatal care are inconsistently applied. Although children are allowed to stay with their mothers until the age of two, designated spaces for mothers in several prisons lack the resources to meet their needs (National Authority for the Prevention of Torture 2024). Pregnant women often report insufficient medical attention and a lack of adequate nutrition, heightening the risks of complications during pregnancy and childbirth.

Moreover, despite a high prevalence of psychological disorders like depression, anxiety, and post-traumatic stress disorder (PTSD), mental health services within Tunisian prisons are nearly non-existent. Reports indicate that Tunisia had only nine mental health workers per 100,000 citizens, reflecting a national shortage that extends into the prison system (World Health Organization 2020). Overall, the lack of physical and mental health services indicates a need for reforms to address these concerns.

Impact on Families and Children

The incarceration of women in Tunisia burdens their families, particularly their mothers, who often provide financial and emotional support. As Ben Arab and Elloumi (2021) found in interviews with inmates at Manouba, women's mothers often deliver food, clothing, and financial aid, while also taking on responsibilities for their grandchildren. In one case, a mother regularly visited her imprisoned daughter, cared for her granddaughter, and sent cash (typically no more than the equivalent of 35 USD) for necessities. Her emotional reassurance was described as a source of strength during confinement. This example illustrates the intergenerational impact of incarceration, reinforcing gendered expectations of unpaid caregiving within already strained families.

Unfortunately, family ties are often broken upon a mother's incarceration due to stigma. Women from impoverished backgrounds or those convicted of crimes like infanticide are often abandoned by their families. This lack of familial support makes it even worse when these women reintegrate into society, stressing the need for reforms to address these disruptions (Ben Arab and Elloumi 2021).

While some children can remain with their mothers in prison until the age of two, the prison environment is not conducive to their development. Incarcerated mothers have inadequate healthcare and limited resources to care for their children, creating distressing conditions for both. For children who end up separated from their mothers, being placed with extended family members or in state institutions often results in emotional trauma, social stigma, and other consequences. These disruptions frequently lead to interrupted education and delayed social development, further marginalizing these children (International Center for Transitional Justice 2018).

An example of the effects of incarceration is the case of Farida, whose husband was the one incarcerated. His imprisonment left her to care for their children in a hostile environment. Her oldest son, Mohamed, faced harassment and was expelled from school. He eventually joined an extremist group before losing his life. This case demonstrates the consequences of incarceration on families, indicating a need for reforms. Improved prison conditions, better access to healthcare, and community-based alternatives to incarceration are needed to reduce these adverse effects and support incarcerated women and their families (International Center for Transitional Justice 2018).

Policy Reforms and Recommendations

Improving the lives of incarcerated women in Tunisia requires reforms that address health and mental health needs, improve prison conditions, and create alternatives to incarceration for non-violent offenses. Women in Tunisian prisons face shortages of medical supplies, including hygiene products for genital infections, which are rarely provided (National Authority for the Prevention of Torture 2024). Pregnant women are entitled to prenatal and postnatal care under Tunisian law, but they report inconsistent implementation of these services, which could cause risks during pregnancy and childbirth. Overcrowding, especially in Manouba Prison, makes these issues worse. Efforts to reduce overcrowding and provide access to hygiene products and medical care are necessary to improve living conditions for these women.

The high prevalence of trauma, depression, and other mental health challenges among incarcerated women indicates a need for gender-specific mental health services. Many have experienced domestic violence, sexual abuse, or other forms of gender-based harm, often without access to adequate support before entering the prison system. Nearly three-quarters suffer from depression, and 40 percent report self-harm or suicide attempts (Boukhayatia 2022). Despite these figures, mental health services are almost non-existent, and prison staff often lack training in trauma-informed care. The absence of such services worsens women's suffering during incarceration and undermines their ability to heal, regain autonomy, and reintegrate after release. Having regular mental health assessments, providing individualized psychological care, and training prison staff on gender-sensitive approaches would improve these issues.

Additionally, alternatives to incarceration are another area for reform. Most women in Tunisian prisons are incarcerated for non-violent offenses, such as debt-related crimes, theft, and drug-related crimes (Human Rights Watch 2024b). Community-based alternatives (e.g., probation, electronic monitoring, and community service) would help with overcrowding, lessen the stigma of incarceration, and allow women to continue caring for their children. Expanding these alternatives would also be beneficial for children, many of whom face trauma and disruption when their mothers are imprisoned.

Finally, efforts must focus on breaking the cycle of stigmatization and exclusion faced by incarcerated women. Many women, particularly those convicted of moral offenses or infanticide, are abandoned by their families and shunned upon release. This isolation makes reintegration into society challenging, often leading to recidivism. Providing rehabilitation and reintegration programs, including vocational training and community support, would help women rebuild their lives after incarceration. Additionally, raising awareness and addressing cultural stigmas would support societal acceptance of formerly incarcerated women. These measures are needed to address issues within Tunisia's criminal justice system and improve the lives of incarcerated women and their families.

Iran

Historical Context

Politics, religion, and social changes have influenced the experiences of women's incarceration in Iran. The Pahlavi dynasty (1925–79) played a considerable role, transforming Iran's prison system by creating modern prisons. During this period, women were typically incarcerated for crimes like theft or fraud. This era also saw improvements in women's rights, as Reza Shah Pahlavi introduced policies to improve women's position in society. For instance, by the mid-1930s, women could attend college, with more than seventy female students enrolled at the University of Tehran in that first year (Sedghi n.d.). These reforms increased the country's literacy rate and improved job opportunities for women.

More progress occurred under Mohammad Reza Shah Pahlavi (1941–79). For example, women could vote and run for parliament by 1963 as part of the White Revolution. Additionally, legal reforms, like the Family Protection Law of 1967 and its amendment in 1975, improved women's marriage, divorce, and child custody rights (Frontline 2010). However, these reforms were limited to wealthier women and those living in urban areas.

The 1979 Islamic Revolution changed women's rights and the justice system in Iran. A stricter interpretation of Sharia law criminalized behaviors once considered private, such as adultery or dress code violations, leading to the imprisonment of women for moral offenses (United States Institute of Peace 2020). Political dissent was also criminalized, with female activists, journalists, and reformers targeted. Among them was Farrokhroo Parsa, a former Minister of Education and advocate for women's rights, who was executed by firing squad inside Tehran's Evin Prison in 1980. Sentenced by the Islamic Revolutionary Court on charges such as "spreading corruption on earth" and collaborating with the former regime, her case is seen as a politically motivated response to her secular and feminist views (Iran Human Rights 2022). As one of the first female politicians executed after the revolution, Parsa's death became a symbol of the regime's repression of women reformers. The revolution also reversed legal protections for women, including repealing the Family Protection Law, lowering the legal age of marriage for girls to nine, and enforcing mandatory **hijab laws**.

Since the revolution, women political prisoners have dealt with severe conditions, including solitary confinement, torture, and denial of medical care. For example, Kurdish political prisoner Varisheh Moradi, who has been sentenced to death, has continually been denied medical treatment in Iran's Evin Prison despite deteriorating health (Medya News 2025). Overall, women's prisons in Iran continue to be known for overcrowding, unsanitary conditions, and inadequate healthcare (Iran Human Rights 2024b).

"Free Iranian Political Prisoners" poster, created by artist Rachael Romero in 1975 (Library of Congress)

Female Incarceration Rates and Trends

Women make up about 3 percent of Iran's prison population, but their numbers have been increasing because of political repression and the enforcement of religious and moral laws. Women expressing political views against the regime have been targeted, especially during events like the 2022 Mahsa Amini protests, after she died in custody for violating hijab laws. The government responded by making mass arrests and subjecting the detained women to abuse (HRA Iran 2024). Since March 2016, at least 715 women and girls have been arrested for their beliefs and activism (Iran Barometer n.d.).

Another trend is an increase in the executions of women in Iran. In 2024, over 1,000 prisoners, including 34 women, were executed, which is the most in 30 years. Moreover, between 2010 and 2024, at least 241 women have been executed. Forty-seven percent were executed for committing homicide, 70 percent of whom were accused of killing abusive husbands or partners. Furthermore, 44 percent were executed on drug-related charges, many of whom were coerced into these crimes, typically from provinces where poverty and discrimination are widespread. These executions are usually carried out by hanging inside prisons, with most cases conducted quietly and without public announcement (Iran Human Rights 2025).

Incarcerated women are housed in facilities across the country. Although the exact number is limited because of a lack of governmental transparency, most of these women are housed in wards within men's prisons. Evin Prison in Tehran houses political prisoners along with people convicted of other crimes, with no

Qarchak Women's Prison

Qarchak Prison is one of Iran's most notorious women's prisons, located in the desert area of Varamin, about 30 kilometers southeast of Tehran. Housing around 2,000 women, it is known for overcrowding, contaminated food, pest infestations, and lack of medical care. Political prisoners and women convicted of minor offences are held together under degrading conditions. Reports describe inadequate drinking water, poor sanitation, and abuse by guards, making Qarchak a symbol of the human rights crisis within Iran's prison system. Former detainees have described it as "a place of exile," noting that prisoners are often sent there as punishment for protesting or speaking out while incarcerated elsewhere.

crime separation and severe overcrowding. Qarchak Prison in Varamin holds about 2,000 women, including political detainees, with reports of abuse and inadequate amenities. Basic needs like clean drinking water, functioning toilets, ventilation, and access to sanitary products are often unmet. Other facilities are also characterized by unsanitary environments, insufficient food, and a lack of healthcare (Women's Network for Community Reporting on Iran 2021a).

Demographics of Incarcerated Women

Many incarcerated women in Iran come from economically disadvantaged backgrounds, and they are often involved in crimes like theft, fraud, and drug-related offenses. They typically have limited access to education, employment, and support systems, which makes them more apt to engage in crime. Even though women make up over 50 percent of college graduates, their workforce participation is low, with only 14 percent employed (Women's Network for Community Reporting on Iran 2021b), compared to 64 percent of men (Human Rights Watch 2017). Economic marginalization and limited opportunities often force women into illegal activities, heightening their risk of incarceration.

Women in Iran are often imprisoned for violating moral and religious laws, which disproportionately affect impoverished women without the resources to navigate the legal system. These women often cannot afford effective representation, making them more likely to receive harsh sentences. Women detained for moral offenses also endure lengthy pre-trial detention and unfair trials, worsening socioeconomic disparities (Amnesty International 2024). Additionally, the enforcement of mandatory veiling laws has led to countless arrests of women from lower socioeconomic backgrounds, who face severe penalties, including imprisonment and fines, which they often cannot contest (Amnesty International 2024).

While data disaggregated by age was limited, one report noted that the average age of incarcerated women in Iran ranges between twenty and thirty-five years (Women's Network for Community Reporting on Iran 2017). Moreover, domestic violence is another factor impacting women in Iran, as two-thirds have experienced domestic abuse. However, specific data on its prevalence among incarcerated women is scarce (Center for Human Rights in Iran 2025).

Furthermore, foreign nationals, especially Afghan women, make up a portion of the female prison population. Approximately 5,400 Afghan nationals, including men and women, are detained in Iranian prisons, often for immigration-related offenses (Rahmati 2024). These women encounter language barriers, isolation, and limited access to legal representation. Additionally, Iran's strict immigration policies contribute to their incarceration, and foreign women are also susceptible to exploitation and trafficking (U.S. Department of State 2021).

Crimes Leading to Incarceration

The government's lack of transparency makes it hard to determine the nature and extent of female incarceration in Iran. However, many women are incarcerated for violating moral and religious laws, including not wearing the mandatory hijab, dressing "immodestly," participating in mixed-gender gatherings, or engaging in acts like public singing, dancing, or expressing dissent online (Human Rights Watch 2024a). Women involved in political activism also face being incarcerated. Those who advocate for human rights, women's rights, or challenge the regime are targeted. A recent example occurred when twelve women in Guilan province received sentences of over sixty years in prison. Additionally, Sharifeh Mohammadi, a workers' rights activist, was recently sentenced to death on charges of "armed rebellion against Islamic rule" (Golshiri 2024). Moreover, on the anniversary of Mahsa Amini's death, thirty-four female political prisoners participated in a hunger strike in Evin Prison to protest governmental repression (Cadena SER 2024).

As noted, women in Iran are increasingly being put to death for their crimes. At least eighty-six women have been executed in Iran for drug-related crimes between 2010 and 2021 (Iran Human Rights 2022). Additionally, some women are incarcerated for violent crimes like murder, usually related to killing their spouses, because they themselves had been victims of continued domestic violence. Between 2010 and 2021, at least sixty women were executed for murder (Iran Human Rights 2022). Lastly, non-violent crimes like theft and fraud, which typically result from economic marginalization, also contribute to women's imprisonment in Iran.

Contributing Laws and Policies

Laws related to moral and religious codes, especially hijab regulations, influence the incarceration of women in Iran. The government has required dress codes since the 1979 revolution, with violations punishable by fines, imprisonment, and physical torture. For instance, the "Protection of the Family through the Promotion of the Culture of Chastity and Hijab" law has penalties of up to fifteen years in prison for breaking these laws (The New Indian Express 2024). Moreover, "Project Nour" has recently led to 644 arrests of women for improper veiling, showing that the government continues to focus on women's appearance and behavior in public (Iran International 2024). In a recent incident, a university student protested the hijab laws by taking off her clothes in public. She was arrested and sent to a psychiatric hospital (Downing 2024). These laws criminalize acts that are not considered crimes in most countries, showing how the government in Iran tries to control women.

In addition, Iran's laws do not properly address gender-based violence or protect women who defend themselves against abuse. Women who act in self-defense in domestic violence cases often face prison time or death. Moreover, the frequency of femicides, with women killed for dishonoring their families or wanting a divorce, indicates a need for reforms to protect women in Iran (Center for Human Rights in Iran 2025). It is estimated that 600 women and girls are killed annually in Iran because of femicide. However, this figure is likely less than the actual number because many cases go unreported or are incorrectly classified (Keypour et al. 2022).

Furthermore, women involved in protests, activism, or journalism are often arrested for "propaganda against the state" and "acting against national security" (Reporters Without Borders 2022). This demonstrates how the Iranian regime continues to use the law to silence dissent, suppress activism, and control women's expression.

Conditions in Women's Prisons

Conditions in women's prisons in Iran are poor, and women encounter overcrowding, inadequate healthcare, and a lack of legal representation. Qarchak Prison is known for overcrowding and often has pest infestations, contaminated food, and insufficient ventilation. Unsatisfactory restroom facilities worsen unsanitary conditions and increase the risk of illness (Iran Human Rights 2024a). Moreover, women housed at Lakan Prison suffer winters without heating, electricity, or proper sewage systems, and illnesses spread due to the lack of medical care (Medya News 2025).

Political prisoners face even worse treatment, including extended stays in solitary confinement, limited contact with their families, and minimal contact with lawyers. For instance, Golrokh Ebrahimi Iraee spent a month and a half in solitary confinement in Evin Prison, and she had no access to a lawyer (Amnesty International 2016). Also, activist Fatemeh Sepehri endured failing health after spending over a month in solitary confinement (Iran International 2023).

Additionally, abuse by prison staff is rampant, with women claiming both physical and emotional torture. For example, a woman from Shiraz province described being beaten by staff, resulting in permanent nerve damage. She also saw other women receiving beatings, including ones that resulted in miscarriages (Bose 2024).

Furthermore, there are limited opportunities for educational and vocational programming for women imprisoned in Iran. There have been collaborations with organizations like the Iran Technical and Vocational Education Organization, but only about one-third of incarcerated people, both men and women, have access to training (Iran Human Rights Documentation Center 2015). Overall, a lack of rehabilitation leaves women without the resources to successfully reintegrate into society.

Health and Mental Health Issues

There are many health and mental health issues for women imprisoned in Iran, mainly because access to these services is limited. Many women arrive at prison with poor health, including diseases and injuries from domestic violence, and these problems are made worse in prison. Few doctors or medical personnel are available to care for these women. To illustrate, women and children in Qarchak Prison face freezing temperatures, with limited heat or hot water. As a result, illnesses spread throughout the prison, but people barely receive care, for instance, two antibiotic pills for each sick person (Hosseini 2024).

Pregnant women also face unsatisfactory conditions. They have minimal prenatal and postnatal care, as well as insufficient nutrition, which puts their and their babies' lives in danger. These shortcomings indicate a need for better care of pregnant women incarcerated in Iran (Alirezaei and Roudsari 2022). Overall, noise, instability, and disease within the prison environment threaten the well-being of incarcerated mothers and their children, who can typically stay with their mothers until age two (Farmand 2022).

Also, incarcerated women in Iran often face mental health challenges, many of whom suffered domestic violence or political repression before imprisonment. Unfortunately, mental health services are nearly non-existent, leaving these women to deal with depression, anxiety, and other conditions on their own. Furthermore, prison staff often abuse incarcerated women to break their will, which can worsen their mental health conditions and lead to long-term consequences like PTSD (Esfandiari 2021).

Impact on Families and Children

The incarceration of women in Iran has a considerable impact on their families and children. The mother's absence leads to emotional, social, and financial challenges, with children often experiencing anxiety, depression, and isolation. A study of incarcerated mothers in Iran showed that their children frequently faced behavioral and mental health challenges because of their mothers' incarceration (Rahimipour Anaraki and Boostani 2014).

Maternal incarceration also affects finances, especially when women contribute heavily to the household income. This can impact children's access to education, healthcare, and other needs, especially for impoverished families (National Council of Resistance of Iran Women's Committee 2021). Additionally, children of incarcerated mothers are stigmatized in a society that values family honor, leading to them having low self-esteem and strained relationships with peers (Moradi 2024).

The separation from their children also causes stress for incarcerated mothers, mainly because there is a lack of contact and limited visitation opportunities. The Center for Human Rights in Iran (2016) found that the most difficult experience for incarcerated women was the denial or limitation of family visits and communication (Center for Human Rights in Iran 2016). Political prisoners are further subjected to restrictions on familial contact, intensifying their negative experiences (Center for Human Rights in Iran 2019).

While some children in Iran can live with their incarcerated mothers until the age of two, prison conditions are damaging to their development. For example, in Sanandaj Prison, children and their mothers suffer from infectious diseases because of unsanitary and overcrowded conditions (National Council of Resistance of Iran Women's Committee 2016). In 2017, approximately 2,300 children were reported to be living in Iranian prisons with their mothers (U.S. Department of State 2019). However, there is a need for improved living conditions and support systems for these families (Qarchak Prison Report 2024).

Policy Reforms and Recommendations

There are several policy reforms and recommendations that would improve the lives of incarcerated women in Iran. First, there are limited legal safeguards for women, especially in cases of domestic violence. Implementing laws that address gender-based violence would better protect women from abuse and prevent their unfair imprisonment. Existing laws do not adequately deal with self-defense in domestic violence cases, leaving women susceptible to long prison sentences or execution. Many women executed in Iran killed their abusive partners, stressing the need for reforms in this area (Center for Human Rights in Iran 2025).

Additionally, conditions in women's prisons, including overcrowding, insufficient healthcare, and poor sanitation, need attention. For instance, facilities like Qarchak and Sanandaj Prisons are known for unsanitary conditions that subject women and children to diseases. There must be investments in infrastructure so that they have access to heat, clean water, and medical care. Reports indicate women often receive only two antibiotic pills for illnesses, and children living with their mothers until age two face developmental risks in these environments (Hosseini 2024).

Furthermore, mental health services are almost non-existent for incarcerated women, many of whom suffer from pre-existing trauma such as domestic violence or political repression. Introducing counseling, therapy, and mental health support would help conditions like PTSD and depression. Additionally, rehabilitation programs, including vocational and educational training, are needed so that women can successfully reintegrate into society. Currently, only about one-third of incarcerated people in Iran have access to these programs (Esfandiari 2021).

Finally, maternal incarceration disrupts families and negatively impacts children, who face stigma, isolation, and financial difficulties. Policies should help maintain family connections through improved visitation rights and enhanced communication. It is also imperative to allow political prisoners visitation with their families (Center for Human Rights in Iran 2019). Additionally, reforms should improve living conditions for children living with their mothers in prison, making sure they have proper nutrition, healthcare, and other support (Qarchak Prison Report 2024). These recommendations provide necessary reforms that address the challenges faced by incarcerated women and their families in Iran.

Conclusion

This chapter has examined the social and political factors that contribute to the incarceration of women in Egypt, Tunisia, and Iran. Across these countries, patriarchal norms, economic marginalization, and political repression have targeted women, criminalizing them for moral offenses, crimes of poverty, and political dissent. In these prison systems, women face severe conditions due to overcrowding, violence, and inadequate healthcare systems. Most of these women also face mental health challenges, which are made worse by the prison environment and lack of mental health services. Furthermore, incarceration does not just affect these women, but it also impacts their children.

Although Egypt, Tunisia, and Iran have some similar issues, each country's social and political factors impact the experiences of incarcerated women differently. In Egypt, women are often imprisoned for economic crimes or engaging in political activism. Tunisia has had more progressive legal reforms, but poverty and social stigma shun incarcerated women, especially those involved in prostitution. The most severe conditions are in Iran, a country that strictly enforces moral and religious laws, leading to mass arrests and executions of women involved in activism or self-defense against abuse. Across all three countries, prisons exhibit overcrowding and inadequate access to health services, but Iran's reliance on incarceration to repress the political voices of women makes it the most severe. While there are differences, all three countries overlook the gender-specific needs of incarcerated women.

Focusing on these needs will help protect their rights and promote justice, and reforms must focus on poverty, domestic violence, and discrimination. Improved prison conditions, access to healthcare and mental health services, along with alternatives to incarceration, are necessary to improve the experiences for these women. It is also essential to protect them from political repression and ensure they have legal representation. By making these changes, Egypt, Tunisia, and Iran can advance gender equity within their prison systems and society.

References

Alirezaei, Somayeh, and Robab Latifnejad Roudsari. 2022. "Imprisoned Pregnant Women's Lived Experience of Prenatal Care: A Phenomenological Inquiry." *Journal of Midwifery and Reproductive Health* 10 (2): 3258–67.

Alkarama. 2020. "Egypt: Life Imprisoned for Photographer and Journalist Alia Awad Is in Danger." *Alkarama*. September 17, 2020. https://www.alkarama.org/en/articles/egypt-life-imprisoned-photographer-and-journalist-alia-awad-danger.

Amnesty International. 2024. "Iran: New Compulsory Veiling Law Intensifies Oppression of Women and Girls." December 2024. https://www.amnesty.org/en/latest/news/2024/12/iran-new-compulsory-veiling-law-intensifies-oppression-of-women-and-girls/.

Amnesty International. 2021a. “Egypt: Abused and Denied Healthcare—Prisoners’ Lives at Risk.” https://www.amnesty.org/en/latest/news/2021/01/egypt-abused-and-denied-heath-care-prisoners-lives-at-risk-2/.

Amnesty International. 2021b. “Egypt: ‘What Do I Care If You Die?’ Negligence and Denial of Health Care in Egyptian Prisons.” https://www.amnesty.org/en/documents/mde12/5094/2021/en/.

Amnesty International. 2016. “Iran: Writer Arrested in Violent Raid on Her House Following Prison Sentence for Story About Stoning.” October 27, 2016. https://www.amnesty.org/en/latest/news/2016/10/iran-writer-arrested-in-violent-raid-on-her-house-following-prison-sentence-for-story-about-stoning-2/.

Badri, Najd. 2017. *Drug Policy in Tunisia: Towards an Evidence-Based Human Rights and Public Health Approach*. C·A·Perspectives on Tunisia No. 02-2017. Center for Applied Policy Research (C·A·P). https://cap-lmu.de.

Beardsley, Eleanor. 2011. “In Tunisia, Women Play an Equal Role in Revolution.” *KPBS*. January 27, 2011. https://www.kpbs.org/news/2011/01/27/tunisia-women-play-equal-role-revolution.

Ben Arab, Maissène, and Ali Elloumi. 2021. “Family Solidarity for Tunisian Women Prisoners and Its Effect on Their Reintegration.” *International Journal of Scientific and Innovative Analysis* 2 (6), November–December 2021: 941–50. https://www.ijscia.com/full-text-volume-2-issue-6-nov-dec-2021-941-950.

Ben Salah, Faïrouz. 2020. “Sex Workers in Tunisia Face ‘Moral Crusade’ of Abuse and Violence.” *Middle East Eye*. November 6, 2020. https://www.middleeasteye.net/news/tunisia-sex-workers-moral-crusade-abuse-violence.

Biancani, Francesca. 2018. *Sex Work in Colonial Egypt: Women, Modernity and the Global Economy*. London: I. B. Tauris.

Booth, Marilyn. 1987. “Women’s Prison Memoirs in Egypt and Elsewhere: Prison, Gender, Praxis.” *MERIP Middle East Report* (149): 35–41.

Bose, Sayan. 2024. “Snatched from Home and Jailed by Iran’s Revolutionary Guard—Victim Tells of Torture and Abuse.” *The Sun*. December 2024. https://www.thesun.ie/news/14406088/snatched-home-jailed-iran-revolutionary-guard-torture/.

Boukhayatia, Rihab. 2022. “Women’s Prisons in Tunisia: Punishment Without Rehabilitation.” *Nawaat*. June 3, 2022. https://nawaat.org/2022/06/03/womens-prisons-in-tunisia-punishment-without-rehabilitation/.

Cadena SER. 2024. “Presas Políticas de Irán Inician una Huelga de Hambre por el Segundo Aniversario de la Muerte de Mahsa Amini.” September 16, 2024. https://cadenaser.com/nacional/2024/09/16/presas-politicas-de-iran-inician-una-huelga-de-hambre-por-el-segundo-aniversario-de-la-muerte-de-mahsa-amini-cadena-ser/.

Center for Human Rights in Iran. 2025. “Killed Because You Are a Woman: Violence Against Women in Iran Reaches New Heights.” Iran Human Rights Documentation Center. January 2025. https://iranhumanrights.org/2025/01/killed-because-you-are-a-woman-violence-against-women-in-iran-reaches-new-heights/.

Center for Human Rights in Iran. 2019. "Another Mother Denied Visits with Children Under Evin Prison's New Director." October 2019. https://iranhumanrights.org/2019/10/another-mother-denied-visits-with-children-under-evin-prisons-new-director/.

Center for Human Rights in Iran. 2016. "Family Visitation and Telephone Communications: Denying Basic Rights to Prisoners in Iran." June 2016. https://iranhumanrights.org/2016/06/wwr-family-visitation-and-telephone-communications/.

Center for Justice and Accountability. 2024. "Egypt: Arrest of 17 Activists in Front of UN Women's Headquarters Protest." *Center for Justice and Accountability*. Last modified April 2024. https://www.cfjustice.org/egypt-arrest-of-17-activists-in-front-of-un-womens-headquarters-protest.

Central Agency for Public Mobilization and Statistics (CAPMAS). 2020. "Poverty Rates in Egypt Decline to 29.7% Within Year." State Information Service (SIS). Last modified July 15, 2020. https://www.sis.gov.eg/Story/159611/CAPMAS-Poverty-rates-in-Egypt-decline-to-29.7%25-within-year.

Charrad, Mounira M. 2001. *States and Women's Rights: The Making of Postcolonial Tunisia, Algeria, and Morocco*. Berkeley: University of California Press.

Committee for Justice. 2023. "Egypt: CFJ Documents Second Suicide Attempt in Custody in September." *Committee for Justice*. September 14, 2023. https://www.cfjustice.org/egypt-cfj-documents-second-suicide-attempt-in-custody-in-september/.

Davis, Diana K. 2007. *Resurrecting the Granary of Rome: Environmental History and French Colonial Expansion in North Africa*. Athens: Ohio University Press.

Douah, Chahrazade. 2023. "In Egypt, Women Become Prisoners of Poverty." *Missing Perspectives*. https://missingperspectives.com/posts/in-egypt-2c-women-become-prisoners-of-poverty/.

Downing, Jared. 2024. "Iran Student Strips Off and Walks Around in Underwear in Apparent Protest at Strict Hijab Laws." *New York Post*. November 3, 2024. https://nypost.com/2024/11/03/world-news/iran-student-strips-off-and-walks-around-in-underwear-in-apparent-protest-at-strict-hijab-laws/.

Egypt Today. 2020a. "How Child Law Treats Babies of Jailed Mothers." https://www.egypttoday.com/Article/1/77709/How-Child-Law-treats-babies-of-jailed-mothers.

Egypt Today. 2020b. "Study: Egypt Soon to Have Zero Debtors in Prison." https://www.egypttoday.com/Article/1/100063/Study-Egypt-soon-to-have-zero-debtors-in-prison.

Egyptian Initiative for Personal Rights (EIPR). 2014. "EIPR Report on Health Conditions in 16 Prisons and Police Stations: Living Conditions and Violations." *Egyptian Initiative for Personal Rights*. June 2014. https://eipr.org/en/press/2014/06/eipr-report-health-conditions-16-prisons-and-police-stations-living-conditions-and.

El Atti, Basma. 2024. “Tunisia: Women Protest Saied’s ‘Misogyny’ on National Women’s Day.” *The New Arab*. August 14, 2024. https://www.newarab.com/news/tunisia-women-protest-saieds-misogyny-national-womens-day.

El Atti, Basma. 2023. “First Female Political Prisoner of Saied’s Tunisia.” *The New Arab*. September 8, 2023. https://www.newarab.com/analysis/first-female-political-prisoner-saieds-tunisia.

Esfandiari, Golnaz. 2021. “Sexual Abuse in Iranian Prisons: The Silent Scourge.” *Radio Free Europe/Radio Liberty (RFE/RL)*. May 27, 2021. https://www.rferl.org/a/women-sexual-abuse-iran-prisons/31282808.html.

Euro-Mediterranean Human Rights Monitor. 2019. *Suppressed and Humiliated: Violence Against Egyptian Women Arbitrarily Locked Behind Bars*. January 2019. https://euromedmonitor.org.

Fahmy, Mona. 2019. “I Chose the Wrong Father for My Children: Stories of Single Mothers in Egypt.” *Egyptian Streets*. October 1, 2019. https://egyptianstreets.com/2019/10/01/i-chose-the-wrong-father-for-my-children-stories-of-single-mothers-in-egypt/.

Fair, Helen, and Roy Walmsley. 2022. *World Female Imprisonment List, Fifth Edition: Women and Girls in Penal Institutions, Including Pre-Trial Detainees/Remand Prisoners*. Institute for Crime & Justice Policy Research. https://www.prisonstudies.org.

Farmand, Hamed. 2022. “The Most Vulnerable Inhabitants of Iran’s Most Famous Women’s Prison.” *Children of Imprisoned Parents International (COIPI)*. March 2022. https://coipi.org/the-most-vulnerable-inhabitants-of-irans-most-famous-womens-prison/.

Frontline. 2010. “Iran Primer: The Women’s Movement.” *PBS*. October 2010. https://www.pbs.org/wgbh/pages/frontline/tehranbureau/2010/10/iran-primer-the-womens-movement.html.

Golshiri, Ghazal. 2024. “In Iran, the Regime Is Cracking Down on Women.” *Le Monde*. August 7, 2024. https://www.lemonde.fr/en/international/article/2024/08/07/in-iran-the-regime-is-cracking-down-on-women_6711035_4.html.

Hosseini, Mehdi. 2024. “Dire Conditions in Qarchak Women’s Prison: Inmates Endure Cold, Illness, and Deprivation.” *Iran Focus*. December 2024. https://iranfocus.com/iran/52839-dire-conditions-in-qarchak-womens-prison-inmates-endure-cold-illness-and-deprivation/.

HRA Iran. 2024. “An Increase in Women’s Activism Alongside Rising Government Hostility in Iran: ‘They Can Imprison Our Bodies, but They Will Never Imprison Our Fight for Justice.’” https://www.hra-iran.org/an-increase-in-womens-activism-alongside-rising-government-hostility-in-iran-they-can-imprison-our-bodies-but-they-will-never-imprison-our-fight-for-justice/.

Human Rights Watch. 2024a. “Iran: New Hijab Law Adds Restrictions and Punishments.” https://www.hrw.org/news/2024/10/14/iran-new-hijab-law-adds-restrictions-and-punishments.

Human Rights Watch. 2024b. "Tunisia: Many Face Prison over Debts." https://www.hrw.org/news/2024/06/10/tunisia-many-face-prison-over-debts.

Human Rights Watch. 2023. "Egypt: Release Prison Population Figures." Last modified February 28, 2023. https://www.hrw.org/news/2023/02/28/egypt-release-prison-population-figures.

Human Rights Watch. 2022. "*So What If He Hit You?": Addressing Domestic Violence in Tunisia*. December 8, 2022. https://www.hrw.org/report/2022/12/08/so-what-if-he-hit-you/addressing-domestic-violence-tunisia.

Human Rights Watch. 2020. "Egypt: Spate of Morality Prosecutions of Women." Last modified August 17, 2020. https://www.hrw.org/news/2020/08/17/egypt-spate-morality-prosecutions-women.

Human Rights Watch. 2017. *It's a Men's Club: Discrimination Against Women in Iran's Job Market*. May 26, 2017. https://www.hrw.org/report/2017/05/26/its-mens-club/discrimination-against-women-irans-job-market.

Human Rights Watch. 2016a. "*All This for a Joint": Tunisia's Repressive Drug Law and a Roadmap for Its Reform*. https://www.hrw.org/report/2016/02/02/all-joint/tunisias-repressive-drug-law-and-roadmap-its-reform.

Human Rights Watch. 2016b. "Tunisia: Widespread Abuses Under Drug Law." https://www.hrw.org/news/2016/02/02/tunisia-widespread-abuses-under-drug-law.

International Center for Transitional Justice (ICTJ). 2018. "*Who Hears My Voice Today?" Tunisia's Forgotten Women Victims and Indirect Victims of the Political Violence of the 1960s–1980s*. https://www.ictj.org/publication/%E2%80%9Cwho-hears-my-voice-today%E2%80%9D-tunisia%E2%80%99s-forgotten-women-victims.

International Federation for Human Rights. 2016. "Tunisia Legislates Against Trafficking in Persons (TIP)." https://www.fidh.org/en/impacts/tunisia-legislates-against-trafficking-in-persons-tip.

Iran Barometer. n.d. "Topic: Women Political Prisoners." https://iranbarometer.org/topic/women-political-prisoners/.

Iran Human Rights. 2025. *Women and the Death Penalty in Iran: A Gendered Perspective*. Oslo, Iran Human Rights. https://iranhr.net/en/reports/25/.

Iran Human Rights. 2024a. "Qarchak Prison: Iran's Notorious Women's Prison." https://www.iranhr.net/en/articles/7185/.

Iran Human Rights. 2024b. "Women Executions in Iran: 2023 Sees the Highest Number in Five Years." https://www.iranhr.net/en/articles/7185/.

Iran Human Rights. 2022. "Annual Report on the Death Penalty in Iran 2021." March 15, 2022. https://www.iranhr.net/en/articles/4910/.

Iran Human Rights Documentation Center. 2015. *Rights Disregarded: Prisons in the Islamic Republic of Iran*. https://iranhrdc.org/rights-disregarded-prisons-in-the-islamic-republic-of-iran/.

Iran International. 2024. "Iranian Police Intensify Crackdowns on Women Through 'Project Nour.'" December 26, 2024. https://www.iranintl.com/en/202412263018.

Iran International. 2023. "Iranian Activist Fatemeh Sepehri Held in Solitary Confinement, Faces Health Deterioration." December 28, 2023. https://www.iranintl.com/en/202312287874.

Joseph, Suad. 2016. *Women Under Colonialism: Egypt.* Encyclopedia of Women and Islamic Cultures (EWIC). University of California, Davis. March 1, 2016. Accessed from EWIC Public Outreach Project funded by the Henry Luce Foundation.

Keypour, Marjan, Silja Aebersold, Zahra Azizi, Ralph Geissen, and Adina G., eds. 2022. *2022 Annual Report: Documented Femicides in Iran.* Alliance for Rights of All Minorities (ARAM). https://stopfemicideiran.org.

Magdy, Solafa. 2023. "Women in Egypt's Prisons: Tales of Oppression, Abuse, and Human Rights Violations." *The Tahrir Institute for Middle East Policy.* April 19, 2023. https://timep.org/2023/04/19/women-in-egypts-prisons-tales-of-oppression-abuse-and-human-rights-violations/?eType=EmailBlastContent&eId=791bc7e6-e08e-43ab-b918-6ff3465205ec.

Medya News. 2025. "Women Behind Bars: Deteriorating Health of Iran's Political Prisoners." https://medyanews.net/women-behind-bars-deteriorating-health-of-irans-political-prisoners/.

Mkaouar, Farah. 2022. "Tunisian Women Are Stuck Between Freedom and Inequality." *Assembly by Malala Fund.* https://assembly.malala.org/stories/tunisian-women-are-stuck-between-freedom-and-inequality.

Moradi, Khadije. 2024. "Analyzing the Rights of Children with Imprisoned Mothers in Iran." *Journal of Human Rights and Social Work* 9: 93–103.

National Authority for the Prevention of Torture. 2024. "Women in Prison: Tumknisia—Analysis from the National Preventive Mechanism." September 2024. https://www.apt.ch/global-report.

National Council of Resistance of Iran Women's Committee. 2021. "The Plight of Women in Iran: A Report to the UN Beijing+25 Forum." *NCRI Women's Committee.* June 14, 2021. https://wncri.org/2021/06/14/the-plight-of-women-in-iran-a-report-to-the-un-beijing25-forum/.

National Council of Resistance of Iran Women's Committee. 2016. "Female Political Prisoners and Conditions of Women's Wards in Iranian Prisons." *NCRI Women's Committee.* August 23, 2016. https://wncri.org/2016/08/23/female-political-prisoners-and-conditions-of-women-s-wards-in-iranian-prisons/.

Nazra for Feminist Studies. 2017. "Violence Has Many Prisons: A Look into Women's Experiences in Prisons and Detention Centers in Egypt." https://nazra.org/en/2017/01/violence-has-many-prisons-look-women%E2%80%99s-experiences-prisons-and-detention-centers-egypt.

Penal Reform International. 2014. *Women Prisoners' Survey Results: Jordan and Tunisia.* https://www.penalreform.org/resource/women-prisoners-survey-results-jordan-tunisia/.

"Qarchak Prison Report: Hell for Women and Children in Iran." 2024. Iranhr.net. https://www.iranhr.net/en/articles/7185/.

Rahimipour Anaraki, Nahid, and Dariush Boostani. 2014. "Living In and Living Out: A Qualitative Study of Incarcerated Mothers' Narratives of Their Children's Living Condition." *Quality & Quantity* 48 (6): 3093–107.

Rahmati, Fidel. 2024. "Majority of Foreign Prisoners in Iran Are Afghan Citizens: Iranian Official." *The Khaama Press News Agency*. https://www.khaama.com/majority-of-foreign-prisoners-in-iran-are-afghan-citizens-iranian-official/.

Reporters Without Borders. 2022. "Unprecedented Number of Women Journalists Are Now Detained in Iran." November 2022. https://rsf.org/en/unprecedented-number-women-journalists-are-now-detained-iran.

Sedghi, Hamideh. n.d. "Feminist Movements III. In the Pahlavi Period." *Encyclopaedia Iranica* 9 (5): 492–8. http://www.iranicaonline.org/articles/feminist-movements-iii.

Tahrir Institute for Middle East Policy. 2023a. "Inside Women's Prisons in Egypt: Conditions and Violations Behind Bars." https://timep.org/2023/11/29/inside-womens-prisons-in-egypt-conditions-and-violations-behind-bars/.

Tahrir Institute for Middle East Policy. 2023b. "Women in Egypt's Prisons: Tales of Oppression, Abuse, and Human Rights Violations." *Tahrir Institute for Middle East Policy*.

The Advocates for Human Rights and Mobilising for Rights Associates. 2022. *Tunisia's Compliance with the Convention Against Torture and Other Cruel, Inhumane or Degrading Treatment or Punishment: Suggested List of Issues Prior to Reporting Relating to Violence Against Women*. https://www.advrights.org.

The New Indian Express. 2024. "Iran Imposes Strict Hijab Laws, Approves Death Penalty for Offenders." December 11, 2024. https://www.newindianexpress.com/world/2024/Dec/11/iran-imposes-strict-hijab-laws-approves-death-penalty-for-offenders.

UN Women. 2021. "Tunisia." https://arabstates.unwomen.org/en/countries/tunisia.

United Nations Office on Drugs and Crime. 2007. *Handbook of Basic Principles and Promising Practices on Alternatives to Imprisonment*. Vienna: United Nations.

United Nations Office on Drugs and Crime (UNODC). 2024. "On International Women's Day, Tunisian Ministry of Justice and UNODC Launch a Joint Project to Improve Gender-Responsive Correctional Services for Female Prisoners in Tunisia." March 2024. https://www.unodc.org/romena/en/press/2024/March/press-release_-on-international-womens-day—tunisian-ministry-of-justice-and-unodc-launch-a-joint-project-to-improve-gender-responsive-correctional-services-for-female-prisoners-in-tunisia.html.

United Nations Population Fund (UNFPA). n.d. "Gender-Based Violence." *UNFPA Egypt*. https://egypt.unfpa.org/en/topics/gender-based-violence-27.

United States Institute of Peace. 2020. "Part 3: Iranian Laws on Women." *The Iran Primer*. December 8, 2020. https://iranprimer.usip.org/blog/2020/dec/08/part-3-iranian-laws-women.

U.S. Department of State. 2024. *2024 Trafficking in Persons Report: Tunisia*. https://www.state.gov/reports/2024-trafficking-in-persons-report/tunisia/.

U.S. Department of State. 2023a. *Egypt 2023 Human Rights Report*. Bureau of Democracy, Human Rights, and Labor. https://www.state.gov.

U.S. Department of State. 2023b. *2023 Trafficking in Persons Report: Egypt*. https://www.state.gov/reports/2023-trafficking-in-persons-report/egypt.

U.S. Department of State. 2021. *Trafficking in Persons Report: Iran*. https://www.state.gov/reports/2021-trafficking-in-persons-report/iran/.

U.S. Department of State. 2019. *2019 Country Reports on Human Rights Practices: Iran*. https://2017-2021.state.gov/reports/2019-country-reports-on-human-rights-practices/iran/.

Van Hout, Marie-Claire, Heba Elsayed, Raghda Elgamil, Menan A. Rabie, Reham Aly, and Mohammad Tariq Sonnan. 2022. *Rapid Situation Assessment of Women Who Use Drugs in Egypt*. Liverpool John Moore's University, National AIDS Program Director, Ministry of Health and Population, Egypt; Addiction Department Director, Secretariat of Mental Health and Addiction Treatment, Egypt; UNODC ROMENA, Egypt.

Vinchon, Timothee. 2017. "Jailed for a Joint: Tunisia's Drug Law Throws Thousands into Hellish Prisons." *Middle East Eye*. https://www.middleeasteye.net/features/jailed-joint-tunisias-drug-law-throws-thousands-hellish-prisons.

Women's Network for Community Reporting on Iran. 2021a. "The Conditions of Women in Iran Prisons." https://wncri.org/2021/12/09/the-conditions-of-women-iran-prisons/.

Women's Network for Community Reporting on Iran. 2021b. "The Effects of Extreme Poverty on the Body and Soul of Iranian Women." https://wncri.org/2021/10/16/the-effects-of-extreme-poverty-on-the-body-and-soul-of-iranian-women/.

Women's Network for Community Reporting on Iran. 2017. "Iran: Average Age of Female Prisoners Ranges Between 20 and 35." April 7, 2017. https://wncri.org/2017/04/07/iran-average-age-of-female-prisoners-ranges-between-20-and-35/.

World Health Organization. 2020. *Mental Health Atlas 2020: Tunisia Country Profile*. https://cdn.who.int/media/docs/default-source/mental-health/mental-health-atlas-2020-country-profiles/tun.pdf.

5

Sub-Saharan Africa

This chapter explores the incarceration of women in Sub-Saharan Africa, specifically in South Africa, Nigeria, and Kenya. Despite distinct socio-legal contexts, all three countries show how poverty, gender inequality, and outdated laws contribute to women's incarceration. The chapter examines historical legacies, incarceration trends, demographic patterns, common offenses, legal frameworks, and the lived experiences of incarcerated women. It also highlights prison conditions, health and mental health challenges, and the impact on families and children. The chapter calls for gender-responsive regional reforms across the three countries.

South Africa

Historical Context

Like many nations, the history of incarcerated women in South Africa is shaped by the country's political and social struggles, especially during apartheid (1948–94). Institutionalized racial segregation defined the legal and penal systems (Lawler 2023). Under repressive laws like the 1963 General Law Amendment Act and the Internal Security Act, Black women were detained without trial, tortured, and denied necessities. Between 1963 and 1989, over 20,000 women were detained under apartheid security laws (SAHA 2025).

Many women were imprisoned for resisting apartheid, particularly those involved in liberation movements like the African National Congress and Pan Africanist Congress. Prominent figures like Winnie Madikizela-Mandela, Albertina Sisulu, and Fatima Meer faced repeated arrests and harsh treatment for their activism, often held in facilities like the Women's Jail at Constitution

Women protest against apartheid by occupying places for white people in public transport in Johannesburg, South Africa, *c.* 1952. (International News Photos [INP]/AFP via Getty Images)

Hill (SAHA 2025). Prisons at the time were notorious for overcrowding, poor sanitation, and gendered abuse, including sexual violence and the denial of hygiene products (Lawler 2023).

In the postapartheid era, reforms such as the Correctional Services Act of 1998 and efforts to align with international standards, like the Bangkok Rules, which you will recall address the needs and treatment of women in the criminal justice system, aimed to improve conditions and promote gender equity (Van Hout and Wessels 2021). However, the legacy of apartheid continues. Many incarcerated women come from economically marginalized backgrounds and are held for poverty-related offenses (e.g., petty theft or drug possession), reflecting the country's social inequalities and high unemployment (World Bank 2025).

Despite these reforms, challenges remain in ensuring equitable treatment. Limited resources and systemic barriers hinder access to gender-responsive programs and healthcare, leaving many women underserved in South Africa's prison system (Van Hout and Wessels 2021).

Female Incarceration Rates and Trends

Women make up a small share of South Africa's prison population—about 4,700 out of 156,600 incarcerated individuals, or 3 percent. Roughly 62 percent of these women have been convicted, while 38 percent are awaiting trial (World Prison Brief 2024b). They are held in nine women's prisons and ninety-one mixed-gender facilities (Kinuthia 2021). Notable sites include Pollsmoor, Worcester, and the Westville women's wing. The Women's Jail at Constitution Hill now serves as a heritage site, commemorating those once imprisoned there (Constitution Hill 2024). Women are classified across all security levels (minimum, medium, and maximum) based on their offenses (Mogatle 2023).

Since 2000, the number of incarcerated women in South Africa has steadily grown, increasing by 17 percent by 2024 (Fair and Walmsley 2023). Most incarcerated women are held for non-violent, poverty-driven offenses. Their criminalization is tied to structural inequalities like unemployment and gender-based violence (GBV) (George et al. 2022). Many commit crimes out of economic necessity (Van Hout and Wessels 2021). Drug-related offenses are also on the rise, with growing numbers of women imprisoned for possession or trafficking. South Africa's role as a global drug transit hub has contributed to this trend, as economically vulnerable women are often recruited into distribution networks (UNODC 2023).

Demographics of Incarcerated Women

The demographics of incarcerated women in South Africa indicate social and economic inequalities. Over 98 percent are people of color—Black African, Colored (or of mixed heritage), and Indian/Asian groups (Makou et al. 2017)—compared to 93 percent in the general population (Statistics South Africa 2023). Common offenses include economic crimes (45 percent), aggressive offenses like assault or homicide (37 percent), and drug-related offenses (10 percent) (Johnson et al. 2012).

Many women come from rural or peri-urban areas shaped by apartheid-era spatial inequities and ongoing underdevelopment. These areas have limited access to education, healthcare, and employment. Nearly two-thirds of South Africans in these areas live below the international poverty line (World Bank 2025). About 2 million households live in informal settlements marked by overcrowding and poor services (Comins 2023).

Educational attainment is low among incarcerated women, with about 50 percent having completed some secondary schooling. The age distribution is even: roughly one-third are in their twenties, one-third in their thirties, and one-third are over forty (Steyn and Booyens 2017). Three-quarters are mothers, many of whom were imprisoned for crimes linked to economic survival to provide for their families (Mamacos 2023).

Furthermore, GBV is pervasive, with over one-third of women reporting physical or sexual abuse in their lifetime, and 24 percent specifically reporting intimate partner violence (Masiko-Mpaka 2024). Mental health challenges are also common, with 90 percent of incarcerated women in Durban reporting psychiatric disorders (Naidoo et al. 2021).

Crimes Leading to Incarceration

As previously discussed, many incarcerated women in South Africa are serving time for non-violent, economically motivated offenses. While these are often minor crimes rooted in poverty and marginalization, more severe and high-profile cases have also drawn public attention. In 2024, Racquel Chantel Smith from Saldanha Bay was sentenced to life in prison for selling her six-year-old daughter, Joshlin, to a traditional healer for approximately $1,000. Her boyfriend, a codefendant, also received life sentences for kidnapping and human trafficking (Associated Press 2025).

Drug-related offenses are another contributor to female incarceration in South Africa. Many women are drawn into trafficking as low-level couriers or mules, often under coercion or manipulation by male partners or organized crime networks (Stanyard 2023). Despite minor roles, women often receive severe sentences. Research from Johannesburg and Kgoši Mampuru II prisons found that many women had been exploited or deceived into unknowingly transporting drugs (Mukoma and Jansen 2022). While the Prevention and Combating of Trafficking in Persons Act (2013) allows for mitigation based on coercion or vulnerability, inconsistent application means many women are criminalized rather than protected (Van Hout and Chimbga 2020). One notable case involved a 21-year-old woman arrested at OR Tambo International Airport after arriving from Brazil. She had ingested over 110 cocaine-filled pellets, far more than the average drug mule. Authorities expressed concern because she was the eleventh mule arrested within two months (Masilela 2024).

Some women are incarcerated for violent crimes, often linked to histories of abuse. Over one-third of women charged with violent offenses in forensic psychiatric settings had experienced prior victimization, illustrating how trauma may lead to violence (Nagdee et al. 2024). South Africa's legal system, like many others, lacks provisions to fully account for the lived experiences of "battered women," limiting access to trauma-informed defenses (Gore 2024).

Finally, extreme cases of violent offending have also emerged. In 2024, police sergeant Rachel Kutumela was charged with murdering six people to claim life and funeral insurance worth over 10 million rand. Her victims were known to her, and the killings were described as premeditated (CBS News 2024).

Contributing Laws and Policies

South Africa's legal framework contributes to the incarceration of women, particularly through harsh sentencing policies and the criminalization of poverty-related offenses. Drug laws under the **Drugs and Drug Trafficking Act 140 of 1992** impose penalties of up to fifteen years for possession and mandatory minimums for trafficking. These women, often coerced into minor roles, are prosecuted like major traffickers with little access to diversion programs that redirect offenders away from prosecution or imprisonment and into community-based treatment or rehabilitation instead (Van Hout and Chimbga 2020). The Prevention and Combating of Trafficking in Persons Act of 2013 allows courts to consider coercion or vulnerability, but implementation is inconsistent, and women continue to be punished (Mukoma and Jansen 2022).

Although the Criminal Procedure Act 51 of 1977 permits noncustodial alternatives like community-based supervision and postponed or suspended sentences, these measures are not consistently applied (Constitutional Law of South Africa 2019). Courts can consider restorative sentences for first-time non-violent offenders, as affirmed in *S v Shilubane* (2008), where the court emphasized rehabilitation and community service over imprisonment for theft. Yet, many women continue to receive custodial sentences for minor property-related crimes. Penal Reform International (2019) emphasizes that theft, fraud, and other "crimes of poverty" are common among women and advocates for gender-sensitive alternatives. However, South Africa's Department of Correctional Services lacks reliable application of rehabilitation programs tailored to women's needs (Samuels et al. 2024).

Additionally, the legal system has failed to adequately protect victims of prolonged abuse. Although common law allows for private defense (i.e., self-defense), courts often require the threat to be immediate and the force proportionate, criteria difficult to meet in cases of long-term abuse. This interpretation ignores the cumulative trauma many women face, leading to imprisonment for acts of survival. Legal Resources Centre (2024) notes that women who kill abusive partners are often criminalized, and courts have been reluctant to recognize frameworks like battered woman syndrome.

Despite reforms introducing parole, probation, and community service, the justice system remains slow to systematically apply these alternatives in a gender-sensitive way. A framework informed by the Bangkok Rules and similar international standards calls for non-custodial responses that reflect women's socioeconomic and familial realities (Penal Reform International 2019). Until these reforms are realized, the system will continue to disproportionately imprison women for poverty- and trauma-related crimes.

Conditions in Women's Prisons

Women's prisons in South Africa face overcrowding, poor healthcare, and limited rehabilitation opportunities. Facilities often lack hygiene and sanitary resources. One review found ninety-four women in poorly ventilated rooms without bedding, sanitary products, or reading materials, which can increase disease risk (Artz et al. 2023) like TB and HIV (Van Hout and Mhlanga-Gunda 2018).

The Department of Correctional Services has been criticized for failing to provide gender-sensitive care or address overcrowding, inadequate ventilation, and healthcare neglect (Commission for Gender Equality 2024). Many incarcerated women arrive with chronic illnesses, untreated injuries, or mental health conditions stemming from past trauma. Despite international standards like the Southern African Development Community Minimum Standards for HIV in Prisons, access to gender-specific healthcare remains insufficient. This is especially true for pregnant women and mothers, who face increased risks due to inadequate prenatal and postnatal care (Van Hout and Mhlanga-Gunda 2018).

Additionally, rehabilitation programs are minimal and often limited to domestic chores such as sewing and Bible study, reflecting a patriarchal approach that limits access to economic skills (University of South Africa 2023). Incarcerated women have little opportunity to participate meaningfully in rehabilitation, with institutional practices reinforcing inequality (Qhogwana and Segalo 2022). Despite the Correctional Services Act 111 of 1998 mandating support for literacy, only 5 percent of women enroll in adult education and 7 percent in mainstream or correspondence courses (Dissel 2008). Programs such as computer literacy or vocational training are lacking, leaving women unprepared for reintegration and more vulnerable to recidivism (Qhogwana and Segalo 2022).

Health and Mental Health Issues

Health and mental health issues are concerns among incarcerated South African women, many of whom enter prison with conditions like tuberculosis, HIV, and untreated psychological disorders. A study in KwaZulu-Natal found that 64 percent of incarcerated women were living with HIV, and 90 percent had at least one psychiatric disorder (Naidoo et al. 2022). Across the region, HIV prevalence in prisons reaches 45 percent, more than double the national average (Naidoo et al. 2021). Additionally, TB rates are up to thirty times higher (Van Hout and Mhlanga-Gunda 2018).

Mental health is an especially pressing concern, given the high rates of trauma, substance use, and psychological distress. One study reported that 71 percent suffered from depression, 47 percent from PTSD, 48 percent from alcohol use disorder, and 32 percent from other substance use disorders. However, only 17 percent had ever received a diagnosis or treatment (Naidoo et al. 2022). Many have endured trauma, including childhood abuse and intimate partner violence, and they often used substances to cope.

Despite these needs, mental health services in correctional facilities remain inadequate. Many prisons, particularly in the Eastern Cape, have no permanent psychological staff, and psychiatric care is lacking. There are also systemic barriers to continuity of care, such as the absence of screening on intake and poor referral systems (Sukeri et al. 2016).

Women and HIV in South African Prisons

In South Africa, HIV prevalence among incarcerated women is much higher than in the general population. Studies show that up to 64 percent of incarcerated women are HIV-positive, which is approximately three times the national average. Many enter prison without access to healthcare or antiretroviral therapy, and overcrowding worsens conditions for managing their condition. Stigma, lack of screening, and shortages of medical staff also prevent treatment. These disparities indicate a need for gender-responsive health services in correctional facilities.

These findings illustrate a cycle. Women enter prison already vulnerable; lack of care worsens their conditions, and untreated mental health and substance use increase the risk of recidivism. Expanding access to prison-based mental health and medical services is a public health issue and is needed for successful rehabilitation, reintegration, and long-term community safety.

Impact on Families and Children

The incarceration of women in South Africa also affects their families, particularly their children. As many imprisoned women were primary caregivers and providers, their absence disrupts emotional and financial stability. A study found that children of mothers imprisoned for killing abusive partners experienced emotional trauma. They lost access to familiar homes, schools, and caregivers, often facing neglect or abuse in new environments (Bhana and Hochfeld 2001). One child said, "I just want to see her," underscoring the pain of separation.

Children under two may stay with mothers in poorly equipped units (Miamingi 2020). In 2010, 129 children lived in such units (Rawoot 2012), but updated data are lacking, reflecting continued accountability issues. Most children live outside prison, often far away, making regular contact nearly impossible (Catholic Parliamentary Liaison Office 2014).

Muriel Mitchell, once incarcerated at Johannesburg Central Prison, gave birth in custody and lived with her daughter in a small cell with minimal resources. Despite efforts to create a safe space, Mitchell acknowledged the limitations: "Tashlyn doesn't know about dogs or cats or birds … All she knows is, 'Wake up, parade, and dankie hek'" (Rawoot 2012).

Female imprisonment worsens household poverty, leaving children at risk of hunger, unstable caregiving, and educational disruption (Masekoameng et al. 2025). Children of imprisoned mothers often have depression, cognitive delays, and academic problems (Magadla-Mateyise and Zenzile 2024). Stigma further isolates these children and discourages relatives from offering support. They are often described as "forgotten victims," suffering in silence due to social judgment and a lack of institutional assistance (Magadla-Mateyise and Zenzile 2024). Limited child-friendly visitation and rigid prison policies make parent–child contact rare and inadequate, particularly after children leave prison units (Sukeri et al. 2016). These structural barriers erode bonds and hinder successful reintegration (Masekoameng et al. 2025).

Policy Reforms and Recommendations

Reforms should focus on building a humane, gender-responsive correctional system. One priority is improving access to medical and mental healthcare, including prenatal and postnatal services and trauma-informed psychological support. Given the high rates of HIV, TB, and psychiatric conditions among incarcerated women, expanding care is essential (Naidoo et al. 2022).

Also important is the development of gender-sensitive rehabilitation and education programs. Vocational and life skills programs must go beyond stereotypical roles (Qhogwana and Segalo 2022). Education must address the large proportion of incarcerated women with limited formal schooling, with only 5 percent enrolled in adult education (Dissel 2008).

Additionally, alternative sentencing should be expanded for non-violent and poverty-related offenses. Community-based sentences can prevent family separation, alleviate overcrowding, and reduce the long-term harms of incarceration, especially for primary caregivers. Courts should apply these options more consistently under the Criminal Procedure Act (Penal Reform International 2019).

Policy should also support family ties during incarceration. Increasing visitation, improving communication, and enabling proximity-based placement can help preserve the parent–child bond. These changes are important for emotional well-being and reintegration (Masekoameng et al. 2025). Barriers like long travel distances and rigid visitation policies weaken familial connections (Sukeri et al. 2016).

Finally, addressing root causes (e.g., poverty, GBV, and lack of education) through coordinated social policy is needed. Most incarcerated women are poor, undereducated, and primary caregivers criminalized for survival-based offenses (George et al. 2022). A gender-equitable justice system must align legal responses with reforms in housing, education, social welfare, and violence prevention to reduce the pipeline into incarceration and promote long-term stability for women and their families.

Nigeria

Historical Context

During British colonial rule in Nigeria, Western-style prisons were introduced, with Broad Street Prison in Lagos incarcerating women as early as 1898 (Nigeria Correctional Service n.d.). Staffed by police and ex-servicemen, they prioritized discipline over rehabilitation. Acts such as vagrancy, pass laws, and moral codes criminalized survival strategies like informal vending, loitering, and sex work (Anaekwe and Oli 2024). These laws targeted poor women, undermining their traditional livelihoods through land dispossession.

After independence in 1960, Nigeria retained many of these punitive legal structures. The Nigerian Civil War (1967–70) deepened poverty and displacement, increasing women's vulnerability as caregivers and heads of households (Akresh et al. 2017). Economic desperation drove many into petty crime or survival-based offenses, still criminalized under outdated laws. Urbanization, unemployment, and weakened family ties have contributed to rising female incarceration (Anaekwe and Oli 2024). Human trafficking has had gendered impacts, with 750,000 to 1 million Nigerians, mostly women, trafficked into forced labor or sexual exploitation (Egbejule 2024).

Adultery is punishable by up to two years in prison under the Northern Penal Code. Additionally, women (especially older women) are still detained over witchcraft accusations, reflecting continuing cultural stigma (Mosadioluwa 2022). Prison conditions remain harsh and overcrowded, with many women lacking access to sanitary products and gender-responsive healthcare (U.S. Department of State 2023). Prolonged pre-trial detention is widespread, disproportionately affecting women charged with nonviolent or poverty-related offenses (Chukwuka 2025). During COVID-19, only one woman received clemency versus over 2,600 men, revealing gender bias (Penal Reform International 2020).

Although the Administration of Criminal Justice Act of 2015 was enacted to improve due process and reduce pre-trial detention, implementation has been inconsistent. Corruption, underfunding, and gender bias continue to weaken justice for women, especially those accused of moral or gender-based crimes (Uzu et al. 2025). Addressing these structural and historical inequities is needed to advance justice and reduce female incarceration in Nigeria.

Female Incarceration Rates and Trends

While women are a small share of the incarcerated, their numbers are rising. As of June 2025, women accounted for 2.4 percent of inmates (approximately 1,964 out of 81,746), with two-thirds still awaiting trial (World Prison Brief 2025). While this proportion is relatively low, the percentage of women admitted to correctional centers rose to nearly 5 percent in 2022, indicating a growing trend (Gazette Nigeria 2023). This increase stems from poverty, unemployment, family instability, and gender inequality, pushing many women, particularly those in rural or low-income urban areas, into survival-based offenses like petty theft, fraud, drug trafficking, and other nonviolent crimes (Anaekwe and Oli 2024). Human trafficking is also a major factor, with Nigerian women and girls frequently coerced into forced labor or sexual exploitation across Africa and beyond (Egbejule 2024).

Women in Nigeria are confined in either one of only three all-female custodial centers or in separate wings within mixed-gender prisons (IAWJ 2024). The most prominent is Kirikiri Women's Prison in Lagos, established in 1963 (Nairaland 2023). Most other facilities lack gender-responsive services like prenatal care or menstrual hygiene support (IAWJ 2024). One trend is the increase in drug-related incarcerations, driven by Nigeria's role as a narcotics transit hub. Many women involved in these offenses are manipulated by partners or traffickers into low-level roles, but they face severe penalties under strict drug laws (Oweibia et al. 2025).

Demographics of Incarcerated Women

Most incarcerated women in Nigeria come from impoverished, marginalized backgrounds and lack formal education or stable employment. As a result, they often commit survival-based crimes (Anaekwe and Oli 2024). Sarki and Lalu (2020) make a direct correlation between a lack of education and incarceration rates, finding that 40 percent of imprisoned women had only informal education, with just 12 percent reaching tertiary education, while Agomoh (2004) reported 33 percent were completely illiterate.

Many are single mothers or primary caregivers. A study of fifty-seven prisons found that 39 percent were single and 65 percent had children at home before their arrest (Agomoh 2004). Lacking a safety net, women often commit nonviolent offenses. As the IAWJ (2024) notes, factors like "unemployment, low wages, divorce, [and] being the breadwinner of the home" are key to understanding female criminality.

Though data are limited, about 87 percent are between eighteen and fifty, the typical working and reproductive age range (Agomoh 2004). However, comprehensive and current demographic data remain scarce, highlighting the need for gender-specific research.

Mental health data on women incarcerated in Nigeria are also limited. Osasona and Koleoso (2015) found high rates of depression (73 percent) and anxiety (78 percent) among the general prison population, but results were not broken down by gender. Similarly, a 2020 study at Makurdi Medium Security Prison found 37 percent of 381 inmates screened positive for depression, though gender-disaggregated data were not provided (Nwefoh et al. 2020). They highlight the mental toll and need for gender-responsive care.

GBV is pervasive in Nigerian society and closely linked to women's criminalization, yet official prison statistics on GBV histories remain unavailable. Substance abuse is another critical factor. A 2022 study found that 58 percent of incarcerated individuals met criteria for substance use disorders, though 98 percent of participants were male, highlighting a gap in understanding women's experiences (Olagunju et al. 2022).

Crimes Leading to Incarceration

The crimes leading to the incarceration of women in Nigeria are mainly non-violent. Theft and petty fraud are the most common offenses, often committed by women from rural or low-income backgrounds to support their families. In 2022, 1,272 women were convicted of theft, reflecting the persistence of economically driven offenses (PM News Nigeria 2024).

Drug-related offenses also represent a large portion of female incarceration. As Nigeria plays a central role in the international drug trade, many women, frequently coerced by criminal networks or intimate partners, serve as couriers or mules. Despite their minor roles, these women face harsh penalties under Nigeria's drug laws. In 2022, the National Drug Law Enforcement Agency (NDLEA) arrested 891 women for drug-related offenses, representing approximately 8 percent of all such arrests (Gazette Nigeria 2023).

Moral and cultural offenses like adultery and witchcraft accusations still disproportionately affect women, especially in rural and conservative areas (Mosadioluwa 2022). One case is that of Amina Lawal, sentenced to death by stoning for adultery in 2002. However, her conviction was overturned in 2003 due to procedural errors and lack of evidence, marking a victory for human rights advocates (Amnesty International 2003). Women make up about 60 percent of those convicted of witchcraft in Nigerian prisons (Eboiyehi 2017). Furthermore, between 2012 and 2023, 555 documented deaths were linked to mob violence related to witchcraft, theft, and blasphemy (Amnesty International 2024).

Although national figures on trafficking-related convictions are not disaggregated by gender, women accounted for about 15 percent of prison admissions for trafficking and related offenses in 2018 (National Bureau of

Witchcraft Accusations

In parts of Nigeria, accusations of witchcraft still result in incarceration, especially for older women. Research indicates that women make up about 60 percent of those convicted of witchcraft in Nigerian prisons. Furthermore, mob violence related to witchcraft accusations has led to hundreds of deaths over the past ten years. These cases indicate that cultural beliefs and weak legal safeguards still criminalize women for noncriminal behaviors. In many communities, traditional healers, widows, and women living alone are particularly vulnerable to such accusations, which are often used to justify social exclusion, property seizure, or violence. Despite advocacy from human rights groups, enforcement of anti-witchcraft laws remains inconsistent, and fear of supernatural harm continues to shape local justice practices.

Statistics 2019). They highlight how women are often both victims and coerced participants.

In addition, some women are criminalized for actions taken in self-defense against domestic violence. Nigeria's legal system offers limited protections for survivors, and enforcement remains inconsistent. The U.S. Department of State (2023) reported that police often fail to intervene in domestic abuse cases and may even blame the victims.

Recent high-profile cases also highlight the criminalization of women's expression. In 2023, Chioma Okoli was detained for three days after posting a negative review of a tomato purée online. Charged under Nigeria's Cybercrime Act, which criminalizes online speech deemed false, offensive, or reputationally harmful, she was forced to sign a confession under duress and was later threatened with rearrest, despite a court restraining order (Salako 2024).

Contributing Laws and Policies

Nigeria's legal and policy frameworks often do not match economic and social realities, leading women to commit non-violent offenses. Harsh drug laws, especially under the NDLEA Act, impose mandatory minimum sentences without considering gendered vulnerabilities, coercion, or the roles women play in drug trafficking. Women coerced into serving as couriers face the same severe penalties as high-level traffickers, including life imprisonment for trafficking and fifteen to twenty-five years for possession, with no option for fines (Nigeria n.d.).

Although the Administration of Criminal Justice Act (2015) and Nigeria Correctional Service Act (2019) authorize non-custodial alternatives such as probation and community service, these are rarely implemented due to limited capacity and judicial apathy (Izevbuwa et al. 2023). Courts often default to imprisonment, incarcerating women for poverty-related offenses instead of using alternatives.

In Nigeria's Sharia-governed northern states, moral and gendered offenses further establish legal inequality. Adultery (zina), fornication, and violations of dress codes are punishable under the Northern Penal Code by up to two years in prison and/or a fine, disproportionately affecting women. Since 1999, twelve northern states have implemented **Sharia-based hudud punishments**, such as flogging or stoning, for these offenses. Courts sometimes bypass Qur'anic evidentiary standards (which require four adult male eyewitnesses to prove zina), instead relying on confessions. In cases of rape, lack of evidence may result in victims being charged with zina themselves (Rabi'u 2016).

At the federal level, the **Violence Against Persons (Prohibition) Act of 2015** criminalizes physical, sexual, emotional, and economic abuse, offering protective measures such as restraining orders and access to shelters (Federal Republic of Nigeria 2015). Yet, enforcement remains weak. Police often fail to intervene in domestic violence cases, and survivors face victim-blaming and bureaucratic indifference (U.S. Department of State 2023). While legally available, restraining orders are rarely enforced. Some women are criminalized for self-defense, exposing enforcement gaps.

Conditions in Women's Prisons

Conditions in women's prisons in Nigeria are often harsh and inadequate, with overcrowding, poor infrastructure, and systemic neglect. Although prisons were originally built to accommodate about 50,000 inmates, they now hold over 81,000, with nearly 70 percent awaiting trial (World Prison Brief 2025). Most incarcerated women are confined in facilities not designed with their needs in mind, resulting in overcrowded cells, a lack of privacy, and limited access to gender-responsive services (IAWJ 2024). Conditions include poor ventilation, insufficient sanitation, and a lack of necessities like clean water and soap, posing health risks (Chukwuka 2025). They were worsened during COVID-19 due to overcrowding and limited hygiene supplies (Penal Reform International 2020).

Access to healthcare is also limited. The U.S. Department of State (2023) reports that pregnant inmates often lack adequate prenatal or postnatal care, and gynecological services are scarce. Chronic conditions and untreated injuries frequently go unaddressed due to shortages of medical staff and supplies. Mental health and trauma are widespread, yet appropriate care is nearly nonexistent (Osasona and Koleoso 2015).

Opportunities for education and rehabilitation are also lacking. Sarki and Lalu (2020) found that 40 percent of female inmates had only informal education. Yet few programs exist to address these deficits. Rehabilitation initiatives often prioritize men, leaving women without access to vocational training or skill-building resources (Agomoh 2004). The IAWJ (2024) confirms that most women leave prison without improved prospects, increasing the risk of recidivism.

Cases of abuse further highlight the dangers incarcerated women face. At Maiduguri Maximum Security Prison and Giwa Barracks in Borno State, Amnesty International (2019) documented widespread sexual violence against women and girls by prison officials and inmates. Detainees were forced to trade sex for food and essentials, and some were raped repeatedly in overcrowded, unsanitary conditions. Despite public outcry, authorities took little action to hold perpetrators accountable.

Similar patterns persist elsewhere. Chukwuka (2025) reports that women in Nigerian prisons often experience harassment, sexual coercion, and physical intimidation by male staff. Without independent oversight or safeguards, abuse often goes unchecked. Beyond prisons, a recent investigation revealed that women who fled Boko Haram were later detained by the Nigerian military, under suspicion of association with the group, where they were beaten, sexually assaulted, and denied food and medical care. Some returned to Boko Haram-controlled areas to escape the violence in detention (Associated Press 2024).

Health and Mental Health Issues

Health and mental health issues are concerns for women incarcerated in Nigeria. Many women enter custody with untreated conditions, including malnutrition, tuberculosis, HIV, and complications from previous pregnancies. A study conducted in Osun State prisons found that HIV prevalence among incarcerated women ranged from 1 percent to nearly 17 percent, and access to preventive measures like condoms was limited to less than 6 percent of the population, highlighting gaps in reproductive and infectious disease care (Olugbenga-Bello et al. 2013).

Pregnant women in Nigerian prisons face heightened risks. A study of two correctional facilities in Osun State found issues with reproductive healthcare, including limited access to antenatal care, maternal nutrition, and gynecological services (Olugbenga-Bello et al. 2013). These deficiencies place mothers and infants at risk of complications. The U.S. Department of State (2023) similarly reports that most facilities lack resources to support prenatal and postnatal care, with chronic underfunding limiting even the most basic maternal health services.

Mental health is another area of concern. Many incarcerated women have experienced trauma before their imprisonment, including domestic violence, sexual assault, and extreme poverty. A study by Osasona and Koleoso (2015) at Benin City prison found that 85 percent of inmates screened positive for at least one mental health condition. These figures were not disaggregated by gender, but they highlight the psychological toll of imprisonment in overcrowded and under-resourced settings.

The prison environment itself worsens physical and mental health challenges. The National Care and Referral Model highlights that most prisons fail to conduct proper intake screenings for HIV, TB, pregnancy, or trauma (National Tuberculosis and Leprosy Control Programme 2021). Additionally, care upon release is limited, leaving women vulnerable to reentry without support. These gaps compromise health outcomes and reduce the chances of successful reintegration.

Impact on Families and Children

The incarceration of women in Nigeria has effects on their families, particularly their children. As primary caregivers, many women leave behind children who face disruptions in care and emotional instability. They are often placed with extended family or in orphanages (Chukwuka 2025). Children usually experience anxiety, abandonment, and stigma, especially in cases where mothers are imprisoned for moral or survival-based offenses (Mosadioluwa 2022).

Economically, the loss of a mother's income, even from informal work, can worsen poverty. Older children may be forced to leave school or take on caregiving roles, especially daughters, further limiting their life chances (Anaekwe and Oli 2024). For incarcerated women, separation from children causes deep emotional distress. High rates of depression and anxiety among female inmates are often linked to this separation, which is worsened by limited visitation opportunities and bureaucratic barriers (Chukwuka 2025).

While Nigerian law allows infants to remain with their mothers in prison up to eighteen months (Federal Republic of Nigeria 2019), few facilities have functioning nurseries (crèches). Most prisons lack dedicated mother–child spaces, forcing mothers to care for infants in unsanitary conditions (IAWJ 2024). A study in Osun State highlighted severe gaps in maternal and infant healthcare (Olugbenga-Bello et al. 2013), and infants often lack access to nutrition, immunizations, and legal recognition (U.S. Department of State 2023).

Conditions are especially dire in conflict zones. At Giwa Barracks and Maiduguri Prison in Borno State, women and children were held in overcrowded, unsanitary cells and subjected to violence, including sexual abuse (Amnesty International 2019). Despite international calls to expand gender-sensitive alternatives such as community-based sentencing for mothers, these options remain underutilized in Nigeria (Izevbuwa et al. 2023).

Policy Reforms and Recommendations

Addressing the incarceration of women in Nigeria requires reforms that reflect the gendered pathways into crime and the disproportionate harms women face in custody. Many women are imprisoned for non-violent, survival-based offenses (Anaekwe and Oli 2024). Expanding non-custodial alternatives like probation, community service, and diversion is essential, especially for low-level offenders. Though authorized under the Administration of Criminal Justice Act and the Nigerian Correctional Service Act, these alternatives are rarely applied due to limited institutional capacity and judicial unwillingness (Izevbuwa et al. 2023).

Laws criminalizing moral offenses like adultery, sex work, or witchcraft must be reviewed and repealed. Such laws disproportionately affect women and reflect outdated colonial and religious norms (Mosadioluwa 2022). Survivors of GBV should be protected from criminalization, especially when acting in self-defense, and legal protections like the Violence Against Persons (Prohibition) Act must be more effectively enforced (U.S. Department of State 2023).

Prison conditions also need reform. Most facilities are overcrowded, lack sanitary provisions, and do not offer gender-responsive healthcare (Chukwuka 2025). Improving access to reproductive, maternal, and mental health services is critical, especially for pregnant women and those with trauma histories (Osasona and Koleoso 2015). Functional mother–child units should be established where infants can safely remain with their mothers up to eighteen months, as allowed by law (Federal Republic of Nigeria 2019).

Finally, data collection must be improved to support evidence-based policy. Disaggregated data on women's health, sentencing, and family status are needed to ensure reforms are targeted and sustainable.

Kenya

Historical Context

The incarceration of women in Kenya has roots in its colonial past. Under British rule (1895–1963), the prison system served as a tool of social control, especially during the Mau Mau uprising of the 1950s. Over 8,000 women were detained under emergency powers. Many were held in Kamiti and Gitamayu detention camps, where they faced abuse, neglect, and unsanitary conditions. Notable examples include Mekatilili wa Menza, exiled in 1913 for anti-colonial activism, and Wambui Otieno, a Mau Mau supporter reportedly raped while in custody (Cambridge University 2018).

Colonial prison infrastructure was built for men, failing to provide adequate healthcare, sanitation, or accommodations for mothers. After independence in 1963, Kenya retained much of this punitive legal framework. Although the political context changed, women continued to be incarcerated for nonviolent offenses (Chepkemoi 2011). From 2009 to 2016, sentenced women rose from 2,081 to 3,762 (81 percent) (Ondeng et al. 2021), with a 25 percent increase in convictions between 2017 and 2018 alone (Njongoro 2024). Today, women comprise about 4.7 percent of Kenya's prison population, a relatively high share regionally (World Prison Brief 2024a). Female incarceration continues to be driven by poverty, unemployment, limited education, and gender inequality.

Recently, there has been growing recognition of the need for gender-sensitive reforms. Some women's prisons now offer vocational programs (often delivered through non-governmental organizations [NGOs]) in tailoring, baking, farming, and hairdressing (Cyrus R. Vance Center for International Justice 2019). Yet, major issues persist. Overcrowding, poor infrastructure, and inadequate maternal care continue to harm incarcerated women. Mental health services are minimal, and structured reintegration programs are rare. As a result, Kenya faces a high female recidivism rate, estimated at nearly 50 percent (Onyango et al. 2021), while stigma and limited job prospects remain barriers to reentry.

Kenya's penal system still reflects many colonial legacies. Though reforms acknowledge women's needs, deeper structural change is required for a rehabilitative, equitable justice model.

Female Incarceration Rates and Trends

Female incarceration in Kenya remains lower than that of men but has steadily increased amid ongoing socioeconomic and legal challenges. As of 2023, women constitute about 4.7 percent of the prison population (roughly 2,820 of 60,000 incarcerated individuals), with nearly 43 percent detained while awaiting trial (World Prison Brief 2024a).

Women in Kenya are incarcerated in both standalone women's prisons and segregated wings within mixed-gender facilities. The largest is Lang'ata Women's Maximum Security Prison near Nairobi, which holds convicted and remand prisoners. It includes gender-responsive services like vocational training, counseling, and a nursery for children up to age four (Clarke and Topete 2023). Additional facilities include Thika, Kilifi, Meru, Kitui, Nyeri, and Eldoret Women's Prisons (IEBC 2022). All are managed by the Kenya Prisons Service under the Ministry of Interior (World Prison Brief 2024a).

Most incarcerated women are serving time for non-violent, poverty-related offenses and minor drug crimes, often driven by economic necessity and lack of support systems (Jeffries et al. 2019). Drug-related incarcerations are rising as Kenya becomes a key trafficking route in East Africa (UNODC 2022).

In rural areas, women are frequently jailed for unpaid fines or debts. The Penal Code permits imprisonment for up to twelve months for failure to pay court-ordered fines, effectively criminalizing poverty (Kenya Law 2025). Additionally, prosecutions under Kenya's **Witchcraft Act** disproportionately target women, especially elderly or marginalized individuals, leading to imprisonment or even extrajudicial violence and displacement (Owusu 2023).

Criminalizing Poverty

Failure to pay court fines or debts can result in up to one year of imprisonment under Kenya's Penal Code. This practice criminalizes poverty, disproportionately impacting women in rural and low-income areas. Many are jailed for minor infractions like unpaid fines, brewing alcohol, or petty theft, indicating how inequalities influence female incarceration. For example, a 94-year-old woman in Kakamega was imprisoned for failing to pay a small fine before being released after an NGO intervened. Reports from Penal Reform International also describe women jailed for selling home-brewed alcohol or being unable to pay fines as low as a few US dollars.

Though gender-sensitive reforms are emerging, such as non-custodial sentencing, basic healthcare, and vocational training (UNODC 2022), challenges remain. Overcrowding, outdated infrastructure, and limited reintegration services continue to affect incarcerated women across Kenya.

Demographics of Incarcerated Women

The demographics of incarcerated women in Kenya reflect poverty, limited education, and gender-based inequality. A study of forty-nine women found most came from poor areas and were driven into crime by hardship, caregiving duties, and few employment options (Jeffries et al. 2019). Many are single mothers or primary caregivers, with 81 percent reporting at least one child (Clarke and Topete 2023).

Low educational attainment is common among incarcerated individuals. A study of people housed at Kamiti and Lang'ata prisons, though not disaggregated by gender, found that 16 percent had no formal education and 26 percent had completed only primary school. Notably, 85 percent of individuals with only basic education expected to reoffend, compared to just 1 percent of those with university-level education (Nyabuto et al. 2023).

Data show incarceration disproportionately affects women in their caregiving years. A 2020 study found that just 2 percent of incarcerated women were under eighteen, while 47 percent were aged eighteen to twenty-five, and 46 percent were twenty-six to fifty. Only 5 percent were over fifty (Kiptoo and Muthee 2020). Younger women from impoverished backgrounds are especially vulnerable to exploitation as drug couriers or involvement in informal criminal activity (Jeffries et al. 2019).

Additionally, substance use is widespread. A study at Eldoret Prison of 395 incarcerated people, 124 of whom were women, found that 66 percent of incarcerated individuals reported lifetime substance use. Sixty-five percent reported alcohol use, and 21 percent reported cannabis use, with other drugs like heroin also noted minimally (Kinyanjui and Atwoli 2013).

Mental health challenges are also prevalent. A 2020 study using the MINI diagnostic tool found that 65 percent of incarcerated women met the criteria for at least one mental disorder, including depression, PTSD, suicidality, and anxiety. Women also reported higher levels of childhood and adult trauma than men, particularly physical and sexual abuse (Museve et al. 2020).

Crimes Leading to Incarceration

The crimes leading to the incarceration of women in Kenya are predominantly non-violent. Petty theft is one of the most common offenses, often committed by women struggling to support their families. While national-level statistics are limited, property crimes and "crimes of poverty" are the most frequent offenses among incarcerated women across East Africa, a pattern mirrored in Kenya (UNODC 2022). A government economic survey similarly found a 25 percent rise in convicted women offenders between 2017 and 2018, primarily linked to poverty-related offenses (Njongoro 2024).

An estimated 70 percent of incarcerated women in Kenya are serving sentences for alcohol- and drug-related offenses. However, gender-disaggregated data remain scarce, a gap acknowledged by the Kenya National Bureau of Statistics (Chepkonga 2020). Women often play minor or coerced roles in the drug trade but face disproportionately harsh penalties under Kenya's strict drug laws. In 2025, one woman received a fifty-year prison sentence for trafficking heroin worth KSh 3 million (approximately 23,000 USD), prompting public debate over extreme sentencing for low-level female couriers (Oduor 2025).

Incarceration for unpaid fines and minor debts is another common pathway into prison. While exact figures specific to Kenya are lacking, regional studies show that such financial penalties frequently criminalize poverty and disproportionately impact vulnerable women (Cyrus R. Vance Center for International Justice 2019).

Cultural and moral offenses also contribute to female incarceration, especially in rural areas where patriarchal norms are strong. Women may be imprisoned for accusations of witchcraft, adultery, or violations of customary moral codes. These prosecutions typically target older, economically marginalized women and reflect gender biases (Owusu 2023). In one high-profile case, four men were convicted in 2023 for lynching two elderly women in Kisii County accused of witchcraft (Nyaberi 2024).

Contributing Laws and Policies

Kenyan laws and policies contribute to women's incarceration by emphasizing punishment over rehabilitation and overlooking the economic and social challenges many women face. Non-violent offenses are often prosecuted under the Penal Code, despite judicial discretion allowing for non-custodial alternatives like probation, community service, or fines (Kenya 2016). Although gender-responsive programs like the ExTRA (Ex-Offender Reintegration and Transitional Assistance) project, which help women transition back into the community after prison, have been piloted, their application remains low. Barriers like childcare responsibilities and inflexible work schedules often prevent compliance with community sanctions, leading many women to serve custodial sentences instead (Penal Reform International and Kenya Probation and Aftercare Service 2016).

Drug-related offenses also contribute to female incarceration. Kenya's Narcotic Drugs and Psychotropic Substances (Control) Act imposes harsh penalties, including life imprisonment, for trafficking, without distinguishing between high-level traffickers and low-level participants. As Chepkonga (2020) notes, many women are first-time offenders coerced into courier roles by partners or criminal networks but still receive disproportionately severe sentences.

The **Alcoholic Drinks Control Act of 2010** (Liquor Act) was intended to regulate alcohol production and consumption. However, it has disproportionately affected women, particularly those in the informal economy. Women who brew or sell traditional alcohol to support their families face barriers like licensing fees, strict premises requirements, and the criminalization of unlicensed sale. Many are pushed into illicit markets, increasing their risk of arrest. Liquor Act violations have accounted for 32 percent of women's convictions (Nyamichaba 2016).

Kenya's Protection Against Domestic Violence Act (2015) provides protective measures like court orders but lacks clear provisions for self-defense in cases of prolonged abuse. Although it prohibits emotional and economic abuse, it does not address psychological factors such as Battered Woman Syndrome, leaving survivors who retaliate against abusers vulnerable to prosecution under criminal laws (Magato 2023). Courts rarely admit expert testimony to contextualize trauma, making self-defense claims difficult. During the COVID-19 pandemic, these issues were worsened. Law enforcement often ignored women seeking help, and in some cases, survivors were arrested instead of being protected (Human Rights Watch 2021).

Conditions in Women's Prisons

Conditions in women's prisons in Kenya remain harsh, marked by overcrowding, inadequate bedding, poor sanitation, and limited access to clean water and sanitary products. Although efforts have been made to provide beds for all women and accompanying children, distribution is inconsistent, and oversight remains weak. These cramped conditions contribute to health problems, especially respiratory infections, undernutrition, and psychological stress, particularly among mothers with young children (CICMN 2023).

Overcrowding is worsened by high rates of pre-trial detention, which strain limited infrastructure (Kenya State Department for Correctional Services 2024). At Kamiti Maximum Security Prison, structural deficiencies in cell design and lack of open space have been linked to increased psychological distress (Kasau et al. 2025). Despite recent infrastructure expansion, prison conditions fall short of international standards (CICMN 2023).

Healthcare in these facilities is limited. Many women arrive with untreated injuries, malnutrition, or infectious diseases such as tuberculosis and HIV. Recent research reports TB and HIV coinfection rates of 10 percent and 19 percent among incarcerated individuals, though the study did not disaggregate by gender, limiting insight into women's specific health needs (Hamza et al. 2024). Mental healthcare is also lacking. At Lang'ata Women's Prison, 43 percent of participants showed severe depressive symptoms, yet psychological services remain largely unavailable (Wainaina and Kuria 2019). Many women, often survivors of domestic or sexual violence, are left to manage trauma and mental illness in isolation.

Rehabilitation and vocational training programs are similarly limited. While the Kenya Prisons Service offers training in carpentry, tailoring, masonry, and mechanics, these programs are often outdated and gender-insensitive. Only 57 percent participate in vocational training and 14 percent in education (Mburu and Gathitu 2022). However, the study does not disaggregate by gender, limiting its relevance to women's experiences.

Incarcerated women also face safety risks. They are vulnerable to sexual abuse by prison guards in both women's and mixed-gender facilities, due to the lack of female staff, gender-sensitive protocols, and effective complaint mechanisms (Cyrus R. Vance Center for International Justice 2019). The U.S. Department of State (2024) continues to document cases of domestic violence, sexual assault, and psychological abuse committed by law enforcement and correctional officers, showing that custodial mistreatment remains an issue in Kenya's prison system.

Health and Mental Health Issues

Health and mental health issues are concerns for incarcerated women in Kenya, where prison conditions and limited access to healthcare services worsen existing vulnerabilities. Facilities often lack sufficient personnel, essential medications, and basic supplies, resulting in treatment delays or denial of care. For HIV-positive individuals, access to antiretroviral therapy is often disrupted by food insecurity; many women report experiencing dizziness and adverse effects when taking medication without food (Bukenya et al. 2019). These challenges reflect broader issues, as Kenya faces a nationwide healthcare workforce shortage, with only about one doctor per 5,000 people (Mwaura 2024).

Mental health needs are also often unmet. A survey of incarcerated women revealed high rates of moderate to severe depression and suicidal ideation (Wainaina and Kuria 2019). Another study found that nearly two-thirds met the criteria for at least one mental disorder (Museve et al. 2020). Many women have experienced physical or sexual abuse before incarceration, and prison conditions often worsen these traumas. However, there are few trained professionals, no routine screening, and no formal suicide prevention programs for these women. Mathari National Teaching and Referral Hospital in Nairobi remains Kenya's only public forensic psychiatric facility, making access to care unattainable for most incarcerated women (Kenya National Commission on Human Rights 2023).

Without adequate healthcare and mental health support, incarcerated women remain vulnerable to deteriorating physical and psychological health. These unmet needs harm them during incarceration and prevent successful reintegration into the community.

Impact on Families and Children

The incarceration of women in Kenya disrupts family life, posing emotional, economic, and social risks to children. Women often serve as primary caregivers, and their imprisonment deprives children, especially those under five, of care and stability (Mutunga 2019). This separation can cause emotional distress, confusion, and abandonment.

Psychological effects are particularly severe when young children live in prison with their mothers. At Lang'ata Women's Prison, children endure overcrowded, unsanitary conditions with limited food, inadequate bedding, and poor sanitation, leading to developmental delays and emotional trauma (CICMN 2023). One mother recalled her son's confusion, relating how he asked if all children in the nursery were his siblings, showing the emotional toll of institutional settings (CICMN 2023). At least 250 children live within the Kenyan prison system (Wangira 2021).

Economically, maternal incarceration worsens family poverty. Their absence strains families' ability to afford food, education, and healthcare. It sometimes even forces children to drop out of school or enter child labor, perpetuating cycles of disadvantage (Mutunga 2019). Institutional support is limited. Families rely heavily on NGOs and volunteers for essentials like diapers and bedding, especially for children in prison nurseries. As of 2023, only ten of Kenya's forty-three women's facilities offered nursery programs, and most were under-resourced (CICMN 2023).

Limited visitation rights and poor prison conditions further strain mother–child bonds. Although the Kenya Prisons Service allows children under four to stay with incarcerated mothers, the daily government allocation of Kshs 410 (about 3.17 USD) per child is insufficient to cover basics like clothing, food, and bedding (Wangira 2021). This policy does not guarantee adequate care, leaving children vulnerable to neglect and developmental harm.

Policy Reforms and Recommendations

Kenya's female incarceration system shows colonial legacies and ongoing socioeconomic inequalities that disproportionately affect women, especially single mothers from marginalized communities (Njongoro 2024). Policy reforms are needed to move toward a rehabilitative and equitable justice model.

The justice system must improve non-custodial sentencing alternatives for non-violent, poverty-related offenses and minor drug crimes (UNODC 2022). Greater judicial discretion to impose probation, community service, or fines can reduce overcrowding and lessen the harm of maternal incarceration on families (Ondeng et al. 2021).

Additionally, there is a need for gender-responsive prison infrastructure and programming. Current facilities inadequately address women's health, safety, and caregiving needs, contributing to poor maternal and child health outcomes (CICMN 2023). Expanding nursery programs, improving sanitary conditions, and providing adequate nutrition and healthcare, including prenatal and mental health services, are essential steps (Hamza et al. 2024).

Moreover, reintegration support must be enhanced through vocational training, education, and counseling to reduce Kenya's high female recidivism rate (Mburu and Gathitu 2022). Programs should address trauma and substance use disorders prevalent among incarcerated women (Museve et al. 2020) and prepare women for sustainable employment upon release.

Finally, reforms must tackle the socio-legal environment by revising punitive laws such as the Alcoholic Drinks Control Act that disproportionately criminalize marginalized women (Owusu 2023). Strengthening protections for survivors of domestic violence, including clear self-defense provisions, will further promote justice and gender equality (Magato 2023). Together, these reforms will support a more just, humane, and effective criminal justice system for women in Kenya, promoting rehabilitation and protecting their families.

Conclusion

The incarceration of women in South Africa, Nigeria, and Kenya indicates patterns rooted in colonial legacies, poverty, and gender-based inequality. In these countries, women make up a small proportion of the total prison population, ranging from 2.4 percent in Nigeria to 4.7 percent in Kenya.

Most of these women are held for non-violent, poverty-related offenses, often committed out of economic desperation or under coercion. Common crimes include petty theft, drug trafficking, and informal alcohol production. Despite their often-minor roles, women in all three countries face disproportionately harsh penalties due to rigid sentencing laws, limited judicial discretion, and underuse of non-custodial alternatives.

While South Africa has made more visible strides toward gender-responsive reform aligned with the Bangkok Rules and improved legal protections, implementation gaps remain. Kenya has also begun piloting vocational programs and maternal care initiatives, but overcrowding, outdated infrastructure, and harsh drug laws continue to undermine progress. Nigeria has been slower to implement reforms, and the persistence of laws criminalizing moral offenses like adultery and witchcraft disproportionately targets women, especially in the north.

Conditions in women's prisons across these nations are harsh. They experience overcrowding, poor sanitation, limited healthcare, and a lack of mental health services. Pregnant women and mothers are especially vulnerable, often receiving inadequate prenatal care or being separated from their children. Reintegration support is also minimal, increasing the risk of recidivism.

Despite some differences, the shared themes are similar. Structural inequality, weak legal protections, and punitive criminal justice systems contribute to the disproportionate harm faced by incarcerated women. Each country must prioritize gender-sensitive sentencing, trauma-informed care, and social support to reduce female incarceration and help with rehabilitation.

References

Agomoh, Uju. 2004. "Assessment and Treatment of Female Prisoners in Africa." *UNAFEI Resource Material Series* No. 94. https://www.unafei.or.jp/publications/pdf/RS_No94/No94_VE_Agomoh1.pdf.

Akresh, Richard, Sonia R. Bhalotra, Marinella Leone, and Una O. Osili. 2017. "First and Second Generation Impacts of the Biafran War." IZA Discussion Paper 10938. Bonn: Institute of Labor Economics (IZA). https://docs.iza.org/dp10938.pdf.

Amnesty International. 2024. *Instantly Killed! How Law Enforcement Failures Exacerbate Nigeria's Wave of Mob Violence.* London: Amnesty International. https://www.amnesty.org/en/wp-content/uploads/2024/10/AFR4484252024ENGLISH.pdf.

Amnesty International. 2019. *Nigeria: Children and Women Face Sexual Violence in Borno Prisons.* April 30, 2019. https://www.amnesty.org/en/latest/press-release/2019/04/nigeria-children-and-women-face-sexual-violence-in-borno-prisons.

Amnesty International. 2003. "Nigeria: Amina Lawal's Death Sentence Quashed—but Questions Remain About Discriminatory Legislation." Amnesty International Press Release. https://www.amnesty.org/en/documents/afr44/032/2003/en/.

Anaekwe, Henry Ebuka, and Nneka Perpetua Oli. 2024. "Socio-Economic Factors Influencing Female Criminality in Nigeria." *UNIZIK Journal of Gender Research* 3: 24–37.

Artz, Lillian, Veronica Filippeschi, and Nokwanda Nzimande. 2023. "Women in Prison Deserve Better Treatment." *South African Human Rights Commission*. February 16, 2023. https://www.sahrc.org.za/index.php/sahrc-media/news-2/item/3447-women-in-prison-deserve-better-treatment.

Associated Press. 2025. "A South African Woman Is Sentenced to Life in Prison for Selling Her Young Daughter." *Yahoo News*. May 29. https://www.yahoo.com/news/south-african-woman-sentenced-life-114353746.html.

Associated Press. 2024. "Nigerian Women Who Escaped Boko Haram Face Sexual Abuse in Military Detention." *Associated Press*. June 18, 2024. https://apnews.com/article/68afedcc76e270543875267d2d0b41a2.

Bhana, Kailash, and Tessa Hochfeld. 2001. *Now We Have Nothing: Exploring the Impact of Maternal Imprisonment on Children Whose Mothers Killed an Abusive Partner.* Johannesburg: Centre for the Study of Violence and Reconciliation. https://www.csvr.org.za/docs/gender/nowhavenothing.pdf.

Bukenya, Danstan, Barbara N. Mayanja, Stella Nakamanya, Rogers Muhumuza, and Janet Seeley. 2019. "What Causes Non-Adherence Among Some Individuals on Long-Term Antiretroviral Therapy? Experiences of Individuals with Poor Viral Suppression in Uganda." *AIDS Research and Therapy* 16 (1): 2.

Cambridge University. 2018. "How the British Treated 'Hardcore' Mau Mau Women." *University of Cambridge Research News*. May 16, 2018. https://www.cam.ac.uk/research/news/how-the-british-treated-hardcore-mau-mau-women.

Catholic Parliamentary Liaison Office. 2014. *Mothers and Babies in Incarceration: A Policy Brief*. May 2014. Cape Town: Catholic Parliamentary Liaison Office. https://www.cplo.org.za/wp-content/uploads/2014/02/BP-352-Mothers-and-Babies-in-Incarceration-May-2014.pdf.

CBS News. 2024. "'Rogue' Policewoman Accused of Murdering 6 People for Insurance Payouts in South Africa." October 11, 2024. https://www.cbsnews.com/news/policewoman-rachel-kutumela-accused-murders-south-africa/.

Chepkemoi, Florence. 2011. *The Challenges Faced by Inmates at Langata Women Prison, Nairobi County*. Nairobi: University of Nairobi. https://erepository.uonbi.ac.ke/handle/11295/4401.

Chepkonga, Mary C. K. 2020. "Women, Drug Policy and the Kenyan Prison System." In *The Impact of Global Drug Policy on Women: Shifting the Needle*, edited by Julia Buxton, Giavana Margo, and Lona Burger, 123–30. Bingley: Emerald Publishing.

Chukwuka, Victory. 2025. "How Prison Disproportionately Affects Women in Nigeria." *Medium*. March 21, 2025. https://medium.com/@HopeBehindBarsAfrica/how-prison-disproportionately-affects-women-in-nigeria-eb1494204b08.

CICMN (Citizenship, Inclusion, and Civic Mobilization Network). 2023. *Kenya Report: Women in Detention*. October 30, 2023. https://cicmn.org/wp-content/uploads/2023/11/CICs-Kenya-Report-10-30-23-FINAL.pdf.

Clarke, Jane, and Socorro Topete. 2023. *Kenya Prison Nursery Country Report*. CICMN. https://cicmn.org/wp-content/uploads/2023/11/CICs-Kenya-Report-10-30-23-FINAL.pdf.

Comins, Lyse. 2023. "The Shifting Landscape of South Africa's Informal Settlements." *Mail & Guardian*. October 30, 2023. https://mg.co.za/news/2023-10-30-the-shifting-landscape-of-south-africas-informal-settlements/.

Commission for Gender Equality. 2024. *Correctional Services Report*. https://cge.org.za/wp-content/uploads/2025/01/Correctional-Services-Report.pdf.

Constitution Hill. 2024. *Women's Jail*. https://www.constitutionhill.org.za/sites/site-womens-jail.

Constitutional Law of South Africa. 2019. "Chapter 49 (Sentencing): Criminal Procedure Act 51 of 1977." *Constitutional Law of South Africa*. December 2019. https://constitutionallawofsouthafrica.co.za/wp-content/uploads/2019/12/Chapter-49-for-Website.pdf.

Cyrus R. Vance Center for International Justice. 2019. *Women in Prison: Africa Regional Initiative*. https://www.vancecenter.org/wp-content/uploads/2019/10/WIP_ARI_Report-Final-10-15-2019-compressed.pdf.

Dissel, Amanda. 2008. *Rehabilitation and Reintegration in African Prisons*. Johannesburg: Centre for the Study of Violence and Reconciliation. https://www.csvr.org.za/wp-content/uploads/2008/04/Rehabilitation_and_reintegration_in_Afri.pdf.

Eboiyehi, Friday A. 2017. "Convicted Without Evidence: Elderly Women and Witchcraft Accusations in Contemporary Nigeria." *Journal of International Women's Studies* 18 (4): 247–65.

Egbejule, Eromo. 2024. "I Miss Home: 13-Year-Old Nigerian Girls Trapped and Exploited in Ivory Coast Sex Industry." *The Guardian*. August 26, 2024. https://www.theguardian.com/global-development/article/2024/aug/26/i-miss-home-13-year-old-nigerian-girls-trapped-and-exploited-ivory-coast-sex-industry.

Fair, Helen, and Roy Walmsley. 2023. *World Female Imprisonment List: Women and Girls in Penal Institutions, Including Pre-Trial Detainees/Remand Prisoners. Fifth Edition*. London: Institute for Crime & Justice Policy Research. https://www.prisonstudies.org/sites/default/files/resources/downloads/world_female_imprisonment_list_5th_edition.pdf.

Federal Republic of Nigeria. 2019. *Nigerian Correctional Service Act*. Abuja: Federal Ministry of Interior. Accessed July 8, 2025. https://www.corrections.gov.ng/storage/report/NCoS_act_2019.pdf.

Federal Republic of Nigeria. 2015. *Violence Against Persons (Prohibition) Act, 2015*. Abuja: Federal Ministry of Justice. https://fida.org.ng/wp-content/uploads/2020/09/Violence-Against-Persons-Prohibition-Act-2015-1.pdf.

Gazette Nigeria. 2023. "Female Inmates in Correctional Centres Rose by 4.82% in 2022—NBS." *Peoples Gazette*. August 23, 2023. https://gazettengr.com/female-inmates-in-correctional-centres-rose-by-4-82-in-2022-nbs.

George, Krinesha, Ephraim K. Sibanyoni, and Jacob T. Mofokeng. 2022. "Fetching Water with a Leaking Container: Female Offenders' Rehabilitation Programme Limitation, South Africa." *International Journal of Research in Business and Social Science* 11 (2): 433–46.

Gore, Rebecca. 2024. "Women Who Kill Their Abusers in South Africa." *Michigan Journal of Gender & Law*, article 1322. https://repository.law.umich.edu/cgi/viewcontent.cgi?article=1322&context=mjgl.

Hamza, Muhammad, Zil-E-Huma Jalil, Abid Jan Abdul Sattar, Hamnah Sohail, and Malik Olatunde Oduoye. 2024. "Comments on: Prevalence and Risk Factors for Tuberculosis and HIV Coinfections in Kenyan Prison Inmates." *Tropical Medicine and Health* 52 (1): 78.

Human Rights Watch. 2021. "I Had Nowhere to Go: Violence Against Women and Girls During the Covid-19 Pandemic in Kenya." September 21. https://www.hrw.org/report/2021/09/21/i-had-nowhere-go/violence-against-women-and-girls-during-covid-19-pandemic-kenya.

IAWJ (International Association of Women Judges). 2024. *Nigeria Association of Women Judges: Country Report for IDWJ 2024*. https://www.iawj.org/idwj-2024-nigeria-association-of-women-judges.

IEBC (Independent Electoral and Boundaries Commission). 2022. *Registered Voters per Prison for the 2022 General Election*. Nairobi: IEBC. https://www.iebc.or.ke/docs/rov_per_prison.pdf.

Izevbuwa, Osaretin George, Rita Abhavan Ngwoke, and Ibiene P. Mbano. 2023. "An Examination of the Statutory and Institutional Frameworks for Implementing Non-Custodial Measures in Nigeria's Criminal Justice Administration." *International Journal of Criminal, Common and Statutory Law* 3 (1): 1–11.

Jeffries, Samantha, Chontit Chuenurah, Prarthana Rao, and Min Jee Yamada Park. 2019. "Women's Pathways to Prison in Kenya: Violence, Poverty, Familial Caretaking and Barriers to Justice." *Women's Studies International Forum* 73: 50–61.

Johnson, Jennifer E., Tracy Carney, Tyler Kline, Felicia A. Browne, and Wendee M. Wechsberg. 2012. "Incarceration History Relative to Health, Substance Use, and Violence in a Sample of Vulnerable South African Women: Implications for Health Services in Criminal Justice Settings." *Substance Abuse and Rehabilitation* 3 (Suppl 1): 59–69.

Kasau, Regina Wango, Gerryshom Munala, and Christine Majale. 2025. "The Built Environment of Kamiti Maximum Security Prison, Nairobi: Implications for Rehabilitation and Psychological Well-being." *East African Journal of Interdisciplinary Studies* 8 (1): 176–91.

Kenya. 2016. *Sentencing Policy Guidelines*. Nairobi: Judiciary of Kenya. https://kenyalaw.org/kl/fileadmin/pdfdownloads/Sentencing_Policy_Guidelines_Booklet.pdf.

Kenya State Department for Correctional Services. 2024. *Strategic Plan 2023–2027*. https://correctional.go.ke/sites/default/files/Correctional/FINAL%20DRAFT%20SDCS%20STRATEGIC%20PLAN%2009.12.2024.pdf.

Kenya Law. 2025. "Section 28 of Penal Code Cap 63: Fines." SheriaPlex. https://www.sheriaplex.com/kenya-acts/495-section-28-of-penal-code-cap-63-fines.

Kenya National Commission on Human Rights. 2023. *Mental Health and the Criminal Justice System*. June 8, 2023. https://www.knchr.org/Portals/0/Disability%20Publications/Mental%20health%20and%20the%20criminal%20justice%20system08_06_2023FINAL.pdf.

Kinuthia, Peter. 2021. "Complete List of Top 10 Female Prisons in South Africa 2021." *Briefly*. August 4, 2021. https://briefly.co.za/104876-complete-list-top-10-female-prisons-south-africa-2021.html.

Kinyanjui, Daniel W. C., and Lukoye Atwoli. 2013. "Substance Use Among Inmates at the Eldoret Prison in Western Kenya." *BMC Psychiatry* 13: 53.

Kiptoo, Beatrice, and John Muthee. 2020. *Coping Mechanisms Adopted by Women Ex-Offenders in Nyeri County, Kenya*. ResearchGate. https://www.researchgate.net/publication/347401278.

Lawler, Justin. 2023. *History of Women in Prisons During Apartheid.* South African History Online. https://sahistory.org.za/article/history-women-prisons-during-apartheid.

Legal Resources Centre (LRC). 2024. "When Survival Becomes a Crime." https://lrc.org.za/when-survival-becomes-a-crime/.

Magadla-Mateyise, Afika Fikiswa, and Enoch Zenzile. 2024. "A Review of Official Documents and Literature on the Forgotten Victims of Parental Incarceration in South Africa." *Research in Social Sciences and Technology* 9 (3): 160–77.

Magato, Valentine. 2023. *To Kill or to Be Killed: Evaluating the Prospect of Situating Battered Woman Syndrome Within the Kenyan Criminal Law.* October 9. SSRN.

Makou, Gopolang, Ina Skosana, and Ruth Hopkins. 2017. *FACTSHEET: The State of South Africa's Prisons.* Africa Check. July 18, 2017. https://africacheck.org/fact-checks/factsheets/factsheet-state-south-africas-prisons.

Mamacos, Elizabeth. 2023. "Mothers in Prison." *News24.* October 30, 2023. https://specialprojects.news24.com/mothers-in-prison/.

Masekoameng, Sello M., Bronwyn R. Parry, and Marlize E. Fourie. 2025. "The Motherhood Experiences of Women Incarcerated at the Johannesburg Maximum Correctional Facility, in the Gauteng Province, South Africa." *International Journal of Offender Therapy and Comparative Criminology* 69 (6–7): 853–68.

Masiko-Mpaka, Nomathamsanqa. 2024. "Confronting South Africa's Crisis of Gender-Based Violence." *Human Rights Watch.* November 25, 2024. https://www.hrw.org/news/2024/11/25/confronting-south-africas-crisis-gender-based-violence.

Masilela, Sinenhlanhla. 2024. "Update: 21-Year-Old Woman Who Landed in SA from Brazil Has Released over 110 Drug Bullets from Her Stomach." *IOL News.* September 30, 2024. https://iol.co.za/news/crime-and-courts/2024-09-30-update-21-year-old-woman-who-landed-in-sa-from-brazil-has-released-over-110-drug-bullets-from-her-stomach/.

Mburu, Hellen Wairimu, and Catherine Gathitu. 2022. "Effect of Prison Programs on Rehabilitation of Inmates in County, Kenya." *International Journal of Research and Innovation in Social Science* 6 (10): 489–95. https://www.rsisinternational.org/journals/ijriss/Digital-Library/volume-6-issue-10/489-495.pdf.

Miamingi, Alina. 2020. "The Applicability of the Best Interests Principle to Children of Imprisoned Mothers in Contemporary Africa: Between Hard and Soft Law." *African Human Rights Law Journal* 20 (2): 831–52.

Mogatle, Lesego. 2023. "Banged Up: Prisons for Women in South Africa." *Right for Education.* April 12, 2023. https://rightforeducation.org/2023/04/12/prisons-women-south-africa/.

Mosadioluwa, Adam. 2022. "Abortion, Adultery, Witchcraft, Suicide: Little Known Actions That Can Land You in Jail in Nigeria." *Tribune Online.* July 10, 2022. https://tribuneonlineng.com/abortion-adultery-witchcraft-suicide-little-known-actions-that-can-land-you-in-jail-in-nigeria/.

Mukoma, Wanjiru, and Gert Jansen. 2022. "Female Offenders in Two South African Prisons: Narratives of Drug-Related Offending." *Cogent Social Sciences* 8 (1): 1–12.

Museve, Judith, Charles Helm, Obiero Angira, and Peter Aloka. 2020. "Prevalence and Associated Factors of Mental Disorders Among Prisoners in Kenya." *International Journal of Research and Innovation in Social Science* 10: 261–71.

Mutunga, Daniel. 2019. "The Forgotten Victims of Our Correction System: The Case of Children of Imprisoned Parents in Kenya." *Interdisciplinary Journal on the African Child* 1 (1): 73–9.

Mwaura, Wambui. 2024. "Kenyans Are Dying Due to Lack of Healthcare—Even as Plans to Export Health Workers Are Underway." *Africa Uncensored*. March 22, 2024. https://africauncensored.online/blog/2024/03/22/kenyans-are-dying-due-to-lack-of-healthcare-even-as-plans-to-export-health-workers-are-underway/.

Nagdee, Mariam, Lillian Artz, Ugasvaree Subramaney, Chantelle Young, Annelize Pieterse, and Janine Pettitt. 2024. "The Gendered Context of Women Charged with Violent Offences in the Forensic Psychiatric Setting." *The South African Journal of Psychiatry* 30: 2222.

Naidoo, Samantha, Liezel Ferreira, Ugasvaree Subramaney, and Saeeda Paruk. 2021. "An HIV Narrative of Female Inmates with a Lifetime History of Mental Illness in Durban, South Africa." *Frontiers in Psychiatry* 12 (August): Article 637387.

Naidoo, Samantha, U. Subramaney, Saeeda Paruk, and Liezel Ferreira. 2022. "Mental Illness and HIV Amongst Female Inmates in Durban, South Africa." *The South African Journal of Psychiatry* 28: 1628.

Nairaland. 2023. "List of Prisons in Nigeria: Facts and Locations." *Nairaland Forum*. July 2023. https://www.nairaland.com/7985133/list-prisons-nigeria-facts-locations.

National Bureau of Statistics (Nigeria). 2019. *2018 Statistical Report on Women and Men in Nigeria*. Abuja: National Bureau of Statistics. https://www.nigerianstat.gov.ng/pdfuploads/Final_2018%20Statistical%20Report%20on%20Women%20and%20Men%20in%20Nigeria_Publication_SG%20OFFICE_29052019.pdf.

National Tuberculosis and Leprosy Control Programme. 2021. *National Care and Referral Model for HIV, TB and Other Health Conditions in Nigerian Correctional Facilities*. Abuja: Federal Ministry of Health. https://ntblcp.org.ng/content/uploads/2023/06/National_Care_and_Referral_Model_1.pdf.

Nigeria. n.d. *National Drug Law Enforcement Agency Act*. Lagos: Federal Ministry of Trade, Industry & Investment. https://nigeriatradeportal.fmiti.gov.ng/media/NDLEA%20Act.pdf.

Nigeria Correctional Service. n.d. "History of the Nigerian Correctional Service." Federal Ministry of Interior, Nigeria. https://cdcfib.gov.ng/history-of-ncs/.

Njongoro, Benson Mwangi. 2024. "Breaking Barriers for Women Offenders in Kenya." *Commonwealth Scholarship Commission (UK)*. April 4, 2024. https://cscuk.fcdo.gov.uk/breaking-barriers-for-women-offenders-in-kenya-2/.

Nwefoh, Emmanuel, Chinwe M. Aguocha, Gillian Ryan, Paul Ocheche, Godfrey M. Onyeama, and Julian Eaton. 2020. "Depression and Experience of Incarceration in

North Central Nigeria: A Situation Analysis at Makurdi Medium Security Prison." *International Journal of Mental Health Systems* 14 (76): 1–13.

Nyaberi, Wycliffe. 2024. "Four Men Found Guilty of Lynching Elderly Women." *Nation*. https://nation.africa/kenya/counties/kisii/four-men-found-guilty-of-lynching-elderly-women-4863580.

Nyabuto, Sukuru Clinton, Thaddaeus Rugar, and Norbert Ogeta. 2023. "Relationship Between Level of Schooling and Incarceration Among Inmates of Kamiti and Langata Maximum Prisons in Kenya." *Journal of Education* 3 (1): 26–35.

Nyamichaba, Edith. 2016. *"Liquor Laws Effect on Women's Conviction."* Institute of Economic Affairs Kenya. December 14, 2016. https://ieakenya.or.ke/blog/liquor-laws-effect-on-womens-conviction/.

Oduor, Frankline. 2025. "Kenyan Woman Sentenced to 50 Years in Jail for Drug Trafficking." *Kenyans.co.ke*. March 19. https://www.kenyans.co.ke/news/110085-kenyan-woman-sentenced-50-years-jail-drug-trafficking.

Olagunju, Andrew T., Abayomi A. Bioku, Chidinma Poluyi, Ibrahim Abdullahi, Titilola O. Olagunju, Yusuf A. Alatishe, Oluwaseun F. Kolawole, Muktar Mela, John M. W. Bradford, and Gary A. Chaimowitz. 2022. "Substance Use Disorders and Antisocial Personality Disorder Among a Sample of Incarcerated Individuals with Inadequate Health Care: Implications for Correctional Mental-Behavioural Health and Addiction Services." *Journal of Health Care for the Poor and Underserved* 33 (3): 1401–18.

Olugbenga-Bello, Abiodun I., Olusegun A. Adeoye, and Kehinde G. Osagbemi. 2013. "Assessment of the Reproductive Health Status of Adult Prison Inmates in Osun State, Nigeria." *International Journal of Reproductive Medicine* 2013: 451460.

Ondeng, Jacinta Mary, Merecia Ann Sirera, and Beatrice Kathungu. 2021. "Gender-Responsive Programming in Kenya: Time Is Ripe." *Women & Criminal Justice* 31 (6): 476–93.

Onyango, Okello Clifford, Ombachi K. Nicholas, and Moses Adama. 2021. "Influence of Gender on Rehabilitation and Reintegration of Recidivists: A Study of Female Inmates in Women's Prisons in Selected Counties in Western Kenya." *Public Policy and Administration Research* 11 (8): 50–61.

Osasona, Segun O., and Oluwakemi N. Koleoso. 2015. "Prevalence and Correlates of Depression and Anxiety Disorder in a Sample of Inmates in a Nigerian Prison." *International Journal of Psychiatry in Medicine* 50 (2): 203–18.

Oweibia, Mordecai, Tarimobowei Egberipou, Gift Cornelius Timighe, Preye David Ogbe, Uchenna Geraldine Elemuwa, and Tuebi Richard Wilson. 2025. "Drug Abuse in Nigeria; The Public Health Impact of Collective Actions and Inactions: A Systematic Review." *medRxiv*. May 13, 2025.

Owusu, Emmanuel S. 2023. "Provocation by Witchcraft: Exploring the Evolution of the Kenyan Courts' Interpretation of the Doctrine of Provocation in Relation to Witchcraft Beliefs." *Journal of Law and Religion* 38 (2): 265–89.

Penal Reform International. 2020. "Coronavirus and Women in Detention: A Gender-Specific Response Is Needed." *Penal Reform International.* May 5, 2020. https://www.penalreform.org/blog/coronavirus-and-women-in-detention-a-gender-specific.

Penal Reform International. 2019. *Rehabilitation of Women Prisoners.* London: Penal Reform International. https://cdn.penalreform.org/wp-content/uploads/2019/05/PRI_Rehabilitation-of-women-prisoners_WEB.pdf.

Penal Reform International & Kenya Probation & Aftercare Service. 2016. *Community Service and Probation for Women in Kenya: Summary Briefing.* Nairobi: Penal Reform International. https://cdn.penalreform.org/wp-content/uploads/2016/12/PRI-Kenya-report-summary-briefing_WEB_rev.pdf.

PM News Nigeria. 2024. "Number of Female Inmates Increased to 4.82% in 2022—NBS." *PM News Nigeria.* May 22, 2024. https://pmnewsnigeria.com/2024/05/22/number-of-female-inmates-increased-to-4-82-in-2022-nbs/.

Qhogwana, Sibulelo, and Puleng Segalo. 2022. "Women Offenders' Experiences of Rehabilitation in a South African Correctional Centre." *Journal of Psychology in Africa* 32 (1): 97–102.

Rabi'u, Sulaiman Olayiwola. 2016. "Shari'ah Hudud and Northern Nigerian Penal Code." *International Journal of Law* 2 (1): 8–12.

Rawoot, Ilham. 2012. "Babies Behind Bars." *Mail & Guardian.* June 28, 2012. https://mg.co.za/article/2012-06-28-babies-behind-bars-2/.

S v Shilubane 2008 (1) SACR 295 (T).

Salako, Pelumi. 2024. "Why a Nigerian Woman Faces Jail Time for Reviewing Tomato Puree." *Al Jazeera.* June 9, 2024. https://www.aljazeera.com/features/2024/6/9/why-a-nigerian-woman-faces-jail-time-for-reviewing-tomato-puree.

Samuels, Julia A., Nadia V. Roman, and Marlene Schoeman. 2024. "A Qualitative Inquiry: Management of Recidivism in South Africa." *Crime, Law and Social Change* 82: 197–218.

Sarki, Zakariyya Muhammad, and Ado Umar Lalu. 2020. "Speaking from Behind Bars: A Survey on Women Inmates in Katsina and Kano Prisons, Nigeria." *African Journal of Social Sciences and Humanities Research* 3 (5): 69–79.

South African History Archive (SAHA). 2025. *Leading Women.* https://www.saha.org.za/women/leading_women.htm.

Stanyard, Julia. 2023. *Women and Drug Policy in Eastern and Southern Africa.* Global Initiative against Transnational Organized Crime. https://globalinitiative.net/wp-content/uploads/2023/11/Julia-Stanyard-Women-and-drug-policy-in-Eastern-and-Southern-Africa-GI-TOC-November-2023.pdf.

Statistics South Africa. 2023. *Census 2022 Statistical Release: P0301.4.* Pretoria: Statistics South Africa. https://census.statssa.gov.za/assets/documents/2022/P03014_Census_2022_Statistical_Release.pdf.

Steyn, Francois, and Karen Booyens. 2017. "A Profile of Incarcerated Female Offenders: Implications for Rehabilitation Policy and Practice." *Acta Criminologica: Southern African Journal of Criminology* 30 (4): 33–44.

Sukeri, Kiran, Orlando A. Betancourt, Robin Emsley, Mohammed Nagdee, and Helmut Erlacher. 2016. "Forensic Mental Health Services: Current Service Provision and Planning for a Prison Mental Health Service in the Eastern Cape." *South African Journal of Psychiatry* 22 (1): a787.

University of South Africa (Unisa). 2023. "Rehab for South Africa's Female Inmates Focuses on Domestic Chores—Instead of Finding Good Work." Unisa. September 13, 2023. https://www.unisa.ac.za/sites/corporate/default/Colleges/Human-Sciences/Schools%2C-departments%2C-centres%2C-institutes-%26-units/Units/Chief-Albert-Luthuli-Research-Chair/News/Articles/Rehab-for-South-Africas-female-inmates-focuses-on-domestic-chores–instead-of-finding-good-work.

UNODC (United Nations Office on Drugs and Crime). 2023. *World Drug Report 2023.* Vienna: UNODC. https://www.unodc.org/unodc/en/data-and-analysis/world-drug-report-2023.html.

UNODC (United Nations Office on Drugs and Crime). 2022. *Annual Project Results Report, 1 January to 31 December 2022: Lang'ata Women's Prison.* Nairobi: UNODC Eastern Africa Regional Office. https://www.unodc.org/documents/easternafrica/Criminal_Justice/Annual_Project_Results_Report_-_1_Jan_to_31_Dec_2022_Langata_Prison.pdf.

U.S. Department of State. 2024. *2023 Country Reports on Human Rights Practices: Kenya.* Bureau of Democracy, Human Rights, and Labor. https://www.state.gov/reports/2023-country-reports-on-human-rights-practices/kenya.

U.S. Department of State. 2023. *Country Reports on Human Rights Practices for 2022: Nigeria.* Washington, DC: Bureau of Democracy, Human Rights, and Labor. https://www.state.gov/reports/2022-country-reports-on-human-rights-practices/nigeria/.

Uzu, Augusta, Obagboye Tomi Grace, Isiaka Jamiu Isiaka, and Adesina Ileola Ibironke. 2025. "Critical Issues in the Administration of Criminal Justice in Nigeria." *International Journal of Law, Policy and Social Review* 7 (1): 48–52.

Van Hout, Marie Claire, and Jakkie Wessels. 2021. "Human Rights and the Invisible Nature of Incarcerated Women in Post-Apartheid South Africa: Prison System Progress in Adopting the Bangkok Rules." *International Journal of Prisoner Health* 18 (3): 300–14.

Van Hout, Marie Claire, and Lucky Chimbga. 2020. "Tackling Intersectionality of Drug Offenses and Violence Against Women in South Africa." *Liverpool John Moores University.* https://researchonline.ljmu.ac.uk/id/eprint/14206/.

Van Hout, Marie Claire, and Rumbi Mhlanga-Gunda. 2018. "Contemporary Women Prisoners' Health Experiences, Unique Prison Health Care Needs and Health Care Outcomes in Sub-Saharan Africa: A Scoping Review of Extant Literature." *BMC International Health and Human Rights* 18: 31.

Wainaina, Gituro, and Nyawira Kuria. 2019. "Art Therapy as a Treatment for Depression: Case of Control Group at Langata Women's Prison Nairobi." *International Journal of Research and Innovation in Social Science* 3 (8): 330–36.

Wangira, Dorcas. 2021. "Born in Prison: Child Experiences in Kenya's Women's Facilities." *Citizen Digital*. October 5. https://www.citizen.digital/lifestyle/born-in-prison-child-experiences-in-kenyas-womens-facilities-n283983.

World Bank. 2025. *South Africa: Macro Poverty Outlook, May 2025*. Washington, DC: World Bank. https://thedocs.worldbank.org/en/doc/bae48ff2fefc5a869546775b3f010735-0500062021/related/mpo-zaf.pdf.

World Prison Brief. 2025. "Nigeria: World Prison Brief Data." *Institute for Crime & Justice Policy Research, University of London*. Accessed July 3, 2025. https://www.prisonstudies.org/country/nigeria.

World Prison Brief. 2024a. "Kenya." Birkbeck, University of London. https://www.prisonstudies.org/country/kenya.

World Prison Brief. 2024b. "South Africa." *World Prison Brief (Institute for Crime & Justice Policy Research)*. https://www.prisonstudies.org/country/south-africa.

6

Central and East Asia

This chapter explores the incarceration of women in Central and East Asia, focusing on Uzbekistan, China, and Japan. Each country has distinct legal systems and cultural histories, but common themes emerge, like the criminalization of poverty, gendered social control, inadequate prison conditions, and limited support for incarcerated mothers. Looking at the historical context, current trends, and policy analysis, the chapter highlights how structural inequalities and punitive laws disproportionately affect women. By examining incarceration patterns across these countries, the chapter stresses the need for gender-responsive reforms throughout the region.

Uzbekistan

Historical Context

Uzbekistan's history of incarcerating women is tied to its Soviet past and influenced by patriarchal norms and political repression. Punishment was emphasized over rehabilitation during Soviet rule (1924–91). Women were imprisoned for political dissent, economic crimes, and moral offenses like prostitution. Campaigns like the **hujum**, aimed at unveiling Muslim women, increased surveillance and punitive responses (Akhrorova 2021). During this time, there were overcrowded facilities, inadequate healthcare, and forced labor (U.S. Department of State 2023).

Additionally, political repression in the Stalinist era influenced women's experiences with incarceration. Sabira Kholdorova, a pioneering journalist, was arrested in 1937, tortured, and exiled for ten years (Akhrorova 2021; Salomova 2023). After Uzbekistan gained independence in 1991, women continued to be incarcerated for economic crimes. UNAIDS (2019) estimates that there are around 22,000 sex workers in Uzbekistan, many of whom are vulnerable to arrest under morality laws.

Women also face pressure for perceived moral transgressions like adultery, though not criminalized. Local authorities may use vague public order laws or rely on traditional community structures to impose punitive consequences outside the law (Mamasolieva 2023). Moreover, domestic violence was not criminalized until 2023, and enforcement is still inconsistent (Human Rights Watch 2023b).

Gendered control continues through the criminal justice system. Women arrested for sex work or moral offenses often lack legal protection and face inadequate conditions (UNAIDS 2019). Political dissent is still met with harsh retaliation. Activists have been imprisoned on questionable charges, and human rights groups have documented abuse against female journalists (Amnesty International 2023).

Despite some reforms, including collaborations with UN agencies (Van Hout et al. 2023), prison conditions remain harsh. Reports highlight inadequate healthcare, poor sanitation, and a lack of gender-responsive services, especially affecting mothers and pregnant women (ACCA 2022; U.S. Department of State 2023). For instance, Muslim women in KIN-7 were punished for seeking care. They also endure flooded cells and religious discrimination (OMCT 2003). These issues show continued neglect of women's rights and health.

Female Incarceration Rates and Trends

Women make up an estimated 3–5 percent of Uzbekistan's prison population, consistent with regional norms (Fair and Walmsley 2022). With a total inmate population of roughly 29,000 as of 2022, this would be approximately 870 to 1,450 incarcerated women (World Prison Brief 2022). However, gender-disaggregated statistics are not routinely published in Uzbekistan (Prison Insider 2024).

Female incarceration is concentrated in a few facilities. KIN 7, in Tashkent, faced international criticism after women advocating for medical care were placed in punishment cells under inhumane conditions (OMCT 2003). The Zangiota Women's Colony, in the Zangiota district, is the country's primary female-only prison, offering limited vocational training and reflecting the lack of adequate facilities for incarcerated women (Kun.uz 2020). Additionally, Colony No. 21, also in the Zangiota district, has drawn concern for forcing pregnant inmates to work under unsafe conditions and pressuring them to terminate pregnancies (ACCA 2022).

Uzbekistan's location along heroin trafficking routes has contributed to rising female incarceration for drug-related offenses. Women, often coerced into courier roles, are swept up in antidrug operations intensified by regional enforcement (OC Index 2023; U.S. Department of State 2022).

Patriarchal norms also shape incarceration trends. Women in rural areas are sometimes prosecuted under vague morality laws for behavior deemed "immoral," such as adultery or defiance of traditional roles (Human Rights Watch 2023b).

Though some reforms have addressed prison overcrowding and harsh conditions, systemic drivers of female incarceration (e.g., poverty, gender inequality, and limited legal protections) remain unaddressed. Experts continue to call for gender-responsive sentencing and greater use of non-custodial alternatives (Van Hout et al. 2023).

Demographics of Incarcerated Women

A considerable portion of incarcerated women in Uzbekistan come from economically disadvantaged backgrounds. This is especially the case in rural areas where access to education, healthcare, and employment is limited. While there is no publicly available data on the exact percentage of incarcerated women from poor households, national statistics help explain their hardships. As of 2023, approximately 50 percent of Uzbekistan's population lived in rural areas (The Global Economy 2025), and the average annual household income per capita was 1,705 USD (CEIC 2025). Rural poverty is common, with around 80 percent of Uzbekistan's poor living in rural areas (World Bank 2021).

Women from low-income rural households are especially at risk of economic marginalization. In 2020, the national employment-to-population ratio was 61 percent, but there was a significant gender gap—73 percent of men were employed compared to just 49 percent of women. Women in the lowest income bracket had the lowest employment rates, and limited educational opportunities further restricted their access to employment. While most rural women complete secondary school, only 8 percent pursue higher education (World Bank 2021).

Demographic data on incarcerated women remains limited. There is no publicly reported breakdown of the female prison population by ethnicity, race, education level, or mental health status (Saida and Scardavilli 2023). Age-related data is also scarce, though qualitative reports from Colony No. 21 indicate that inmates range from girls as young as fourteen to women over seventy (ACCA 2022). Similarly, while no official statistics exist on incarcerated mothers, it is known that up to thirty children are born each year in Colony KIN 21, where infants can remain with their mothers until the age of three (ACCA 2022).

Data on the prevalence of substance use and mental illness among incarcerated women is also lacking. While global patterns suggest these issues are widespread in female prison populations, no Uzbekistan-specific statistics are available. Likewise, while 43 percent of women surveyed in Uzbekistan reported experiencing domestic violence (Anhor 2023), no prison-specific data exists to determine how many incarcerated women are survivors of such abuse.

Crimes Leading to Incarceration

Poverty, marginalization, and limited economic opportunities drive the incarceration of women in Uzbekistan, especially for non-violent offenses. A joint report by the International Harm Reduction Association and WHO (2013) found that over 28 percent of incarcerated women in Europe and Central Asia were imprisoned for non-violent drug offenses, many linked to small-scale sales or possession. While Uzbekistan-specific data is lacking, this regional pattern is likely reflected locally, where the country's proximity to Afghanistan has fueled domestic drug availability and led to a rise in minor drug-related arrests (OC Index 2023). A UNODC (2008) report noted that of the 5,490 drug-related convictions in Uzbekistan in 2006, 2,305 were for sale and only 122 for trafficking. This finding suggests that many defendants, including women, were low-level participants.

Women are also commonly incarcerated for petty property crimes like theft or robbery, often tied to economic hardship. National amnesty releases often include women convicted of such offenses, reinforcing the prevalence of small-scale, non-violent crimes in the female prison population (Facts and Details 2016).

Prostitution is illegal in Uzbekistan, and there were approximately 22,000 women engaged in sex work as of 2019, largely due to poverty and lack of employment (UNAIDS 2019). Though no public statistics specify how many are incarcerated for prostitution, enforcement tends to be inconsistent. Police often extort sex workers or pressure them into becoming informants rather than pursuing formal charges (Bureau of Democracy 2009). Still, some women are prosecuted for related offenses. In 2022, a female sex worker in Bukhara received a three-year prison sentence for allegedly infecting over twenty-one men with HIV (HIV Justice Network 2022).

Uzbekistan is also a source country for sex trafficking, with women frequently lured abroad under false promises of employment. A 22-year-old woman was recently arrested in Tashkent for trafficking another woman to St. Petersburg for prostitution (Zamin 2025). These cases show how sex workers are caught between criminalization and coercion.

Political imprisonment remains another concern. While gender-specific data is unavailable, an estimated 1,800 to 2,000 individuals (about 6 percent of Uzbekistan's total prison population) are detained for political or religious reasons (USCIRF 2021). Documented cases include Elena Urlaeva, a human rights defender repeatedly arrested and institutionalized for protesting forced labor. Also, sisters Mehriniso and Zulkhumor Hamdamova were imprisoned in 2010 for offering private religious instruction outside of state-approved structures (Norwegian Helsinki Committee 2021). These cases reflect the Uzbek government's suppression of activism and religious expression, including among women.

Contributing Laws and Policies

Uzbekistan's punitive laws play a role in female incarceration, especially for drug and economic crimes. The country's proximity to Afghanistan has led to increased availability of drugs and increased law enforcement efforts. Under Uzbek law, even small-scale possession or transport of narcotics is treated as a serious crime, with penalties ranging from several years to up to twenty years in prison depending on the quantity and context (U.S. Department of State 2022). The law does not differentiate between levels of involvement, meaning women coerced into acting as low-level couriers often receive the same harsh sentences as high-level traffickers.

Economic crimes such as theft, fraud, and embezzlement are also treated severely under Uzbekistan's Criminal Code. Embezzlement and fraud carry sentences ranging from fines and correctional labor to as much as ten years in prison (VERTIC 2023). In 2023, the government reinforced its punitive approach by declaring that even first-time offenders convicted of these crimes would be ineligible for parole or early release (Daryo 2023). Although alternatives like community service and conditional release exist, they are rarely used, leaving most female offenders incarcerated (Tursunmurodov 2024).

Some progress toward reform has been proposed. In 2023, a draft law proposed turning minor economic crimes into administrative offenses if the financial loss is below a specific amount (Kun 2023). If implemented, these reforms could reduce the prison population by diverting economically motivated women away from prison. Until then, women committing petty crimes from financial desperation still face incarceration.

Additionally, Uzbekistan's legal system is often used to suppress political dissent. The Criminal Code includes provisions criminalizing defamation and insult, including statutes prohibiting insulting the president. These laws are often used against journalists, activists, and critics (Commission on Security and Cooperation in Europe 2023). Other statutes address extremism and threats to public safety and are routinely applied to peaceful forms of dissent. Recent amendments have expanded the state's ability to punish people involved in protests or "mass unrest," silencing independent voices (International Partnership for Human Rights 2025). One example is Sitora Bozorova, a 24-year-old woman sentenced to five years for social media posts criticizing President Shavkat Mirziyoyev's family. Her charges included calling for the "dynasty" to "burn" and making a disparaging remark about the president's daughter (Rickleton and Babadjanov 2024).

Conditions in Women's Prisons

According to the U.S. Department of State (2023), prison conditions in Uzbekistan are often harsh. They exhibit overcrowding, inadequate sanitation, and food shortages. Cells are cramped, unhygienic spaces with little privacy and increased risks of disease transmission. Women often enter these facilities with preexisting health issues like malnutrition, untreated injuries, or infectious diseases, which the prison system is poorly equipped to manage. In some facilities, sewage overflows and filthy communal punishment cells compromise basic hygiene. People are frequently denied access to clean water, sufficient nutrition, and medical care, even in cases of severe illness (OMCT 2003).

One example comes from KIN 7, where at least seven Muslim women were confined in a punishment cell after demanding medical attention for a seriously ill inmate. The cell was overcrowded and unsanitary, with waterlogged floors and overflowing sewage, creating unsafe and degrading conditions. One woman with a heart condition was denied medical treatment throughout her detention. These women also faced religious persecution. Prison staff forcibly removed modest clothing worn for religious reasons and punished them for practicing their faith. Family visits were restricted to once every six months, worsening their isolation and psychological distress (OMCT 2003).

Women at KIN-7

At Colony KIN-7, a women's penal colony in Uzbekistan, several inmates protested after one of their fellow prisoners fell seriously ill and was denied medical attention. When they demanded care for her, prison officials accused them of insubordination and placed them in a punishment cell flooded with sewage for several days. The women were denied medical treatment, stripped of their religious clothing, and permitted family visits only twice a year. One detainee with a heart condition reportedly received no care at all. Their eventual release from solitary confinement came only after advocacy groups raised concerns about their treatment, yet no officials were held accountable. The case highlights how Uzbek prisons neglect women's health and punish them for asserting their rights.

Furthermore, rehabilitation and reintegration support for women is lacking. Penal Reform International (2021) reports that Uzbekistan's prison system offers few educational, vocational, or psychological services tailored to women's needs. While a few programs like sewing or tailoring workshops have been piloted with support from outside organizations, they are not consistently available. Most incarcerated women have no access to meaningful rehabilitation or psychological counseling.

Health and Mental Health Issues

Health and mental health issues are concerns for incarcerated women in Uzbekistan. Many women enter the prison system with preexisting health problems, including malnutrition, untreated injuries, tuberculosis, and hepatitis. The U.S. Department of State (2023) reports high rates of tuberculosis in Uzbek prisons, where access to proper treatment remains inadequate. Hepatitis C is also a serious concern. Its prevalence in Central Asian prisons ranges from 7 percent to 50 percent, with a median of 32 percent, and Uzbekistan-specific figures fall within this range (Botheju et al. 2019).

Overcrowded and poorly ventilated cells, often holding up to ten women, create conditions for the spread of disease. Former inmates and prison workers have described routine denial of care, with even seriously ill prisoners receiving medications like aspirin (Institute for War and Peace Reporting 2014).

Women are vulnerable due to the lack of gender-specific health services and psychological support. Many have histories of trauma, including domestic violence, sexual abuse, and poverty, yet no trauma-informed mental healthcare is available. Psychological abuse by security forces, including threats against inmates' families, has also been reported (U.S. Department of State 2023).

At Colony No. 21, women have reportedly been forced to perform manual labor until childbirth in unsanitary conditions, with inadequate prenatal and postnatal care. Some former inmates reported being pressured to terminate pregnancies without medical oversight, raising human rights concerns (ACCA 2022). After childbirth, mothers are often allowed only brief contact with their infants. Furthermore, reports of staff neglect and abuse toward infants stress the failures that endanger mothers and children in Uzbekistan's prisons.

Impact on Families and Children

The incarceration of women in Uzbekistan has consequences for families, especially their children. As primary caregivers in many households, women's imprisonment can lead to anxiety, depression, and behavioral issues among children. According to UNICEF (2019), children (especially until the age of six) are often placed with extended family, where emotional and developmental needs are unmet. Institutional care also poses risks due to its lack of individualized attention. The U.S. Department of State (2023) has noted that families of prisoners often face housing, childcare, and financial instability.

The loss of a mother's income can force families into deeper poverty, sometimes driving children out of school and into labor. These pressures, particularly in rural areas with limited state support, reinforce cycles of disadvantage. Social stigma worsens these challenges. In Uzbekistan's conservative society, families of incarcerated women may be ostracized, and children excluded from school activities or community life (UNICEF 2019).

Visitation rights are also limited. Most incarcerated individuals are allowed only two short and one long visit per year. Moreover, visits can be denied or delayed (U.S. Department of State 2023). This limited contact disrupts the mother–child bond and complicates post-release reintegration. Families are also expected to bring essentials like food and medicine, making visits even more important. These challenges stress the need for reforms like expanded visitation and alternative sentencing.

In some facilities, such as Colony No. 21, mothers are permitted to keep infants with them until age three. However, overcrowded and under-resourced conditions offer little support, and children are typically separated and sent to relatives or state institutions afterward. While this allows for some early bonding, the lack of structured nursery programs places mothers and children in vulnerable situations (ACCA 2022).

Policy Reforms and Recommendations

Uzbekistan should expand non-custodial alternatives to incarceration for women, especially for non-violent and economic crimes. A 2023 draft law proposing the reclassification of minor economic crimes as administrative violations is a promising step (Kun 2023). Gender-responsive sentencing, especially for pregnant women or primary caregivers, should be formalized to reduce imprisonment and its impact on families (Van Hout et al. 2023).

Prison conditions and healthcare must also be improved. Overcrowding, poor sanitation, and medical neglect are widespread (U.S. Department of State 2023). Women often arrive with untreated conditions, yet healthcare and trauma support are largely absent (ACCA 2022). Targeted medical services and gender-specific facilities are needed.

Rehabilitation programs remain limited and inconsistent. While vocational workshops exist in some prisons, they are underdeveloped, and psychological support is rare despite high rates of trauma among incarcerated women (Penal Reform International 2021). Without meaningful training or mental healthcare, women face barriers to reintegration (Van Hout et al. 2023).

Family contact is also restricted, with only a few visits allowed each year, which are often delayed or denied (U.S. Department of State 2023). Mothers need greater access to visits and communication to preserve relationships with their children. While infants may remain with mothers until age three in some facilities, poor conditions and lack of nursery programs make this support inadequate (ACCA 2022).

The imprisonment of women also deepens economic hardship for families. Many incarcerated women were primary earners. Their absence can force children into labor or early school dropout, especially in rural areas. Social stigma compounds these challenges, isolating children and families (UNICEF 2019).

Uzbekistan should also publish gender-disaggregated data on prisoners to better inform policy (Saida and Scardavilli 2023). In addition, laws criminalizing moral behavior and dissent, like insulting the president, should be reformed.

Addressing these structural issues would promote a more humane, equitable justice system focused on rehabilitation.

China

Historical Context

The incarceration of women in China has been influenced by patriarchal norms, political ideologies, and evolving laws. In traditional society, Confucian doctrine reinforced the subordination of women through ideals like the *Three Obediences and Four Virtues*, which confined women to domestic roles and moral expectations (Dikotter 2002). Under imperial laws like the Tang Code and Qing Code, women were punished harshly for acts that disrupted family harmony (e.g., adultery or defiance of male authority), often through public shaming, beatings, or exile (Bakken 2005).

With the fall of the Qing Dynasty in 1912 and the rise of the Republic of China, reformers began modernizing the justice system by adopting elements of Western legal systems, especially from Germany and Japan (MacCormack 1990). However, women continued to be disproportionately punished for "crimes of immorality," including prostitution and behaviors considered socially deviant. Female incarceration was framed as moral correction, and the first women's prisons emphasized domestic rehabilitation over legal justice (Hershatter 2014).

After the founding of the People's Republic of China in 1949, the Communist Party restructured the penal system around socialist principles, including the goal of gender equality. Women were subjected to labor reform (**laogai**) and re-education through labor (**laojiao**), which combined physical labor with ideological training (Dikotter 2002). However, during the Cultural Revolution (1966–76), incarceration was increasingly used for political repression. Women labeled as "counter-revolutionaries" were detained for defying moral or ideological norms like wearing makeup or questioning collectivist values. Many were imprisoned without trial or subjected to "struggle sessions" (e.g., public humiliation, abuse, forced confessions) and forced labor (Hershatter 2014). By the 1970s, an estimated 1–2 million people were held in the laogai system, with women comprising a significant but undocumented portion (Walmsley 2017).

In the reform era beginning in the 1980s, China's rapid development and legal modernization brought greater attention to women's rights. Legal amendments in 1996 and 2012 introduced protections for pregnant women and those with young children in detention (Dui Hua Foundation 2012a).

However, the effects of the **one-child policy** (1979–2015) continue to influence women's experiences with state control. Women were frequently subjected to forced abortions, sterilizations, or detention for violating population mandates (Greenhalgh 2008). Today, incarcerated women still face overcrowding, inadequate gynecological care, and poor sanitation, despite government commitments to improve conditions through policy reforms (Dui Hua Foundation 2014). Implementation remains inconsistent, and women's incarceration continues to reflect tensions between legal reform and gendered control.

Female Incarceration Rates and Trends

The number of incarcerated women in China has increased significantly over the past few decades. Yet, women represent a relatively small portion (approximately 6.6 percent) of the total prison population (Fair and Walmsley 2022). As of 2022, approximately 145,000 women were held in Chinese prisons, making China the nation with the second-largest female prison population after the United States (Fair and Walmsley 2022). This figure excludes women in pre-trial and administrative detention. Due to the lack of gender-disaggregated data, the proportion of women in pre-trial detention remains unknown.

Most incarcerated women are housed in dedicated women's prisons managed at the provincial or municipal level. These facilities increased from 31 in 2015 to 41 by 2018, showing the state's response to the growing female prison population (Dui Hua Foundation 2020). Major institutions include Beijing Women's Prison, Shanghai Women's Prison, and Sichuan Provincial Women's Prison (Dui Hua Foundation and Renmin University 2014). Women awaiting trial are held in pre-trial detention centers, which are often coed facilities with gender-segregated sections. Facilities like Guangzhou No. 1 Detention Center are reported to house women in designated wings (Dui Hua Foundation 2020).

The increase in female incarceration has been driven by the enforcement of laws targeting non-violent offenses, especially drug-related crimes, economic offenses, and violations of family planning policies. Between 2003 and 2013, the number of incarcerated women rose by 46 percent (Dui Hua Foundation 2015). According to the International Drug Policy Consortium (2015), female incarceration rates increased ten times faster than male rates during the early 2000s, largely due to strict sentencing for low-level drug offenses that disproportionately affect women.

Many women have also been convicted of petty financial crimes (e.g., fraud, embezzlement, and theft), often due to participation in informal economic activities driven by poverty and limited opportunities (Dui Hua Foundation 2014). Additionally, the legacy of the one-child policy contributed to the detention of women in administrative facilities like reeducation through labor (laojiao) and family planning detention centers, which often operated outside the formal criminal justice system (Greenhalgh 2008).

Reforms have aimed to improve prison oversight and reduce custodial sentencing, but challenges remain. Incarcerated women face inadequate healthcare, poor sanitation, overcrowding, and a lack of rehabilitation programs (Penal Reform International 2019). The continued growth in female incarceration has outpaced the prison system's ability to address women's needs, emphasizing the need for more gender-responsive criminal justice reforms.

Demographics of Incarcerated Women

Most incarcerated women in China come from economically disadvantaged backgrounds, often from rural areas or impoverished urban neighborhoods. Over 90 percent of the country's poor population resides in rural regions, where women experience significantly higher poverty rates than men. One study found that 30 percent of rural women lived in multidimensional poverty, lacking access to education, healthcare, and basic rights (Xia et al. 2022).

Low educational attainment is another common characteristic. Many incarcerated women have only basic literacy or have not completed secondary school. In southwest China, rural girls made up just 22 percent of female university students (Liu 2008). These educational disadvantages are compounded by the hukou (household registration) system, which limits rural residents' access to urban education, employment, and social services (Chan 2015).

A large-scale study of Hunan Provincial Female Prison found that the average age of incarcerated women was approximately forty, with ages ranging from fifteen to eighty-one (Zhong et al. 2019). Women over sixty accounted for nearly 2 percent of the total female prison population (Dui Hua Foundation 2024).

China does not publish gender-disaggregated data on incarcerated parents, but a Ministry of Justice survey reported that roughly 30 percent of all incarcerated individuals were parents of minor children (Dui Hua Foundation 2012b).

Educational attainment also intersects with health outcomes. A mental health survey conducted in Hunan Women's Prison found that women with six to twelve years of education were more likely to report substance use disorders than those with higher or lower levels of education (Zhong et al. 2020), suggesting that education influences both health and pathways into the criminal justice system.

In the same study, Zhong and colleagues (2020) reported that nearly two-thirds of incarcerated women met the criteria for at least one lifetime DSM-IV psychiatric disorder, and almost 17 percent were diagnosed with a drug use disorder.

Crimes Leading to Incarceration

While China does not publish gender-disaggregated national statistics on offense types, available research indicates that most women are serving sentences for non-violent crimes. These patterns are linked to poverty, unemployment, and limited education, which leave many women vulnerable to low-level survival crimes.

Property-related offenses like petty theft, fraud, illegal fundraising, and extortion are among the most frequent crimes committed by women, especially among low-wage, undereducated populations (Dui Hua Foundation 2015). Similarly, many women convicted of drug offenses are from poor backgrounds and serve as low-level couriers, often working alone and without decision-making power. These roles are often assumed out of economic necessity and coercion (Liang et al. 2009).

A provincial study in Hunan found that only 13 percent of incarcerated women had committed violent offenses, compared to 33 percent among men, emphasizing that most women are imprisoned for non-violent property or drug crimes (Story FM 2022).

Economic crimes like fraud and embezzlement are also on the rise, particularly among women entering financial sectors in urban areas. Wu Ying, a rural entrepreneur turned multimillionaire, was convicted in 2009 for illegally raising over RMB 770 million (about 107.34 million USD). Initially sentenced to death, her punishment was later commuted to twenty-five years in prison, becoming a widely publicized example of the legal risks faced by women in illegal private lending (Reuters 2018). As Cheng (2016) notes, women's growing economic participation has increased their exposure to financial criminal liability.

Wu Ying—From Entrepreneur to Prisoner

Once one of China's richest women, Wu Ying rose from humble beginnings to become a successful entrepreneur in Zhejiang Province, building a business empire that included beauty salons, hotels, and real estate ventures. She was convicted in 2009 for illegally raising over RMB 770 million (about 107 million USD) through informal lending. Initially sentenced to death, her penalty was later reduced to twenty-five years. Her case became a symbol of how women in business, often operating outside formal banking systems, face severe punishment under China's financial crime laws. Supporters argued that her case reflected the barriers women face in accessing credit and the harsh penalties imposed on private entrepreneurs in China's tightly controlled economy.

Although less common today, some women have been incarcerated for violating family planning policies under the former one-child policy. Enforcement measures included forced abortions, sterilizations, and detention (Congressional-Executive Commission on China 2022). Notable cases include Mao Hengfeng, who was repeatedly detained for protesting forced abortions (Amnesty International 2012), and Feng Jianmei, who was forcibly aborted at seven months after failing to pay a state-imposed fine (Branigan 2012). While national policy has shifted, such enforcement continues in regions like Xinjiang, where family planning violations are still used to justify the detention of Uyghur women (Congressional-Executive Commission on China 2022).

Contributing Laws and Policies

China's legal framework affects the incarceration of women through strict drug laws, economic regulations, and family planning policies. The *Anti-Drug Law of the People's Republic of China*, adopted in 2007 and implemented in 2008, imposes severe penalties, including long prison terms and, in some cases, capital punishment, for a range of drug-related activities (Supreme People's Court of China 2008). Women with minimal involvement (e.g., couriers) often face the full weight of these laws. Many are coerced into these roles by criminal networks and lack the legal resources or social capital to avoid prosecution. A study by Liang and colleagues (2009) found that women were more likely than men to operate alone and in low-level roles yet still received disproportionately harsh sentences.

Economic crimes like fraud, embezzlement, and illegal fundraising are also common pathways into prison for women. As female workforce participation has increased, so has exposure to China's financial regulations (Cheng 2016). China's Criminal Law (Article 176) prohibits individuals or entities from illegally raising funds from the public without proper licensing. Violators who absorb a *relatively large* amount face three to ten years in prison plus fines. Those involved in *serious cases* may receive ten-plus years or life imprisonment, with additional financial penalties (Supreme People's Procuratorate 2020).

This broadly defined law has been used to prosecute rural entrepreneurs (often low-educated women) who run informal lending schemes or private fundraising, even when these activities support small business or community financing. Although such women typically never operated formal financial institutions, a lack of regulatory guidance means they often violate the law by default (Liu et al. 2018).

Family planning enforcement under the one-child policy also led to the criminalization and incarceration of women. The 2002 Family Planning Law enabled local authorities to impose fines, enforce sterilizations or abortions, and detain women for unauthorized pregnancies (UK Home Office 2018). While these policies were relaxed in 2015 and abolished in 2021, the legacy of coercive enforcement remains significant (Congressional-Executive Commission on China 2022).

Conditions in Women's Prisons

Conditions in women's prisons in China are frequently harsh, affected by overcrowding, inadequate healthcare, and limited access to rehabilitation. On average, women's facilities in China hold 14 percent more people than men's facilities, with some, like Guangdong Women's Prison, even more severely overcrowded (Dui Hua Foundation 2015). Reports describe cramped and unsanitary conditions, with up to fourteen women confined in cells as small as three square meters, contributing to illness, bedsores, and heightened tensions (Dui Hua Foundation 2015).

Additionally, healthcare delivery remains inadequate. In some prisons, official budgets reportedly cover only one-sixth of actual medical needs, and costs for elderly prisoners have risen sharply (77 percent over three years) without matching resources (Dui Hua Foundation 2024). Overcrowding further stretches medical infrastructure, worsening the impact of chronic illnesses and poor sanitation.

Rehabilitation programs are also limited and rarely gender-specific. While vocational and counseling programs exist in some prisons, they are often generic, inconsistently offered, and poorly attended due to overcrowding and rigid labor schedules. Studies indicate that although Chinese prison law emphasizes punishment and reform, actual practice prioritizes productivity and discipline over rehabilitation (Zhao et al. 2019).

These problems are especially evident in documented cases of extreme abuse. One of the most well-documented cases of abuse comes from the Liaoning Women's Labor Camp. Detainees, particularly political prisoners and Falun Gong practitioners (i.e., a practice of meditation and moral teachings), have reported torture, chaining, and sexual assault by guards and inmates acting on official orders (Amnesty International 2013). A report revealed cases of rape, electrocution, and solitary confinement in windowless cells, revealing the gap between official claims of reform and the reality of punitive control (Luo 2013).

Health and Mental Health Issues

Incarcerated women in China face physical and mental health challenges, which are made worse by overcrowding, limited medical resources, and a lack of gender-responsive care. Many enter prison with preexisting conditions, but the prison system is often unable to meet their needs, with medical care often limited to emergencies (U.S. Department of State 2020).

Pregnant women and mothers face risks due to insufficient prenatal and postnatal care, often administered by untrained staff. Additionally, there is often limited access to hygiene products and clean environments during menstruation, pregnancy, and postpartum recovery. Drinking water is provided, but there is often inadequate hot water for sanitary hygiene. Moreover, meals frequently lack the nutrition needed during pregnancy (Dui Hua Foundation 2014). These conditions increase the likelihood of infections, discomfort, and maternal health complications.

Mental health conditions are also common but largely untreated. In one study, two-thirds of incarcerated women met the criteria for at least one psychiatric disorder, with depression (37 percent) and PTSD (22 percent) being the most prevalent (Zhong et al. 2020). Although China's Mental Health Law (2013) mandates that prisons provide psychological counseling when necessary, most facilities do not have mental health wards or specialists, leaving incarcerated individuals without access to mental healthcare (Zhong et al. 2020). The prison environment makes trauma worse, increases emotional suffering, and makes it harder for women to recover and rebuild their lives.

One of the most revealing examples of these failures is the case of Masanjia Women's Labor Camp. Masanjia housed many women in forced labor conditions where medical care was nearly nonexistent. One former detainee, Liu Hua, described months of isolation in a small cell without access to a toilet or medical attention. She was physically restrained for hours and exhibited severe stress and physical deterioration (Amnesty International 2013).

Impact on Families and Children

The incarceration of women in China has consequences for their children, leading to emotional, social, and economic hardship. A Ministry of Justice survey estimated that 600,000 children had incarcerated parents, yet nearly 95 percent received no formal support (Dui Hua Foundation 2012b). Without state assistance, many are cared for by elderly relatives, contributing to an 82 percent school dropout rate due to financial instability. Children of incarcerated mothers often face stigma, bullying, and exclusion. In one study, children described themselves as "orphans" and reported strained relationships with caregivers (Xia and Lam 2020).

Maintaining family contact is also difficult. Although two visits per month are legally permitted, access is often restricted by staff discretion (Dui Hua Foundation 2012b). Children are not allowed to live in prison with their mothers, compounding emotional distress and attachment issues. These conditions point to the need for family-centered reforms and alternative sentencing for non-violent female offenders.

Some efforts to maintain maternal bonds exist, but they are rare. Shanghai Women's Prison runs maternal-focused programs, including poetry, films, and drama centered on mother-daughter relationships. "Mary," a 36-year-old serving a reduced sentence for drug trafficking, began reconnecting with her mother through these classes (Yang 2015). Each year on International Women's Day, the prison invites mothers of selected inmates for visits. For example, Liu, convicted of fraud, reconciled with her estranged mother during an event. For these women, taking photos with their aging mothers is meaningful, especially when family reunification may never come.

Though limited in scope, these programs offer opportunities for emotional healing and reflection. While children are still not permitted to live with their mothers in custody, such initiatives represent an awareness of the importance of preserving family ties during incarceration (Yang 2015).

Policy Reforms and Recommendations

To address the rising incarceration of women in China, most of whom are convicted of non-violent, poverty-driven crimes, policymakers should expand non-custodial alternatives (e.g., probation, community service, and suspended sentences) (Penal Reform International 2019). These reforms would help reduce overcrowding and target the causes of women's criminalization.

Legal and correctional practices must become more gender-responsive. Courts should consider factors like caregiving responsibilities, pregnancy, and histories of trauma when sentencing. Prisons should offer rehabilitation programs tailored to women, including education, trauma-informed care, and job training (Dui Hua Foundation 2024).

Overcrowding, inadequate healthcare, and poor sanitation remain problems. Many women's prisons operate over capacity, with limited access to prenatal care, menstrual hygiene products, and chronic illness treatment, especially for elderly and pregnant inmates (Dui Hua Foundation 2024). Enhanced health infrastructure and oversight are needed to protect basic rights.

Mental healthcare is severely lacking despite a high need. Two-thirds of incarcerated women meet the criteria for psychiatric disorders, particularly depression and PTSD (Zhong et al. 2020). Prisons should implement screenings, provide access to counseling, and fulfill their obligations under China's Mental Health Law.

China must also end legacy practices of coercive family planning enforcement, which continue in regions like Xinjiang (Congressional-Executive Commission on China 2022). These violations of bodily autonomy require legal prohibition and accountability.

Additionally, reform of Article 176 is needed to protect women criminalized for informal economic activity, especially those lacking regulatory knowledge (Liu et al. 2018). Clarifying how the law is applied could help separate serious fraud from small-scale borrowing.

Lastly, with 600,000 children affected by parental incarceration and most receiving no formal support, China should implement child welfare programs and promote alternatives to maternal imprisonment to preserve family bonds (Xia and Lam 2020). Expanding visitation rights and supporting family reunification efforts would help mitigate the emotional and developmental harm experienced by these children.

Japan

Historical Context

The historical context of women's incarceration in Japan has been shaped by traditional gender norms, evolving legal systems, and socioeconomic change. Historically, Confucian ideals kept women in domestic roles, emphasizing obedience and moral virtue. Texts like *Onna Daigaku* ("The Great Learning for Women") instructed women to obey their husbands and in-laws, reinforcing patriarchal social structures (Kaibara 1914). Female deviance was viewed as a moral failing instead of a violation of the law, so punishments emphasized shame over incarceration. Public shaming rituals such as *hikimawashi* (parading offenders through the streets) and the use of the *cangue* (a wooden collar) were common, especially for women accused of dishonor (Terazawa 2018).

The Meiji era (1868–1912) brought Western-style legal reforms and the creation of formal prisons, including Abashiri Prison. Women began to be incarcerated for economic crimes (e.g., theft and fraud), often tied to poverty and industrialization (Botsman 2005). Yet, they continued to be framed as morally deviant. Abortion was criminalized, and women could be incarcerated for terminating their pregnancies. Activists like Kishida Toshiko and Kanno Sugako were imprisoned for challenging gender norms, the latter executed for alleged treason (Mackie 2003).

Another example of gendered criminalization is the case of Iva Toguri, a Japanese American woman accused of being "Tokyo Rose," a wartime radio propagandist. Although she was in Japan during the Second World War, Toguri was not prosecuted there. Instead, she was convicted of treason in the United States in 1949 due to coerced witness testimony and anti-Japanese sentiment (Iovino 2020). Her case illustrates how women have been framed as political threats and punished for symbolic betrayals.

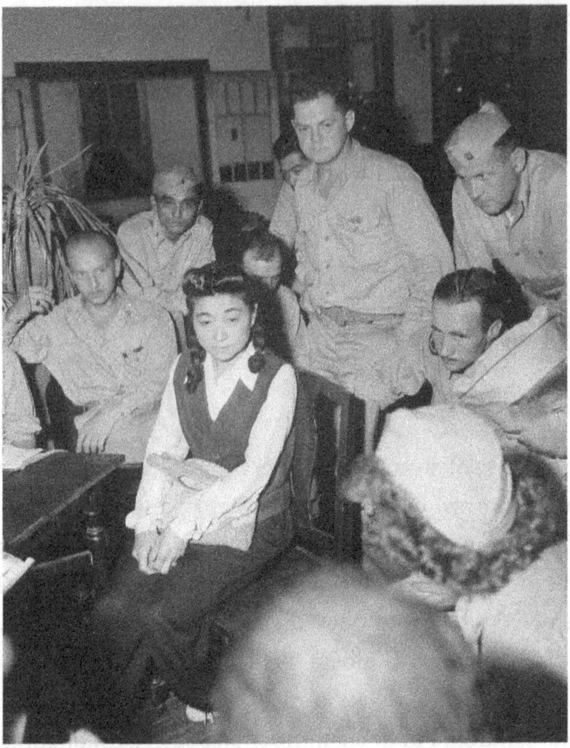

Iva Toguri, identified as "Tokyo Rose," being interviewed by journalists in Tokyo, 1945 (US National Archives and Records Administration)

After the Second World War, US-led reforms introduced a new constitution and modern criminal procedures, emphasizing rights and equality (Japan Society 2023). Nevertheless, female incarceration rose in the postwar period, driven first by property crimes and later by strict drug laws. By the 1990s, stimulant-related offenses became a leading cause of female imprisonment. As of 2021, 80 percent of incarcerated women had been convicted of theft or drug crimes (Human Rights Watch 2023a).

Today, women imprisoned in Japanese prisons face inadequate mental healthcare, poor medical treatment, and family separation. Most mothers are separated from their newborns shortly after birth, despite legal stipulations allowing joint incarceration, which are rarely granted (Human Rights Watch 2023a). Elderly women, who are often isolated and impoverished, sometimes view prison as a place of refuge (Fukada 2018). Overall, there is a need for more gender-responsive, supportive criminal justice policies.

Female Incarceration Rates and Trends

Female incarceration rates in Japan are low compared to their male counterparts, but they have fluctuated in response to changing laws and socioeconomic conditions. Women comprise approximately 9.1 percent of the total prison population, up from 5.4 percent in 2000 (World Prison Brief 2024). The percentage of women entering prison has also risen, more than doubling from 4.8 percent in 1996 to 10.3 percent in 2021 (Human Rights Watch 2023a). The number of incarcerated women peaked at around 5,343 in 2010, but it has declined to approximately 3,671 in 2024 (World Prison Brief 2024). These women are housed within 11 dedicated women's prisons, with a combined capacity of around 6,500 people (Human Rights Watch 2023a).

Most are imprisoned for non-violent offenses, especially economically motivated crimes like theft and drug violations. These patterns are associated with poverty, social isolation, and marginalization. Many of the women incarcerated for drug crimes are first-time offenders driven by financial desperation. Although overall drug use in Japan remains low, the country enforces strict anti-narcotics laws, and those arrested for possession or trafficking face harsh penalties (Human Rights Watch 2023a).

A notable trend in recent years is the rise in the incarceration of elderly women. Between 2004 and 2023, the proportion of incarcerated women aged sixty-five or older rose from 5.4 percent to 22.7 percent (Kyodo News 2024). Many of these women commit petty theft as a means of survival. They often view prison as a safe place because of inadequate pensions, poor health, or a lack of family support (Fukada 2018). These developments demonstrate some of the challenges tied to Japan's aging population and insufficient social safety nets.

Another growing concern is the high rate of repeat offenses among incarcerated women, especially those convicted of theft. Recidivism is driven by economic instability, homelessness, and the lack of gender-responsive programming. After release, many women struggle to access employment, housing, and healthcare, increasing their risk of reoffending (Human Rights Watch 2023a).

Demographics of Incarcerated Women

The demographics of incarcerated women in Japan indicate strong links between poverty, aging, and social isolation. Women aged sixty-five and older account for nearly 23 percent of the female prison population (Kyodo News 2024).

Many are repeatedly incarcerated for minor crimes like shoplifting, often driven by financial desperation or loneliness. A Tokyo study found that more than half of elderly female shoplifters lived alone, and nearly 40 percent had little to no contact with family (Fukada 2018). For many, prison is seen as a place of stability, providing food, shelter, and medical care in the absence of sufficient support systems. Reflecting these trends, incarcerated women in Japan tend to be older than their counterparts in other countries. Only about 25 percent are in their twenties or thirties, around 23 percent are in their forties, and approximately 29 percent fall between fifty and sixty-four (Ministry of Justice 2023).

Low educational attainment also contributes to women's vulnerability to incarceration. Sasaki and colleagues (2022) found that women with histories of substance use or early-life adversity often had lower educational and economic status. Their study also revealed that nearly 65 percent of incarcerated women were mothers, emphasizing the overlap of caregiving responsibilities, economic marginalization, and criminal justice involvement.

Furthermore, mental illness and trauma are widespread among this population. A 2022 Ministry of Justice report found that 28 percent of women admitted to prison had a psychosocial disability (OHCHR 2022). Interviews with formerly incarcerated women further show that many experienced childhood abuse or domestic violence, and that their trauma was often worsened by the harsh conditions of incarceration (Human Rights Watch 2023a).

Elderly Women and Shoplifting

Nearly one in four incarcerated women in Japan is over sixty-five. Many elderly women repeatedly commit petty theft, often viewing prison as safer than the outside. A Tokyo survey found over half of these women lived alone, and 40 percent had almost no family contact. Incarceration provides them with food, shelter, and medical care missing from the community. Outside prison, many struggle with poverty, social isolation, and inadequate pensions. They also have trouble finding stable housing or employment after release. With few social supports and growing loneliness, some intentionally reoffend to return to the structure and care they receive behind bars.

Crimes Leading to Incarceration

In Japan, most women are incarcerated for non-violent, economically motivated offenses. As of 2023, over 80 percent of female inmates were convicted for either theft (48 percent) or drug-related offenses (33 percent) (Human Rights Watch 2023a). Shoplifting, particularly among older women, is especially prevalent. In one case, an 81-year-old woman deliberately broke the law to go to prison, stating she did not want to "die alone" and saw incarceration as a source of shelter and companionship (Singh 2025). Her story reflects the trend that poverty, loneliness, and a lack of family support drive elderly women to commit petty crimes, with prison substituting for the social services they lack.

Drug offenses are the second most common cause of women's incarceration, and Japan's anti-narcotics laws impose harsh penalties. Even minor involvement in possession or low-level trafficking can lead to long prison sentences (Human Rights Watch 2023a). Recently, Australian grandmother Donna Nelson was sentenced to six years in prison in 2024 after being convicted of importing methamphetamine into Japan. Nelson claimed a romance scammer had deceived her, but the court ruled that she bore sufficient responsibility for the offense (Oaten 2024).

While theft and drug charges dominate incarceration patterns, a smaller share of women are sentenced for other non-violent crimes such as fraud, embezzlement, and administrative violations. Violent offenses remain rare among women in Japan (Ministry of Justice 2022).

Contributing Laws and Policies

Japan's laws contribute to the incarceration of women, especially for non-violent economic crimes, drug offenses, and repeat offending. Under the Penal Code (Article 13), minor violations like petty theft or simple drug possession can result in prison sentences ranging from one month to twenty years (Japanese Law Translation 2025). Japan's zero-tolerance drug laws, especially the **Stimulant Control Act**, impose harsh penalties for low-level or first-time offenses. Nearly 60 percent of women incarcerated under this law are repeat offenders, often struggling with drug dependence, coercion, or financial instability (Human Rights Watch 2023a).

The Act for the Prevention of Recidivism (Act No. 104 of 2016) establishes coordinated support to aid ex-offenders with housing, employment, and community rehabilitation (Government of Japan 2016). However, despite their well-intended provisions, these programs are rarely gender-responsive. Evaluations show that they often overlook the needs of elderly, economically vulnerable women, resulting in repeated short-term incarcerations without reintegrative support. Consequently, many women cycle through short-term sentences without escaping the conditions (i.e., loneliness, financial strain, lack of social support) that led them to crime in the first place (UNODC 2023).

Despite endorsing international standards like the Bangkok Rules, Japan has been slow to implement community-based, trauma-informed alternatives to incarceration. Existing programs often lack structural support to address the root causes of women's criminal behavior. As a result, prison has become a safety net for women without access to adequate housing, healthcare, or social support (UNODC 2023). Expanding non-custodial sentencing, improving gender-specific probation services, and investing in rehabilitation and community reentry programs would provide more effective alternatives to incarceration.

Conditions in Women's Prisons

Women's prisons in Japan are structured and regimented. Women follow strict daily schedules, maintain silence during designated periods, and participate in labor like sewing, cleaning, and factory work. Workdays often last up to eight hours on weekdays, and refusal to comply can result in disciplinary action (U.S. Embassy & Consulates in Japan 2024). Cells are small and sparsely furnished, with limited privacy and personal possessions, indicating a system prioritizing discipline and control over comfort and rehabilitation. Solitary confinement is used during pre-trial detention or as punishment, often with restricted communication (Human Rights Watch 2023a).

Although this environment contributes to low violence and orderly management, it raises human rights concerns. Reports document verbal abuse by staff, arbitrary use of solitary confinement, and inadequate mental health services, particularly for women with trauma histories, disabilities, or preexisting mental health conditions (Human Rights Watch 2023a).

Additionally, the aging prison population presents challenges. Some prisons have introduced eldercare services, including assistance with bathing, toileting, and mobility. However, most facilities lack appropriate infrastructure and trained personnel, turning prisons into nursing homes (Fukada 2018). The Program for Reintegration into Society offers limited post-release support for elderly or disabled inmates, but implementation is inconsistent and insufficient (UNODC 2023).

Transgender individuals also face heightened risks in Japan's prisons. Transgender women often experience misgendering, verbal abuse, denial of hormone therapy, and invasive searches by staff (Human Rights Watch 2023a). Japan's Act on Penal Detention (Article 34.2) requires that female detainees be examined by female staff. This mandate extends to transgender women, even those who have begun but not completed legal gender recognition (Amnesty International 2017). However, there remains a lack of anti-discrimination provisions and protective measures, so transgender inmates remain vulnerable to staff abuse, extended solitary confinement, and a lack of gender-affirming medical care (Human Rights Watch 2025).

Health and Mental Health Issues

Incarcerated women in Japan face physical and mental health challenges, especially as this population ages. Many enter prison with chronic conditions or mobility issues, but the system struggles to meet their needs because of physician shortages and outdated infrastructure. Older women, who often view prison as a source of stability and healthcare, often encounter inadequate support once they are inside (Human Rights Watch 2023a).

Mental health services are also lacking. Most incarcerated women have experienced trauma before imprisonment, yet counseling and psychological care are rarely provided. Many women are unaware of available services or face barriers to receiving them, worsening conditions like depression, anxiety, and PTSD. Strict prison discipline, rigid routines, and the use of solitary confinement worsen mental health, especially for those with preexisting trauma (Human Rights Watch 2023a).

Stigma surrounding mental illness in Japan intensifies the problem. Cultural attitudes that frame mental health issues as personal failings discourage women from seeking help, in and out of prison (Ando et al. 2013). These factors contribute to a cycle of untreated trauma, emotional deterioration, and increased risk of recidivism (Human Rights Watch 2023a).

Pregnant women face additional barriers. Until recently, there were cases of women being shackled during transport and even postpartum, violating international norms like the Mandela and Bangkok Rules (Human Rights Watch 2023a). Although a 2014 directive limited restraints during labor, reform in

2024 was needed to extend protections to transportation and postpartum care (Human Rights Watch 2024).

Furthermore, medical care for pregnant women remains limited. With only 291 doctors serving 73 correctional facilities for both men and women, access to prenatal and postnatal care is often delayed or insufficient (Takino 2023). Japan has expanded community-based maternal healthcare through reforms like the 2018 Basic Law for Child and Maternal Health. However, these reforms have not been extended to incarcerated women (Suzuki 2024).

Impact on Families and Children

Women's incarceration in Japan has consequences for their families, especially their children. Many of these women were primary caregivers, and their imprisonment disrupts family dynamics. Children often experience anxiety, depression, and social withdrawal, while mothers report guilt and emotional distress over their inability to care for their children (Sasaki et al. 2022).

Stigma around incarceration adds to this burden. In Japan's honor-focused society, children of incarcerated women often face bullying, social exclusion, and shame, increasing the effects of separation (Human Rights Watch 2023a). Caregiving often falls on extended family (typically grandparents), whose households may already be under economic and emotional strain (Sasaki et al. 2022). These dynamics increase the risk of long-term disadvantages for children, complicating their integration into school and community life.

Limited visitation rights and restricted communication further weaken mother–child bonds. Mothers may go months or years without seeing their children, making reunification after release more challenging. Advocates stress the importance of family-centered support programs, child-friendly visitation policies, and alternative sentencing for non-violent offenses to preserve family relationships (Sasaki et al. 2022).

Although Japanese law permits infants to reside with their mothers in prison for up to eighteen months with warden approval (Article 66 of the Act on Penal Detention Facilities), this right is rarely granted. As of 2019, seven penal institutions had mother–child units. However, between 2011 and 2017, only three women were permitted to stay with their newborns, and even then, for no more than twelve days. Many mothers were never even informed of their right to apply (Human Rights Watch 2023a).

These practices are counter to Japanese law and international standards. Immediate separation denies mothers the opportunity to bond with their infants during a critical period and has been described as traumatizing. Such practices can cause lasting emotional and developmental harm to mothers and children (Human Rights Watch 2023a).

Policy Reforms and Recommendations

To address the gendered and structural causes of women's incarceration in Japan, policymakers should expand non-custodial alternatives and trauma-informed, gender-responsive sentencing. Courts must consider caregiving responsibilities, trauma histories, and poverty when sentencing, especially for non-violent and first-time offenses. Diversion programs, probation, and home detention would offer more effective responses while reducing the reliance on incarceration (UNODC 2023).

Reentry support is also critical. Although the 2016 Act for the Prevention of Recidivism provides a framework for reintegration, current programs often neglect the needs of elderly and economically marginalized women. These supports should include housing, employment, and trauma-informed services, especially for mothers and older adults (UNODC 2023).

Additionally, prison conditions require reform. Human Rights Watch (2023a) has documented solitary confinement, verbal abuse, and limited mental healthcare. Incarcerated women, many of whom have experienced abuse or mental illness, need access to counseling rather than punishment. Staff should be trained in trauma-informed care and gender sensitivity. Moreover, societal efforts to reduce mental health stigma and increase treatment access are also essential (Ando et al. 2013).

Healthcare inside prisons is inadequate, particularly for elderly and pregnant women. With only a few hundred doctors serving the national prison system, delays in treatment are common (Takino 2023). Maternal and geriatric care must be improved, and reforms like the 2018 Basic Law for Child and Maternal Health should be extended to incarcerated populations (Suzuki 2024).

Transgender inmates also face serious risks, including misgendering and denial of medical care. Despite legal mandates for gender-appropriate searches, enforcement is inconsistent. Japan must implement antidiscrimination protections, ensure access to hormone therapy, and train staff to uphold human rights standards (Human Rights Watch 2025).

Family separation is another major harm. Although the law permits infants to stay with their mothers in prison, this is rarely granted (Human Rights Watch 2023a). Expanding visitation, bonding programs, and family-centered alternatives can support maternal well-being and reduce harm to children (Sasaki et al. 2022).

Finally, Japan must address the incarceration of elderly women driven by poverty and isolation. Expanding pension access, elder care, and community outreach can reduce reliance on prison as a substitute for social services (Fukada 2018).

Conclusion

The experiences of incarcerated women in Uzbekistan, China, and Japan uncover similarities related to poverty, gender inequality, and inadequate social supports. Across all three countries, women are usually imprisoned for non-violent offenses like theft, drug possession, and minor economic crimes. Their crimes are often driven by financial desperation, coercion, or social isolation. Many of these women come from marginalized backgrounds, with limited education, poor access to healthcare, and histories of trauma. These patterns demonstrate that criminal justice systems in the region frequently punish women for survival-based crimes but neglect the structural conditions that influence women to commit them.

Despite these similarities, each country has distinct legal frameworks and cultural factors that affect women's incarceration. Uzbekistan's legacy of Soviet authoritarianism, moral policing, and the late criminalization of domestic violence has extended harsh conditions and political repression within women's prisons. China, while undergoing legal modernization, still uses incarceration as political and population control, primarily through punitive responses to economic crimes and family planning violations. Japan faces a rising share of elderly women in prison, reflecting the shortcomings of its aging welfare system and the punitive handling of social isolation.

Institutional conditions also differ across these countries. Uzbek prisons suffer from neglect, overcrowding, and religious discrimination. Chinese women's prisons experience overcrowding, forced labor, and poor mental healthcare, especially for political detainees. Japan's highly regulated prisons impose strict routines and discipline. However, they often fail to provide trauma-informed support, especially for elderly or transgender inmates.

While reform efforts exist in all three countries, they are insufficient. A shift toward gender-responsive sentencing, non-custodial alternatives, and trauma-informed, rehabilitative care is needed to address the root causes of women's incarceration across Central and East Asia.

References

ACCA (Analytical Center for Central Asia). 2022. "Uzbekistan: Women in Prisons Are Forced to Terminate Their Pregnancies." September 8, 2022. https://acca.media/en/16406/uzbekistan-women-in-prisons-are-forced-to-terminate-their-pregnancies/.

Akhrorova, Aziza Nigmanovna. 2021. "Repression of Uzbek Women Journalists." *The American Journal of Social Science and Education Innovations* 3 (11): 81–5.

Amnesty International. 2023. *Uzbekistan: Human Rights in the Spotlight.* https://www.amnesty.org/en/location/europe-and-central-asia/eastern-europe-and-central-asia/uzbekistan/report-uzbekistan.

Amnesty International. 2017. *Human Rights Law and Discrimination Against LGBT People in Japan.* https://www.amnesty.org/es/wp-content/uploads/2021/05/ASA2259552017ENGLISH.pdf.

Amnesty International. 2015. *No End in Sight: Torture and Forced Confessions in China.* November 2015. Index ASA 17/2730/2015. https://www.amnesty.org/en/documents/asa17/2730/2015/en/.

Amnesty International. 2013. *"Masanjia Re-Education Through Labor Camp: Deprivation of Freedom and Health."* ASA 17/042/2013, May 22. Amnesty International. https://www.amnesty.org/en/wp-content/uploads/2021/06/asa170422013en.pdf.

Amnesty International. 2012. "China: Rights Defender Mao Hengfeng Detained." *Amnesty International USA*. October 4. https://www.amnestyusa.org/cases/mao-hengfeng/.

Ando, Shuntaro, Sosei Yamaguchi, Yuta Aoki, and Graham Thornicroft. 2013. "Review of Mental-Health-Related Stigma in Japan." *Psychiatry and Clinical Neurosciences* 67 (7): 471–82.

Anhor. 2023. "Study: 43% of Surveyed Women in Uzbekistan Are Victims of Domestic Violence." *Anhor.uz*. May 12, 2023. https://anhor.uz/news/research/.

Bakken, Børge. 2005. *Crime, Punishment, and Policing in China.* Lanham, MD: Rowman & Littlefield.

Botheju, Wasantha S. P., Fatima Zghyer, Salman Mahmud, Yvan J. F. Hutin, and Philippa Easterbrook. 2019. "The Epidemiology of Hepatitis C Virus in Central Asia: Systematic Review, Meta-Analyses, and Meta-Regression Analyses." *Scientific Reports* 9: 2090.

Botsman, Daniel V. 2005. *Punishment and Power in the Making of Modern Japan.* Princeton, NJ: Princeton University Press.

Branigan, Tania. 2012. "Photograph of Woman with Aborted Foetus Sparks Fury in China." *The Guardian*. June 14. https://www.theguardian.com/world/2012/jun/14/china-forced-abortion-photograph.

Bureau of Democracy, Human Rights, and Labor. 2009. *2008 Country Reports on Human Rights Practices: Uzbekistan*. U.S. Department of State. February 25, 2009. https://2009-2017.state.gov/j/drl/rls/hrrpt/2008/sca/119143.htm.

CEIC. 2025. "Uzbekistan Annual Household Income Per Capita." https://www.ceicdata.com/en/indicator/uzbekistan/annual-household-income-per-capita.

Chan, Kam Wing. 2015. "Five Decades of the Chinese Hukou System." In *Handbook of Chinese Migration: Identity and Wellbeing*, edited by Robyn R. Iredale and Fei Guo, 23–47. Northampton, MA: Edward Elgar.

Cheng, Hongming. 2016. *Financial Crime in China: Developments, Sanctions, and the Systemic Spread of Corruption*. 1st ed. Basingstoke: Palgrave Macmillan.

Commission on Security and Cooperation in Europe. 2023. "Uzbekistan's Litany of Violations." *U.S. Helsinki Commission*. https://www.csce.gov/statements/uzbekistans-litany-violations/.

Congressional-Executive Commission on China. 2022. Population Control in Xinjiang. https://www.congress.gov/117/chrg/CHRG-117jhrg47949/CHRG-117jhrg47949.pdf.

Daryo. 2023. "Fraud-Related Crimes in Uzbekistan Jumped, Senator Says." *Daryo.uz*. April 10, 2023. https://daryo.uz/en/2023/04/10/fraud-related-crimes-in-uzbekistan-jumped-senator-says.

Dikotter, Frank. 2002. *Crime, Punishment and the Prison in Modern China*. New York: Columbia University Press.

Dui Hua Foundation. 2024. "Gray Matters: China's Aging Prisoners." *Dui Hua Human Rights Journal*. April. https://www.duihuahrjournal.org/2024/04/gray-matters-chinas-aging-prisoners.html.

Dui Hua Foundation. 2020. "Big Increase in Women Behind Bars in China." *Dui Hua Human Rights Journal*. September 14, 2020. https://www.duihuahrjournal.org/2020/09/big-increase-in-women-behind-bars-in.html.

Dui Hua Foundation. 2015. "China: Women Prisoner Numbers Rise 10 Times Faster than Men." *Dui Hua Human Rights Journal*. June 23, 2015. https://www.duihuahrjournal.org/2015/06/china-women-prisoner-numbers-rise-10.html.

Dui Hua Foundation. 2014. "China's Women's Prisons: Areas for Improvement." *Dialogue* (54). https://duihua.org/dialogue-issue-54-chinas-womens-prisons-areas-for-improvement/.

Dui Hua Foundation. 2012a. "Bridging the Legal Gap for China's Incarcerated Women." *Dui Hua Journal*. April 24, 2012. https://www.duihuahrjournal.org/2012/04/bridging-legal-gap-for-chinas.html.

Dui Hua Foundation. 2012b. "Dialogue—Issue 46: Sino-US Comparison: Children of Incarcerated Mothers." *Dui Hua Dialogue*. https://duihua.org/dialogue-issue-46-sino-us-comparison-children-of-incarcerated-mothers/.

Facts and Details. 2016. "Crime in Uzbekistan." https://factsanddetails.com/central-asia/Uzbekistan/sub8_3f/entry-4726.html.

Fair, Helen, and Roy Walmsley. 2022. *World Female Imprisonment List*. 5th ed. London: Institute for Crime & Justice Policy Research. https://www.prisonstudies.org/sites/default/files/resources/downloads/world_female_imprisonment_list_5th_edition.pdf.

Fukada, Shiho. 2018. "For Many of Japan's Elderly Women, Prison Is a Haven." *Pulitzer Center*. March 18, 2018. https://pulitzercenter.org/stories/many-japans-elderly-women-prison-haven.

Government of Japan. 2016. *Act for the Prevention of Recidivism (Act No. 104 of 2016)*. Japanese Law Translation. https://www.japaneselawtranslation.go.jp/en/laws/view/3425/en.

Greenhalgh, Susan. 2008. *Just One Child: Science and Policy in Deng's China*. Berkeley, CA: University of California Press.

Hershatter, Gail. 2014. *The Gender of Memory: Rural Women and China's Collective Past*. Berkeley: University of California Press.

HIV Justice Network. 2022. "Uzbekistan: Female Sex Worker Sentenced to Three Years for Alleged HIV Transmission." November 3, 2022. https://www.hivjustice.net/cases/uzbekistan-woman-sex-worker-sentenced-to-3-years-for-alleged-hiv-transmission/.

Human Rights Watch. 2025. "Japan Should End Abusive Detention Conditions for Transgender People." *Human Rights Watch*. June 11, 2025. https://www.hrw.org/news/2025/06/11/japan-should-end-abusive-detention-conditions-transgender-people.

Human Rights Watch. 2024. "Japan: Broadens Ban on Restraints for Jailed Women in Labor." March 29, 2024. https://www.hrw.org/news/2024/03/29/japan-broadens-ban-restraints-jailed-women-labor.

Human Rights Watch. 2023a. "They Don't Treat Us Like Human Beings: Abuse of Imprisoned Women in Japan." November 14, 2023. https://www.hrw.org/report/2023/11/14/they-dont-treat-us-human-beings/abuse-imprisoned-women-japan.

Human Rights Watch. 2023b. *World Report 2023: Uzbekistan*. https://www.hrw.org/world-report/2023/country-chapters/uzbekistan.

Institute for War and Peace Reporting. 2014. "TB Scourge in Uzbek Prisons." March 1, 2014. https://iwpr.net/global-voices/tb-scourge-uzbek-prisons.

International Drug Policy Consortium (IDPC). 2015. "China: Women Prisoner Numbers Rise 10 Times Faster than Men." *IDPC News*. August 4, 2015. https://idpc.net/news/2015/08/china-women-prisoner-numbers-rise-10-times-faster-than-men.

International Harm Reduction Association and World Health Organization. 2013. *Women in Prison: A Review of the Conditions in Male and Female Prisons in Europe and Central Asia*. August 2013. https://www.hri.global/files/2014/08/06/IHRA_WomenInPrisonReport_Aug2013_A5_Web.pdf.

International Partnership for Human Rights. 2025. "Freedoms Under Threat as Uzbekistan Continues to Put Pressure on Journalists and Human Rights Defenders."

https://iphronline.org/articles/freedoms-under-threat-as-uzbekistan-continues-to-put-pressure-on-journalists-and-human-rights-defenders/.

Iovino, Nicholas. 2020. "Tokyo Rose: The Woman Wrongfully Convicted of Treason." *Courthouse News*. November 18, 2020. https://www.courthousenews.com/tokyo-rose-the-woman-wrongfully-convicted-of-treason/.

Japan Society. 2023. "The Allied Occupation of Japan." Japan Society. November 6, 2023. https://japansociety.org/news/the-allied-occupation-of-japan/.

Japanese Law Translation. 2025. *Penal Code (Act No. 45 of 1907, as Amended)*. Ministry of Justice, Japan. https://www.japaneselawtranslation.go.jp/en/laws/view/3581.

Kaibara, Ekiken. 1914. *Women and Wisdom of Japan*. Translated by Basil Hall Chamberlain. London: J. Murray. https://archive.org/details/womenwisdomofjap00kaib_1.

Kun. 2023. "Uzbekistan to Decriminalize Certain Types of Crimes with Low Social Risk." *Kun.uz*. November 14, 2023. https://www.kun.uz/en/news/2023/11/14/uzbekistan-to-decriminalize-certain-types-of-crimes-with-low-social-risk.

Kun.uz. 2020. "Women Behind Bars: Special Photo Report from Zangiota Women's Colony." February 14, 2020. https://kun.uz/en/news/2020/02/14/women-behind-bars-special-photo-report-from-zangiota-womens-colony

Kyodo News. 2024. "80% of Female Inmates in Japan Convicted on Theft, Drug Charges." https://english.kyodonews.net/articles/-/51570?phrase=%2Cspi&words=.

Liang, Bin, Hong Lu, and Melanie Taylor. 2009. "Female Drug Abusers, Narcotics Offenders, and Legal Punishment in China." *Journal of Criminal Justice* 37 (2): 133–41.

Liu, Jinghuan. 2008. *The Most Disadvantaged: An Examination and Analysis of Rural Girls' Access to Higher Education in China*. MA thesis, Kent State University. https://etd.ohiolink.edu/acprod/odb_etd/ws/send_file/send?accession=kent1207896230&disposition=inline.

Liu, Xinmin, Flora Huang, and Horace Yeung. 2018. "The Regulation of Illegal Fundraising in China." *Asia Pacific Law Review* 26 (1): 77–100.

Luo, Chris. 2013. "Women 'Chained Up and Tortured' in Labour Camp: Dark Secrets of Female Labour Camp Revealed." *South China Morning Post*. April 8. https://www.scmp.com/news/china/article/1210058/dark-secrets-female-labour-camp-revealed.

MacCormack, Geoffrey. 1990. *Traditional Chinese Penal Law*. Edinburgh: Edinburgh University Press.

Mackie, Vera. 2003. *Feminism in Modern Japan: Citizenship, Embodiment and Sexuality*. Cambridge: Cambridge University Press.

Mamasolieva, Shaxrizoda. 2023. "Women's Rights in Uzbekistan: Legislative Problems and Their Solutions." *Uzbekistan Law Blog*. https://uzbekistanlawblog.com/womens-rights-in-uzbekistan-legislative-problems-and-their-solutions/.

Ministry of Justice. 2023. "Trends in Age Composition of Female Inmates." *White Paper on Crime 2023*. https://hakusyo1.moj.go.jp/jp/71/nfm/images/full/h2-4-2-4.jpg.

Ministry of Justice. 2022. White Paper on Crime 2022. https://hakusyo1.moj.go.jp/en/71/WHITE_PAPER_ON_CRIME2022.pdf.

Norwegian Helsinki Committee. 2021. *Release of Women Political Prisoners in Uzbekistan Urged*. https://nhc.no/en/release-woman-political-prisoners/.

Oaten, James. 2024. "Donna Nelson Found Guilty of Importing Methamphetamine into Japan." *ABC News*. December 4, 2024. https://www.abc.net.au/news/2024-12-04/donna-nelson-guilty-drug-smuggling-trial-japan/104679648.

OC Index—Organized Crime Index. 2023. "Uzbekistan: Criminal Markets and Heroin Trade." *Criminality in Uzbekistan—The Organized Crime Index*. https://ocindex.net/country/uzbekistan.

Office of the High Commissioner for Human Rights (OHCHR). 2022. *Submission to the UN on Persons with Psychosocial Disabilities in Detention*. https://www.ohchr.org/sites/default/files/documents/issues/ohchr-cfis/accelerating-eliminate-vawgs/subm-accelerating-efforts-eliminate-cso-hrw.pdf.

OMCT (World Organisation Against Torture). 2003. "Uzbekistan: Violence Against Women in Prison." Urgent Intervention UZB 310703.VAW. https://www.omct.org/en/resources/urgent-interventions/uzbekistan-violence-against-women-in-prison.

Penal Reform International. 2021. *Брошюра Узбекистан Final Сентябрь 2021* [Uzbekistan Penitentiary System Baseline Study]. London: Penal Reform International. https://cdn.penalreform.org/wp-content/uploads/2021/09/Брошюра_Узбекистан_Final_Сентябрь2021.pdf.

Penal Reform International. 2019. *Global Prison Trends 2019: Special Focus on Women in Prison*. London: PRI. https://www.penalreform.org/resource/global-prison-trends-2019/.

Prison Insider. 2024. "Uzbekistan: Prison Profile." https://www.prison-insider.com/en/countryprofile/ouzbekistan-2024?s=populations-specifiques-5d9b19c2d4a4f#populations-specifiques-5d9b19c2d4a4f.

Reuters. 2018. "Chinese Businesswoman's Sentence Reduced to 25 Years in Jail." *Reuters*. March 24. https://www.reuters.com/article/business/chinese-businesswomans-sentence-reduced-to-25-years-in-jail-idUSKBN1H001M.

Rickleton, Chris, and Khurmat Babadjanov. 2024. "Jail for Insulting Uzbek President Mirziyoev." *Radio Free Europe/Radio Liberty*. May 12, 2024. https://www.rferl.org/a/jail-insulting-uzbek-president-mirziyoev-uzbekistan/32940015.html.

Saida, Niginakhon, and Sara Scardavilli. 2023. "A Gender Perspective on HIV Prevalence in Uzbekistan." *The Diplomat*. February 2, 2023. https://thediplomat.com/2023/02/a-gender-perspective-on-hiv-prevalence-in-uzbekistan/.

Salomova, Barchinoy J. 2023. "Formation and Development of Women's Journalism in Uzbekistan." *Journal of Social Sciences and Humanities Research* 3 (11). https://doi.org/10.5564.

Sasaki, Ayako, Daiki Yoshihara, and Akemi Mochizuki. 2022. "Gender-Responsive Needs and Vulnerabilities Among Incarcerated Mothers in Japan: Comparisons with Non-Mothers and Fathers." *Journal of Drug Abuse* 8 (7): 105.

Singh, Simran. 2025. "81-Year-Old Japanese Woman Purposely Breaks Law to Go to Jail: 'Don't Want to Die Alone.'" *Hindustan Times.* February 2, 2025. https://www.hindustantimes.com/trending/81yearold-japanese-woman-purposely-breaks-law-to-go-to-jail-don-t-want-to-die-alone-101738481996252.html.

StoryFM. 2022. "My Decade of Studying Female Inmates in Prison." *The World of Chinese.* December 16. Translated by Ana Padilla Fornieles. https://www.theworldofchinese.com/2022/12/my-decade-of-studying-female-inmates-in-prison/.

Supreme People's Court of China. 2008. *Anti-Drug Law of the People's Republic of China* (English translation). Effective June 1, 2008. Supreme People's Court. https://english.court.gov.cn/2015-07/17/c_761568_8.htm.

Supreme People's Procuratorate. 2020. "Criminal Law of the People's Republic of China." *Supreme People's Procuratorate.* December 26, 2020. https://en.spp.gov.cn/2020-12/26/c_948417_10.htm.

Suzuki, Satoru. 2024. "Current Strategies for Perinatal Mental Health Care in Japan." *JMA Journal* 7 (1): 5–9.

Takino, Yūsaku. 2023. "Medical Care Behind Bars: Author Ōtawa Fumie on Being a Prison Doctor." *Nippon.com.* February 28, 2023. https://www.nippon.com/en/japan-topics/g02245/.

Terazawa, Yuki. 2018. *Knowledge, Power, and Women's Reproductive Health in Japan, 1690–1945.* Genders and Sexualities in History series. Cham: Palgrave Macmillan.

The Global Economy. 2025. "Uzbekistan: Rural Population, Percent of Total Population." https://www.theglobaleconomy.com/Uzbekistan/rural_population_percent/.

Tursunmurodov, Komron. 2024. "Affirmative Actions: Promotion of Women's Rights or Social Injustice?" *Uzbekistan Law Blog.* July 4, 2024. https://uzbekistanlawblog.com/affirmative-actions-promotion-of-womens-rights-or-social-injustice/.

UK Home Office. 2018. *Country Policy and Information Note: China—Contravention of National Population and Family Planning Laws.* Version 3.0, November. Refworld. https://www.refworld.org/reference/countryrep/ukho/2018/en/122355.

UNAIDS. 2019. *UNAIDS Data 2019: State of the Epidemic—Uzbekistan.* Geneva: UNAIDS. https://www.unaids.org/sites/default/files/media_asset/2019-UNAIDS-data_en.pdf.

UNICEF Uzbekistan. 2019. *Effects of Migration on Children of Uzbekistan.* Tashkent: UNICEF. https://www.unicef.org/uzbekistan/media/2936/file/Effects-of-migration-on-children-of-Uzbekistan-EN.pdf.

UNODC. 2023. "Measures to Reduce Reoffending in Japan." *UNODC Justice Section Report.* https://www.unodc.org/documents/justice-and-prison-reform/ReducingReoffending/MS/Japan_-_Input_on_reducing_reoffending.pdf.

UNODC. 2008. *Illicit Drug Trends in Central Asia.* Central Asia Regional Office. https://www.unodc.org/documents/regional/central-asia/Illicit%20Drug%20Trends_Central%20Asia-final.pdf.

U.S. Department of State. 2023. *Uzbekistan 2022 Human Rights Report.* Washington, DC: U.S. Government Printing Office. https://www.state.gov/wp-content/uploads/2023/03/415610_UZBEKISTAN-2022-HUMAN-RIGHTS-REPORT.pdf.

U.S. Department of State. 2022. *2022 Trafficking in Persons Report: Uzbekistan.* Washington, DC. https://2021-2025.state.gov/reports/2022-trafficking-in-persons-report/uzbekistan/?safe=1.

U.S. Department of State. 2020. *2019 Country Reports on Human Rights Practices: China (Includes Tibet, Hong Kong, and Macau).* Section on Prison Conditions. https://china.usembassy-china.org.cn/china-2018-human-rights-report/.

U.S. Embassy & Consulates in Japan. 2024. "Prisons." *U.S. Embassy in Japan.* https://jp.usembassy.gov/services/prisons/.

USCIRF (U.S. Commission on International Religious Freedom). 2021. *Report on Uzbekistan's Religious and Political Prisoners.* https://www.uscirf.gov/publication/report-uzbekistans-religious-and-political-prisoners/.

Van Hout, Marie Claire, Simon Fleißner, and Heino Stöver. 2023. "'Women's Right to Health in Detention': United Nations Committee Observations Since the Adoption of the United Nations Rules for the Treatment of Women Prisoners and Non-custodial Measures for Women Offenders (Bangkok Rules)." *Journal of Human Rights Practice* 15 (1): 138–55.

VERTIC. 2023. *Criminal Code of the Republic of Uzbekistan.* https://www.vertic.org/media/National%20Legislation/Uzbekistan/UZ_Criminal_Code.pdf.

Walmsley, Roy. 2017. *World Female Imprisonment List.* 4th ed. London: Institute for Crime & Justice Policy Research. https://www.prisonstudies.org/news/world-female-imprisonment-list-fourth-edition.

World Bank. 2021. *Uzbekistan: Enhancing Economic Opportunities for Rural Women Project.* https://documents1.worldbank.org/curated/en/441871643297027306/pdf/Uzbekistan-Enhancing-Economic-Opportunities-For-Rural-Women-Project-Grant.pdf.

World Prison Brief. 2024. "Japan." Institute for Crime & Justice Policy Research. https://www.prisonstudies.org/country/japan.

World Prison Brief. 2022. "Uzbekistan." https://www.prisonstudies.org/country/uzbekistan.

Xia, Lily, and Ching Man Lam. 2020. "Where Is Home? The Lived Experiences of Chinese Children After Their Parents Have Been Incarcerated." *Journal of Social Work Practice* 34 (2): 191–203.

Xia, Yu, Shuo Wang, and Yaping Hu. 2022. "Multidimensional Poverty of Rural Women in China." *Frontiers in Psychology* 13: 1–15.

Yang, Meiping. 2015. "Women's Prison Invites Mothers to See Their Daughters." *Shanghai Daily.* May 21, 2015. Archived at *Shine.* https://jyj.sh.gov.cn/n263/20180725/0042-6439.html.

Zamin. 2025. "'Zulya' Scheme Leading to Prostitution Exposed: Human Trafficking Stopped in Tashkent." *Zamin.uz.* May 27, 2025. https://zamin.uz/en/society/150780-

zulya-scheme-leading-to-prostitution-exposed-human-trafficking-stopped-in-tashkent.html.

Zhao, Yuning, Steven F. Messner, Jianhong Liu, and Chuncheng Jin. 2019. "Prisons as Schools: Inmates' Participation in Vocational and Academic Programs in Chinese Prisons." *International Journal of Offender Therapy and Comparative Criminology* 63 (15–16): 2713–40.

Zhong, Shaoling, Xiaomin Zhu, Yanan Chen, Huijuan Guo, Chenyuli Luo, Xiaoxi Liang, Fanglan Wang, Hui Chen, Jiansong Zhou, and Xiaoping Wang. 2020. "High Psychiatric Morbidity and Comorbidity Among Female Prisoners in Hunan, China." *Frontiers in Psychiatry* 11 (April): 1–7.

Zhong, Sihui, Xueqin Zhu, Graham Mellsop, Hong Guo, Yuhua Chen, Chunhui Luo, Qian Li, Jie Zhou, and Xiaoping Wang. 2019. "Mental Health Problems, History of Drug Use, and Violent Offending Are Associated with Increased Suicide Risk in Imprisoned Females." *Frontiers in Psychiatry* 10: 395.

7

South and Southeast Asia

Women's incarceration in South and Southeast Asia reflects injustices rooted in colonialism, patriarchy, and socioeconomic disparities. Across India, the Philippines, and Cambodia, women are incarcerated for non-violent, poverty-driven crimes, often shaped by gender-based violence, coercion, and limited opportunity. Conditions in prison are harsh, and women frequently lack access to adequate healthcare, legal aid, or family support. This chapter examines the unique historical, legal, and social contexts influencing women's incarceration in each country. It explores how policies, institutions, and cultural norms neglect, and often harm, this population.

India

Historical Context

Colonial legacy, patriarchal norms, and post-independence legal evolution shape the context of women's incarceration in India. During British rule (1858–1947), the Indian Penal Code of 1860 introduced a uniform criminal justice system. Prisons were modeled after Victorian England and failed to meet women's needs (Naik 2019). Women were often jailed for poverty-related offenses like theft and prostitution. Additionally, marginalized communities were disproportionately targeted through colonial laws like the Criminal Tribes Act of 1871. This law branded entire communities as criminals by birth, subjecting them to police surveillance and discrimination (Radhakrishna 2001). During this period, political activists were also detained under sedition laws for being involved in the freedom movement (Singh 2023).

After independence in 1947, India kept most of the colonial penal code but introduced constitutional guarantees for equality. However, gender norms continued to influence women's incarceration. Many women were imprisoned for issues related to domestic violence, dowry disputes, or economic survival (Singh 2023). **Section 498A** of the code, designed to protect women from dowry-related harms, such as harassment and violence by husbands or in-laws over dowry demands, has been used in family disputes that sometimes criminalize women. Many incarcerated women end up being victims and offenders, punished for actions related to their abuse (Singh and Tripathi 2025).

Despite reforms, prison conditions for women are still inadequate, with little focus on reproductive health, childcare, or rehabilitation (Naik 2019). While Alipore Central Jail in Kolkata was converted into a museum after it closed in 2019, recent investigations in other West Bengal prisons show ongoing abuses, including sexual violence, with documented cases of pregnancy and denial of medical care (Safi 2024).

Overall, women's incarceration in India indicates intersecting injustices of class, caste, and gender. While reform efforts exist, the system has been slow to address the needs of incarcerated women.

Bengali Hindu women in Alipore Prison, India. Nineteenth-century depiction (Robert Schlagintweit via Picryl.com)

Female Incarceration Rates and Trends

Although women make up a small share of India's total prison population, their number has increased over the past two decades. While the proportion of women in prison has remained relatively stable—from 3.3 percent in 2000 to 4.3 percent in 2015 (Vasudha 2020) and 4.2 percent in 2023 (Shanid 2023)—the growth in actual numbers signals socioeconomic and structural inequalities. As of 2022, approximately 22,500 women were incarcerated in India, and nearly 76 percent of the prison population consists of people awaiting trial (Institute for Crime and Justice Policy Research 2025b).

Women in custody are housed in either exclusive women's prisons or segregated sections within male facilities. There are thirty-four dedicated women-only prisons across India offering some gender-responsive services, such as childcare units and gynecological care (Shah 2024). However, about 81 percent of incarcerated women are held in gender-segregated areas within general prisons (Viji 2023), where infrastructure and services are frequently inadequate. In rural areas, women may be confined in sub-jails or temporary lockups not designed for long-term detention or equipped to meet the needs of pregnant women, nursing mothers, or those accompanied by young children. Some facilities offer under-resourced mother–child units for children under six, contributing to deprivation (Shanid 2023).

The high proportion of pre-trial detainees among incarcerated women indicates a systemic challenge. Many spend months or years in pre-trial detention because of delays in judicial proceedings and limited access to legal aid (Vasudha 2020). This burden is especially severe for rural and marginalized women, who often lack the financial and social capital to navigate the justice system (Shanid 2023).

Demographics of Incarcerated Women

The demographics of incarcerated women in India indicate socioeconomic inequalities. Most are illiterate, poor, and socially marginalized, with limited access to defense (Kanwal et al. 2025). Twenty-seven percent of all incarcerated people in India are completely illiterate, and 42 percent have not studied beyond Class 10 (Economic Times 2021). Among undertrial (pre-trial detainees) prisoners, nearly 70 percent have minimal formal education, making them especially vulnerable to prolonged detention and legal disadvantage (Rai 2020). As a result, many women are imprisoned for poverty-driven offenses like petty theft, dowry-related disputes, or coerced involvement in drug trafficking.

Marginalized caste groups are also disproportionately represented in the prison system. In 2022, approximately two-thirds of undertrial detainees belonged to Scheduled Castes (oppressed Dalit communities) (21 percent), Scheduled Tribes (Indigenous groups) (9 percent), or Other Backward Classes (socially and economically disadvantaged groups) (35 percent) (Paliath 2023), reflecting how entrenched caste inequality influences incarceration in India. Intersecting disadvantages of caste, poverty, education, and gender worsen women's overrepresentation in custody.

Most women imprisoned in India are between thirty and fifty years old (52 percent), followed by those aged eighteen to thirty (28 percent) (Viji 2023). A significant portion of incarcerated women are also mothers. As of 2022, 1,537 mothers were held with 1,764 children in Indian prisons (approximately 6.5 percent of the female prison population) (Shah 2024). This underrepresents incarcerated mothers, many of whom have children living outside prison, often in conditions without adequate support.

Compounding these social and economic hardships are high rates of mental health disorders among incarcerated women. A study of women in Mandoli and Tihar prisons, two of the largest facilities in Delhi, found that 88 percent of participants experienced psychological distress (Kaur and Roy 2021). These findings suggest the need for trauma-informed mental health services in women's facilities.

Crimes Leading to Incarceration

Women in India are often incarcerated for non-violent, economically motivated crimes driven by financial hardship, gender inequality, and survival-based decisions. These crimes are often committed to support their families (Samridhi 2024). They are rarely the result of premeditated criminal intent. Instead, they illustrate the structural disadvantages many women face, including poverty, limited social support, and exposure to domestic violence (Pandey 2020).

Although the National Crime Records Bureau does not publicly provide disaggregated data on offense types by gender, research and reports suggest that a substantial proportion of incarcerated women are imprisoned for low-level, financially driven crimes. At the same time, broader prison data show that 37 percent of incarcerated women are held for murder and 15 percent for dowry deaths. This shows that serious charges, often linked to partner violence, are common (Viji 2023).

Drug-related offenses are another reason for the imprisonment of women, especially in certain regions. While national statistics remain limited, reporting from Punjab demonstrates this trend. In some prisons, over 90 percent of incarcerated women are held under the **Narcotic Drugs and Psychotropic Substances Act** (Dhaliwal 2025). Many of these women are coerced into low-level trafficking roles, like acting as couriers, by male partners or criminal networks.

The prevalence of homicide and dowry-related charges also demonstrates the gendered aspects of violence and victimization. Women's involvement in these cases is often the effect of cycles of abuse and economic dependence (Pandey 2020). A recent example includes the conviction of Vina Dabhi in Ahmedabad, who was sentenced to life imprisonment for the dowry-related murder of her 22-year-old daughter-in-law, Mittal. Dowry refers to money or property demanded by a husband or his family from the bride's family, often leading to harassment or violence when expectations are unmet. Although initially treated as an accidental death, the case was reclassified as murder and dowry harassment after Mittal's father reported a pattern of abuse (Times of India 2024).

Contributing Laws and Policies

Several laws and policies in India, intended to protect women, also contribute to their incarceration. The Dowry Prohibition Act of 1961 and Section 498A of the Indian Penal Code, introduced in 1983 to address cruelty related to dowry, are among the most significant. While these laws aim to prevent violence and exploitation, they have led to unintended legal consequences by criminalizing family disputes and exposing some women to imprisonment.

Section 498A, a non-bailable offense, is sometimes invoked in retaliatory or cross-FIRs (first information reports) during family disputes, resulting in the arrest of female relatives like mothers-in-law or sisters-in-law. In Bengaluru, a review of 2,202 cases filed under 498A between 2017 and 2022 showed that over 1,500 resulted in arrest. However, only 1 percent ended in conviction, indicating a disconnect between accusations and guilt (Times of India 2025). Courts have also flagged misuse. In a 2024 ruling, the Nagpur bench of the Bombay High Court cancelled charges against extended relatives, noting that complaints were increasingly used "to teach a lesson" to the husband's family (Ganjapure 2025). These patterns contribute to the undertrial population of incarcerated women.

India's Narcotic Drugs and Psychotropic Substances Act (NDPS) of 1985 is another reason for female incarceration. The law imposes strict penalties, even for minor involvement, such as carrying small quantities (India Code 1985). In Uttarakhand, a northern Himalayan state of India, there was a 79 percent increase in women arrested under the NDPS Act over three years, reflecting the growing use of female couriers in trafficking (Das 2023). Sentencing under this law often overlooks factors like coercion, poverty, or caregiving roles, resulting in disproportionately harsh punishment for women with minor or coerced involvement (Penal Reform International 2020). These trends indicate the need for reform, including alternative sentencing for non-violent offenses and more attention to the conditions that influence women's entry into the justice system.

Conditions in Women's Prisons

Conditions in women's prisons in India are harsh and inadequate. They exhibit overcrowding, poor sanitation, and limited access to basic services. Most prisons were designed for men and remain ill-equipped to address the needs of women. As the number of incarcerated women has grown, infrastructure and staffing have not kept up, resulting in cramped, under-resourced facilities that compromise health and safety (Naik 2019).

Overcrowding is among the most urgent challenges. Indian prisons operate at 131 percent of their capacity, with district jails being the most overcrowded (Institute for Crime and Justice Policy Research 2025b). This strains limited resources, including toilets, bathing areas, and clean water. It also often forces male correctional officers into roles that should be gender specific (Naik 2019).

Menstrual hygiene also remains a concern. Incarcerated women frequently lack access to sanitary products and must rely on family members or purchase supplies themselves. When unavailable, women often resort to unhygienic alternatives like cloth or ash, posing health risks (Commonwealth Human Rights Initiative 2023).

Vocational training and rehabilitation programs, which are needed for post-release reintegration, are limited and often consist of gender-stereotyped tasks like sewing or crafts. Many women come from communities with little education or employment. Without access to job-readiness training or literacy programs, they face higher risks of recidivism (National Commission for Women 2018).

An example of the system's failures occurred in 2017 at Byculla Jail, Mumbai. Here, 38-year-old Manjula Shetye was stripped, beaten, and sexually assaulted by staff after she complained about food shortages. Her death sparked a protest

The Byculla Jail Protest

In 2017, Manjula Shetye, a 38-year-old inmate at Mumbai's Byculla Jail, was beaten to death after protesting food shortages. Reports revealed she was stripped, assaulted, and denied medical care. Her death sparked an uprising, and over 200 women banged plates, shouted slogans, and climbed prison walls in protest. The case exposed systemic abuse and the lack of accountability in India's prisons, highlighting calls for reform and oversight. Following public outrage and media attention, six female prison guards were arrested and charged with murder, though the trial has faced repeated delays. Despite this, activists note that conditions in women's prisons remain largely unchanged.

by fellow inmates and brought national attention to the abuse incarcerated women often face (JusCorpus 2023). Overall, improving prison conditions requires investment in infrastructure, gender-sensitive staff, and access to rehabilitation.

Health and Mental Health Issues

Incarcerated women in India face health and mental health challenges, mainly due to inadequate medical services, overcrowded conditions, and a high prevalence of trauma before imprisonment. Many women enter prison suffering from malnutrition, reproductive health issues, and untreated diseases like HIV. One national study found that 1.7 percent of incarcerated men and women in India were HIV positive, highlighting an elevated risk within prison settings (Dolan and Larney 2010).

Most prisons lack sufficient healthcare personnel, including female doctors, and commonly fail to offer diagnostic services for serious medical conditions. As a result, chronic illnesses often go untreated, exacerbating immediate and long-term health risks (Naik 2019). Conditions are especially severe for pregnant women and mothers, who are legally entitled to prenatal and postnatal care but frequently lack access to balanced diets, routine medical exams, or safe delivery facilities. Studies also report that breastfeeding mothers experience nutritional deficiencies, placing them and their children at risk (Borah and Baishya 2023). For children permitted to live with their mothers in prison, inadequate nutrition and limited access to pediatric care are common. These deficiencies, compounded by overcrowding and understaffing, contribute to long-lasting physical and emotional harm for mothers and children (Paliath and Acharya 2020).

Mental healthcare in prisons is also lacking. Many incarcerated women have experienced domestic violence, sexual abuse, or extreme poverty, yet few receive counseling or psychiatric support. A study of women incarcerated in Mandoli and Tihar prisons found that 88 percent reported psychological distress, with 73 percent experiencing depression and 78 percent anxiety (Kaur and Roy 2021). Broader research estimates that 21–33 percent of women in India's prisons have a diagnosable mental illness, and substance use disorders affect up to 56 percent (Dhillon and Sasidharan 2024). Addressing these challenges requires gender-responsive, trauma-informed care, improved infrastructure, and consistent access to physical and mental health services during and after incarceration.

Impact on Families and Children

Women's incarceration in India disrupts families, with children bearing the worst effects of the consequences. As primary caregivers, imprisoned women leave behind children who often experience abandonment, anxiety, depression, aggression, or withdrawal (Ranta 2018). These emotional effects are intensified by unstable caregiving arrangements and social stigma, which lead to ostracism by peers and communities (Kaur and Roy 2021).

The economic impact is also significant. Incarcerated women are often the primary earners in their households. Their absence can force children into caregiving roles or child labor, perpetuating intergenerational poverty (Borah and Baishya 2023). The social stigma surrounding maternal incarceration further isolates children and erodes support systems (Kaur and Roy 2021).

Furthermore, limited visitation rights and a lack of child-friendly spaces make it difficult for mothers and children to maintain emotional bonds. Incarcerated mothers report psychological distress, fearing custody loss and emotional estrangement, while their children often suffer from attachment issues (Shah 2024).

Legally, Indian prisons are required to provide nurseries and basic education to children under six residing with incarcerated mothers. This was established in *R.D. Upadhyay v. State of A.P.* (2006) and reinforced in the Model Prison Manual (2016). However, implementation is inconsistent. Many prisons lack dedicated child-friendly spaces or educational programs. While some offer these services, they are frequently under-resourced or non-functional (Shah 2024). Children in prisons often have limited or no access to formal schooling or developmentally appropriate activities. For example, in central prisons like Tihar, children live in overcrowded, unsanitary conditions without consistent access to early learning or outdoor play (Paliath and Acharya 2020). A survey revealed that 6 percent of children received no education. Many others were only partially enrolled in government or open schools. Common barriers include logistical difficulties and insufficient staffing (Murti 2021).

Policy Reforms and Recommendations

To address the inequities and hardships faced by incarcerated women in India, policy reforms must be gender-responsive and grounded in human rights principles. A priority should be reducing the number of women in prison through alternatives to incarceration, especially for non-violent, poverty-driven crimes. Sentencing practices under laws like the NDPS Act often fail to consider mitigating factors like coercion, caregiving responsibilities, and economic hardship, leading to harsh penalties for women with little involvement in crime (Das 2023). Expanding community-based alternatives like restorative justice and probation could decrease the female prison population and support rehabilitation.

Legal protections like Section 498A, although intended to safeguard women, must be enforced with greater judicial discretion. Data demonstrating low conviction rates and high arrest rates, especially among female relatives, indicate a need for protections preventing misuse, pre-trial overreach, and the unnecessary criminalization of women during familial disputes (Ganjapure 2025). Access to legal aid must be improved, especially for undertrial women from marginalized communities who remain imprisoned due to a lack of representation (Shanid 2023).

Prison conditions also demand reform. Overcrowding, poor sanitation, and a lack of gender-specific health services harm women (Naik 2019). Steps must be taken to ensure the availability of sanitary products, female healthcare personnel, and reproductive and mental healthcare (Borah and Baishya 2023). Manjula Shetye's death in Byculla Jail illustrates the consequences of abuse, reinforcing the need for stronger oversight and accountability (JusCorpus 2023).

Children of incarcerated women must also be better protected. Although Indian law mandates nurseries and educational support for children under six living with their mothers in prison, these services are poorly implemented (Shah

2024). Strengthening child-friendly visitation policies, expanding nursery and educational services, and offering post-release family reintegration support are needed to preserve family bonds and break the cycle of poverty and incarceration (Murti 2021).

Reform requires the Indian criminal justice system to move beyond punishment and prioritize rehabilitation and the dignity of women in custody. Investments, legal safeguards, and reforms must work together to reduce incarceration, improve prison conditions, and support successful reentry.

Philippines

Historical Context

The history of women's incarceration in the Philippines is influenced by colonial legacies and socioeconomic inequalities. Under Spanish rule (1521–1898), the legal system criminalized women for moral indiscretions like adultery, enforcing patriarchal norms that policed female behavior. Prisons like the Old Bilibid (established in 1865), also known today as Manila City Jail, were overcrowded, unsanitary, and did not provide for the needs of women, who were often detained alongside men without access to healthcare, hygiene, or legal protection (UNAFEI 2013).

After the Philippines was ceded to the United States in 1898, the administration overhauled its penal system, establishing formal courts and expanding prison infrastructure (Bureau of Corrections n.d.). Despite these reforms, the penal approach remained fixed on punishment rather than rehabilitation. Women were often imprisoned for property and morality crimes like theft or adultery, disproportionately targeting poor women (Commission on Human Rights 2022).

The Correctional Institution for Women (CIW), located in Mandaluyong City, Metro Manila, was established in 1931 to separate women from men. However, its services remained limited, with vocational training focused on gendered roles and minimal health or rehabilitation programs (Correctional Institution for Women n.d.). Following independence in 1946, the legal system continued to reflect both Spanish civil law and American criminal justice procedures (National WWII Museum 2021). Socioeconomic drivers like poverty, domestic violence, and lack of education persisted, and most imprisoned women were detained for non-violent, survival-related offenses (Amnesty International 2001). Legal aid and healthcare access remained scarce, and prison infrastructure showed little improvement for women's needs (Commission on Human Rights 2022).

Since 2016, the government's aggressive anti-drug campaign has led to a surge in women's incarceration, especially for low-level drug offenses. Many women are arrested as couriers or for possession, often coerced by partners or driven by desperation (Human Rights Watch 2017). This has overwhelmed under-resourced detention facilities, emphasizing the need for reform (Commission on Human Rights 2022).

Female Incarceration Rates and Trends

Female incarceration in the Philippines has risen in recent years, especially after the start of President Rodrigo Duterte's war on drugs in 2016. Before this, women comprised 6.6 percent of the prison population in 2015. By 2024, that figure had increased to approximately 9.8 percent, with around 16,782 women imprisoned. Sixty-five percent of all incarcerated people across the country are pre-trial detainees (Institute for Crime and Justice Policy Research 2025c). This increase is driven by the enforcement of drug laws, which have disproportionately impacted low-income women involved in minor offenses like possession. For instance, in Baguio City Jail, over 55 percent of women behind bars face drug-related charges, a trend that is similar throughout the Philippines (Pas-iwen et al. 2024).

This trend has further strained prisons. On average, facilities in the Philippines operated at 362 percent capacity as of 2021 (Institute for Crime and Justice Policy Research 2025c). CIW in Mandaluyong, the country's primary women's prison, suffers from severe overcrowding and limited resources (Torres-Tupas 2023). Women convicted of serious crimes or serving longer sentences are typically housed at CIW, which is managed by the Bureau of Corrections under the Department of Justice (Montealegre and Pineda 2023).

Women awaiting trial or serving shorter sentences, typically under three years, are held in city and municipal jails administered by the Bureau of Jail Management and Penology, under the Department of the Interior and Local Government. These include the Quezon City Female Dormitory, Cebu City Jail, and Manila City Jail's women's wing (Bureau of Jail Management and Penology 2015). Despite gender segregation, these facilities often lack services and are overcrowded. In rural areas, women may be detained in old buildings, with minimal separation or gender-responsive services (Commission on Human Rights 2022).

While some community-based alternatives to incarceration have been proposed for non-violent offenders, their availability is scarce. Reducing the female prison population requires correctional reform, investment in poverty reduction, gender-sensitive legal responses, and diversion programs (UN Women Asia Pacific 2022).

Demographics of Incarcerated Women

The demographics of incarcerated women in the Philippines indicate socio-economic disadvantages. Most come from impoverished communities with little access to education, employment, and services. A qualitative study found that many formerly incarcerated women returned to the same disadvantaged neighborhoods after release, highlighting cycles of poverty (Veloso 2023).

Occupational and educational profiles also illustrate these susceptibilities. Before imprisonment, 18 percent of women at the CIW worked as informal traders, 12 percent as vendors, and 6 percent as housewives or caretakers. Additionally, 15 percent were unemployed (DIGNITY 2013). Educational attainment was low among these women. Twenty percent had only completed elementary school, 40 percent had some high school, and 30 percent had attended college (DIGNITY 2013).

Over 90 percent of incarcerated women are held for non-violent, low-level offenses, often linked to survival, including drug possession or theft of necessities like soap or clothing (UN Women Asia Pacific 2022). A study at Baguio City Jail found that 60 percent of female detainees were aged 20–39 years old. Over half faced drug-related charges, emphasizing the intersection of vulnerability and criminalization (Pas-iwen et al. 2024).

While most incarcerated women are under forty years old, 21 percent are over fifty (Pas-iwen et al. 2024), with ages increasing due to harsh drug sentencing and prolonged pre-trial detention. For instance, DIGNITY (2013) documented cases of women held pre-trial for over six years.

No official statistics are available on the percentage of incarcerated women in the Philippines who are mothers, but qualitative studies highlight that a significant proportion were primary caregivers before their imprisonment (Ceballo and Absin 2022). These patterns show that women's involvement is shaped by inequality and gendered vulnerability.

Crimes Leading to Incarceration

The crimes leading to the incarceration of women in the Philippines are predominantly non-violent and linked to poverty and punitive anti-drug policies. Since the launch of the drug war in 2016, drug-related charges have risen. Nearly 70 percent of the country's prison population is imprisoned for these offenses, many involving minor possession or low-level trafficking (UNODC 2023).

Most of these women come from impoverished backgrounds and are drawn into the drug trade out of financial desperation or through coercion by partners, family members, or organized crime networks. Many women arrested were involved at the lowest levels of distribution, often as couriers or small-scale sellers, and were manipulated or pressured into these roles (Alvarez 2018). Interviews confirm that some were charged because of their association with romantic partners or community figures (Veloso 2023).

Legal penalties for drug offenses in the Philippines are harsh, even for lesser violations. Mandatory sentencing and limited plea bargaining options contribute to long prison terms, especially for women without financial resources or legal support (Alvarez 2018). Some women have been jailed while pregnant or shortly after childbirth. For instance, Rosemarie Santiago was arrested on drug charges while four months pregnant. She gave birth to her son, Jericho, in a Manila hospital while in custody, and was separated from him for nine months before being reunited (Cabato 2021).

Additionally, theft and fraud are the next most common offenses (Pas-iwen et al. 2024). Often committed by single mothers or informal workers, these crimes reveal attempts to meet basic needs through shoplifting or minor scams. These patterns reflect how inequalities shape women's criminalization in the Philippines.

Contributing Laws and Policies

The Comprehensive Dangerous Drugs Act (RA 9165) of 2002 is a contributor to women's incarceration. It imposes harsh, mandatory sentences for a range of drug-related offenses, including minor possession, with no room for probation or judicial discretion (Alvarez 2018). Under President Duterte's war on drugs, incarceration increased, with nearly 70 percent of the prison population held on drug charges (UNODC 2023). Despite lesser involvement, like serving as couriers or small-scale sellers, many women face lengthy sentences without access to plea bargaining or legal alternatives (Penal Reform International and Linklaters 2020).

Economic crimes like theft and fraud are also common pathways to incarceration for women in the Philippines. These offenses are often committed by single mothers or informal workers attempting to meet their needs, like buying food (Pas-iwen et al. 2024). The Revised Penal Code offers limited opportunities for non-custodial alternatives, even for non-violent or first-time offenses, resulting in imprisonment rather than rehabilitation (UN Women Asia Pacific 2022).

Additionally, the legal system also fails to protect survivors of domestic violence, contributing to women's incarceration. The **Anti-Violence Against Women and Their Children Act of 2004 (RA 9262)** exists, but its implementation is inconsistent. A study of Metro Manila's local governments found uneven enforcement of Barangay Protection Orders, which are temporary restraining measures meant to shield victims from their abusers, along with limited access to legal aid (Matahum and Tanigue 2025). Women who retaliate against abusers are often prosecuted for violent crimes without consideration of Battered Woman Syndrome or the context of prolonged abuse.

The lack of trauma-informed practices in legal proceedings and sentencing results in survivors being punished instead of protected (DIGNITY 2013). Consequently, there is a need for reforms that incorporate domestic violence histories into legal decision-making and expand access to community-based alternatives for women.

Conditions in Women's Prisons

Conditions in women's prisons in the Philippines are generally poor. They exhibit overcrowding, inadequate healthcare, and a lack of gender-sensitive facilities. The increase in arrests from the war on drugs has overwhelmed the prison system. For instance, Manila City Jail held nearly 4,800 inmates in a facility built for 1,100, operating at over 400 percent capacity (UNODC 2023). Many people are forced to sleep on the floor, in bathrooms, or share cramped bedding.

Prisons often lack clean water, soap, and working toilets. Women report using torn clothing as makeshift sanitary pads, and bathrooms frequently have no locks, exposing them to health risks and humiliation. Despite international standards like the UN Bangkok Rules which guide the humane treatment of women in custody, gender-responsive spaces, like private hygiene areas, are limited (DIGNITY 2013). For instance, it was reported that there were around 130 women in a room the size of a classroom at Manila City Jail. With just one electric fan for ventilation, women had to pay unofficial fees to guards to secure sleeping space on mats or floors (Beltran 2024). During the COVID-19 pandemic, conditions worsened. Each woman received only four liters of water daily for drinking, bathing, laundry, and toilet use. Some days, detainees relied on collected rainwater, passed between buckets, to meet basic needs (Beltran 2024).

Rehabilitation programs are also lacking. While CIW offers livelihood and literacy programs, serving over 2,000 women in areas like sewing, baking, and computer skills, space and staffing limitations mean that only a minority can access them consistently (DIGNITY 2013). Many programs are underfunded, limited in scope, and do not provide marketable skills needed to be successful in the community (UN Women Asia Pacific 2022). These conditions violate international human rights standards and hinder incarcerated women's chances for reintegration. Without reforms, the Philippine prison system will continue to perpetuate cycles of neglect, inequality, and institutional harm.

Health and Mental Health Issues

Incarcerated women in the Philippines face health and mental health challenges. These are compounded by overcrowded and unsanitary conditions, poor nutrition, and little access to care. Many enter prison with preexisting conditions, including malnutrition, HIV, hepatitis C, sexually transmitted infections, and reproductive health issues (Hermosa 2024). The spread of communicable diseases like tuberculosis (TB) and skin infections is worsened by poor hygiene. TB rates in facilities like New Bilibid Prison and Quezon City Jail have been reported at eight to thirteen times higher than in the general population (ICRC 2016).

Maternal healthcare is especially lacking. A study of pregnant detainees found that many women lacked regular checkups, balanced nutrition, and access to skilled birth attendants. Some gave birth in prison without medical professionals present, increasing risks of complications (Nieva Jr. 2024). Prenatal vitamins, emergency obstetric care, and postnatal support are frequently unavailable, and birthing conditions are often unhygienic (Hermosa 2024). Prisons typically lack maternity units, recovery areas, and breastfeeding spaces, offering little assistance for mothers (UN Women Asia Pacific 2022). Women are separated from their newborns shortly after birth, and there are limited policies ensuring hospital deliveries or professional supervision (Cabato 2021).

Women who are not pregnant also face unmet health needs, including inadequate access to gynecological exams, screenings for cervical and breast cancer, and menstrual hygiene products (Hermosa 2024). These gaps violate international standards and contribute to poor health outcomes (Penal Reform International 2023). Mental health needs are also underserved. Histories of trauma, including domestic violence, sexual abuse, and substance dependence, are common among incarcerated women (Hermosa 2024). Yet, most prisons lack trained professionals, and access to therapy or psychiatric care is rare (UN Women Asia Pacific 2022). The prison environment itself worsens depression, anxiety, and PTSD (Penal Reform International 2023).

Impact on Families and Children

Women's incarceration in the Philippines has consequences for their families, especially their children. Many women are the primary caregivers, and their absence leaves children without emotional and material support. Children often experience feelings of abandonment, sadness, and anxiety. A study in South Cotabato found that children of incarcerated mothers struggled with academic decline, social stigma, and emotional distress (Soriao and Balongoy 2025). Some must leave school or take on adult responsibilities, like caring for siblings or contributing financially (Ceballo and Absin 2022).

Additionally, families often fall deeper into poverty. Many imprisoned women come from low-income backgrounds, and their imprisonment creates a financial void, making it harder for families to afford food, healthcare, and education (Hermosa 2024). This often forces children or other family members to leave school or overextend themselves. Moreover, the stigma associated with incarceration isolates families. Children may face bullying, and caregivers, often grandparents or older siblings, struggle with added responsibilities (Ceballo and Absin 2022). Without support, these families become socially and economically marginalized, reinforcing caregiving burdens (UN Women Asia Pacific 2022).

Incarcerated mothers also suffer from the toll of separation. Limited visitation rights and poor communication make it hard to maintain relationships with their children, complicating reunification after release (Hermosa 2024). These weakened bonds can damage rehabilitation and reintegration efforts (Penal Reform International 2023). Mother–baby units are rare in the Philippines. Most prisons separate mothers from infants shortly after birth, although the

Correctional Institution for Women in Mandaluyong allows babies to stay up to one year. Still, the ward is overcrowded and underfunded, with just ₱85 (1.49 USD) per day allotted for mother and child (Prison Insider 2024). Overall, women's incarceration goes beyond prison walls, highlighting the need for family-centered policies that protect the well-being of mothers and children.

Policy Reforms and Recommendations

The incarceration of women in the Philippines calls for reforms. Its prison system is shaped by colonialism and reinforced by punitive modern laws, and it has disproportionately affected women from marginalized backgrounds. A shift toward humane, rehabilitative, and inclusive policies is needed to protect women's rights, reduce overcrowding, and prevent the intergenerational harms of prison.

Expanding non-custodial alternatives is critical. Many women are incarcerated for minor drug offenses, petty theft, or crimes committed for survival. Diversion programs like community service, probation, or restorative justice should be prioritized, especially for first-time and non-violent offenders. This requires reforms to the Comprehensive Dangerous Drugs Act and the Revised Penal Code to allow judicial discretion and plea bargaining (Alvarez 2018).

Also, legal proceedings must be trauma-informed. Histories of domestic violence and coercion often influence women's pathways to prison. Courts should consider mitigating factors like Battered Woman Syndrome. Moreover, law enforcement, prosecutors, and judges must receive training in gender-sensitive approaches. The inconsistent application of protective laws like RA 9262 emphasizes the need for institutional reform (Matahum and Tanigue 2025).

Conditions inside women's prisons must be improved to meet international human rights standards. Overcrowding, inadequate healthcare, poor sanitation, and a lack of gender-responsive facilities are pervasive. Prisons should provide clean water, menstrual hygiene products, private bathing spaces, and mental and physical health services. Rehabilitation opportunities must be enhanced to include vocational and literacy programs that offer reintegrative support (Prison Insider 2024).

Protecting the rights of incarcerated mothers is another priority. Women should not be automatically separated from their infants, especially during the postpartum period. Existing mother–baby units like the one at CIW should be expanded, with consistent policies for co-residence and child-friendly visitation areas (Prison Insider 2024).

Legal aid and post-release support must also be strengthened. Many incarcerated women lack legal representation, especially during pre-trial detention. They also face stigma and poverty upon release. Expanding access to public defenders and establishing reintegration services (e.g., transitional housing, employment assistance, and trauma counseling) can reduce recidivism and promote long-term stability (Veloso 2023).

Lastly, investment in social protection is necessary to prevent women's criminalization in the first place. Lack of education, gender-based violence, and economic exclusion are drivers of women's imprisonment. Policy responses should include targeted poverty alleviation, universal education, domestic violence prevention, and support for informal workers and single mothers. By addressing the roots of incarceration, the Philippines can move toward a more equitable and humane justice system (Pas-iwen et al. 2024).

Cambodia

Historical Context

The historical context of women's incarceration in Cambodia is influenced by its colonial past, conflict, and the Khmer Rouge regime. Under French rule (1863–1953), Cambodia adopted French civil law, but gender norms continued. Women were limited to domestic roles with little access to education or employment (Dim 2018). Female criminalization was often linked to poverty or moral offenses like theft or prostitution (Sandy 2006). Colonial prisons were undeveloped, and records suggest that female inmates were rarely documented (Anderson 2022).

In the decades following independence, the prison system remained weak, and women continued to be imprisoned for minor offenses. Facilities exhibited overcrowding, poor sanitation, and limited healthcare (UN Office of the High Commissioner for Human Rights 2015). Under the Khmer Rouge (1975–9), these issues intensified. The legal system was dismantled, courts were abolished, and people were detained for minor infractions like dissent or wearing Western clothing (Killean 2018). Women were targeted for moral crimes and suffered torture, sexual violence, and execution, including while pregnant. At sites like Tuol Sleng and Kraing Ta Chan, survivors reported abuse, including disembowelment and mutilation (Peace Institute of Cambodia 2016). These crimes have been documented by the Extraordinary Chambers in the Courts of Cambodia, a UN-backed court established to prosecute Khmer Rouge leaders for genocide and international crimes (International Crimes Database 2025).

After the regime's fall, Cambodia began rebuilding its legal institutions. In the post-conflict era, poverty and displacement drove many women into survival-based offenses like petty theft, drug activity, or labor-related migration (UN OHCHR 2015). Vulnerability was high for single mothers and abuse survivors (Penal Reform International 2019).

Although reforms like the 1993 Constitution and gender-based violence laws were introduced to promote equality and protect women's rights, enforcement remains inconsistent. Many incarcerated women are pre-trial detainees charged with non-violent drug offenses, often as users or couriers (UN OHCHR 2015). Others are detained for actions stemming from victimization, such as fleeing abuse (PRI 2019). Persistent issues include overcrowding, inadequate medical care, and neglect of gender-specific needs. These trends reflect Cambodia's legacy of gender inequality, poverty, and institutional neglect.

Female Incarceration Rates and Trends

Female incarceration rates in Cambodia have risen in recent years, mainly due to strict drug laws and socioeconomic challenges. Women comprise a small percentage of the total prison population (6.1 percent) (Institute for Crime and Justice Policy Research 2025a), but their numbers have increased significantly. In 2000, there were 288 women behind bars, but there are now approximately 3,500 (Institute for Crime and Justice Policy Research 2025a).

Many incarcerated women are first-time, non-violent offenders, often charged with low-level drug offenses like possession (UN Office of the High Commissioner for Human Rights 2015). Women are also frequently imprisoned for crimes like theft and fraud, typically linked to poverty and caregiving responsibilities. Moral offenses like prostitution and adultery also contribute, reflecting the influence of patriarchal social norms (Sandy 2006). In addition, women have been detained for peaceful activism or political dissent, including environmental defenders and housing rights advocates who often receive harsh sentences under vague laws like "incitement" or "plotting" (Ratcliffe 2024).

Cambodia's primary women's facility is Correctional Centre 2 (CC2), or Prey Sar Women's Prison, located in Phnom Penh. It has served as a pilot site for ASEAN's "Model Prison" initiative under the UN Bangkok Rules (TIJ

2019). Despite reform efforts, overcrowding and gender-specific challenges continue. As of 2024, the facility also held forty-three pregnant women and ninety-two children living with their incarcerated mothers (Seoung and Narim 2025). Women are also held in provincial prisons, such as Kandal Provincial Prison, which transferred forty inmates to CC2 in early 2025 due to overcrowding at nearly four times its capacity (Sotheary 2025). In 2024, eighteen of nineteen monitored prisons exceeded capacity, eleven by at least 200 percent (LICADHO 2025).

Demographics of Incarcerated Women

The demographics of incarcerated women in Cambodia reflect the country's socioeconomic inequalities. While specific statistical breakdowns are lacking, multiple sources indicate that most imprisoned women come from poor, rural, and marginalized communities where poverty, limited education, and few employment opportunities increase their vulnerability to criminalization. According to the UN Office of the High Commissioner for Human Rights (2015), many of these women have histories of substance abuse, gender-based violence, or economic desperation, and their offenses are typically non-violent, often related to survival.

Rural poverty is a driver of female incarceration. As of 2020, 23 percent of rural residents lived below the national poverty line, compared with just 4 percent in Phnom Penh (Theavy 2023). Since most incarcerated women are believed to come from these areas (UN OHCHR 2015), the connection between rural hardship and imprisonment is strong. Educational attainment also plays a role. As of 2022, nearly 68 percent of girls in Cambodia completed lower-secondary school (World Bank 2023). These trends reflect barriers that reduce women's economic opportunities and increase criminalization.

Most incarcerated women in Cambodia are young adults, and recent trends suggest a rise in younger women entering the criminal justice system, especially for drug-related offenses (Penal Reform International 2019). A national gender assessment also found that 22–25 percent of married Cambodian women reported experiencing physical abuse by a spouse, highlighting the intersection of domestic violence and economic vulnerability as pathways to incarceration (Ministry of Women's Affairs 2014). These patterns demonstrate how poverty, gender inequality, and trauma contribute to women's involvement in Cambodia's justice system.

Crimes Leading to Incarceration

The crimes leading to women's incarceration in Cambodia are mostly non-violent and linked to poverty, gender-based violence, and strict drug laws. Approximately 77 percent of incarcerated women are held for non-violent offenses (TIJ 2025), with drug-related charges comprising the majority. As of 2020, 73 percent of women in prison were serving time for drug offenses, typically possession or small-scale trafficking (Amnesty International and LICADHO 2020). Cambodia's position as a regional drug transit country has led to aggressive enforcement, with poor and rural women often coerced or recruited into acting as couriers (Jeffries and Chuenurah 2019). One notable case involved Ve Thi Tran, an Australian woman sentenced in 2019 to thirty years in prison for attempting to smuggle nearly 2 kilograms of heroin out of Phnom Penh International Airport (The Cambodia Daily 2019). Another example is Noor Yuni, who was arrested en route to Hong Kong after unknowingly carrying methamphetamine (Jha 2020). These cases show how women, who are often exploited by trafficking networks, receive severe penalties despite their minor roles.

A smaller number of women are incarcerated for violent crimes committed in response to long-term abuse. Jeffries and Chuenurah (2018) describe this "domestic violence pathway" to prison, citing the case of Tevy, a woman who killed her abusive partner during an attack after years of suffering. Her story highlights how acts of self-defense are often criminalized despite lengthy victimization.

Moral offenses, including adultery and prostitution, are still prosecuted under conservative legal norms. In 2022, a woman named Soun Pov was detained for alleged adultery after her husband filed a complaint (Cambodia Expats Online 2022). Additionally, in 2018, Hun Chansen, a massage parlor owner in Siem Reap, was arrested and charged with procurement of prostitution, demonstrating the legal targeting of women in sex work (Raksmey 2018).

Lastly, Cambodian women activists have faced politically motivated incarceration. For instance, in 2024, Phuon Keoraksmey, a 23-year-old member of the environmental activist group Mother Nature Cambodia, was sentenced to six years in prison on charges of "plotting against the government" and insulting the king (Ratcliffe 2024). This case represents a crackdown on female voices, where female activists are criminalized for peaceful activism.

Note that publicly available data does not provide detailed statistical breakdowns by offense type for women in Cambodia.

Contributing Laws and Policies

Laws and policies related to drug enforcement, economic crimes, and gender-based offenses have contributed to women's incarceration. Cambodia's Law on Drug Control of 2012 outlines the penalties for drug offenses. Under **Article 40**, possession carries two to five years' imprisonment, and repeat offenses are punishable by up to ten years. Trafficking charges can lead to two to twenty years in prison (Amnesty International and LICADHO 2020). Cambodia's role as a regional transit hub has intensified enforcement, and women have become easy targets due to poverty, limited education, and lack of legal representation (Amnesty International and LICADHO 2020). Courts rarely consider mitigating factors like coercion, caregiving, or prior victimization, resulting in a system that punishes vulnerability (Cots Fernandéz and Nougier 2021).

Economic crimes are another reason for women's imprisonment, often the result of poverty. Cambodia has non-custodial measures like probation and community-based rehabilitation. However, their implementation is limited because of insufficient judicial training and unclear guidelines (IDPC 2024). Consequently, women convicted of minor crimes are often imprisoned, worsening overcrowding and failing to address the root causes of their offending.

Cambodia has protections like the 2005 Domestic Violence Law and constitutional guarantees against gender-based violence. However, enforcement is weak, especially in rural and marginalized areas (Resource Hub 2024). Survivors who act in self-defense are often criminalized due to the justice system's lack of trauma-informed approaches (Penal Reform International 2019). Police and prosecutors frequently divert cases to mediation rather than prosecution, discouraging women from seeking help and enabling abuse to continue (Nimol 2023).

Legal reforms are needed to promote gender-sensitive practices, including community-based alternatives to incarceration. The Bangkok Rules emphasize reducing reliance on prison for low-risk women, which can help reduce overcrowding and address the root causes of offending (Penal Reform International 2019). Most incarcerated women in Cambodia are non-violent and pose minimal public safety risks, making them suitable for community-based responses rather than imprisonment. Expanding alternatives and consistently enforcing domestic violence laws could reduce women's incarceration and align Cambodia's justice system with international standards (UNODC 2019).

Conditions in Women's Prisons

Conditions in Cambodia's women's prisons are often harsh and inadequate. Overcrowding is among the most severe problems. For instance, Kandal Prison has more than 650 percent of its intended capacity, housing nearly 3,900 inmates in a facility built for 600 (Khuon 2025).

Cramped, poorly ventilated cells contribute to the spread of infections and illnesses (Human Rights Watch 2021). Sanitation is poor, and access to hygiene products like sanitary pads is unreliable, with many women depending on overpriced commissary items or donations (Pou and Sreypich 2024). The Ministry of Interior has acknowledged that underfunding limits the prison system's ability to provide basic services. An example is Prey Sar Women's Prison in Phnom Penh. During the COVID-19 pandemic, Amnesty International described the facility as a "ticking time bomb" due to extreme overcrowding and the absence of health safeguards (Amnesty International 2020). People have reported only 30–40 centimeters of floor space, and food shortages can be so severe that some women resorted to eating insects and rats (Prisoners Abroad 2019).

Another infamous site was Koh Romdual, an island facility that held mentally ill and socially marginalized women without trial. Conditions included overcrowded bamboo shelters, lack of medical care, and abuse. UN intervention led to its closure in 2008 following reports of torture, neglect, and detention for non-criminal behavior (Jackson 2014).

Pregnant women and mothers face additional risks. Between the end of 2015 and mid-2018, the number of children living with their mothers in Cambodian prisons increased from 30 to 138 (with 55 additional pregnant women) by late 2018 (Amnesty International and LICADHO 2020). In 2020, a five-month-old baby died in custody from pneumonia and malnutrition after her mother was jailed for allegedly possessing $3.60 worth of methamphetamine (Handley 2020).

Lastly, rehabilitation programs are minimal and inconsistent. Without access to education or job training, most women leave prison with few resources, increasing their risk of recidivism (Penal Reform International 2019). Consequently, reform is urgently needed.

Health and Mental Health Issues

Incarcerated women in Cambodia face health and mental health challenges due to inadequate healthcare services and the prison environment. Many enter prison with pre-existing conditions like malnutrition, infectious diseases, and reproductive health complications, which are often worsened behind bars (Amnesty International 2020).

Access to medical care is limited. Prisons have persistent shortages of healthcare staff, essential medicines, and sanitary supplies. During the COVID-19 pandemic, Amnesty International (2020) described Cambodia's prisons as grossly underprepared to handle routine illnesses, let alone infectious outbreaks in overcrowded, poorly ventilated cells. Nutritional deficiencies are widespread, and meals lack sufficient vitamins and nutrients, weakening immune systems and increasing susceptibility to illness (Amnesty International 2020).

Pregnant women and mothers with infants are especially vulnerable. Prenatal and postnatal care is lacking, and living conditions are unsafe. Pregnant inmates are not routinely provided basic healthcare, and babies sometimes return from hospitals to overcrowded cells without proper follow-up (Amnesty International and LICADHO 2020). The lack of screenings, adequate nutrition, bedding, and maternal care places mothers and infants at risk. These failures emphasize the system's inability to meet gender- and age-specific health needs.

Mental health is another overlooked concern. Many incarcerated women have experienced trauma before incarceration, including domestic violence, sexual abuse, and human trafficking. However, mental health services in prison are virtually nonexistent. TPO Cambodia, one of the few organizations offering support, operates in only four of the country's twenty-six prisons. It provides assessments, crisis intervention, and counseling on a limited basis (TPO Cambodia 2023). As a result, most women must cope with depression, anxiety, PTSD, and trauma-related symptoms without professional support. Human Rights Watch (2021) reported that the fear, surveillance, lack of privacy, and general neglect within Cambodian prisons compound mental distress. Former detainees have described widespread emotional suffering, which goes largely unacknowledged and untreated.

Impact on Families and Children

The incarceration of women in Cambodia has consequences for their families, especially their children. Many incarcerated women are primary caregivers, and their absence leaves children without support. Some children are placed with extended family, while others are institutionalized or left to fend for themselves, leading to long-term emotional instability (This Life Cambodia 2019).

Cambodian law allows children under age three to live with their mothers in prison. However, implementation is inconsistent and often left to the discretion of prison staff. As of 2024, ninety-two children (fifty girls and forty-two boys) were living in prison with their mothers. They are often housed in overcrowded

> ### Motherhood Behind Bars
>
> Cambodian law allows children under age three to live with their mothers in prison, but conditions are unsafe. In 2020, a five-month-old baby died of pneumonia and malnutrition after her mother was jailed for possessing methamphetamine worth less than four dollars. Such tragedies show how punitive drug policies and poor prison conditions endanger children's lives.

and unsanitary conditions with poor access to healthcare, nutrition, and early education (Yalirozy 2025). Children frequently stay past the legal age limit due to the absence of alternative care options (Gorter 2019). In response, a 2025 decree introduced small cash subsidies for pregnant prisoners and children under two, though support is limited (Yalirozy 2025).

For mothers separated from children living outside prison, emotional distress is compounded by limited visitation opportunities, which are often restricted by distance, poverty, and prison discretion (Pandya 2022). In one study, only two of seven mothers reported monthly visits from children living outside, while four received sporadic visits and one had never been visited at all (This Life Cambodia 2019). Stigma and economic instability worsen these challenges. The loss of a mother's income drives families further into poverty, forcing children to drop out of school or enter the labor force. Social discrimination isolates these families, and Cambodia lacks organized reintegration and support programs (Gorter 2019). One woman, Bopha, gave birth while in pre-trial detention and lived with her infant in a severely overcrowded cell. Denied access to a phone to check on her other children, she recalled, "I wait—with my child, behind bars—to find out what my sentence is from a judge" (Cambodianess 2020).

Policy Reforms and Recommendations

Cambodia has constitutional commitments and endorsement of international norms like the Bangkok Rules. However, the prison system continues to punish vulnerable women while offering few rehabilitative or gender-sensitive alternatives. A shift toward non-custodial measures, trauma-informed approaches, and coordinated support is needed.

Expanding community-based alternatives to incarceration would help reduce overcrowding and ensure more proportionate responses to low-level offenses. Cambodia has some non-custodial options like probation, but their use is limited because of vague implementation guidelines and a lack of judicial training (IDPC 2024). Most incarcerated women are non-violent and pose little public safety risk, making them suitable candidates for these alternatives (Penal Reform International 2019).

Additionally, drug reform is needed. Cambodia's anti-drug laws impose harsh penalties even for minor possession or acting as a courier. They disproportionately affect poor, rural women (Amnesty International and LICADHO 2020), and courts rarely consider mitigating factors (Cots Fernandéz and Nougier 2021). Revising Article 40 of the 2012 Law on Drug Control to incorporate these realities could reduce incarceration and promote rehabilitation.

Stronger enforcement of existing protections against gender-based violence is also needed. Cambodia has a Domestic Violence Law (2005), but enforcement is weak, and many survivors are diverted into mediation rather than formal legal processes (Resource Hub 2024). Training police and prosecutors in trauma-informed, victim-centered approaches would improve access to justice and prevent the criminalization of survivors acting in self-defense (Penal Reform International 2019).

Maternal and child health inside prisons also requires attention. The 2025 decree offering cash subsidies to pregnant inmates and children under two is a step forward but remains insufficient (Yalirozy 2025). Expanded funding, healthcare services, and education programs within prisons would improve the development of children living behind bars (Seoung and Narim 2025).

Finally, reintegration support is necessary to prevent recidivism. Women released from prison face social discrimination and limited economic opportunity (Gorter 2019). Family-centered policies, transitional housing, and vocational training programs could improve post-release outcomes.

Conclusion

Across India, the Philippines, and Cambodia, women's incarceration demonstrates inequalities influenced by poverty, gender-based violence, and punitive legal systems. Despite differences in laws and incarceration rates, several similarities emerge. In all three countries, most incarcerated women are poor, marginalized, and imprisoned for non-violent, survival-based offenses, especially low-level drug crimes or theft. Many are primary caregivers, and their imprisonment harms children and families. Pre-trial detention is widespread, and prison conditions are overcrowded, unsanitary, and lacking in gender-sensitive care.

Each country also faces unique challenges. India's large pre-trial population and overuse of laws like Section 498A and the NDPS Act result in the criminalization of victims and minor offenders. In the Philippines, the war on drugs has led to a dramatic increase in women's imprisonment, overwhelming the system and intensifying human rights concerns. Cambodia continues to criminalize poverty, sex work, and political dissent, with minimal enforcement of existing gender protections and few rehabilitation options.

Despite some legislative safeguards, implementation remains inconsistent, and trauma-informed approaches are rare. To improve outcomes, all three countries must prioritize non-custodial alternatives for non-violent women offenders, especially those driven to crime by poverty, coercion, or abuse. Drug laws must account for low-level roles and mitigating factors. Gender-specific prison services, including maternal care, mental health support, and vocational programs, must be expanded. Finally, reintegration efforts, child-protection policies, and legal aid services should be strengthened to reduce recidivism and support families.

A shift toward rehabilitation, rather than punishment, is needed. Without systemic reform, these nations will continue to incarcerate vulnerable women for social failures better addressed through community support, legal reform, and investment in gender equity.

References

Alvarez, Mary Catherine A. 2018. *Incarceration and Drug Policies in South East Asia: Promoting Humane and Effective Responses.* IDPC Project on Women, Incarceration and Drug Policy in South East Asia. International Drug Policy Consortium. https://www.aidsdatahub.org/sites/default/files/resource/idpc-philippines-policy-guide-women-2018.pdf.

Amnesty International. 2020. *Cambodia: Overcrowded Detention Centres a "Ticking Time Bomb" for COVID-19.* March 27, 2020. https://www.amnesty.org/en/latest/news/2020/03/cambodia-overcrowded-detention-centres-covid-19-raft-fake-news-arrests.

Amnesty International. 2001. *Philippines: Fear, Shame and Impunity—Rape and Sexual Abuse of Women in Custody.* AI Index: ASA 35/001/2001. London: Amnesty International. https://www.amnesty.org/es/wp-content/uploads/2021/06/asa350012001en.pdf.

Amnesty International and LICADHO (Cambodian League for the Promotion and Defense of Human Rights). 2020. *Arbitrary Detention Related to Drug Policies in Cambodia: Joint Submission.* June 2020. https://www.amnesty.org/en/wp-content/uploads/2021/05/ASA2325062020ENGLISH.pdf.

Anderson, Clare. 2022. "Convicts from French Indochina in the Global French Empire." *Convicts, Creolization and Cosmopolitanism in the British and French Empires.* July 15, 2022. https://www.convictscc.le.ac.uk/2022/07/15/remembering-convicts-from-french-indochina-in-the-global-french-empire/.

Beltran, Michael. 2024. "Women's Stories from the 'Graveyard of the Living' in the Philippines." *The Diplomat.* March 9, 2024. https://thediplomat.com/2024/03/womens-stories-from-the-graveyard-of-the-living-in-the-philippines/.

Borah, Rashmita, and Bimal Kumar Baishya. 2023. "Living Conditions of Prisoners in India: The Right to Adequate Food and Proper Nutrition." *International Journal of Food and Nutritional Sciences (IJFANS)* 12 (1): 7244–54.

Bureau of Corrections (Philippines). n.d. "History." Philippine Bureau of Corrections. https://bucor.gov.ph/?page_id=492.

Bureau of Jail Management and Penology. 2015. *Comprehensive Operations Manual.* Department of the Interior and Local Government—Bureau of Jail Management and Penology. Revised November 2024. https://car.bjmp.gov.ph/wp-content/uploads/2024/11/BJMP-Comprehensive-Operations-Manual-2015-Edition.pdf.

Cabato, Regine. 2021. "The Philippines' Drug War Is Putting More Pregnant Women Behind Bars. What Happens to Their Children?" *The Washington Post.* April 9, 2021. https://www.washingtonpost.com/world/2021/04/06/women-jail-births-philippines-duterte/.

Cambodia Expats Online. 2022. "Husband Sick of Cheating Wife, Files Police Complaint for Adultery." *Cambodia Expats Online.* January 19, 2022. https://cambodiaexpatsonline.com/general-chatter/husband-sick-cheating-wife-files-police-complaint-for-adultery-t48239.html.

Cambodianess. 2020. "Surviving the System and Building a Life After Prison in Cambodia." June 4, 2020. https://cambodianess.com/article/surviving-the-system-and-building-a-life-after-prison-in-cambodia.

Ceballo, Emma C., and Faith Ann Joy C. Absin. 2022. "Phenomenology of Incarcerated Mothers: What About Their Children?" *European Journal of Social Sciences Studies* 7 (4): 139–67.

Commission on Human Rights, Center for Gender Equality and Women's Rights. 2022. *Inside Stories: A Report on the Situation of Women Deprived of Liberty from Select Detention Facilities.* Quezon City: Commission on Human Rights. https://cdn1.chr.gov.ph/wp-content/uploads/2022/01/08155554/Inside-Stories-A-Report-on-the-Situation-of-Women-Deprived-of-Liberty-from-Select-Detention-Facilities.pdf.

Commonwealth Human Rights Initiative. 2023. "Periods in Prison—A Short Report on Menstrual Hygiene Management in India's Women Prisons." *Commonwealth Human Rights Initiative.* May 3, 2023. https://www.humanrightsinitiative.org/publication/

periods-in-prison-a-short-report-on-menstrual-hygiene-management-in-indias-women-prisons.

Correctional Institution for Women. n.d. *Correctional Institution for Women*. Scribd. https://www.scribd.com/document/492860300/CORRECTIONAL-INSTITUTION-FOR-WOMEN.

Cots Fernandéz, Adrià, and Marie Nougier. 2021. *Punitive Drug Laws: 10 Years Undermining the Bangkok Rules*. February 2021. https://womenanddrugs.wola.org/wp-content/uploads/2021/02/Punitive-Drug-Laws-10-years-undermining-the-Bangkok-Rules.pdf.

Das, Kalyan. 2023. "Female Drug Traffickers: 79 % Rise in Women Held Under NDPS Act in State." *The Times of India*. May 28, 2023. https://timesofindia.indiatimes.com/city/dehradun/female-drug-traffickers-79-rise-in-women-held-under-NDPS-Act-in-state/articleshow/100560079.cms.

Dhaliwal, Ravi. 2025. "Punjab: Amid Tightening of Noose Around Male Drug Smugglers, Women Fill the Void in Illicit Trade." *The Tribune (India)*. July 21, 2025. https://www.tribuneindia.com/news/punjab/punjab-amid-tightening-of-noose-around-male-drug-smugglers-women-fill-the-void-in-illicit-trade-546520.

Dhillon, Harpreet Singh, and Shibu Sasidharan. 2024. "Prison Mental Health—An Indian Perspective." *Annals of Indian Psychiatry* 8 (1): 80–2.

DIGNITY. 2013. *Conditions for Women in Detention in the Philippines: Needs, Vulnerabilities and Good Practices*. Copenhagen: DIGNITY—Danish Institute Against Torture. https://dignity.dk/wp-content/uploads/publication-series-11.pdf.

Dim, Phirun. 2018. "Cambodian Women's Roles in Education and Leadership: Empowerment." *Cambodian Journal of International Studies* 2: 217–31.

Dolan, Kate, and Sarah Larney. 2010. "HIV in Indian Prisons: Risk Behaviour, Prevalence, Prevention & Treatment." *The Indian Journal of Medical Research* 132: 696–700.

Economic Times. 2021. "India's 27.37 Per Cent Prison Inmates 'Illiterate', Over 5,600 Techies: Govt Data." *The Economic Times*. April. https://m.economictimes.com/news/politics-and-nation/indias-27-37-per-cent-prison-inmates-illiterate-over-5600-techies-govt-data/articleshow/80908764.cms.

Ganjapure, Vaibhav. 2025. "Police Complaints Being Increasingly Used to Teach Lesson to Husband's Family, Says HC." *The Times of India*. June 19, 2025. https://timesofindia.indiatimes.com/city/nagpur/police-complaints-being-increasingly-used-to-teach-lesson-to-husbands-family-says-hc/articleshow/121939052.cms.

Gorter, Billy. 2019. "Women in Cambodian Prisons: The Challenges of Caring for Their Children." *Penal Reform International Blog*. November 4, 2019. https://www.penalreform.org/blog/women-in-cambodian-prisons-the-challenges-of-caring/.

Handley, Erin. 2020. "Cambodia's Drug War Has Seen Prisoner Numbers Skyrocket During Coronavirus Pandemic." *ABC News*. May 30, 2020. https://www.abc.net.au/news/2020-05-31/cambodia-war-on-drugs-human-rights-abuses-torture-women/12288860.

Hermosa, Allona. 2024. "Seeing Through the Prison Walls: The SRHR Situation of Women Deprived of Liberty (WDL)." Likhaan Center for Women's Health. January 4, 2024. https://www.likhaan.org/articles/seeing-through-the-prison-walls-the-srhr-situation-of-women-deprived-of-liberty-wdl.

Human Rights Watch. 2021. "Cambodia: Urgently Address Covid-19 Outbreak in Prisons." May 23, 2021. https://www.hrw.org/news/2021/05/23/cambodia-urgently-address-covid-19-outbreak-prisons.

Human Rights Watch. 2017. *License to Kill: Philippine Police Killings in Duterte's 'War on Drugs'.* https://www.hrw.org/report/2017/03/02/license-kill/philippine-police-killings-dutertes-war-drugs.

ICRC (International Committee of the Red Cross). 2016. "Philippines: Intensifying the Detection of Tuberculosis in Jails and Prisons." https://www.icrc.org/en/document/philippines-intensifying-detection-tuberculosis-jails-and-prisons.

IDPC (International Drug Policy Consortium). 2024. *Cambodia: Barriers to Accessing Alternatives to Incarceration for Women and Young People Who Use Drugs.* https://idpc.net/publications/2024/09/cambodia-barriers-to-accessing-alternatives-to-incarceration-for-women-and-young-people-who-use.

India Code. 1985. *The Narcotic Drugs and Psychotropic Substances Act, 1985.* Government of India. https://www.indiacode.nic.in/bitstream/123456789/18974/1/narcotic-drugs-and-psychotropic-substances-act-1985.pdf.

Institute for Crime & Justice Policy Research. 2025a. "Cambodia." World Prison Brief. https://www.prisonstudies.org/country/cambodia.

Institute for Crime & Justice Policy Research. 2025b. "*India.*" World Prison Brief: PrisonStudies.org. https://www.prisonstudies.org/country/india.

Institute for Crime & Justice Policy Research. 2025c. "Philippines—World Prison Brief." *World Prison Brief.* Birkbeck, University of London. https://www.prisonstudies.org/country/philippines.

International Crimes Database. 2025. "Case 002/01 Judgment (Case 3312)." https://www.internationalcrimesdatabase.org/Case/3312.

Jackson, Will. 2014. "Surviving the Island of Widows, a 'Prison Without Walls' for Women." *Phnom Penh Post.* April 28, 2014. https://www.phnompenhpost.com/7days/surviving-island-widows-%E2%80%98prison-without-walls%E2%80%99-women.

Jeffries, Samantha, and Chontit Chuenurah. 2019. "Vulnerabilities, Victimisation, Romance and Indulgence: Thai Women's Pathways to Prison in Cambodia for International Cross Border Drug Trafficking." *International Journal of Law, Crime and Justice* 56: 39–52.

Jeffries, Samantha, and Chontit Chuenurah. 2018. "Pathways to Prison in Cambodia for Homicide Offending: Exploring Women's Life History Narratives." *South East Asia Research* 26 (2): 109–31.

Jha, Preeti. 2020. "Asia's Prisons Are Filling up with Women. Many Are Victims of the War on Drugs." *CNN*. August 16, 2020. https://www.cnn.com/2020/08/16/asia/women-drug-trafficking-mules-hnk-intl-dst-as-equals/index.html.

JusCorpus. 2023. "The Condition of Women Prisoners in India." July 2, 2023. https://www.juscorpus.com/the-condition-of-women-prisoners-in-india/#:~:text=India%20has%20seen%20a%20worrying, … while%20undergoing%20a%20heavy%20flow.

Kanwal, Garima, Richa Ranjan, and Jyoti. 2025. "The Status of Women Prisoners in India." *International Journal for Legal Research & Analysis* 2 (7), June: 5–27.

Kaur, Navdeep, and Sanjoy Roy. 2021. "Mental Health Status of Incarcerated Women in India: A Perspective from a Social Worker." *Indian Journal of Gender Studies* 29 (1): 1–15.

Khuon, Narim. 2025. "Cambodia Now Ranks Second in Prison Overcrowding, Calls for Reform." *CamboJA News*. February 19, 2025. https://cambojanews.com/cambodia-now-ranks-second-in-prison-overcrowding-calls-for-reform/.

Killean, Rachel. 2018. "Selective Justice and Constructions of Victimhood at the Khmer Rouge Tribunal." In *Transitional and Transformative Justice: Critical and International Perspectives*, edited by Susanne Buckley-Zistel, and Annika Björkdahl, 21–8. London: Routledge.

LICADHO (Cambodian League for the Promotion and Defense of Human Rights). 2025. "Cambodia's Capacity Crisis: Overcrowded Prisons and the Need for Reform." https://www.licadho-cambodia.org/topic/prison_detention.

Matahum, Ferolini T., and Yolanda G. Tanigue. 2025. "The Extent of Implementation of RA 9262 in the National Capital Region." *International Journal of Multidisciplinary: Applied Business and Education Research* 6 (4): 1890–912.

Ministry of Women's Affairs. 2014. *Violence Against Women and Girls: Cambodia Gender Assessment*. Phnom Penh: Ministry of Women's Affairs. https://www.undp.org/sites/g/files/zskgke326/files/migration/kh/Neary-Rattanak-4—Violence-against-Women-and-Girls_Eng.pdf.

Montealegre, Janyn Mariella, and Jan Krianne Pineda. 2023. *Assessing the Correctional Institution for Women's (CIW) Safety and Security: Gender-Sensitive Prison Management in Compliance with the United Nations Bangkok Rules*. Philippine Statistics Authority. https://psa.gov.ph/sites/default/files/ncs/paper-presentations-manuscripts/Assessing%20The%20Correctional%20Institution%20for%20Women%E2%80%99s%20%28CIW%29%20Safety%20And%20Security%20Gender-Sensitive%20Prison%20Management%20In%20Compliance%20With%20The%20United%20Nations%20%20Bangkok%20Rules.pdf.

Murti, Aditi. 2021. "Children of Women Prisoners Receive Little Education, Institutional Support: Govt Survey." *The Swaddle*. April 7, 2021. https://www.theswaddle.com/children-of-women-prisoners-receive-little-education-institutional-support-govt-survey.

Naik, Kiran R. 2019. "Women in Prisons India." *International Journal of Research and Analytical Reviews (IJRAR)* 6 (2, June): IJRAR1AXP008.

National Commission for Women. 2018. *A Report on Improving the Condition of Women Inmates in Prisons*. New Delhi: NCW. https://www.ncw.gov.in/reports/a-report-on-improving-the-condition-of-women-inmates-in-prisons.

National WWII Museum. 2021. "July 4, 1946: The Philippines Gained Independence from the United States." *The National WWII Museum*. July 2, 2021. https://www.nationalww2museum.org/war/articles/july-4-1946-philippines-independence.

Nieva Jr., Romulo Fernandez. 2024. "Navigating Pregnancy in Detention: Lived Experiences in a Philippine Women's Prison." *International Journal of Prisoner Health* 20 (3): 286–98.

Nimol, Seoung. 2023. "Report Points to Inadequate Enforcement, Legal Flaws as Reasons for Entrenched Domestic Violence." *Camboja News*. March 10, 2023. https://cambojanews.com/report-points-to-inadequate-enforcement-legal-flaws-as-reasons-for-entrenched-domestic-violence/.

Paliath, Shreehari. 2023. "#DataViz: Prison Occupancy Rose in 2022, Despite Campaign to Release Undertrials—Three in Four Prisoners Continue to Be Undertrials, a Majority of Whom Belong to Oppressed Caste Groups." *IndiaSpend*. December 5, 2023. https://www.indiaspend.com/data-viz/dataviz-prison-occupancy-rose-in-2022-despite-campaign-to-release-undertrials-884179.

Paliath, Shreehari, and Preety Acharya. 2020. "Living with Imprisoned Mothers, Children Struggle for Normal Childhood." *IndiaSpend*. October 6, 2020. https://www.indiaspend.com/8-women-prisoners-children-live-with-them-heres-how-the-system-fails-them.

Pandey, Diksha. 2020. *Female Prisoners in India: The Consequences of Triple Marginalisation*. Issue Brief 06.20. New Delhi: Social and Political Research Foundation. https://sprf.in/wp-content/uploads/2021/02/Female-Prisoners.pdf.

Pandya, Khushi. 2022. *A Desktop Assessment of the Situation of Women and Children in Cambodian Prisons*. January 24, 2022. SSRN. https://ssrn.com/abstract=4016092.

Pas-iwen, Jevilyn, Acelyn Attaban, Athena Camacho, Carl Daguing, Jaime Lumiqued III, John Rey Danli Antiyag, and Nelson Saingan. 2024. "Ensuring Equity in Addressing Rising Female Incarceration: Exploring Profile Trends and Overcoming Systemic Challenges." December 19, 2024. *SSRN*.

Peace Institute of Cambodia. 2016. *Story from the Ground: Memory Sketch of Kraing Ta Chan Security Center*. Phnom Penh: Peace Institute of Cambodia. https://www.sitesofconscience.org/wp-content/uploads/2018/04/Kraing-Ta-Chan-Booklet-English.pdf.

Penal Reform International. 2023. *Global Prison Trends 2023*. https://cdn.penalreform.org/wp-content/uploads/2023/06/GPT-2023.pdf.

Penal Reform International. 2020. *Sentencing of Women Convicted of Drug-Related Offences: A Multi-Jurisdictional Study*. Linklaters LLP. https://cdn.penalreform.org/wp-content/uploads/2020/02/LinklatersPRI_Sentencing-of-women-convicted-of-drug-related-offences_WEB.pdf.

Penal Reform International. 2019. *The Rehabilitation and Social Reintegration of Women Prisoners: Implementation of the Bangkok Rules*. London: Penal Reform International. https://cdn.penalreform.org/wp-content/uploads/2019/05/PRI_Rehabilitation-of-women-prisoners_WEB.pdf.

Penal Reform International and Linklaters. 2020. *Sentencing of Women Convicted of Drug-Related Offences*. International Drug Policy Consortium. https://cdn.penalreform.org/wp-content/uploads/2020/02/LinklatersPRI_Sentencing-of-women-convicted-of-drug-related-offences_WEB.pdf.

Pou, Soreachny, and Sovann Sreypich. 2024. "Cambodia's Prisons Struggle to Meet Women's Basic Health Needs, Campaign Highlights." *CamboJA News*. December 11, 2024. https://cambojanews.com/cambodias-prisons-struggle-to-meet-womens-basic-health-needs-campaign-highlights/.

Prison Insider. 2024. "Philippine Inmates: In Prison, Mother and Baby Share ₱85 a Day for Food and Medicine." *Prison Insider*. January 2024. https://www.prison-insider.com/en/articles/philippine-in-prison-mother-and-baby-share-p85-a-day-for-food-medicine.

Prisoners Abroad. 2019. "Captive in Cambodia: Life Inside Prey Sar Prison." https://www.prisonersabroad.org.uk/blog/captive-in-cambodia-life-inside-prey-sar-prison.

Radhakrishna, Meena. 2001. *Dishonoured by History: "Criminal Tribes" and British Colonial Policy*. Hyderabad: Orient Longman.

Rai, Sandeep. 2020. "Nearly 70% of Prisoners Lodged in Indian Jails Are Either Illiterate or Semi-Literate." *The Times of India*. October 8, 2020. https://timesofindia.indiatimes.com/city/meerut/nearly-70-of-prisoners-lodged-in-indian-jails-are-either-illiterate-or-semi-literate/articleshow/78540769.cms.

Raksmey, Kongkea. 2018. "Cambodia: Judicial Authorities Charge Two Massage Shop Owners with Procurement of Prostitution." *Business & Human Rights Resource Centre*. December 9, 2018. https://www.business-humanrights.org/en/latest-news/cambodia-judicial-authorities-charge-two-massage-shop-owners-with-procurement-of-prostitution/.

Ranta, Randhir Singh. 2018. "Rights of Children of Incarcerated Parents: A Constitutional Perspective." *Journal of Emerging Technologies and Innovative Research (JETIR)* 5 (3): 618–22.

Ratcliffe, Rebecca. 2024. "Cambodia Jails 10 Environmentalists in 'Crushing Blow to Civil Society.'" *The Guardian*. July 2, 2024. https://www.theguardian.com/world/article/2024/jul/02/cambodia-jails-10-environmentalists-in-crushing-blow-to-civil-society.

Resource Hub. 2024. "Legal Provisions | Cambodia | Fighting Domestic Violence." *Baker McKenzie Resource Hub*. https://resourcehub.bakermckenzie.com/en/resources/fighting-domestic-violence/asia/cambodia/topics/1legal-provisions.

Safi, Michael. 2024. "Dozens of Women Raped and Made Pregnant in Indian Jails, Inquiry Finds." *The Guardian*. February 23, 2024. https://www.theguardian.com/

global-development/2024/feb/23/rape-sexual-abuse-women-babies-indian-prisons-west-bengal.

Samridhi. 2024. "Unveiling Complexity: Factors Influencing Women's Involvement in Crime." *International Journal for Multidisciplinary Research (IJFMR)* 6 (3): 1–14.

Sandy, Larissa Jane. 2006. *My Blood, Sweat and Tears: Female Sex Workers in Cambodia—Victims, Vectors or Agents?* Canberra: Australian National University. https://openresearch-repository.anu.edu.au/items/f8c56f52-a9e1-4988-9838-356b8316affa.

Seoung, Nimol, and Khuon Narim. 2025. "Govt. Committee Reports Improved Conditions for Women Prisoners, Concerns Persist." *CamboJA News*. January 10, 2025. https://cambojanews.com/govt-committee-reports-improved-conditions-for-women-prisoners-concerns-persist/.

Shah, Stuti. 2024. *India Prison Nursery Report*. April 12, 2024. Children of Incarcerated Caregivers. https://cicmn.org/wp-content/uploads/2024/05/India-Report-Finalized-Version.docx.pdf.

Shanid, Padanna. 2023. "Locked Up and Forgotten: The Stories of Incarcerated Women in India." *Reflections.Live*. https://reflections.live/articles/11328/locked-up-and-forgotten-the-stories-of-incarcerated-women-in-india-an-article-by-padanna-shanid-11635-lmj0qjb7.html.

Singh, Manvir. 2023. "How Dowries Are Fuelling a Femicide Epidemic: Every Year in India, Many Thousands Are Killed in Marriage-Payment Disputes. Why Does This War on Women Persist?" *The New Yorker*. June 12, 2023. https://www.newyorker.com/magazine/2023/06/19/how-dowries-are-fuelling-a-femicide-epidemic.

Singh, Rajeev Kumar, and Sameeksha Tripathi. 2025. "From Legislation to Reality: A Critical Examination of Dowry Law Enforcement Using NCRB Data." *IJCRT*, April 2025 13 (4): 105–15.

Soriao, Johnly G., and Albert P. Balongoy. 2025. "The Invisible Victims: A Narrative Inquiry on the Experiences of Children with Incarcerated Mothers." *International Journal of Innovative Science and Research Technology* 10 (6), June: 1760–74.

Sotheary, Som. 2025. "40 Female Inmates Transferred to CC2 to Ease Overcrowding." *Khmer Times*. March 5, 2025. https://www.khmertimeskh.com/501648843/40-female-inmates-transferred-to-cc2-to-ease-overcrowding/.

The Cambodia Daily. 2019. "Cambodia Sentences Australian to 30 Years for Drug Trafficking." *The Cambodia Daily*. April 26, 2019. https://english.cambodiadaily.com/2019/04/26/cambodia-sentences-australian-to-30-years-for-drug-trafficking/.

Theavy, Chhom. 2023. *Poverty and Covid-19 in Cambodia: Lessons and Future Preparedness*. Policy Brief No. 03. Phnom Penh: Cambodia Development Research Institute. https://cdri.org.kh/storage/pdf/PB2023E-Poverty_1686039465.pdf.

This Life Cambodia. 2019. *Why Children Accompany Mothers into Prison*. Phnom Penh. https://thislife.ngo/wp-content/uploads/2019/04/Why-Children-Accompany-Mothers-into-Prison-2019.pdf.

TIJ (Thailand Institute of Justice). 2025. *Asia and Pacific Regional Preparatory Meeting for the Fifteenth United Nations Congress on Crime Prevention and Criminal Justice, Bangkok, 21–23 January 2025: Conference Room Paper*. https://digitallibrary.un.org/record/4078205/files/A_CONF.241_RPM.1_CRP.1-EN.pdf.

TIJ (Thailand Institute of Justice). 2019. "The Model Prison Project." https://www.tijthailand.org/en/highlight/detail/the-tij-carried-out-a-model-prison-project-in-asean-first-piloted-in-cambodia.

Times of India. 2025. "Domestic Violence: Low Rates of Conviction Flag Systemic Gaps." *The Times of India*. July 20, 2025. https://timesofindia.indiatimes.com/city/bengaluru/domestic-violence-low-rates-of-conviction-flag-systemic-gaps/articleshow/122788123.cms.

Times of India. 2024. "Woman Gets Life Term for Dowry Killing." *The Times of India*. December 15, 2024. http://timesofindia.indiatimes.com/articleshow/116325243.cms.

Torres-Tupas, Tetch. 2023. "Correctional Institution for Women to Close in 5 Years." *INQUIRER.net*. May 15, 2023. https://newsinfo.inquirer.net/1769465/correctional-institution-for-women-to-close-in-5-years.

TPO Cambodia. 2023. "Mental Health Care and Psychosocial Support for Cambodian Prisoners." *Transcultural Psychosocial Organization Cambodia*. https://tpocambodia.org/mental-health-care-psychosocial-support-for-cambodian-prisoners.

UN Office of the High Commissioner for Human Rights. 2015. *A Paradigm Shift for Incarcerated Women with Children*. Phnom Penh: UN OHCHR. https://cambodia.ohchr.org/sites/default/files/SS%204-Women%20and%20children%20in%20prison%20-%20final.pdf.

UN Women Asia Pacific. 2022. *Pilot Factsheet—Philippines*. December 2022. UN Women. https://asiapacific.unwomen.org/sites/default/files/2022-12/UNW_Pilot-Factsheet-Philippines.pdf.

United Nations Asia and Far East Institute (UNAFEI). 2013. *Annual Report for 2012 and Resource Material Series No. 90*. Fuchu: UNAFEI. https://www.unafei.or.jp/publications/pdf/RS_No90/No90_00All.pdf.

UNODC. 2023. "Jails and Prisons in the Philippines Are Severely Overcrowded." United Nations Office on Drugs and Crime. December 18, 2023. https://www.unodc.org/roseap/en/philippines/2023/12/jails-prisons-overcrowding/story.html.

UNODC (United Nations Office on Drugs and Crime). 2019. *Report on the Global Webinar Series on "Gender-Responsive Criminal Justice and Prison Reform"*. https://www.unodc.org/documents/justice-and-prison-reform/Report_on_the_Global_Webinar_Series_on_Gender-Responsive_Criminal_Justice_and_Prison_Reform.pdf.

Vasudha. 2020. "The State of Women Prisoners in India." *Together Magazine*. https://www.togethermagazine.in/thestateofwomenprisoners.php.

Veloso, Diana Therese M. 2023. "The Experiences of Currently and Formerly Incarcerated Women in a Time of Pandemic: Implications for Life-Giving Communities." *Acta Theologica* 43 (suppl. 35): 97–122.

Viji. 2023. "Women in Prisons." *Social-Welfare—Women and Child Development.* Vikaspedia, Government of India. https://en.vikaspedia.in/viewcontent/social-welfare/women-and-child-development/women-development-1/women-in-prisons.

World Bank. 2023. *Cambodia Gender Data Portal.* https://genderdata.worldbank.org/en/economies/cambodia.

Yalirozy, Teng. 2025. "Cash Program Rolled Out for Pregnant Prisoners." *Cambodianess.* June 13, 2025. https://cambodianess.com/article/cash-program-rolled-out-for-pregnant-prisoners.

8

Oceania

This chapter explores the incarceration of women across Oceania, focusing on Australia, Papua New Guinea, and New Zealand. Each country has its own legal system and colonial history, but women's imprisonment throughout the region is influenced by poverty, trauma, gender inequality, and systemic discrimination. Indigenous women are disproportionately impacted, often incarcerated for non-violent, survival-based offenses linked to addiction, abuse, or social marginalization. By examining their histories, laws, and prison conditions, this chapter highlights the need for gender-responsive reforms and community-based alternatives that prioritize healing, family preservation, and social justice.

Australia

Historical Context

The history of women's incarceration in Australia is rooted in the country's colonial origins. From 1788 to 1868, Britain transported over 160,000 convicts to Australia, including an estimated 25,000 women, many of whom were sentenced for minor, poverty-related offenses like theft or vagrancy (Oxley 1997). Upon arrival, women were sent to institutions known as *female factories*, such as those in Parramatta and Cascades, which served as prisons, workhouses, hospitals, and assignment depots (Smith 2008). Over 9,000 women passed through these facilities, where harsh conditions and moral regulation reinforced gender norms (Oxley 1997).

As the penal colonies evolved into settler states, women continued to be incarcerated for behaviors seen as moral failings, including prostitution, drunkenness, and petty theft (Carrington 1993). Indigenous women were disproportionately criminalized under colonial legal systems that policed their mobility, autonomy, and family life (Cunneen and Libesman 2000). By the late nineteenth century, Aboriginal women were already being incarcerated at disproportionate rates compared to non-Indigenous women (Baldry and Cunneen 2014).

One example of institutional punishment was Boggo Road Gaol in Brisbane, with a women's section active in the early 1900s. It incarcerated women primarily for crimes of poverty and enforced moral correction through labor in laundries and sewing rooms. Conditions were harsh. Women were confined in overcrowded cells, subjected to strict discipline, and separated from their children. The prison became symbolic of Australia's punitive approach to "fallen" women, emphasizing moral reform instead of rehabilitation. (Boggo Road Gaol Historical Society 2015).

In the twentieth century, Australia's prison system modernized, but poverty, addiction, and domestic violence remained key drivers of women's incarceration. Up to 98 percent of incarcerated women report histories of abuse (Sisters Inside 2021), and many also face mental illness, housing instability, and substance dependence. These vulnerabilities are most starkly reflected in the persistent overrepresentation of Indigenous women, who make up 39 percent of Australia's

Exterior of the women's prison at Boggo Road Gaol, Brisbane, *c.* 1903. (State Library of Queensland)

female prison population (Australian Institute of Health and Welfare and National Indigenous Australians Agency 2024), despite making up less than 4 percent of the total female population (Australian Human Rights Commission 2024).

Female Incarceration Rates and Trends

Female incarceration in Australia has increased in recent decades. Although women account for just 7.7 percent of the prison population (approximately 3,419 individuals), they represent the fastest-growing segment of incarcerated people (Institute for Crime & Justice Policy Research 2024). Between 2009 and 2019, the number of women in prison rose by 64 percent, compared to a 45 percent increase among men (Wahlquist 2020). More recently, from 2023 to 2024, the female imprisonment rate grew by 8.3 percent, while the male rate increased by only 5.7 percent (Australian Bureau of Statistics 2024). Much of this rise is linked to socioeconomic disadvantage and punitive criminal justice policies that disproportionately impact women, particularly those experiencing poverty, trauma, and housing instability (Edwards et al. 2024).

One of the most alarming trends is the overrepresentation of Indigenous women, who are twenty-one times more likely to be incarcerated than non-Indigenous women (Australian Human Rights Commission 2024). Often imprisoned for low-level offenses, Indigenous women face structural disadvantages rooted in intergenerational trauma, systemic racism, family violence, and the criminalization of poverty (ALRC 2017).

Each Australian jurisdiction governs its correctional system, and all eight states and territories operate at least one facility that detains women (Justice Reform Initiative 2024). There is also a legal system for the Commonwealth (Australian Institute of Health and Welfare 2024).

While some jurisdictions have introduced gender-responsive initiatives, many women's prisons remain under-resourced. Overcrowding and limited access to mental healthcare, parenting support, and trauma-informed services persist (ALRC 2017). These ongoing challenges highlight the need for expanded alternatives to incarceration and culturally appropriate, gender-specific support for women in contact with the justice system.

Demographics of Incarcerated Women

The demographics of incarcerated women in Australia indicate socioeconomic disadvantage, mental health challenges, and systemic inequality. Only 32 percent of women were employed in the thirty days before incarceration, and

43 percent reported being homeless upon entering prison (Australian Institute of Health and Welfare 2023). Many have not completed secondary education, which limits their employment prospects and increases vulnerability to survival-based offenses. Among Indigenous people and incarcerated women, fewer than half have completed schooling beyond Year 9 (Sisters Inside 2023).

Mental health conditions are also widespread. Up to 74 percent of incarcerated women experience disorders like depression, PTSD, or psychosis (Australian Institute of Health and Welfare 2023). Additionally, up to 98 percent report histories of abuse, including sexual and domestic violence (Sisters Inside 2021). Despite these high rates of trauma and mental illness, prison mental health services are under-resourced, and disciplinary responses often emphasize punishment over care (Colahan 2023).

Indigenous women are particularly overrepresented in the prison system. They are more likely to be held on remand (pre-trial detention) and more frequently incarcerated for low-level offenses like unpaid fines, reflecting the criminalization of poverty and systemic barriers to bail (ALRC 2017).

Parenting is also a defining feature of women's incarceration. Approximately two-thirds of women in prison self-identify as mothers of at least one dependent child (Breuer et al. 2021), and many are their primary caregivers or also care for non-biological children (Australian Institute of Health and Welfare 2023). Most incarcerated women are in their prime caregiving years—54 percent are aged twenty-five to thirty-nine, with a median age of thirty-four (Australian Institute of Health and Welfare 2020).

Substance use is another significant issue. Nearly three-quarters (74 percent) of female prison entrants reported using illicit drugs in the twelve months before custody, and 78 percent were daily smokers at the time of entry (Australian Institute of Health and Welfare 2020). These patterns highlight the need for trauma-informed, gender-responsive policies that address the social and health-related contexts contributing to women's incarceration.

Crimes Leading to Incarceration

The crimes leading to women's incarceration in Australia are predominantly non-violent and often rooted in socioeconomic disadvantage, substance dependency, and trauma. According to the Australian Institute of Health and Welfare (2024), common offenses for incarcerated women are acts intended to cause injury (29 percent), illicit drug offenses (16 percent), and offenses against justice (7 percent).

Substance use plays a major role in women's offending. The Australian Institute of Criminology's Drug Use Careers of Offenders study, based on interviews with 470 incarcerated women, found that 55 percent of female property offenders met the criteria for drug dependency, rising to 87 percent among heroin users (Johnson 2004). Additionally, 42 percent of participants reported being under the influence of drugs, alcohol, or both at the time of their most serious offense, and half of property offenders said they committed their crimes to fund drug use. These patterns suggest that many women engage in non-violent, survival-based offenses driven by addiction and poverty rather than premeditated criminal intent.

Some women are incarcerated because of prolonged domestic abuse. Police narrative analysis from the Australian Institute of Criminology found that in 153 incidents involving female persons of interest, about half were engaged in reactive or situational violence linked to intimate partner abuse (Boxall et al. 2020). Others have been imprisoned for breaching domestic violence orders (DVOs), often issued under circumstances that failed to protect the victim. As Gleeson (2019) reports, women have been jailed for DVO breaches involving abusive partners, highlighting shortcomings in recognizing self-defense or coercion. A 2024 Victorian Court of Appeal case illustrates this dynamic. Rebecca Payne, who killed her abusive husband after years of violence, had her sentence reduced in recognition of the long-term abuse she suffered (Australian Associated Press 2024).

Finally, economic marginalization remains a driver. In Western Australia, over one-third of women imprisoned in 2013 were jailed for unpaid fines. Between 2006 and 2015, 64 percent of them were Indigenous, and 73 percent were unemployed at the time (Australian Law Reform Commission 2017).

Contributing Laws and Policies

Several laws and policies in Australia contribute to the incarceration of women, especially Indigenous women and those with socioeconomic disadvantages. Drug laws, fine enforcement, bail practices, and domestic violence frameworks often criminalize women for non-violent or survival-based offenses.

Drug laws disproportionately affect women with histories of trauma, addiction, and poverty. While diversion programs exist, access is limited and unevenly applied. In New South Wales, only 2.6 percent of Indigenous people caught with small quantities of illicit drugs were diverted, compared to 6.9 percent overall—the vast majority were criminalized instead (Beasley 2024). Under federal law, the Criminal Code Act 1995 imposes severe penalties for drug importation, including life imprisonment for commercial quantities and twenty-five years for marketable amounts (Commonwealth Director of Public Prosecutions 2025). At the state and territory level, drug laws criminalize possession and supply, often using threshold-based presumptions of trafficking that shift the burden of proof to the defendant, regardless of personal circumstances (Hughes et al. 2014).

Women are also frequently imprisoned for unpaid fines. In one widely cited case, Ms Dhu, a 22-year-old Aboriginal woman, died in police custody in 2014 after being detained for unpaid fines. Despite pleas for help, her symptoms were dismissed, and she died of septicemia and pneumonia from a prior rib fracture. The State Coroner ruled the death was from natural causes but criticized police and medical staff, recommending reforms including cultural competency training, improved custodial healthcare, and the abolition of imprisonment for fine default (Coroner's Court of Western Australia 2016).

Restrictive bail laws also contribute to women's imprisonment, especially for Indigenous women facing barriers like housing instability. Nearly half of the women in Victorian prisons are pre-trial detainees awaiting trial (Russell et al. 2022). Additionally, domestic violence laws can criminalize women acting in self-defense, with Indigenous women especially vulnerable to being misidentified as aggressors (Boxall et al. 2020). Without trauma-informed legal frameworks, these laws keep punishing marginalized women.

The Legacy of Ms Dhu

Ms Dhu's 2014 death in police custody after being jailed for unpaid fines became a national rallying point for Indigenous justice reform in Australia. Her story exposed how the criminalization of poverty and systemic racism intersect in the treatment of Aboriginal women. In the years since, her family and advocacy groups have continued to demand accountability, leading to public campaigns and renewed calls to end fine-default imprisonment and improve healthcare in custody.

Conditions in Women's Prisons

Conditions in women's prisons in Australia are marked by overcrowding, inadequate healthcare, and limited rehabilitation services. For instance, the Brisbane Women's Correctional Centre (BWCC) was found to be operating at 48 percent above its intended single-cell capacity, forcing women to share cells or sleep on mattresses next to exposed toilets (Queensland Ombudsman 2016). In Western Australia, overcrowding at Greenough Regional Prison has pushed women into facilities originally designed for men, leading to heightened stress, program cancellations, and staffing shortages (Henville 2025).

Healthcare services within prisons are often insufficient to meet women's needs. Sixty-one percent of female prison entrants report chronic physical conditions. Furthermore, psychological distress is widespread, with 63 percent of women reporting high or very high levels. However, fewer than half said they could access a doctor easily while incarcerated (Australian Institute of Health and Welfare 2023).

Overcrowding also limits access to programs. At BWCC, the rise in inmate numbers was not matched by expanded vocational or educational services, and some programs were even reduced or declined altogether (Queensland Ombudsman 2016). Programming remains uneven and often under-resourced, offering limited support for education, rehabilitation, or vocational training. Women are less likely than men to access these programs, constrained by prison wage structures, security regimes, and insufficient staffing, despite the well-established link between education and reduced reoffending (Justice Action 2019).

An exception is **Wandoo Rehabilitation Prison** in Western Australia, which operates as a therapeutic community model with campus-style living tailored to women with substance-use disorders. Wandoo emphasizes trauma-informed care, multidisciplinary case management, and integrated rehabilitation planning. Residents learn life skills, receive counselling, education, and work opportunities. Overall, it offers a "unique opportunity to heal" and provides strong pre-release services so that women can successfully return to the community (Office of the Inspector of Custodial Services 2023).

Health and Mental Health Issues

Incarcerated women in Australia experience high health and mental health needs. Many enter prison with chronic illnesses, mental health concerns, and substance use histories. These conditions are often worsened by overcrowded facilities, understaffed medical teams, and reactive rather than preventive care (Australian Institute of Health and Welfare 2023).

Mental illness is particularly prevalent. A recent meta-analysis of seventeen studies involving over 10,000 incarcerated individuals in Australia and New Zealand found that 54 percent had a current mental health disorder and 69 percent had a lifetime diagnosis (Yee et al. 2024). Substance use is similarly widespread, with 74 percent of incarcerated women reporting illicit drug use before imprisonment (Australian Institute of Health and Welfare 2020). The overlap of trauma, addiction, and mental illness means many women enter custody unwell and unsupported. Without access to trauma-informed counselling, detox services, or continuity-of-care planning, the risk of relapse and recidivism remains high (Edwards et al. 2022).

Mental health services in prison are often crisis-driven, fragmented, and under-resourced. Staffing levels fall below accepted standards, there is no national healthcare framework, and people in prison are excluded from Medicare, resulting in unequal health service quality across jurisdictions (Australian Institute of Health and Welfare 2023). These deficits point to the need for gender-responsive reforms, including culturally safe care for Indigenous women, adequate staffing, and integrated care models.

A diagnostic study of 396 Indigenous prisoners found that 86 percent of women had at least one mental health disorder in the past year, including anxiety, depression, or psychosis (Heffernan et al. 2012). Yet only 26 percent received care from an Aboriginal Medical Service or Aboriginal Community Controlled Health Organization (Australian Institute of Health and Welfare and National Indigenous Australians Agency 2024). Veronica Nelson, an Aboriginal woman, was held on remand for minor offenses at the Dame Phyllis Frost Centre in Victoria. She died in her cell after thirty-six hours of vomiting and unanswered pleas for medical help. Her 2020 death in custody exposed how systemic neglect, inadequate healthcare, and institutional indifference can result in a preventable tragedy (Dunstan 2022).

Impact on Families and Children

In Australia, the incarceration of women disrupts families and imposes strain on their children. A matched cohort study in Western Australia found that maternal imprisonment in infancy increased the likelihood of out-of-home care by age two by twenty-seven times, especially among Indigenous children (Dowell et al. 2018).

Some jurisdictions offer Mother–Baby Units (MBUs), which allow children, up to age five, to live with their mothers in prison. These units exist in seven of Australia's eight jurisdictions. They aim to reduce the trauma of maternal separation and support attachment during early development. However, MBUs remain underutilized because of eligibility criteria and limited capacity. Access is often restricted by sentence length, security classification, and administrative discretion. Mothers also report stress from constant surveillance and limited decision-making over parenting, which can weaken the benefits of the programs (Breuer et al. 2021).

Beyond MBUs, few support systems exist for families affected by maternal incarceration. South Australia's Stronger Families program supports incarcerated mothers in reconnecting with their children and preparing for reunification post-release. As of 2024, the program has formally worked with at least forty women, helping them build parenting capacity and stay informed about their children's circumstances through contact with child protection staff (South Australia 2024). Aimed at reducing the overrepresentation of Aboriginal women and children in the child protection and justice systems, the program also links mothers to services like Mothers Matter, which helps incarcerated women strengthen parenting skills and maintain bonds with their children. It aligns with Closing the Gap targets focused on improving health, education, and justice outcomes for Indigenous communities. While early outcomes are promising, the program operates on a small scale within Adelaide Women's Prison and its Pre-Release Center, stressing the need for broader implementation (South Australia 2024).

Policy Reforms and Recommendations

Addressing the incarceration of women in Australia requires a comprehensive, gender-responsive, and culturally safe reform agenda. Historically, women, especially Indigenous women, have been overrepresented in the justice system because of colonialism and the criminalization of poverty, trauma, and survival-based behaviors (Baldry and Cunneen 2014). Today, they remain the fastest-growing prison demographic, despite being more likely to commit non-violent offenses rooted in addiction, socioeconomic hardship, and victimization (Australian Institute of Health and Welfare 2024).

Reform should begin by diverting women away from incarceration through expanded access to community-based alternatives. Sentencing for low-level drug, property, or breach offenses, especially where addiction or trauma is present, should prioritize treatment and support instead of prison (Boxall et al. 2020). Policies that criminalize fine default or breach of domestic violence orders must be revised to reflect contextual factors and avoid punishing victims.

Mental health and substance use treatment within prisons must shift from crisis response to long-term, trauma-informed care. Greater investment in mental health staffing, care planning, and access to culturally safe providers for Indigenous women is also needed (Australian Institute of Health and Welfare 2023).

Programs supporting women as mothers should be expanded. Mother–Baby Units should have more flexible criteria, and initiatives like South Australia's *Stronger Families* should be available nationally to promote reunification and reduce intergenerational harm (South Australia 2024).

Finally, structural change requires national coordination. Australia must establish gender- and culture-sensitive justice standards across jurisdictions, supported by consistent data collection and program evaluation. By focusing on diversion, equity, and family preservation, Australia can disrupt the cycles of incarceration that impact women and their children.

Papua New Guinea

Historical Context

Before European colonization, Papua New Guinea's (PNG) diverse tribal societies resolved wrongdoing through customary reconciliation practices (e.g., compensation payments, public apology, or ritual cleansing) instead of incarceration. Women's roles varied across groups, but confinement was not a typical sanction (IDLO 2013). This changed with colonization, as German, British, and later Australian administrations introduced European-style legal systems and formal prisons that largely ignored indigenous norms. Under these imposed frameworks, behaviors previously handled through communal justice, like adultery, interpersonal disputes, or accusations of sorcery, were criminalized, leading to the increased incarceration of women (Sikani 1991).

Colonial courts often functioned through dual systems. There were statutory courts and "Courts of Native Affairs," the latter of which were overseen by kiaps (patrol officers) who served as the judge, jury, and jailer. These systems imposed foreign laws without legal representation or understanding among local populations, especially women. A report by the Papua New Guinea Law Reform Commission noted that many women brought before the courts had never heard of the law and were confused by the foreign proceedings (Borrey 1992).

Imprisonment during the colonial era disproportionately affected women for moral offenses, reflecting patriarchal customs and colonial values (Borrey 1992). Despite independence in 1975, there are reminders of these systems. Many rural communities still rely on village courts, which emphasize customary law but often fail to protect women's rights, especially in cases involving family or sexual violence (Amnesty International 2006).

Women navigating PNG's legal systems continue to face barriers, including a lack of legal representation, fear of community retaliation, and stigma. These obstacles indicate a history in which women's dealings with the justice system have been influenced by colonialism, gender inequality, and limited institutional reform (IDLO 2013). Understanding this context is necessary to address the current challenges incarcerated women face in PNG.

Female Incarceration Rates and Trends

Female incarceration rates in PNG are low compared to men, with women comprising approximately 4.4 percent of the total prison population. As of 2023, there were about 238 women imprisoned (Institute for Crime & Justice Policy Research 2023). Most women are imprisoned for non-violent offenses, often linked to poverty, limited education, and little access to formal employment (DFAT 2025). Some offenses stem from interpersonal disputes in polygamous households or socioeconomic desperation, including petty theft and drug transport roles (Amnesty International 2006).

Drug offenses represent a growing area of concern. PNG's emergence as a transit point in regional trafficking networks has resulted in the coercion of women into low-level roles, like couriers, which carry harsh penalties under PNG's strict drug laws (Faa 2025). Without legal representation or economic alternatives, many women serve long sentences for non-violent, survival-driven actions (Antara News 2024).

Women from rural and Indigenous communities are overrepresented in PNG's prisons. They often face systemic disadvantages, including illiteracy, poor health access, and geographic isolation. These factors and under-resourced local courts increase their vulnerability to criminalization and pre-trial detention (DFAT 2025). Anecdotal reports confirm that many incarcerated women originate from remote Highland or Sepik regions (Jolly et al. 2012).

Incarcerated women are primarily housed in general correctional institutions with minimal gender-specific infrastructure. Bomana Prison, the country's largest, holds around 40 women in a small, segregated ward (Dozier 2018). In rural areas, women are sometimes held in overcrowded police lockups or facilities lacking proper sanitation and separation (DFAT 2025). Newer prisons like Beon, developed with Australian assistance, offer more humane accommodations for women and mothers, but these facilities are rare (Australian High Commission 2008).

Demographics of Incarcerated Women

The demographics of incarcerated women in PNG reflect social and economic inequalities. Although there are no publicly available statistics disaggregated by region, ethnicity, age, or parental status, qualitative evidence suggests that most incarcerated women come from rural and Indigenous communities marked by poverty and few employment opportunities (DFAT 2025). With 86 percent of the population living in rural areas (World Bank 2025), many women face disadvantages because of limited access to healthcare, education, infrastructure, and legal protections. These conditions are especially severe for girls growing up in remote or patriarchal communities. Female literacy in PNG is only 19 percent (CARE Australia 2011).

Additionally, approximately 75 percent of PNG's labor force works in the informal economy (i.e., unregulated, non-contract employment like street vending), which offers little legal protection and increases susceptibility to survival-driven offenses like theft or low-level drug trafficking (OC Index 2023). These conditions often overlap with high rates of domestic violence and sorcery-related accusations, which isolate women and increase their risk of arrest, especially in areas where legal infrastructure is weak or inaccessible (Jolly et al. 2012).

Though PNG's population is overwhelmingly Indigenous Melanesian, correctional data does not record racial or clan identity, limiting the ability to assess disparities. Still, correctional officers and NGOs observe that women from under-resourced, remote provinces are overrepresented (DFAT 2025). There is also no available data on the age distribution of incarcerated women or how many are mothers, making it difficult to understand the impact of their imprisonment.

Likewise, there are no statistics on mental health, trauma, or substance use among incarcerated women in PNG. However, international research shows high rates of these issues among women in prison globally (Edwards et al. 2022), and given PNG's widespread gender-based violence and limited mental healthcare, similar patterns are likely present but unreported (DFAT 2025).

Crimes Leading to Incarceration

Women incarcerated in PNG are commonly convicted of non-violent offenses, often tied to poverty, unemployment, and a lack of access to formal employment or legal protections. With nearly three-quarters of the workforce functioning in the informal economy, women frequently engage in survival-driven behavior (e.g., petty theft or fraud) to support themselves (OC Index 2023). Interpersonal disputes, particularly in polygamous households, also contribute to female incarceration. These cases often arise from domestic and economic strain that escalates into criminal charges (Amnesty International 2006).

Drug-related offenses are also a growing concern. For instance, in 2024, two Portuguese women were arrested at Port Moresby's airport attempting to smuggle 15 kilograms of cocaine to Australia. While not PNG nationals, their case reflects a broader trend. PNG's role as a drug transit hub has exposed many women, often poor or coerced, to low-level trafficking (Zarriga 2024). Strict sentencing laws and a lack of gender-responsive rehabilitation programs mean that women receive harsh penalties without adequate support for addiction or trauma (DFAT 2025).

Some women are incarcerated for abortion-related offenses. Abortion remains criminalized except in cases where the mother's life or health is at risk. In one known case, Leoba Devana and her husband were sentenced to four years in prison after terminating a pregnancy due to health concerns. She had recently endured a traumatic childbirth complicated by obstructed labor and feared that carrying another pregnancy to term would be life-threatening, as she was still recovering (Human Rights Watch 2016).

Violent offenses also contribute to female incarceration, particularly in the context of domestic abuse or polygamous conflict. Polygamy, though formally outlawed under the 2014 Civil Registration Act, remains common under customary practice, especially in rural Highlands and Sepik regions (The National 2023). Roughly 19 percent of married women were in polygamous

Polygamy and Women's Incarceration

Although outlawed under the 2014 Civil Registration Act, polygamy remains common in rural areas of Papua New Guinea, with nearly one in five married women in polygamous unions. These arrangements often foster jealousy and conflict between co-wives, leading to violence and, in some cases, imprisonment. Legal records, such as *The State v Drikore Yuana Peter (2000)*, show how domestic disputes linked to polygamy have resulted in criminal convictions. In this case, a second wife in a polygamous union killed the new (third) wife by stabbing her twice while she lay asleep. The court noted that the addition of a third wife created jealousy and violence within the polygamous household, sentencing the perpetrator to twelve years' imprisonment with hard labor. Women caught in these conflicts are doubly disadvantaged. They are criminalized while also lacking protection from abuse.

unions as of 2016 (Mambon and Howes 2024). These arrangements often promote jealousy, competition, and strain among co-wives, sometimes leading to violence and prosecution. In *The State v Drikore Yuana Peter* (2000), a co-wife was convicted for stabbing another following a household conflict (Papua New Guinea 2000). Despite legal reforms, polygamy continues to influence the experiences of women in PNG.

Contributing Laws and Policies

Papua New Guinea's laws play a role in the incarceration of women, primarily through harsh drug and property laws and the weak enforcement of protections against gender-based violence. The Controlled Substance Act 2021, which replaced the 1952 Drugs Act, imposes stricter penalties, including life imprisonment or fines up to K2 million (around 490,000 USD) for serious trafficking offenses (Ligaiula 2021). These laws disproportionately affect economically vulnerable women who are often coerced into low-level roles within trafficking networks. Without access to legal representation or gender-responsive sentencing, many women face severe punishment despite minimal involvement (DFAT 2025).

Similarly, under the Criminal Code Act 1974, property crimes like theft and fraud carry prison terms of five to ten years for offenses involving K2,000 or more (Papua New Guinea 1974). While the judiciary occasionally exercises leniency, such discretion is inconsistently applied. For instance, in *The State v Nancy Leah Uviri*, a woman convicted of embezzling approximately K6,000 received a suspended sentence due to financial hardship (Papua New Guinea 2017). Women from disadvantaged backgrounds frequently engage in survival-based offenses, yet PNG is lacking in diversion programs or noncustodial alternatives (DFAT 2025).

Legal protections for women facing domestic violence in PNG remain weak despite the passage of the **Family Protection Act 2013**, which criminalizes such abuse. Implementation has been slow and inconsistent, especially in rural areas where courts lack resources and gender sensitivity (Human Rights Watch 2015). Cultural norms, inadequate policing, and pressure to pursue customary reconciliation often deter women from seeking legal redress (Amnesty International 2006). As a result, women who retaliate against prolonged abuse may be prosecuted themselves, with courts frequently failing to consider self-defense or cumulative trauma (Human Rights Watch 2020). Barr (2015) highlights this systemic failure through the case of "Jenella," a domestic violence survivor who sought help from police 17 times. Each time, officers dismissed her complaints as a "family problem" and advised her to return home, denying her meaningful protection or access to justice. Though she was never charged with a crime, she remained trapped in an abusive marriage until years of violence left her permanently injured, showing how state inaction can worsen harm and prevent victims from escaping abuse.

Conditions in Women's Prisons

Conditions in women's prisons in PNG are harsh, reflecting systemic neglect and chronic underfunding. Facilities like Bomana Prison operate beyond capacity, with women often sleeping on cement floors in cramped, poorly ventilated spaces lacking basic sanitation (U.S. Department of State 2024). In rural provinces, women are often held in police lockups or juvenile centers without adequate bedding, hygiene facilities, or privacy, increasing their vulnerability to illness and emotional stress (DFAT 2025).

Reports of mistreatment are common. The UN Human Rights Council (2011) documented women being beaten during arrest, detained in vermin-infested cells without bedding or access to clean water, and sometimes housed alongside male detainees, conditions that heighten the risk of abuse and trauma. Human Rights Watch (2015) further reported instances of sexual assault and denial of medical care for women in custody, with few avenues for redress.

Rehabilitation and vocational programs are limited and inconsistently implemented. While PNG's Department of Correctional Services adopted a Detainee Rehabilitation Policy in 2016, most prisons offer only basic skills training or correspondence courses with few programs tailored to women, especially mothers or trauma survivors (DFAT 2025). At Wewak Prison, a trauma-healing initiative supported by Mission Aviation Fellowship (MAF) is one of the few available gender-sensitive efforts. MAF volunteers report that female inmates often sleep without beds or blankets and survive on a single bowl of rice per day with irregular water access, yet still benefit from literacy classes, trauma support, and vocational training (Mission Aviation Fellowship UK 2022).

Health and Mental Health Issues

Incarcerated women in PNG face health and mental health challenges, compounded by unsanitary, overcrowded prison conditions. While gender-disaggregated prison health data is lacking, national health statistics reflect a high risk. PNG's tuberculosis (TB) incidence was 432 per 100,000 people in 2022, more than three times the global average (The Global Economy 2025). Many women enter custody with untreated illnesses, including TB, malnutrition, or chronic diseases, and receive minimal or delayed care.

The U.S. Department of State (2024) reports that detention facilities lack basic medical infrastructure, including regular staffing, isolation procedures, and hygiene supplies. The UN Human Rights Council (2011) observed that female detainees were held in unsanitary, overcrowded cells without clean water or bedding. These conditions increase the spread of disease and the likelihood of untreated physical health issues.

Mental health services are also virtually absent. According to DFAT (2025), psychiatric care and trauma-informed counseling are unavailable in most prisons. Many incarcerated women have histories of domestic violence, sexual assault, or severe poverty, which are risk factors for mental illnesses like depression, anxiety, and PTSD. There are reports of women being held with men, denied medical attention, or subjected to violence during arrest, all of which worsen psychological distress (Human Rights Watch 2015).

Substance abuse further complicates health issues. Despite being a known coping mechanism for trauma and poverty, there are no structured addiction treatment programs in PNG's correctional facilities (DFAT 2025). International research confirms that female prisoners are especially vulnerable to substance use disorders, and they need gender-responsive interventions (Fazel et al. 2017).

These intersecting health and psychological burdens stress the need for correctional healthcare reform. Addressing physical and mental health through gender-sensitive medical services, trauma counseling, and addiction treatment is essential to improving outcomes for incarcerated women in PNG.

Impact on Families and Children

Maternal incarceration in PNG has consequences for families, particularly children, in a context marked by poverty, weak welfare systems, and limited institutional support. Although there is no official data on the number of incarcerated mothers, many women in PNG prisons are believed to be primary caregivers. With few formal social services, children are often placed in the care of relatives who may lack the resources to provide adequate support, especially in rural areas (DFAT 2025).

Some women are permitted to keep their infants in prison until the child reaches around age three. This arrangement, seen at facilities like Bomana Prison, is informal and reflects a lack of alternatives rather than a comprehensive policy. Journalist Deborah Pranis documented the presence of several children living with their mothers at Bomana, noting that they brought emotional relief despite the harsh conditions (Maykin et al. 2022). However, prisons are not equipped with proper nursery spaces, sanitation, or child-specific health services, leaving mothers to care for children in highly inadequate conditions (U.S. Department of State 2024).

For children living outside, maintaining contact with their incarcerated mothers is difficult. Visiting hours are inconsistent, prisons are often far from home, and facilities lack child-friendly spaces. The cost and logistics of travel further limit visitation (DFAT 2025). There is no formal policy in PNG that guarantees children the right to visit incarcerated parents, and the Child Welfare Act of 1961 makes no such provision (Child Welfare Act 1961). Humanitarian organizations have facilitated family visits at facilities like Kerevat, highlighting the importance and the rarity of these interactions (ICRC 2017).

Policy Reforms and Recommendations

PNG's correctional and legal systems require gender-sensitive reforms to address the structural conditions that contribute to women's incarceration.

Rooted in colonial and patriarchal frameworks, these systems disadvantage women, especially those from rural and Indigenous communities (IDLO 2013). Reforms should reduce the reliance on imprisonment for non-violent and survival-based offenses.

Most women in PNG prisons are convicted of offenses linked to poverty and limited opportunity (OC Index 2023). Diversion programs and non-custodial alternatives, particularly for first-time offenders and mothers, would promote justice and ease overcrowding. Judicial discretion should be applied more equitably, as seen in *The State v Nancy Leah Uviri* (Papua New Guinea 2017).

Many women lack legal representation, and they often do not understand their rights (DFAT 2025). Expanding legal aid and outreach services would improve access to justice. Sentencing laws should also be revised to reflect women's socioeconomic vulnerabilities and the role of coercion in low-level trafficking (Ligaiula 2021).

Rehabilitation programs are limited and rarely address trauma, abuse, or substance dependence. One exception is the program at Wewak Prison, supported by Mission Aviation Fellowship, which offers vocational training and support (Mission Aviation Fellowship UK 2022). Expanding such models could help reduce recidivism.

Enforcement of the Family Protection Act 2013 remains inconsistent, leaving survivors of abuse vulnerable to prosecution when they retaliate (Human Rights Watch 2020). Police and court personnel should receive training in trauma-informed responses, especially in rural areas.

Also, for incarcerated mothers, PNG lacks a formal visitation policy for children (DFAT 2025). ICRC-supported family visits in facilities like Kerevat demonstrate the importance of structured visitation programs (ICRC 2017).

Prison conditions remain poor, with overcrowding, inadequate sanitation, and minimal healthcare (U.S. Department of State 2024). Investment in gender-specific infrastructure and services is critical. The absence of disaggregated data on incarcerated women also hinders reform efforts. Improved data collection is essential to guide evidence-based policy and ensure accountability (DFAT 2025).

New Zealand

Historical Context

The historical context of women's incarceration in New Zealand reflects the country's colonial past, shifting social norms, and evolving understandings of gender and crime. In the nineteenth century, the penal system focused on male offenders, and women were typically imprisoned in male facilities without gender-specific accommodations, often alongside their children. The first facility designed for women was established in Addington, primarily incarcerating those convicted of minor offenses like theft, vagrancy, or prostitution, behaviors often viewed as moral failings rather than crimes (Nicholson et al. n.d.).

Reformers like the Women's Christian Temperance Union advocated for separate women's prisons in the late nineteenth century. This eventually led to institutions like Point Halswell (1920) and Arohata (1944), though women were still often confined in male-dominated settings into the mid-twentieth century. Historical records show women made up a small portion of the prison population, but Māori and working-class women were disproportionately affected by colonial legal structures (Clayworth 2012).

As legal structures modernized, many women were imprisoned for offenses rooted in poverty, addiction, and trauma. These patterns prompted calls for a more rehabilitative and individualized response. By the mid-twentieth century, reforms introduced probation, community sentencing, and a growing focus on rehabilitation, particularly for female offenders (Bevan and Wehipeihana 2015).

Today, New Zealand continues to address the legacy of gendered incarceration through policies like the **Wāhine—E rere ana ki te pae hou** strategy, launched in 2021, which emphasizes trauma-informed, culturally responsive care, especially for Māori women (Department of Corrections 2021). Yet, challenges persist, as Māori women remain dramatically overrepresented in incarcerated populations. Ongoing reforms acknowledge the need for improved prison conditions and societal change to reduce the drivers of women's incarceration.

Female Incarceration Rates and Trends

Female incarceration in New Zealand has fluctuated over recent decades, with a notable increase since the early 2000s. Between 1960 and 2018, the number of women in prison rose by 470 percent, more than double the growth rate for men over the same period. This trend peaked in 2018, when 809 women were incarcerated (Ministry of Justice 2022). As of 2025, women comprise about 7.5 percent of the total prison population, with approximately 797 incarcerated women (Institute for Crime & Justice Policy Research 2025).

While still a minority, women are increasingly imprisoned for offenses linked to poverty, addiction, and trauma. Public order and property crimes, like drug possession, traffic violations, and theft, comprise a large share of their charges. Additionally, substance misuse, mental health issues, and intimate partner violence are drivers of women's pathways into the justice system (Adair 2023). In 2022, about half of all incarcerated women were held on remand (i.e., awaiting trial), highlighting ongoing inequities in bail access and pretrial detention (Ministry of Justice 2022).

One of the most significant disparities is the overrepresentation of Māori women. Although they comprise roughly 9 percent of the national population (Environmental Health Intelligence New Zealand 2024), Māori women accounted for 63 percent of women in custody as of 2022 (Adair 2023). Structural inequality, systemic bias, and the effects of colonization continue to influence these figures.

Currently, incarcerated women are held primarily in three dedicated women's prisons: Auckland Region Women's Corrections Facility, Arohata Women's Prison near Wellington, and Christchurch Women's Prison in the South Island. These facilities include mothers-with-babies units and rehabilitative programs (Department of Corrections n.d.). However, calls for greater investment in alternatives to prison, including community-based treatment and support, reflect a growing awareness of the need for gender-responsive approaches (Adair 2023).

Demographics of Incarcerated Women

The demographics of incarcerated women in New Zealand indicate patterns influenced by socioeconomic inequality, trauma, and caregiving roles. Most incarcerated women are relatively young, with around 69 percent aged 20–40 (Adair 2023). This age profile reflects a concentration of offending influenced by limited opportunities and cumulative disadvantage.

Educational disadvantage is a major factor. A 2021 report by the Office of the Inspectorate found that 67 percent of incarcerated women had limited literacy and 74 percent had low numeracy, as measured by national assessment tools. Furthermore, 25 percent had links to gang affiliations (Office of the Inspectorate 2021). These limitations often constrain employment options before and after prison and are frequently compounded by unstable living conditions and limited access to support services.

Most incarcerated women in New Zealand also have a history of trauma and health challenges. Approximately 62 percent have both mental health and substance use disorders, 75 percent have a recent mental health diagnosis, 68 percent experienced family violence, and 53 percent were survivors of sexual assault (APT 2024). These overlapping issues are prevalent among women charged with non-violent, survival-related offenses, often tied to poverty and domestic instability.

Motherhood is another defining feature. Approximately 85 percent of incar cerated women in New Zealand are mothers, many of whom were primary caregivers at the time of arrest (Mothers Project n.d.). As of 2021, 64 percent had children under eighteen, with an average of 2.7 children each (Oranga Tamariki 2021). The disruption of maternal caregiving has lasting effects on mothers and children, highlighting the need for gender-responsive and family-centered justice interventions that prioritize rehabilitation and family cohesion.

Crimes Leading to Incarceration

The types of crimes for which women are incarcerated in New Zealand have shifted over recent decades, reflecting changes in policy and social context. In 1980, property offenses, like burglary, theft, and fraud, made up 64 percent of female prison admissions. By 2022, this figure had dropped to 24 percent. However, these offenses still represent a substantial share of female incarceration and are often tied to poverty, unstable housing, and coercion linked to domestic instability (Ministry of Justice 2022).

Violent offenses among incarcerated women in New Zealand rose from 15 percent in 1980 to 49 percent in 2022. This was not due as much to a surge in violent behavior but largely because of a shift in sentencing practices (Ministry of Justice 2022). Since the **Sentencing Act 2002**, the justice system has expanded community-based alternatives (e.g., community work, supervision, and home detention), especially for women convicted of non-violent, survival-based offenses linked to poverty or addiction (Department of Corrections 2009). As more women are diverted into non-custodial pathways, those who remain in prison tend to be those convicted of serious or violent crimes, altering the composition of the female prison population (Ministry of Justice 2022).

Drug-related offenses are another significant category. In 2022, they accounted for 14 percent of women's prison placements. In 1980, this figure was just 12 percent, but it rose dramatically during the early 2000s as drug enforcement laws were strengthened and has since declined (Ministry of Justice 2022). Many of the women imprisoned for these offenses come from socioeconomically disadvantaged backgrounds and may be involved in low-level trafficking or possession due to addiction, coercion, or survival needs (APT 2024).

Despite the growth in violent offending, non-violent offenses (i.e., property and drug-related) still made up 38 percent of women's imprisonment as of

2022. These patterns highlight how women's criminalization is often rooted in structural inequality, economic desperation, and trauma rather than premeditated violence (Ministry of Justice 2022).

Contributing Laws and Policies

Legal frameworks in New Zealand, especially the Misuse of Drugs Act 1975, have influenced female incarceration by preserving a punitive stance on drug offenses. Under this legislation, possession, use, and supply of controlled substances remain criminalized. Drug-related convictions disproportionately affect women, especially Māori women, because of systemic bias and socio-economic vulnerability (Rapana et al. 2022). Women are more likely than men to be imprisoned for public order offenses, including low-level drug charges linked to addiction, poverty, or coercion (Adair 2023). Corrections data show that substance dependence often drives related crimes like theft or drug supply, indicating how addiction contributes to criminalization (Office of the Inspectorate 2021).

Property offenses, including theft, dishonesty, and fraud, also account for a significant portion of women's imprisonment. These are often survival-based acts stemming from poverty, housing insecurity, or domestic instability. However, the justice system does not always have access to diversion programs or community-based alternatives that might better address the root causes of offending. Consequently, many women are incarcerated for non-violent crimes (Office of the Inspectorate 2021). An example is the case of Jennifer Gordon, a repeat shoplifter from Auckland. In 2025, she was sentenced to two and a half years in prison for stealing over $25,000 worth of goods. Despite mental health issues and over 150 prior convictions, mostly for shoplifting, the court prioritized deterrence over rehabilitation (Stevens 2025). Gordon's case illustrates how women may still receive prison sentences even when their actions are driven by distress or necessity.

Family violence laws also contribute to women's incarceration. While meant to protect victims, they can penalize women who retaliate against their abusers in self-defense. Legal defenses like duress often fail to reflect the cumulative impact of abuse (Tolmie and Norton 2022). However, in *R v Ruddelle* (2020), a Māori woman who killed her abusive partner was convicted of manslaughter instead of murder, with the court acknowledging her history of violence (Tolmie 2020). Still, many survivors face conviction. About two-thirds of incarcerated women report family violence histories, and 62 percent struggle with co-occurring substance use and mental health issues (APT 2024), demonstrating the complexities of family violence.

Conditions in Women's Prisons

Conditions in women's prisons in New Zealand indicate a combination of progress and challenges. The Department of Corrections has implemented gender-responsive reforms, and facilities have been designed to be safer and more rehabilitative than men's prisons. They include mothers-with-babies units, kaupapa Māori services, and therapeutic programs such as the Making Choices (**Kowhiritanga**) Program, which uses cognitive-behavioral therapy to help women understand and change offending behavior (Office of the Inspectorate 2021).

Despite these reforms, many incarcerated women continue to face substandard conditions that hinder rehabilitation. Healthcare, particularly mental healthcare, remains reactive rather than preventive. Most women in custody have co-occurring mental health and substance use disorders. However, access to psychiatric care is limited, and wait times can be long due to staffing shortages. These gaps disproportionately affect Māori and Pacific women, who comprise 93 percent of all women subjected to prolonged segregation, raising equity and human rights concerns (APT 2024).

Rehabilitation programs, which are important for reducing recidivism, are inconsistently accessible. While facilities offer kaupapa Māori services, parenting courses, and trauma-informed support, women serving short sentences often miss out because of eligibility restrictions or disrupted access (Office of the Inspectorate 2021). Additionally, a review found that educational and vocational opportunities for women were notably fewer than those offered to men (Bentley 2017).

Many incarcerated women desire more practical training to support employment after release, including trades, business skills, and tertiary education courses. In interviews with women who completed at least one program, many reported frustration over limited access and inconsistent delivery. Some spoke about the lack of continuity when transferred between facilities or the discouragement they felt when placed on long waitlists, only to be released before participation began. Others emphasized how programs grounded in Māori values offered a rare opportunity for cultural connection and personal transformation but noted that such options were not widely available across all sites (Office of the Inspectorate 2021).

Health and Mental Health Issues

Incarcerated women in New Zealand face high rates of health and mental health challenges. These issues often intersect with experiences of trauma, substance use, and systemic healthcare exclusion before incarceration. Furthermore, they disproportionately affect Māori and Pacific women (Shalev 2021). Cultural disconnection and mistrust of institutional care further complicate health outcomes for these populations.

Women entering New Zealand prisons often arrive with complex health burdens stemming from long-standing socioeconomic disadvantage and inadequate community-based care. Over half report one or more chronic conditions, while many also face unresolved reproductive health issues and dental neglect. Nearly 50 percent of inmates have previously experienced tooth pain while eating or drinking, highlighting the high prevalence of untreated dental problems in custody settings. Routine healthcare needs, such as cervical screening and infection control, may also go unmet due to delays or resource constraints within the prison system (Wakem and McGee 2012).

Mental health services in prison, while improved in some areas, remain reactive rather than preventive. Reports highlight long wait times, under-resourced staffing, and poor access to counselling, especially for severe or co-occurring disorders. Māori and Pacific women are more likely to be subjected to restrictive practices like prolonged segregation, which can exacerbate existing mental health conditions (APT 2024). These punitive measures undermine rehabilitation and worsen existing trauma.

Substance abuse is also a major concern. Forty-six percent of women incarcerated in New Zealand have lifetime alcohol dependence (APT 2024), and 44 percent report drug dependence (Office of the Inspectorate 2021). Many of these women have experienced addiction as a cause and consequence of marginalization. Despite the scale of addiction issues, in-prison treatment remains limited. Access to drug treatment units and structured addiction support is especially limited for women serving short sentences (Office of the Inspectorate 2021). Without access to consistent care, many leave prison without addressing the root causes of their offending.

Impact on Families and Children

The incarceration of mothers in New Zealand has implications for their children and families. Mothers are more likely than fathers to have their children placed in formal care or receive government assistance during incarceration, disrupting household stability and emotional well-being (Ning et al. 2023).

Children separated from their mothers often experience anxiety, depression, and academic difficulties because of the loss of maternal care during important developmental periods. These children also face increased risks of behavioral issues, child protection involvement, and exposure to the justice system (Ning et al. 2023). Many mothers report feeling they lose their parental authority while in custody, complicating reunification after release. Separation frequently results in siblings being split or children being placed with unfamiliar caregivers, compounding trauma (Kingi 2001). In some cases, the fear of permanent custody loss adds psychological strain on mothers and children, especially when communication is limited.

To mitigate such harms, New Zealand offers Mothers with Babies Units at Auckland Region Women's Corrections Facility, Arohata, and Christchurch Women's Prison. These units allow eligible mothers to live with their infants up to twenty-four months of age, provided they meet safety and caregiving criteria (Office of the Inspectorate 2021). These home-like units support bonding, parenting skills, and improved post-release outcomes, though access remains limited due to space, eligibility, and infrastructure issues (Office of the Children's Commissioner 2021).

Visitation policies also affect maternal bonds. Visitors, including children under eighteen, must undergo an application and approval process. Minimum visitation is one thirty-minute session per week (Department of Corrections 2022). Child-focused visitation programs, like Storytime Foundation, allow incarcerated mothers to record themselves reading books to their children, helping maintain connection through shared storytelling. The aim is to reduce stress and promote emotional connection, but they are not widely available (Department of Corrections 2023). Māori children, who are disproportionately affected by maternal imprisonment, also face the effects of systemic inequity and cultural disconnection (Oranga Tamariki 2021). While efforts exist to maintain family ties, consistent implementation and equitable access are challenges.

Policy Reforms and Recommendations

Policy reforms addressing women's incarceration in New Zealand must prioritize equity, cultural responsiveness, and alternatives to custody. Women, especially Māori, are overrepresented in the prison system because of intergenerational trauma, poverty, and systemic inequities (Adair 2023). Most are incarcerated for non-violent offenses linked to addiction, coercion, or survival needs. Legal reforms should expand community-based alternatives for women charged with public order or property offenses, including changes to the Misuse of Drugs Act 1975 to support a health-centered approach (Rapana et al. 2022).

Additionally, trauma-informed and culturally responsive rehabilitation must be expanded. Around 75 percent of incarcerated women have a mental health diagnosis, and many face co-occurring substance use disorders. Māori and Pacific women are particularly affected by punitive responses like segregation, which worsen trauma (APT 2024). Initiatives like *Kowhiritanga*, which integrates kaupapa Māori values into cognitive-behavioral therapy, should be consistently available across all women's prisons (Office of the Inspectorate 2021).

Support for incarcerated mothers is also essential. Approximately 64 percent of women in prison have dependent children, and their incarceration can cause major disruptions in caregiving and emotional well-being (Ning et al. 2023). Mothers with Babies Units (MBUs) allow eligible mothers to remain with their infants up to twenty-four months. Still, access is limited due to space and eligibility (Office of the Children's Commissioner 2021). Visitation policies requiring formal approvals and limited weekly access also strain maternal bonds and family reintegration (Department of Corrections 2023).

Finally, educational and vocational programs for women remain underdeveloped. Many express a desire for skills in trades, business, and tertiary education. However, they face barriers because of short sentence lengths and restricted availability (Office of the Inspectorate 2021). Expanding trauma-informed, culturally grounded education and addiction treatment options would reduce recidivism and promote successful reentry into society.

Conclusion

The experiences of incarcerated women in Australia, Papua New Guinea, and New Zealand indicate shared struggles and country-specific challenges. Across all three nations, women are disproportionately imprisoned for non-violent, survival-based crimes rooted in poverty, addiction, trauma, and inequality. In each context, Indigenous or rural women are especially overrepresented and underserved.

Australia and New Zealand have more formal prison systems with dedicated women's facilities, mother–baby units, and some gender-responsive reforms. Yet, in both countries, Indigenous women face significant disparities in incarceration rates, access to services, and exposure to punitive legal frameworks. New Zealand has made strides toward culturally grounded rehabilitation through initiatives like *Kowhiritanga*, while Australia has focused on programs like Wandoo Rehabilitation Prison.

In contrast, PNG's prison system remains underdeveloped and influenced by colonialism. Facilities lack basic infrastructure, healthcare, and gender-specific programming. Legal protections are inconsistently applied, and many women, especially from remote areas, enter prison without legal representation. Still, PNG shares with Australia and New Zealand a pattern of incarcerating women for minor, poverty-driven offenses, often with consequences for families and children.

While the scale and institutional capacity differ, the need for reform is universal. Each country must prioritize alternatives to incarceration, trauma-informed care, and support for incarcerated mothers. Policies must address the root causes of women's offending and ensure systems are responsive to gender, culture, and caregiving roles. By doing this, Oceania can move toward a more humane and equitable approach to women's incarceration.

References

Adair, Janis. 2023. "Shining a Light on Women in New Zealand Prisons." *Office of the Inspectorate | Te Tari Tirohia*. February 3, 2023. https://inspectorate.corrections.govt.nz/news/news_items/shining_a_light_on_women_in_new_zealand_prisons.

ALRC (Australian Law Reform Commission). 2017. *Pathways to Justice—Inquiry into the Incarceration Rate of Aboriginal and Torres Strait Islander Peoples*. Report 133. https://www.alrc.gov.au/publication/pathways-to-justice-inquiry-into-the-incarceration-rate-of-aboriginal-and-torres-strait-islander-peoples-alrc-report-133/.

Amnesty International. 2006. *Papua New Guinea: Violence Against Women: Not Inevitable, Never Acceptable!* AI Index ASA 34/002/2006. https://www.amnesty.org/es/wp-content/uploads/2021/08/asa340022006en.pdf.

Antara News. 2024. "PNG Police Seeks Collaboration with Papua to Fight Drug Trafficking." April 4, 2024. https://en.antaranews.com/news/310041/png-police-seeks-collaboration-with-papua-to-fight-drug-trafficking.

APT (Association for the Prevention of Torture). 2024. *Women in Prison: New Zealand—Analysis from the National Preventive Mechanism*. Geneva: Association for the Prevention of Torture. https://www.apt.ch/sites/default/files/2024-12/new_zealand_country_report.pdf.

Australian Associated Press (AAP). 2024. "Jail Time Slashed for Victorian Woman Who Killed Abusive Husband After Feeding Him Drug-Laced Biscuits." *The Guardian*. November 19, 2024. https://www.theguardian.com/australia-news/2024/nov/20/rebecca-payne-murder-sentence-reduced-husband-freezer-death-ntwnfb.

Australian Bureau of Statistics. 2024. *Prisoners in Australia, 2024*. Canberra: Australian Bureau of Statistics. https://www.abs.gov.au/statistics/people/crime-and-justice/prisoners-australia/latest-release.

Australian High Commission. 2008. "Beon Prison." *Australian Government Department of Foreign Affairs and Trade*. https://png.highcommission.gov.au/pmsb/Speech080708.html.

Australian Human Rights Commission. 2024. "Statistics About Aboriginal and Torres Strait Islander Women and Girls." *Statistics and Facts*. October 9, 2024. https://humanrights.gov.au/education/stats-facts/statistics-about-aboriginal-and-torres-strait-islander-women-and-girls.

Australian Institute of Health and Welfare. 2024. *Adults in Prison*. Based on Australian Bureau of Statistics data. Canberra: AIHW. https://www.aihw.gov.au/reports/australias-welfare/adults-in-prison.

Australian Institute of Health and Welfare. 2023. *The Health of People in Australia's Prisons 2022*, catalogue number PHE 33. Canberra: AIHW. https://www.aihw.gov.au/getmedia/e2245d01-07d1-4b8d-81b3-60d14fbf007f/aihw-phe-33-health-of-people-in-australias-prisons-2022.pdf?v=20231108163318&inline=true.

Australian Institute of Health and Welfare. 2020. *The Health and Welfare of Women in Australia's Prisons*. Catalogue no. PHE 281. Canberra: AIHW. https://www.aihw.gov.au/getmedia/32d3a8dc-eb84-4a3b-90dc-79a1aba0efc6/aihw-phe-281.pdf.aspx.

Australian Institute of Health and Welfare and National Indigenous Australians Agency. 2024. "Measure 2.11 Contact with the Criminal Justice System." In *Aboriginal and Torres Strait Islander Health Performance Framework*. Canberra: AIHW & NIAA. https://www.indigenoushpf.gov.au/measures/2-11-contact-with-the-criminal-justice-system.

Australian Law Reform Commission. 2017. *Pathways to Justice: Inquiry into the Incarceration Rate of Aboriginal and Torres Strait Islander Peoples*. Report 133: "Fines and Infringement Notices." Updated February 5, 2018. Canberra: Commonwealth of Australia. https://www.alrc.gov.au/publication/pathways-to-justice-inquiry-into-the-incarceration-rate-of-aboriginal-and-torres-strait-islander-peoples-alrc-report-133/12-fines-and-driver-licences/fines-and-infringement-notices-3/.

Baldry, Eileen, and Chris Cunneen. 2014. "Imprisoned Indigenous Women and the Shadow of Colonial Patriarchy." *Australian & New Zealand Journal of Criminology* 47 (2): 276–98.

Barr, Heather. 2015. "2 Years Later, Papua New Guinea's Domestic Safety Law MIA." *Human Rights Watch*. November 12, 2015. https://www.hrw.org/news/2015/11/12/2-years-later-papua-new-guineas-domestic-safety-law-mia.

Beasley, Jordyn. 2024. "More than 90% of People Caught with Small Amounts of Illicit Drugs Criminalised in NSW Despite Diversion Reforms." *The Guardian*. December 3, 2024. https://www.theguardian.com/australia-news/2024/dec/04/more-than-90-of-people-caught-with-small-amounts-of-illicit-drugs-criminalised-in-nsw-despite-diversion-reforms.

Bentley, Hannah. 2017. "Women's Prison Education." *Practice: The New Zealand Corrections Journal* 5 (1) (July 2017). Department of Corrections. https://www.corrections.govt.nz/resources/research/journal/volume_5_issue_1_july_2017/womens_prison_education.

Bevan, Marianne, and Nan Wehipeihana. 2015. *Women's Experiences of Re-Offending and Rehabilitation*. Wellington: Department of Corrections. November 2015. https://www.corrections.govt.nz/__data/assets/pdf_file/0013/13405/Women_s_Experiences_of_Re-offending_and_Rehabilitation_Final.pdf.

Boggo Road Gaol Historical Society. 2015. "Life in the 1903 Women's Prison." *Boggo Road Gaol Historical Society*. October 28, 2015. https://www.boggoroadgaol.com.au/2015/10/life-in-1903-women-prison.html.

Borrey, Anne. 1992. *Ol Kalabus Meri: A Study of Female Prisoners in Papua New Guinea*. Occasional Paper no. 21. Port Moresby: Papua New Guinea Law Reform Commission. https://www.paclii.org/pg/lawreform/PGLawRComm/1992/1.pdf.

Boxall, Hayley, Crystal Dowling, and Anthony Morgan. 2020. *Female Perpetrated Domestic Violence: Prevalence of Self-Defensive and Retaliatory Violence*. Trends & Issues in Crime and Criminal Justice No. 584. Canberra: Australian Institute of Criminology.

Breuer, Erica, Marc Rémond, Stacey Lighton, Jane Passalaqua, Jennifer Galouzis, Kelly-Anne Stewart, and Elizabeth Sullivan. 2021. "The Needs and Experiences of Mothers While in Prison and Post-Release: A Rapid Review and Thematic Synthesis." *Health & Justice* 9 (1): Article 10.

CARE Australia. 2011. *Rural Poverty in Remote Papua New Guinea*. Canberra: CARE Australia. https://www.care.org.au/wp-content/uploads/2014/12/PNG-rural-pverty-in-remote-PNG-case-study-report.pdf.

Carrington, Kerry. 1993. *Offending Girls: Sex, Youth and Justice*. Sydney: Allen & Unwin.

Child Welfare Act. 1961. *Child Welfare Act 1961 (Papua New Guinea)*. https://www.paclii.org/pg/legis/consol_act/cwa1961115/.

Clayworth, Peter. 2012. "Prisons—Women in Prison." *Te Ara—The Encyclopedia of New Zealand*. June 11, 2012. https://teara.govt.nz/en/prisons.

Colahan, Mackenzie. 2023. "Experts, Lawyers Lift Lid on Australia's 'Woefully Under-Funded' Prison Mental Health Services." *ABC News*. March 22, 2023. https://www.abc.net.au/news/2023-03-23/prison-mental-health-woefully-under-funded-experts-say/101972274.

Commonwealth Director of Public Prosecutions. 2025. "Importing and Exporting Border Controlled Drugs or Precursors." *Crimes We Prosecute*. https://www.cdpp.

gov.au/crimes-we-prosecute/serious-drugs/importing-and-exporting-drugs-or-precursors.

Coroner's Court of Western Australia. 2016. *Inquest into the Death of Ms Dhu.* Delivered December 16, 2016. https://www.coronerscourt.wa.gov.au/I/inquest_into_the_death_of_ms_dhu.aspx.

Cunneen, Chris, and Terry Libesman. 2000. "Postcolonial Trauma: The Contemporary Removal of Indigenous Children and Young People from Their Families in Australia." *Australian Journal of Social Issues* 35 (2): 99–115.

Department of Corrections. 2023. *Mothers with Babies Units Providing Warm and Supportive Environments.* Wellington: New Zealand Department of Corrections. https://www.corrections.govt.nz/news/2023/mothers_with_babies_units_providing_warm_and_supportive_environments.

Department of Corrections. 2022. *Becoming an Approved Visitor.* Wellington: New Zealand Department of Corrections. https://www.corrections.govt.nz/our_work/in_prison/staying_connected_with_people_in_prison/visits/becoming_an_approved_visitor.

Department of Corrections. 2021. *Wāhine—E Rere Ana ki te Pae Hou: Women's Strategy 2021–2025. An Oranga-Focused Framework for Restoration and Reclamation.* Wellington: New Zealand Department of Corrections. https://www.corrections.govt.nz/__data/assets/pdf_file/0004/44644/Corrections_Wahine_-_E_rere_ana_ki_te_pae_hou_2021_-_2025.pdf.

Department of Corrections. 2009. *Offender Volumes Report 2009.* Wellington: Department of Corrections. https://www.corrections.govt.nz/__data/assets/pdf_file/0009/10710/offender-volumes-report-2009.pdf.

Department of Corrections. n.d. "Women in Prison." *Ara Poutama Aotearoa / New Zealand Department of Corrections.* https://www.corrections.govt.nz/our_work/in_prison/being_in_prison/women_in_prison.

DFAT (Australian Department of Foreign Affairs and Trade). 2025. *Country Information Report: Papua New Guinea.* Canberra: DFAT. https://www.dfat.gov.au/sites/default/files/country-information-report-papua-new-guinea.pdf.

Dowell, Carly M., Gloria C. Mejia, David B. Preen, and Fiona J. Stanley. 2018. "Maternal Incarceration, Child Protection, and Infant Mortality: A Descriptive Study of Infant Children of Women Prisoners in Western Australia." *Health & Justice* 6 (1): 2.

Dozier, Marc. 2018. "Papua New Guinea: Women in Bomana Prison." *Hemis.fr.* https://www.hemis.fr/reportages/7538/papouasie-nouvelle-guinee-les-femmes-de-la-prison-de-bomana-par-marc-dozier.html?idLangue=2.

Dunstan, Joseph. 2022. "Veronica Nelson Was a Kind Woman. An Inquest Heard She Died an 'Appallingly Undignified' Death in Prison." *ABC News.* May 27, 2022. https://www.abc.net.au/news/2022-05-28/veronica-nelson-coronial-inquest-aboriginal-prison-death-custody/101103922.

Edwards, Layla M., Sungwon Chang, Reem Zeki, Sacha Kendall Jamieson, Julia Bowman, Craig Cooper, Elizabeth Sullivan, Louisa Degenhardt, Tim Slade, Sharon

L. Browne, and Tony Butler. 2024. "The Associations Between Social Determinants of Health, Mental Health, Substance-Use and Recidivism: A Ten-Year Retrospective Cohort Analysis of Women Who Completed the Connections Programme in Australia." *Harm Reduction Journal* 21 (1): 2.

Edwards, Layla, Sacha K. Jamieson, Julia Bowman, Sungwon Chang, Josie Newton, and Elizabeth Sullivan. 2022. "A Systematic Review of Post-Release Programs for Women Exiting Prison with Substance-Use Disorders: Assessing Current Programs and Weighing the Evidence." *Health & Justice* 10 (1): 1.

Environmental Health Intelligence New Zealand. 2024. "Ethnic Profile." *Population Vulnerability to Environmental Hazards*. Environmental Health Intelligence New Zealand. https://www.ehinz.ac.nz/indicators/population-vulnerability/ethnic-profile/.

Faa, Marian. 2025. "Papua New Guinea Police Say They Caught NSW Man with 60 Kilograms of Cocaine in Port Moresby Hotel." *ABC News*. July 2, 2025. https://www.abc.net.au/news/2025-07-02/australian-nsw-man-allegedly-caught-cocaine-png-port-moresby/105487368.

Fazel, Seena, Ingrid A. Yoon, and Amy J. Hayes. 2017. "Substance Use Disorders in Prisoners: An Updated Systematic Review and Meta-Regression Analysis in Recently Incarcerated Men and Women." *Addiction* 112 (10): 1725–39.

Gleeson, Hayley. 2019. "What Happens When an Abused Woman Fights Back?" *ABC News*. July 29, 2019. https://www.abc.net.au/news/2019-07-30/the-women-behind-bars-breaching-domestic-violence-order/11330408.

Government of South Australia. 2024. "New Program Creates Stronger Family Bonds Between Women in Custody and Their Children." Department for Child Protection, South Australia, media release. https://www.childprotection.sa.gov.au/news-and-events/news-and-media-releases/dcp-news/new-program-creates-stronger-family-bonds-between-women-in-custody-and-their-children#:~:text=A%20new%20program%20is%20working,program%20will%20work%20to%20achieve.

Heffernan, Edward B., Kimina C. Andersen, Abhilash Dev, and Stuart Kinner. 2012. "Prevalence of Mental Illness Among Aboriginal and Torres Strait Islander People in Queensland Prisons." *Medical Journal of Australia* 197 (1): 37–41.

Henville, Chloe. 2025. "Female Inmates 'Disadvantaged' by Overcrowding at Greenough Regional Prison." *ABC News*. May 25, 2025. ABC Midwest & Wheatbelt. https://www.abc.net.au/news/2025-05-26/women-indigenous-men-hit-by-prison-overcrowding-staff-shortages/105315494.

Hughes, Caitlin E., Alison Ritter, Nicholas Cowdery, and Benjamin Phillips. 2014. *Evaluating Australian Drug Trafficking Thresholds: Proportionate, Equitable and Just?* Report to the Criminology Research Advisory Council, March 2014. Australian Institute of Criminology, Canberra. https://www.aic.gov.au/sites/default/files/2020-05/35-1112-FinalReport.pdf.

Human Rights Watch. 2020. "Papua New Guinea." In *World Report 2020*. New York: Human Rights Watch. https://www.hrw.org/world-report/2020/country-chapters/papua-new-guinea.

Human Rights Watch. 2016. "Dispatches: Life and Death in Papua New Guinea." *Human Rights Watch*. March 8, 2016. https://www.hrw.org/news/2016/03/08/dispatches-life-and-death-papua-new-guinea.

Human Rights Watch. 2015. *Bashed Up: Family Violence in Papua New Guinea*. November 4, 2015. https://www.hrw.org/report/2015/11/04/bashed/family-violence-papua-new-guinea.

ICRC (International Committee of the Red Cross). 2017. "Papua New Guinea: Family Visit Brings Hope in East New Britain." *International Committee of the Red Cross*. August 14, 2017. https://www.icrc.org/en/document/papua-new-guinea-family-visit-brings-hope-kerevat.

IDLO (International Development Law Organization). 2013. *Accessing Justice: Models, Strategies and Best Practices on Women's Empowerment*. Rome: International Development Law Organization. https://www.idlo.int/sites/default/files/Womens_Access_to_Justice_Full_Report.pdf.

Institute for Crime & Justice Policy Research. 2025. "New Zealand." In *World Prison Brief*. Birkbeck: University of London. https://www.prisonstudies.org/country/new-zealand.

Institute for Crime & Justice Policy Research. 2024. "Australia." *World Prison Brief*. https://www.prisonstudies.org/country/australia.

Institute for Crime & Justice Policy Research. 2023. "Papua New Guinea: Female Prison Population Trend." *World Prison Brief*. https://www.prisonstudies.org/country/papua-new-guinea.

Johnson, Holly. 2004. *Key Findings from the Drug Use Careers of Female Offenders Study*. Research and Public Policy Series No. 289. Canberra: Australian Institute of Criminology.

Jolly, Margaret, Christine Stewart, and Carolyn Brewer, eds. 2012. *Engendering Violence in Papua New Guinea*. Canberra: ANU Press. https://library.oapen.org/bitstream/handle/20.500.12657/33584/459830.pdf?sequence=1.

Justice Action. 2019. "Education and Training." https://justiceaction.org.au/education-and-training/.

Justice Reform Initiative. 2024. *Adult Imprisonment in Australia: Overview April 2024*. Justice Reform Initiative. https://assets.nationbuilder.com/justicereforminitiative/pages/410/attachments/original/1746070902/2024_JRI_Adult_Imprisonment_Overview_April25.pdf.

Kingi, Te Kani. 2001. *Children of Women in Prison: A New Zealand Study (Women in Corrections: Staff and Clients, pp. 1–9)*. Australian Institute of Criminology. NCJRS Abstract No. 187959. https://www.ojp.gov/ncjrs/virtual-library/abstracts/children-women-prison-new-zealand-study-women-corrections-staff-and.

Ligaiula, Pita. 2021. "New Drug Laws Passed in PNG Parliament." *Pacific Islands News Association (PINA)*. December 6, 2021. https://pina.com.fj/2021/12/06/new-drug-laws-passed-in-png-parliament/.

Mambon, Kingtau, and Stephen Howes. 2024. "Polygamy Is Spreading in PNG." *Devpolicy Blog*. February 6, 2024. https://devpolicy.org/polygamy-is-spreading-in-png-20240206/.

Maykin, Melissa, Inga Stünzner, and Hilda Wayne. 2022. "When Jessica Hill Saw the 'Ladies in Pink' in a Fijian Prison, She Feared the Worst. Instead, She Gained Forgiveness and a Passion for Fashion." *Sistas, Let's Talk*, ABC Radio Australia. June 17, 2022. https://www.abc.net.au/news/2022-06-18/women-incarcerated-in-prison-with-children-in-pacific-islands-/101135920.

Ministry of Justice, Ara Poutama Aotearoa, Crown Law Office, Serious Fraud Office, and Oranga Tamariki. 2022. *Long-Term Insights on Imprisonment, 1960 to 2050: A Systemic Approach*. Justice Sector Long-Term Insights Briefing. Wellington: Crown Law Office. https://www.crownlaw.govt.nz/assets/Uploads/Publications/LTIB_Report_extended_Web.pdf.

Mission Aviation Fellowship UK. "MAF Offers Hope to PNG's Prisoners as Global Rate of Female Inmates Rises." April 5, 2022. https://maf-uk.org/news/maf-offers-hope-to-pngs-prisoners-as-global-rate-of-female-inmates-rises/.

Mothers Project. n.d. "Helping Imprisoned Mothers." *Mothers Project | New Zealand*. https://www.mothersproject.org/.

Nicholson, Ellie, Kiani Duffull, Charlee Reveley, and Katarina Tominiko. n.d. *Women in Aotearoa Prisons: The Reality of Life Within the Aotearoa Prison System*. University of Otago Shorthand Stories. Accessed July 29, 2025. https://otago.shorthandstories.com/women-in-aotearoa-prisons/index.html.

Ning, Bo, Kai Faasen, Georgia Jackson, and Gabrielle Jenkin. 2023. *Evidence Brief: Care of Children of Incarcerated Sole Caregivers*. Wellington: Oranga Tamariki—Ministry for Children. https://www.orangatamariki.govt.nz/assets/Uploads/About-us/Research/Latest-research/Youth-Justice-research/Evidence-Brief-Care-of-Children-of-Incarcerated-Sole-Caregivers.pdf.

OC Index (Global Initiative Against Transnational Organized Crime). 2023. "Papua New Guinea." https://ocindex.net/country/papua_new_guinea.

Office of the Children's Commissioner. 2021. *Arohata Women's Prison Monitoring Report: Mothers with Babies Unit*. Wellington: Office of the Children's Commissioner. https://www.manamokopuna.org.nz/documents/534/20211007_Arohata_MBU_Report__Redacted.pdf.

Office of the Inspector of Custodial Services. 2023. *Inspection of Wandoo Rehabilitation Prison*, Report 147, June 13, 2023. Perth: Office of the Inspector of Custodial Services, Western Australia. https://www.oics.wa.gov.au/wp-content/uploads/2023/05/00.2-Clean-Copy-of-Report-Inspection-Report-147-Wandoo-Rehabilitation-Prison.pdf.

Office of the Inspectorate. 2021. *Thematic Report: The Lived Experience of Women in Prison*. Wellington: Ara Poutama Aotearoa. https://inspectorate.corrections.govt.nz/__data/assets/pdf_file/0003/44571/Inspectorate_Womens_Thematic_Report_-_FINAL.pdf.

Oranga Tamariki. 2021. *Descriptive Analysis of Parents in Prison in Aotearoa New Zealand.* Wellington: Ministry for Children. https://www.orangatamariki.govt.nz/assets/Uploads/About-us/Research/Latest-research/Youth-Justice-research/Descriptive-Analysis-of-Parents-in-Prison.pdf.

Oxley, Deborah. 1997. *Convict Maids: The Forced Migration of Women to Australia.* Cambridge: Cambridge University Press.

Papua New Guinea. 2017. *The State v Miriam Hevelawa, Jacob Hevelawa and Timothy Numara (No. 2)*, CR (FC) 221–223 of 2016, N6875. National Court of Justice, Waigani, January 24–September 15. https://d6mljhs7208w9.cloudfront.net/uploads/2017/10/NC2017N6875.pdf.

Papua New Guinea. 2000. *The State v Drikore Yuana Peter* (PNGLR 307). National Court, June 15, 2000. Accessed via vLex at https://vlex.com/vid/the-state-v-drikore-922795606.

Papua New Guinea. 1974. *Criminal Code Act 1974*, Section 383A. Accessed via PacLII. https://www.paclii.org/pg/legis/consol_act/cca1974115/.

Queensland Ombudsman. 2016. *Overcrowding at Brisbane Women's Correctional Centre.* Report tabled in the Queensland Parliament, September 27, 2016. Brisbane: Office of the Queensland Ombudsman. https://www.parliament.qld.gov.au/Work-of-the-Assembly/Tabled-Papers/docs/5516t1587/5516t1587.pdf.

Rapana, Wiremu, Tina Winter, Rachael Fox, Chris Wilkins, Josef Norris, Rose Crossin, Rangimarie Hunia, Hine McGregor, and Khylee Quince. 2022. "Indigenous People in Aotearoa New Zealand Are Overrepresented in Cannabis Convictions." *Harm Reduction Journal* 19: 28.

Russell, Emma K., Bree Carlton, and Danielle Tyson. 2022. "'It's a Gendered Issue, 100 Per Cent': How Tough Bail Laws Entrench Gender and Racial Inequality and Social Disadvantage." *International Journal for Crime, Justice and Social Democracy* 11 (3): 107–21.

Shalev, Sharon. 2021. *First, Do No Harm: Segregation, Restraint, and Pepper Spray Use in Women's Prisons in New Zealand.* Wellington: New Zealand Human Rights Commission. https://hrc-nz-resources.s3.ap-southeast-2.amazonaws.com/files/1516/3593/2021/First_do_no_harm_report.pdf.

Sikani, Richard C. 1991. *Australia and Papua New Guinea: A Comparison of Correctional Systems: Summary Report.* Canberra: Australian Institute of Criminology. https://www.aic.gov.au/sites/default/files/2020-05/australia-and-papua-new-guinea-a-comparison-of-correctional-systems.pdf.

Sisters Inside. 2023. *Submission to the Senate Standing Committees on Community Affairs: The Extent and Nature of Poverty in Australia.* South Brisbane: Sisters Inside. https://www.aph.gov.au/DocumentStore.ashx?id=28265ea7-346b-4264-88c6-af37091fd9d5&subId=735328.

Sisters Inside. 2021. "*Women and Girls' Experience of the Criminal 'Justice' System: Sisters Inside's Response to Discussion Paper 2, Women's Safety and Justice Taskforce, Queensland.*" PDF. Australian Human Rights Commission redacted version. December 2, 2021. https://humanrights.gov.au/sites/default/files/sisters_inside_attachment3_redacted_0.pdf.

Smith, Babette. 2008. *Australia's Birthstain: The Startling Legacy of the Convict Era.* Sydney: Allen & Unwin.

South Australia. Department for Child Protection. 2024. "New Program Creates Stronger Family Bonds Between Women in Custody and Their Children." *News and Media Releases. South Australian Government.* https://www.childprotection.sa.gov.au/news-and-events/news-and-media-releases/dcp-news/new-program-creates-stronger-family-bonds-between-women-in-custody-and-their-children

Stevens, Ric. 2025. "Prolific Auckland Shoplifter Jennifer Gordon in Jail for $25,000 Worth of Stealing." *RNZ.* April 10, 2025. https://www.rnz.co.nz/news/national/557759/prolific-auckland-shoplifter-jennifer-gordon-in-jail-for-25-000-worth-of-stealing.

The Global Economy. 2025. "Papua New Guinea: Tuberculosis Incidence (per 100,000)." *The Global Economy.* https://www.theglobaleconomy.com/Papua-New-Guinea/Tuberculosis/.

The National. 2023. "Outlaw Polygamy Immediately." *The National.* September 19, 2023. https://www.thenational.com.pg/outlaw-polygamy-immediately/.

Tolmie, Julia. 2020. "How We Pre-Package Victims of Domestic Violence." *University of Auckland Law School.* February 26, 2020. https://www.auckland.ac.nz/en/news/2020/02/26/pre-package-victims-domestic-violence.html.

Tolmie, Julia, and Jane Calderwood Norton. 2022. "Victim-Survivors of Intimate Partner Violence Forced to Participate in Crimes: Some Thoughts on the Potential Application of Discrimination Law." *University of Auckland Faculty of Law Research Paper Series.* January 1, 2022.

U.N. Human Rights Council. 2011. *Report of the Special Rapporteur on Torture and Other Cruel, Inhuman or Degrading Treatment or Punishment, Addendum: Mission to Papua New Guinea (A/HRC/16/52/Add.5).* New York: United Nations. Accessed via Refworld. https://www.refworld.org/reference/countryrep/unhrc/2011/en/78225.

U.S. Department of State. 2024. *Papua New Guinea 2023 Human Rights Report.* Washington, DC: Bureau of Democracy, Human Rights, and Labor. https://www.state.gov/wp-content/uploads/2024/02/528267_PAPUA-NEW-GUINEA-2023-HUMAN-RIGHTS-REPORT.pdf.

Wahlquist, Calla. 2020. "A Mass Imprisonment Crisis: Why More Women Are Doing Time." *The Guardian.* November 16, 2020. https://www.theguardian.com/australia-news/2020/nov/17/a-mass-imprisonment-crisis-why-more-women-are-doing-time.

Wakem, Beverley, and David McGee. 2012. *Investigation of the Department of Corrections in Relation to the Provision, Access and Availability of Prisoner Health Services.* Wellington, NZ: Office of the Ombudsman. https://www.ombudsman.parliament.nz/sites/default/files/2019-03/Own%20motion%20prisoner%20health.pdf

World Bank. 2025. "Rural population (% of total population), Papua New Guinea." Trading Economics. https://tradingeconomics.com/papua-new-guinea/rural-population-percent-of-total-population-wb-data.html.

Yee, Natalia, Christie Browne, Farzana Rahman, and Kimberlie Dean. 2024. "Prevalence of Mental Illness Among Australian and New Zealand People in Prison: A Systematic Review and Meta-Analysis of Studies Published over Five Decades." *Australian and New Zealand Journal of Psychiatry* 58 (12): 1034–46.

Zarriga, Mirriam. 2024. "Two Arrested for Cocaine Smuggling." *Post-Courier*. December 15, 2024. https://www.postcourier.com.pg/two-arrested-for-cocaine-smuggling/.

Glossary

Alcoholic Drinks Control Act (2010)—Kenyan law regulating alcohol production and sale, disproportionately impacting women in the informal economy by criminalizing unlicensed traditional alcohol brewing.

Article 40 of Cambodia's Law on Drug Control (2012)—Cambodian statute that mandates 2–5 years' imprisonment for drug possession, with harsher penalties for repeat offenses. It disproportionately affects poor women and offers little judicial discretion.

Article 58—Section of the Soviet Penal Code used during Stalin's regime to charge individuals with counter-revolutionary activities. Many women were imprisoned under Article 58 during the Great Purges, contributing to their incarceration in the Gulag system.

Code Red Law—2019 Italian law designed to respond to gender-based violence. It allows victims to report abuse to police and triggers immediate protective measures, though its enforcement has been criticized for inconsistency.

Drug Mule—Person who transports illegal drugs, typically across borders, often under coercion or economic pressure.

Drugs and Drug Trafficking Act 140 of 1992—South African law imposing harsh penalties for drug-related offenses, disproportionately impacting women coerced into minor trafficking roles.

EQUAL Act—Legislation aimed at ending the federal sentencing disparity between crack and powder cocaine offenses in the United States, which has resulted in disproportionately harsher penalties for crack cocaine, affecting communities of color.

Family Protection Act 2013—Law criminalizing family and sexual violence in Papua New Guinea; however, enforcement is inconsistent, especially in rural or traditional areas.

FARC (Fuerzas Armadas Revolucionarias de Colombia)—Guerrilla group involved in Colombia's internal armed conflict. Women's involvement in, or victimization by, FARC has shaped incarceration patterns and reintegration challenges post-conflict.

Gender-responsive approach—Strategies considering the unique needs, experiences, and social contexts of individuals based on their gender, aiming to create equitable and effective outcomes. It emphasizes addressing gender-specific challenges and reducing barriers, particularly for women and girls, in areas like healthcare, education, and justice systems.

Gharemat—Women imprisoned in Egypt for failing to repay debts, often incurred for necessities like medical care or family expenses. Their incarceration reflects the criminalization of poverty and the absence of economic safety nets.

Gulag—System of forced labor camps established during the Soviet era, particularly under Stalin, where tens of thousands of women were imprisoned. Women in Gulags faced severe conditions, including hard labor, inadequate food, and sexual abuse, and were often imprisoned for political dissent or minor crimes.

Heinous Crimes Law—Brazilian statute that classifies drug offenses alongside violent crimes like murder, imposing harsher penalties and limiting parole, with disproportionate effects on poor women.

Hijab Laws—Laws that mandate women wear Islamic dress in public, and violations are punishable by fines, imprisonment, or corporal punishment. These laws are a tool to control women's bodies and behavior, leading to widespread arrests and repression.

Hujum—Soviet-era campaign in Uzbekistan (1927–30s) to unveil Muslim women and enforce Soviet gender norms. It was carried out through mass rallies, propaganda, and the public removal and burning of veils, often enforced by local officials and party activists. It increased the surveillance and punishment of women seen as resisting state control.

Indian Act of 1896—Amendment to the original 1876 Indian Act, which governed aspects of Indigenous life, including land use, education, and identity, often in a restrictive and assimilative manner. The amendments entrenched government control over Indigenous peoples, limiting their rights and autonomy, and imposing policies aimed at assimilation into Canadian society.

Kowhiritanga Program—Cognitive-behavioral therapy program grounded in Māori values, designed to help incarcerated women in New Zealand address the causes of their offending.

Laogai (Reform through Labor)—System of forced labor camps in the People's Republic of China, established in the 1950s to punish and re-educate offenders. Women held in the laogai were often subjected to hard labor, ideological indoctrination, and poor living conditions. Although the official term was abolished in 2013, similar practices persist in other forms of detention.

Laojiao (Re-education through Labor)—Now-abolished Chinese system of administrative detention used to imprison individuals—often without trial—for "minor offenses." Commonly used to control political dissent, including among women.

Mandatory Minimum Penalties (MMPs)—Legislatively imposed minimum sentences that judges in Canada must apply for certain offenses, regardless of individual case circumstances. Originally intended to deter serious crimes, MMPs have faced criticism for limiting judicial discretion and disproportionately affecting marginalized groups within the justice system.

Moral Offenses—Acts considered violations of cultural or religious codes like adultery, prostitution, or dress code violations. These offenses disproportionately impact women and are often used to enforce patriarchal norms, with punishments including imprisonment and public shaming.

Narcotic Drugs and Psychotropic Substances (NDPS) Act—1985 Indian law that imposes strict penalties for drug offenses, including minor possession. It contributes significantly to the incarceration of women coerced into low-level trafficking roles.

Narkotikaprogram med domstolskontroll (ND)—Norway's Drug Court Program that allows people convicted of drug-related offenses to receive community-based treatment instead of prison. Participants engage in individual and group therapy, medication-assisted treatment, vocational training, housing support, and regular judicial reviews designed to monitor progress and encourage rehabilitation. This initiative reflects Norway's rehabilitative justice philosophy and is implemented nationwide.

One-Child Policy—China's population control policy (1979–2015) that restricted most families to having only one child, leading to coercive enforcement, including forced abortions and sterilizations, disproportionately affecting women and resulting in incarceration.

Political Prisoners—Those who have been incarcerated for political activism, protest, or criticism of the government. They are often held without fair trials and subjected to abuse.

Pretrial Detention—The confinement of individuals accused of crimes before trial, often without a conviction, disproportionately impacting marginalized women due to delays and lack of legal resources.

Prison Rape Elimination Act (2003)—Federal law enacted to address and prevent sexual assault and abuse in US correctional facilities, including prisons, jails, and juvenile detention centers. PREA establishes standards for prevention, detection, and response to sexual abuse, mandates regular facility audits, and requires facilities to provide support and protection for victims, aiming to create safer environments and reduce sexual violence in corrections.

RA 9262 - Anti-Violence Against Women and Their Children Act—Philippine law passed in 2004 to protect women and children from domestic violence. Despite its intent, enforcement is inconsistent, and women who retaliate against abusers are sometimes imprisoned instead of protected.

Residential schools—Government-funded, church-run institutions established in the nineteenth and twentieth centuries to forcibly assimilate Indigenous children by removing them from their families and suppressing their cultural identities. These schools subjected children to harsh living conditions, abuse, and cultural erasure, leaving a lasting and traumatic impact on Indigenous communities across Canada.

Restorative justice—Approach to addressing harm that focuses on repairing relationships and meeting the needs of victims, offenders, and the community. It emphasizes accountability, dialogue, and collaboration to foster healing and prevent future harm.

Section 498A—Section of the Indian Penal Code introduced in 1983 to protect women from cruelty and abuse by husbands and in-laws, particularly related to dowry. While intended to safeguard women, it has also led to the incarceration of women during retaliatory family disputes.

Sentencing Act 2002—Law that expanded the use of community-based sentences (e.g., community work, intensive supervision, and home detention) in New Zealand, affecting how women are sentenced for non-violent offenses.

Sharia-based Hudud Punishments—Fixed Islamic penalties (e.g., flogging, stoning) applied in northern Nigerian states for offenses like adultery and fornication, disproportionately used against women.

Sixties Scoop—Period from the 1960s to the 1980s when thousands of Indigenous children were forcibly removed from their families and placed into foster care or adopted by non-Indigenous families. This practice disrupted Indigenous communities, led to the loss of cultural identity for many children, and has had lasting impacts on Indigenous families and communities across Canada.

Stimulant Control Act—Japanese law regulating methamphetamine use, which has contributed to female incarceration in the country, especially for low-level drug offenses.

Systemic inequality—Institutionalized disparities in resources, opportunities, and treatment experienced by individuals based on factors like race, gender, socioeconomic status, and other identities, perpetuated through societal structures like education, healthcare, and the justice system.

Trauma-informed strategy—Approach that recognizes and responds to the impact of trauma on individuals, aiming to create safe, supportive environments that promote healing, resilience, and empowerment by avoiding re-traumatization.

Violence Against Persons (Prohibition) Act (VAPP), 2015—Nigerian federal law intended to prevent physical, sexual, and psychological abuse. Despite its promise, enforcement remains weak, especially in protecting women.

Wāhine – E Rere Ana ki te Pae Hou—Women's justice strategy launched by the New Zealand Department of Corrections (2021–5) focused on restoration and culturally responsive care, particularly for Māori women. The strategy includes initiatives like marae-based rehabilitation programs, culturally grounded counseling, and strengthened connections to whānau and iwi, aiming to support Māori women's healing and reintegration into their communities.

Wandoo Rehabilitation Prison—Therapeutic, trauma-informed prison for women in Western Australia, focused on addiction recovery, mental health, and reintegration. Its programming includes cognitive-behavioral therapy, substance-use treatment, life-skills and parenting classes, vocational training, and post-release transition support within a structured therapeutic community.

Witchcraft Act—Colonial-era law used in Kenya to prosecute women, especially in rural areas, for alleged witchcraft, often leading to imprisonment or community violence.

Bibliography

ACLU. 2007. "Facts About the Over-Incarceration of Women in the United States." American Civil Liberties Union. December 12, 2007. https://www.aclu.org/documents/facts-about-over-incarceration-women-united-states.

ALRC (Australian Law Reform Commission). 2017. "Pathways to Justice—Inquiry into the Incarceration Rate of Aboriginal and Torres Strait Islander Peoples." Report 133. https://www.alrc.gov.au/publication/pathways-to-justice-inquiry-into-the-incarceration-rate-of-aboriginal-and-torres-strait-islander-peoples-alrc-report-133/.

Amnesty International. 2024. "Iran: New Compulsory Veiling Law Intensifies Oppression of Women and Girls." December 2024. https://www.amnesty.org/en/latest/news/2024/12/iran-new-compulsory-veiling-law-intensifies-oppression-of-women-and-girls/.

Amnesty International. 2019. *Nigeria: Children and Women Face Sexual Violence in Borno Prisons*. https://www.amnesty.org/en/latest/press-release/2019/04/nigeria-children-and-women-face-sexual-violence-in-borno-prisons.

Amnesty International. 2006. "Papua New Guinea: Violence Against Women: Not Inevitable, Never Acceptable!" AI Index ASA 34/002/2006. https://www.amnesty.org/es/wp-content/uploads/2021/08/asa340022006en.pdf.

Amnesty International and LICADHO. 2020. "Arbitrary Detention Related to Drug Policies in Cambodia: Joint Submission." June. https://www.amnesty.org/en/wp-content/uploads/2021/05/ASA2325062020ENGLISH.pdf.

Anaekwe, Henry Ebuka, and Nneka Perpetua Oli. 2024. "Socio-Economic Factors Influencing Female Criminality in Nigeria." *UNIZIK Journal of Gender Research* 3: 24–37.

Ancira, Daniela. 2017. "La Cana, Mexico: Providing Female Prisoners with Employment and Reintegration Opportunities." *Penal Reform International Blog*. https://www.penalreform.org/blog/la-cana-mexico-how-prison-labour-programmes-with/.

Antigone Onlus Association. 2023. *By the Side of Antigone: First Report on Detained Women in Italy, Press Kit*. Rome: Antigone Onlus Association. https://www.antigone.it.

APT (Association for the Prevention of Torture). 2024. "Women in Prison: New Zealand—Analysis from the National Preventive Mechanism." Geneva: APT. https://www.apt.ch/sites/default/files/2024-12/new_zealand_country_report.pdf.

Artz, Lillian, Veronica Filippeschi, and Nokwanda Nzimande. 2023. "Women in Prison Deserve Better Treatment." *South African Human Rights Commission*. February 16.

https://www.sahrc.org.za/index.php/sahrc-media/news-2/item/3447-women-in-prison-deserve-better-treatment.

Baldry, Eileen, and Chris Cunneen. 2014. "Imprisoned Indigenous Women and the Shadow of Colonial Patriarchy." *Australian & New Zealand Journal of Criminology* 47 (2): 276–98.

Borrey, Anne. 1992. "Ol Kalabus Meri: A Study of Female Prisoners in Papua New Guinea." Occasional Paper no. 21. Port Moresby: Papua New Guinea Law Reform Commission. https://www.paclii.org/pg/lawreform/PGLawRComm/1992/1.pdf.

Britto, Lina. 2020. "The Drug Wars in Colombia." Oxford Research Encyclopedia of Latin American History. https://doi.org/10.1093/acrefore/9780199366439.013.504.

Bucerius, Sandra, and Sveinung Sandberg. 2022. *Women in Prisons*. Chicago: University of Chicago Press.

Budd, Kristen. 2023. "Incarcerated Women and Girls." The Sentencing Project. April 3, 2023. https://www.sentencingproject.org/fact-sheet/incarcerated-women-and-girls/.

Cabato, Regine. 2021. "The Philippines' Drug War Is Putting More Pregnant Women Behind Bars. What Happens to Their Children?" The Washington Post. April 9. https://www.washingtonpost.com/world/2021/04/06/women-jail-births-philippines-duterte/.

Canada. 2021. "Pathways to Safe Indigenous Communities Initiative." Sac-Isc.gc.ca. 2021. https://sac-isc.gc.ca/eng/1646747630193/1646747651080.

Canada Correctional Service. 2024. "Crime, Punishment, and Prison for Women." March 4, 2024. https://www.canada.ca/en/correctional-service/lets-talk/read/2024/03-04-prison-for-women.html.

Center for Human Rights in Iran. 2016. "Family Visitation and Telephone Communications: Denying Basic Rights to Prisoners in Iran." https://iranhumanrights.org/2016/06/wwr-family-visitation-and-telephone-communications/.

Chukwuka, Victory. 2025. "How Prison Disproportionately Affects Women in Nigeria." *Medium*. March 21. https://medium.com/@HopeBehindBarsAfrica/how-prison-disproportionately-affects-women-in-nigeria-eb1494204b08.

CICMN (Citizenship, Inclusion, and Civic Mobilization Network). 2023. *Kenya Report: Women in Detention*. October 30. https://cicmn.org/wp-content/uploads/2023/11/CICs-Kenya-Report-10-30-23-FINAL.pdf.

Colombia 2023 Human Rights Report. 2024. State.gov. https://www.state.gov/wp-content/uploads/2024/02/528267_COLOMBIA-2023-HUMAN-RIGHTS-REPORT.pdf.

Colombia—Penal Reform International. 2023. Penal Reform International. https://www.penalreform.org/issues/women/bangkok-rules/bangkok-rules-map/colombia/.

Crewe, Helen. 2020. "No Babies in Prison: Norway's Exception Explained." Cambridge Core. https://www.cambridge.org/engage/api-gateway/coe/assets/orp/resource/item/5f94c2a58f3ba900111bdc84/original/no-babies-in-prison-norway-s-exception-explained.pdf.

Department of Corrections. 2021. "Wāhine—E Rere Ana ki te Pae Hou: Women's Strategy 2021–2025." Wellington: New Zealand Department of Corrections. https://www.corrections.govt.nz/__data/assets/pdf_file/0004/44644/Corrections_Wahine_-_E_rere_ana_ki_te_pae_hou_2021_-_2025.pdf.

Department of Justice. 2023. "Understanding the Overrepresentation of Indigenous People—State of the Criminal Justice System Dashboard." Justice.gc.ca. Government of Canada. April 13, 2023. https://www.justice.gc.ca/socjs-esjp/en/ind-aut/uo-cs.

DIGNITY. 2013. *Conditions for Women in Detention in the Philippines: Needs, Vulnerabilities and Good Practices*. Copenhagen: DIGNITY—Danish Institute Against Torture. https://dignity.dk/wp-content/uploads/publication-series-11.pdf.

Dui Hua Foundation. 2020. "Big Increase in Women Behind Bars in China." *Dui Hua Human Rights Journal*. September 14, 2020. https://www.duihuahrjournal.org/2020/09/big-increase-in-women-behind-bars-in.html.

Edwards, Layla M., Sungwon Chang, Reem Zeki, Sacha Kendall Jamieson, Julia Bowman, Craig Cooper, Elizabeth Sullivan, Louisa Degenhardt, Tim Slade, Sharon L. Browne, and Tony Butler. 2024. "The Associations Between Social Determinants of Health, Mental Health, Substance-Use and Recidivism: A Ten-Year Retrospective Cohort Analysis of Women Who Completed the Connections Programme in Australia." *Harm Reduction Journal* 21 (1): 2.

Euro-Mediterranean Human Rights Monitor. 2019. *Suppressed and Humiliated: Violence Against Egyptian Women Arbitrarily Locked Behind Bars*. https://euromedmonitor.org.

European Prison Observatory. 2015. *Alternatives to Prison in Europe: Italy*. By Susanna Marietti. Rome: Antigone Edizioni.

Fukada, Shiho. 2018. "For Many of Japan's Elderly Women, Prison Is a Haven." *Pulitzer Center*. March 18, 2018. https://pulitzercenter.org/stories/many-japans-elderly-women-prison-haven.

Hershatter, Gail. 2014. *The Gender of Memory: Rural Women and China's Collective Past*. Berkeley: University of California Press.

HRW: Behind Bars in Brazil (Women Prisoners). 2024. Hrw.org. https://www.hrw.org/legacy/reports98/brazil/Brazil-12.htm.

Human Rights Watch. 2024. "Tunisia: Many Face Prison over Debts." https://www.hrw.org/news/2024/06/10/tunisia-many-face-prison-over-debts.

Human Rights Watch. 2023. "They Don't Treat Us like Human Beings: Abuse of Imprisoned Women in Japan." *Human Rights Watch*. November 14, 2023. https://www.hrw.org/report/2023/11/14/they-dont-treat-us-human-beings/abuse-imprisoned-women-japan.

International Crisis Group. 2023. "Partners in Crime: The Rise of Women in Mexico's Illegal Groups." Latin America Report No. 103. November 28, 2023. International Crisis Group. https://www.crisisgroup.org.

Iran Human Rights. 2025. *Women and the Death Penalty in Iran: A Gendered Perspective*. Oslo: Iran Human Rights. https://iranhr.net/en/reports/25/.

Jamaica. 2023. United States Department of State. https://www.state.gov/reports/2023-country-reports-on-human-rights-practices/jamaica/.

Jeffries, Samantha, Chontit Chuenurah, Prarthana Rao, and Min Jee Yamada Park. 2019. "Women's Pathways to Prison in Kenya: Violence, Poverty, Familial Caretaking and Barriers to Justice." *Women's Studies International Forum* 73: 50–61.

Jolly, Margaret, Christine Stewart, and Carolyn Brewer, eds. 2012. *Engendering Violence in Papua New Guinea.* Canberra: ANU Press. https://library.oapen.org/bitstream/handle/20.500.12657/33584/459830.pdf.

Kanwal, Garima, Richa Ranjan, and Jyoti. 2025. "The Status of Women Prisoners in India." *International Journal for Legal Research & Analysis* 2 (7), June: 5–27.

Leslie, Dacia. 2022. "Reassessing Conditions of 'Prison' in Jamaica." *International Criminal Justice Review* 32 (1): 48–67.

Medeiros, Leonardo. 2021. "Brazil Has the World's 3rd Largest Prison Population." Conectas. https://www.conectas.org/en/noticias/brazil-worlds-3rd-largest-prison-population/.

Mexico's Long War: Drugs, Crime, and the Cartels. 2022. Council on Foreign Relations. https://www.cfr.org/backgrounder/mexicos-long-war-drugs-crime-and-cartels.

Mkaouar, Farah. 2022. "Tunisian Women Are Stuck Between Freedom and Inequality." *Assembly by Malala Fund.* https://assembly.malala.org/stories/tunisian-women-are-stuck-between-freedom-and-inequality.

Montanari, Linda. 2020. "Women Offenders in Europe: Drug Problems and Drug Offences and/or Gender-Based Violence." *European Journal of Public Health* 30, Supplement 5: 501.

Museve, Judith, Charles Helm, Obiero Angira, and Peter Aloka. 2020. "Prevalence and Associated Factors of Mental Disorders Among Prisoners in Kenya." *International Journal of Research and Innovation in Social Science* 10: 261–71.

Naik, Kiran R. 2019. "Women in Prisons India." *International Journal of Research and Analytical Reviews (IJRAR)* 6 (2), June: IJRAR1AXP008.

Nazra for Feminist Studies. 2017. "Violence Has Many Prisons: A Look into Women's Experiences in Prisons and Detention Centers in Egypt." https://nazra.org/en/2017/01/violence-has-many-prisons-look-women%E2%80%99s-experiences-prisons-and-detention-centers-egypt.

OMCT (World Organisation Against Torture). 2003. "Uzbekistan: Violence Against Women in Prison." Urgent Intervention UZB 310703.VAW. https://www.omct.org/en/resources/urgent-interventions/uzbekistan-violence-against-women-in-prison.

Penal Reform International. 2021. "Double Punishment: The Situation, Challenges and Adversities Faced by Mothers in Prison Around the World." https://www.penalreform.org/blog/double-punishment-the-situation-challenges-and-adversities-faced-by-mothers-in-prison-around-the-world/.

Sasaki, Ayako, Daiki Yoshihara, and Akemi Mochizuki. 2022. "Gender-Responsive Needs and Vulnerabilities Among Incarcerated Mothers in Japan: Comparisons with Non-Mothers and Fathers." *Journal of Drug Abuse* 8 (7): 105.

Siegler, Alison. 2021. "End Mandatory Minimums | Brennan Center for Justice." Brennan Center for Justice at NYU Law. https://www.brennancenter.org/our-work/analysis-opinion/end-mandatory-minimums.

Steyn, Francois, and Karen Booyens. 2017. "A Profile of Incarcerated Female Offenders: Implications for Rehabilitation Policy and Practice." *Acta Criminologica: Southern African Journal of Criminology* 30 (4): 33–44.

Ukrainchik, Alevtina V., Natalia M. Selezneva, Valentina V. Gorbunova, Kira D. Bondarenko, and Svetlana I. Bondarenko. 2022. "Female Crime in Modern Russia: Features, Main Trends, and Problems of Prevention." In *Business 4.0 as a Subject of the Digital Economy*, edited by Elena G. Popkova, 1195–202. Advances in Science, Technology & Innovation. Cham: Springer.

U.S. Department of State. 2023. *Uzbekistan 2022 Human Rights Report*. Washington, DC: U.S. Government Printing Office. https://www.state.gov/wp-content/uploads/2023/03/415610_UZBEKISTAN-2022-HUMAN-RIGHTS-REPORT.pdf.

Van Hout, Marie Claire, and Jakkie Wessels. 2021. "Human Rights and the Invisible Nature of Incarcerated Women in Post-Apartheid South Africa: Prison System Progress in Adopting the Bangkok Rules." *International Journal of Prisoner Health* 18: 300–15.

Van Hout, Marie Claire, Simon Fleißner, and Heino Stöver. 2023. "'Women's Right to Health in Detention': United Nations Committee Observations Since the Adoption of the United Nations Rules for the Treatment of Women Prisoners and Non-custodial Measures for Women Offenders (Bangkok Rules)." *Journal of Human Rights Practice* 15 (1): 138–55.

White, Heather. 2023. "Born Inside: Montessori Gives Hope to Children Living Their First Years of Life in Mexico's Prisons." *Montessori Life Blog*. American Montessori Society. https://amshq.org/Blog/2023-08-18-Montessori-in-Prisons-in-Mexico.

Zhong, Shaoling, Xiaomin Zhu, Yanan Chen, Huijuan Guo, Chenyuli Luo, Xiaoxi Liang, Fanglan Wang, Hui Chen, Jiansong Zhou, and Xiaoping Wang. 2020. "High Psychiatric Morbidity and Comorbidity Among Female Prisoners in Hunan, China." *Frontiers in Psychiatry* 11 (April). https://www.frontiersin.org/articles/10.3389/fpsyt.2020.00234/full.

Index Term List

1963 General Law Amendment Act 149
2006 Drug Law 55

Abashiri Prison 203
Aboriginal women 258, 262, 264–5
abuse by correctional officers 20, 87, 120, 134, 138, 171, 192, 208
Act for the Prevention of Recidivism (2016) 207, 211
addiction and incarceration 18–19, 26, 30, 36, 54, 61, 63, 69, 85, 88–90, 92, 94, 96, 118–19, 257–8, 261, 264–6, 269, 272–3, 275, 277–8, 280, 282
Administration of Criminal Justice Act (2015) 158, 162, 165
Afghan women in prisons 135
African National Congress 149
Alcoholic Drinks Control Act (2010) 170, 174
Alipore Central Jail 222
Al-Qanater Women's Prison 117
alternatives to incarceration 7, 30, 37, 39, 55, 57, 59, 62, 64–5, 70–1, 84, 86, 89–90, 97–9, 102, 105–6, 120, 123, 128, 131, 141, 193, 203, 208, 229, 232, 242, 245, 259, 276, 281, 283
Amina Lawal case 160
Amnesty Law 33
Anti-Violence Against Women and Their Children Act 234
apartheid 5, 149–51
armed conflict in Colombia 55, 58, 61, 63, 71
Arohata Women's Prison 275–6, 281
Article 176, Criminal Law 199, 202

bail laws 262
Bangkok Rules 1, 150, 154, 174, 208–9, 234, 239, 242, 245
battered woman syndrome 93, 154, 170, 234, 237
Bedford Hills Correctional Facility 21–2
Black women and incarceration 3, 48, 50–1, 149
Boggo Road Gaol 258
Brittney Griner case 4, 86
Broad Street Prison, Lagos 157

caregivers and incarceration 21, 37, 50, 54, 62, 71, 97, 104, 118, 156–9, 164, 168, 172, 192–3, 201, 210, 228, 232, 236, 244, 246, 260, 273, 277, 281
caste and incarceration 7, 222, 224
Centro Femenil de Readaptación y Rehabilitación Social Femenil Tepepan 31
children of incarcerated mothers
- child-friendly visitation 97, 105, 156, 210, 228, 230, 237, 273
- children living in prison with mothers 37, 140, 156, 172, 224, 229, 240, 243, 246, 273
- conjugal visits and children 62
- Mother–Baby Units (MBUs) 236–7, 265–6, 282
- mother-child programs 29, 105
- separation of mothers and children 65, 69–70, 91, 96–7, 104, 122, 139, 156–7, 164, 172, 204, 210–11, 236, 281

Código Penal Federal 34
colonial influence on justice systems 25, 38, 47, 63, 71, 115, 124, 157, 165–6, 173–4, 221, 230, 237–8, 257, 265–7, 274–5, 283
Colony No. 21 186–8, 191–2
community-based sentencing 30, 98, 131, 153, 157, 165, 208, 229, 232, 234, 242, 245, 265, 277–8, 282
Constitution Hill Women's Jail 151
convict criminology 23
Correctional Centre 2 / Prey Sar 239
Correctional Service of Canada 24
Correctional Services Act of 1998 150

criminalization
  debt 116, 118–19, 126, 131, 167, 169
  dissent 6, 98, 116, 119–20, 124, 127, 132, 136–7, 141, 185–6, 190, 193, 238–9, 246
  poverty 51, 117, 153, 169, 185, 246, 259–60, 262, 265
cultural stigmatization of women 132, 158

domestic violence 9, 18, 34, 50–1, 54, 58, 64–7, 85–6, 88, 90, 93–4, 100–2, 126, 131, 135–8, 140–1, 161–2, 164, 171, 174, 186, 188, 192, 206, 212, 222, 224, 228, 230, 234, 236–8, 240–2, 244, 258, 260–2, 266, 268, 271–2
Donna Nelson case 207
dowry-related imprisonment 222, 224–5
drug laws and policies
  Anti-Drug Abuse Act 18
  Anti-Drug Law of 2008 (China) 198
  Canada's Controlled Drugs and Substances Act 27
  Dangerous Drugs Act 4, 67
  Misuse of Drugs Act 1975 278, 282
  NDPS Act 226, 229, 247
  Stimulant Control Act 207
drug treatment courts 65, 70
drug-related crimes 4, 24, 26, 33, 48, 50–1, 57–9, 65–7, 70–1, 84–5, 91–2, 99–100, 116–17, 127–8, 131, 134, 136, 151–2, 160, 167, 169–70, 187–8, 195, 198, 207, 225, 232–3, 240–1, 269, 277–8

economic inequality 47, 276
education and vocational training programs 4, 20, 35, 39, 57, 63, 70, 83–4, 87, 89–90, 95, 98, 103, 106, 132, 138, 140, 155, 157, 163, 166–8, 171, 173–4, 186, 191, 193, 200, 226, 230, 237, 246–7, 263, 272, 274, 279, 282
Egyptian Initiative for Personal Rights 120, 122
Eldoret Women's Prison 167
EQUAL Act 22

Fair Sentencing Act 19
FARC and female incarceration 55–6
Federal Law Against Organized Crime 35
federal penitentiary system in Canada 23
female factories (Australia) 257
female political prisoners 5, 7–8, 116, 119–20, 127, 133–4, 136–7, 139–40, 200
forced labor 81, 83, 87, 89–90, 100, 106, 158–9, 185, 189, 194, 201, 212
forced sterilization 195, 198–9
foreign-born women in prisons 92–3, 99–101, 118, 126, 135–6

gender inequality 66, 149, 159, 166, 187, 212, 224, 239–40, 257, 267
gender-responsive 6, 8, 15, 22, 39, 47, 100, 106, 118–19, 125, 149–50, 155, 157–60, 162, 165, 167, 170, 173–4, 186–7, 193, 196, 200, 202, 204–5, 208, 211–12, 223, 229, 232, 234, 237, 257, 259–60, 264–5, 269–70, 273, 276–7, 279, 282
gender-specific 3, 8, 64, 125, 131, 141, 154, 159, 189, 192, 200, 229, 239–40, 247, 259, 268, 275, 283
Giwa Barracks 163, 165
Greenough Regional Prison 263

Hamdamova sisters 189
HEART/NSTA Trust 68, 70
Hijab laws and incarceration 133–4, 136–7
Hikimawashi punishment 203
house arrest 54–5, 62, 64, 70, 84, 101–2
hujum campaign 185
hukou system and incarceration 196
human rights violations 1, 4–5, 8
human trafficking 33, 85, 92, 100, 126, 128, 152, 158–9, 244
Hunan Provincial Women's Prison 196–7

Indian Act of 1896 25
Indiana Women's Prison 15
Indigenous women 2, 9, 15, 24–30, 33, 35, 38–9, 224, 257–62, 264–8, 274, 282
intergenerational trauma 130, 228, 237, 259, 266, 281
intimate partner violence 26–7, 64, 66, 118, 152, 155, 261, 275–6
Islamic law (Sharia) 5, 132

Jervolino-Vassalli Act 101
Johannesburg Central Prison 156

Kamiti Maximum Security Prison 171
Kaupapa Māori rehabilitation 279, 282
Kgoši Mampuru II Prison 152
Khmer Rouge 238–9
KIN-7 women's prison 186, 190–1
Kingston Prison for Women 23–4
Kirikiri Women's Prison 159
Koh Romdual 243
Kowhiritanga program 279, 282–3

La Cana program 38
Lang'ata Women's Prison 167–8, 171–2
laogai system 194
laojiao system 194, 196
Law 1760 59
Law 30 59
legal aid 221, 223, 229, 231, 234, 238, 247, 274

Mahsa Amini protests 134, 136
mandatory minimums 16, 18–19, 22, 24, 34, 38, 51, 67, 128, 153, 161
Manouba Prison 125, 128, 130–1
Māori women 9, 275–6, 278–82
marginalized women 7–8, 15, 24–5, 27, 37, 47–8, 51, 55, 84, 89, 99, 115, 117, 125, 127, 150, 159, 167, 169, 173–4, 211–12, 221, 223–4, 229, 236–7, 240, 242–3, 246, 262
Masanjia Women's Labor Camp 201
Mathari National Teaching and Referral Hospital 172
mixed-gender facilities 103, 151, 159, 167, 171
model prison initiatives 228, 239
moral offenses and imprisonment 115–16, 124–5, 127, 132, 135, 141, 165, 169, 174, 185–6, 238–9, 241, 267
Mother Nature Cambodia 241
Mount Pleasant Female Prison 15

Nigeria Correctional Service Act (2019) 162
non-violent offenses 18–19, 22, 24, 26–7, 30, 34, 37–8, 55–9, 62–5, 70–1, 82–3, 86, 89–91, 93–4, 98–101, 105–6, 116–17, 120, 123–6, 131, 136, 151–3, 157, 161, 165, 167, 169, 173–4, 188, 193, 195, 197, 202, 205, 207, 210–11, 221, 224, 226, 229, 231–4, 237, 239–42, 246–7, 257, 260–1, 265, 267, 269, 274, 277–8, 282
Northern Penal Code (zina laws) 158, 162
Norway's rehabilitation model 93, 95

Okimaw Ohci Healing Lodge 30
one-child policy 195–6, 198–9
organized crime 2, 31–5, 38, 57, 59, 152, 233
over-policing 27

parenting programs 21, 39, 265, 279
Pathways to Safe Indigenous Communities 27
patriarchal justice systems 6, 16, 47, 81, 98, 115, 124, 140, 154, 169, 185, 187, 194, 203, 221, 230, 239, 267, 274
Penal Code Article 13 207
physical and sexual abuse in prisons 3, 15, 20, 35, 53, 61, 120, 122, 165, 171
pretrial detention 3–4, 6–7, 35, 49, 59, 125, 135, 158, 171, 195, 208, 223, 231–2, 238–9, 245, 260, 262, 268, 276
prison nursery programs 21, 64, 68, 70, 104, 122, 167, 172–3, 193, 230, 273
prison sanitation and hygiene 3, 6–7, 9, 19, 22, 35, 52, 55, 60, 63–4, 68, 71, 83, 86–7, 103, 120–3, 128, 131, 134, 140, 150, 154, 159, 162, 166, 170, 172, 174, 186, 190, 193, 195–6, 200, 202, 226, 229–30, 234–8, 243, 268, 271–4
progressive penal approaches 4–5, 81, 90, 93, 95
property crimes 18, 24, 26, 34, 38, 85, 92, 100, 153, 169, 188, 197, 204, 230, 261, 270, 275, 277–8, 282
public order crimes 18, 26, 275, 278, 282

Qarchak Prison 134–5, 137–8, 140

R. v. Gladue 27
racism and incarceration 25, 259, 262
recidivism 4, 19, 21, 30, 37, 39, 64, 71, 84–5, 87, 90, 94, 106, 155, 166, 173, 205, 209, 226, 238, 243, 247, 264, 282
religious laws 134–6, 141
remand 167, 260, 264, 276

reproductive healthcare 19, 28, 38, 60, 104, 163, 229
restorative justice 30, 37, 91, 94, 120, 229, 237

S v Shilubane (2008) 153
Section 498A (India) 222, 225, 229, 247
self-defense and domestic violence 34, 51, 58, 66–7, 85, 93–4, 101–2, 118, 127, 140–1, 153, 161–2, 170, 174, 241–2, 246, 261, 271, 278
single mothers and crime 2–3, 33, 36–7, 64–5, 100–1, 118, 159, 168, 173, 233–4, 238–9
sorcery accusations 266, 268
Stride Circles 30
substance abuse 8, 18, 26, 36, 54, 61, 84, 90, 95, 118, 160, 272, 280
transgender inmates 7, 20, 28, 50, 209, 211–12
trauma-informed care 15, 20, 22, 39, 93, 105, 131, 157, 175, 192, 202, 211–13, 224, 228, 259–60, 263–4, 266, 272, 275, 279, 282
tuberculosis in prisons 87, 89, 121, 123, 155, 163, 171, 191, 235, 272

Violent Crime Control and Law Enforcement Act 19

Wandoo Rehabilitation Prison 263, 283
War on Drugs 2–3, 16, 18–19, 21–2, 31–2, 34, 38, 231, 233–4, 247
Witchcraft Act 167
women of color 2, 16–18, 22–3, 38
Wu Ying case 197–8

Zangiota Women's Colony 186

About the Author

Francesca Spina, Ph.D., is Chair and Associate Professor of Criminal Justice at Westfield State University. Her research focuses on gender, incarceration, and criminal justice policy. She is the editor of *The Routledge Companion to Gender and Crime* and has published widely on corrections, sentencing, and social inequality. A former department chair at Springfield College, she brings a commitment to research-informed justice reform and to amplifying the experiences of women and marginalized populations within carceral systems.